Genesis, Structure, and Meaning in Gary Snyder's *Mountains and Rivers Without End*

Western Literature Series

ANTHONY HUNT

Genesis, Structure, and Meaning in Gary Snyder's *Mountains and Rivers Without End*

University of Nevada Press / Reno & Las Vegas

Western Literature Series
University of Nevada Press
Reno, Nevada 89557 USA
www.unpress.nevada.edu

Manufactured in the United States of America
Composition by Wilsted & Taylor
Publishing Services
The paper used in this book meets the requirements of American National Standard for Information Sciences—Permanence of Paper for Printed Library Materials, ANSI Z39.48–1984.
Binding materials were selected for strength and durability.

This book has been reproduced as a digital reprint.

Library of Congress
Cataloging-in-Publication Data
Hunt, Anthony, 1938–
Genesis, Structure, and meaning in Gary Snyder's Mountains and rivers without end/ Anthony Hunt.
p. cm. — (Western literature series)
Includes bibliographical references (p.) and index.
ISBN 978–0–87417–545–5 (cloth: alk. paper)
ISBN 978–0–87417–478–6 (pbk. : alk. paper)
ISBN 978–0–87417–476–2 (ebook)
1. Snyder, Gary. Mountains and rivers without end. I. Title. II. Series.
PS3569.N88M6234 2004 2003017449

Dedicated to

THE BAUM SISTERS

Miriam Elsebiene Baum (1901–1995)

Anna Josephine Baum (1906–1996)

high-spirited, demanding

hardworking

cultured and curious

they passed it on . . .

Contents

Key to Frequent Abbreviations

DAC B :F	Donald Allen Collection, Mandeville Special Collections Library, Geisel Library, University of California, San Diego. Accession number MSS 0003. Citations include references to box and folder numbers.
EHH	*Earth House Hold: Technical Notes & Queries to Fellow Dharma Revolutionaries.* New York: New Directions, 1969.
GSP B :F	Gary Snyder Papers, Department of Special Collections, Shields Library, University of California, Davis. Accession number D50. Processed by Pamela Pearl Wilson. March 1995. Citations include references to box and folder numbers according to the Shelf List, 213–460.
MRWE	*Mountains and Rivers Without End.* Washington: Counterpoint, 1996.
Passage	*Passage Through India.* San Francisco: Grey Fox Press, 1983.
Place	*A Place in Space: Ethics, Aesthetics, and Watersheds: New and Selected Prose.* Washington: Counterpoint, 1995.
Practice	*The Practice of the Wild: Essays by Gary Snyder.* San Francisco: North Point Press, 1990.
Reed-PWP	Philip Whalen Collection, Special Collections Library, Eric V. Hauser Memorial Library, Reed College, Portland, Oregon.

Genesis, Structure, and Meaning in Gary Snyder's *Mountains and Rivers Without End*

1

Finding the Paths

Bearings

"I'm sixty-eight" he said,
"I first bucked hay when I was seventeen.
I thought, that day I started,
I sure would hate to do this all my life.
And dammit, that's just what
I've gone and done."

from "Hay for the Horses"(*Riprap, & Cold Mountain Poems* 13)

At what point in time does one recognize what one has "gone and done"? Where, among the events of the past, did diverse flows of energy come together to culminate in the making of a significant lifetime? Remarkably, in the case of Gary Snyder, much of what he has come to represent as an elder of the tribe has always been *there.*

Raised on a dairy farm just outside of Seattle on the edge of an old clear-cut forest, as a child Snyder played among huge twelve-by-twelve-foot stumps of ancient trees that struck him as ghosts from the past, some that even "spoke" to him. Remembering his childhood, Snyder recalls several trees close to his home that he had climbed, "especially one Western Red Cedar (*xelpai'its* in Snohomish) that I fancied became my advisor" (*Practice* 117). Rocks, trees, sheep, rabbits, coyotes, eagles, bear, deer, and ravens all speak to him, for him, and through him. Even "grass-seed-buddhas" and rain drops—"tiny people gliding slanting down" (*MRWE* 81)—are alive in his poems. Snyder's knowledge of the land, especially that of his immediate community and the bioregion encircling it, extends to an interaction over time of its geology, plants, animals, and humans. In this vast planetary web of being, as he continually reminds us, humans share in the irrevocable fact of edibility. Linked by the food chain, all beings provide nourishment, literal and otherwise, for other beings. Conversely, the richness and diversity of the nonhuman world only deepens Snyder's felt responsibility for the human one.

Work has always been a primary force in the poet's life, as it was in the life of his father who split shakes to make money in the depression years, or in the lives of other relatives and friends, male and female, dead or alive, who have known what it was and is to work to live. His poems often celebrate the intensity of work; the words capture the pure musical rhythm, the "riprap" of those who labor with their hands. Male voices, especially in earlier poems, speak in various ethnic accents: seamen, loggers, trail crewmen, farmers, truck drivers, cowboys. Hard-drinking, earthy, frequently carnal, they live close to the edge, their Dionysian wisdom that of people who have managed to persevere, even celebrate, in difficult times.

Notwithstanding the elbow grease and eroticism, Snyder is, and always has been, a scholar-poet. Wherever he goes he takes notes as he studies the animals, the trees, the flowers, the herbs. He contemplates the religious, the philosophical, the cultural, and the historical. He knows both the Paleolithic and the present; he is as informed about the old ways—the traditions, artifacts, and tools of both ancient and contemporary inhabitory peoples—as he is about modern technology and culture. His mother, he says, gave him his love for literature and poetry. She enrolled him at Lincoln High in Portland and later urged him to attend Reed College where his scholarship was energized by the tutelage of teachers like Lloyd Reynolds, Stanley Moore, and David French. Reed also provided intellectual classmates like Philip Whalen, his lifelong friend, and the challenge, in 1951, of writing a senior thesis, "He Who Hunted Birds in His Father's Village," that, even today, is comparable to some doctoral dissertations. Yet Snyder's is a Zen intellect: hours spent in gathering knowledge, complemented by physical labor and meditations on the tangibility of emptiness. The intellect is never a goal in itself.

Never claiming to speak for Native Americans, Snyder surely identifies with many of their traditions. Long before most non–Native Americans knew of the Hump-backed Flute Player, Snyder had incorporated Kokop'ele into his poetry and thought. "Turtle Island"—the "old/new name for the continent, based on many creation myths of the people who have been living here for millennia, and reapplied by some of them to 'North America' in recent years"—became the title of Snyder's Pulitzer Prize-winning book of poems. The phrase clearly took hold of an American consciousness replete with "Anglos, Black people, Chicanos, and others beached up on these shores" who hardly knew such names had been there all the time (*Turtle Island* [xi]). Like the old-growth trees that stood on the edge of his father's farm, the Native American traditions, rituals, and factual history are ghostlike presences lurking in the corners of the modern mind waiting to reassert themselves.

Similarly, Snyder has meditated at length on the mythical and/or prehistorical artifacts of civilization's past. For him, these are the palpable ghosts of the Paleolithic: the ageless mythical time of oral narratives; the magico-mystical power of the healing shaman; the expressive link between human and animal found in the "language" of 40,000-year-old cave paintings; the sophistication of prehistory's technology; and a profound encounter with what some have called a "Great Goddess."

Snyder's poetry is filled with the feminine: the Magna Mater, Lady of the Animals, the Bear Mother, Mother *Bos*, Kuan-yin, Māyā, Pārvāti, Kali, Tārā, Yamamba, the Moon, Gaia, Mother Earth, and so many others. Although he reverently traces his matriarchal lineage to a modest Kansas gravestone where he plants a kiss on a rock inscribed with the name of Harriet Callicotte, his maternal great-grandmother (Halper 169–73), Snyder often depicts the feminine in a conflicted manner. He credits his mother with being an advanced thinker for her time and for inspiring him to be a poet; but in interviews and correspondence he sometimes refers to her as domineering and aggressive, even manic-depressive. Like Actaeon observing Artemis bathing at her virgin spring in the forest, deep in Snyder's mythological consciousness there is an ongoing—and enigmatic—encounter with Swan Maiden, a mysterious naked beauty who bathes in a mountain lake or by a river. Her presence was the impulse for his Reed thesis, a work that he acknowledged in 1978 as "*really*" about "lost love" (*He Who Hunted* xi). She may correspond to Alison, his first wife, whom he portrays as a literal bathing forest maiden in "For the Boy Who Was Dodger Point Lookout Fifteen Years Ago," yet the mysterious aspects of this mythical woman are more strongly reminiscent of Robin Collins, a classmate at Reed, whose haunting image emerges in correspondence, journal notations, or in early poems ("Four Poems for Robin"). The ecstasy of the erotic, whether sacred or secular, is frequent in Snyder's life and writing, and the oppositional energy of the feminine is easily traced in the record of his marriages and liaisons. Joanne Kyger's published journal depicts their four-year marriage as one of both passionate attachment and a clash of egos. Named in an early version of "The Elwha River," Kyger, like so much else in that early poem, becomes a "lost thing" for Snyder. Masa Uehara, his third wife, becomes an emblem of woman as sexual partner, wife, and mother in the poems of *Regarding Wave.* Carole Koda's presence is explicit among the pages of *Mountains and Rivers Without End;* she is named in "Cross-Legg'd" and "Macaques in the Sky"; she is the other "soul" or "paddle" or "wing" in the double kayak of "Afloat." She is the lover and wife mentioned in "Finding the Space in the Heart." Literal associations aside, Snyder's creativity unquestionably drinks at the well of feminine inspiration. The poetic power of The Goddess, whoever she is, whether fearsome or beatific, derives in part from her ability to walk the line between mythology and actuality; she is the perennial dancing partner for the ascetic god-hero of the mountain. Encounters with her lead to enlightenment.

Perhaps Asia entered the web of Snyder's imagination merely because as a spatially oriented person he lived on one side of the Pacific and dreamed of the other, but it is more likely that it had to do with wilderness and mountaineering. Snyder himself has pointed to a significant moment when, barely a teenager, he saw an exhibit of Chinese landscape paintings in the Seattle Art Museum and marveled at the ephemeral reality they depicted. Summer times during high school years were spent exploring the high country of the Cascades. Later, as he sat, like Han Shan, in his lookout's post on the top of Sourdough Mountain, he consciously emulated the life of an Asian mountain ascetic. Throughout these years his technical skill and scholarship continued: at Reed, Chinese calligraphy and poetry with Lloyd Reynolds and Charles Leong; at Berkeley, the study of Oriental languages, and lessons in *sumi* painting under Chiura Obata. Still, it was the mountains that provided him with the "call" to the journey he would undertake. In a journal entry, written several years (1954) after the event, Snyder recorded a moment of direct insight into nature's ways. He was twenty years old at the time:

> Walking out of the Olympics in 1950: the sudden realization of order & chaos, chaos in nature: the paths and gardens are not trimmed and ordered. Everything falls everwhich way, the birds swoop all directions, the deer go crashing off through the brush, & the glaciers fall down & smash the trees: but NOTHING IS OUT OF PLACE. That is why they say: The Tao is like (=)? Nature. Here is a koan for you. order & chaos. . . .

He goes on to ask himself:

> why?? did I at so early an age become a nature-mystic? it wa'nt anything I read?? what did it. This puzzles me. . . . (Robertson, "Real Matter" 224)

A similar experience apparently took place in mid-1951. According to Allen Ginsberg, while Snyder was sitting on the banks of the Willamette River shortly after turning in the final version of his Reed thesis, he experienced a *satori* in which he was overwhelmed by a consciousness that "the entire universe is alive" (Ginsberg 150; Ginsberg incorrectly states the year as 1948).[1] Given the gift of hindsight, these intimations of interconnectedness helped push Snyder in the direction of Zen Buddhism and the formulation of *Mountains and Rivers Without End.* By the age of twenty-four, without knowing exactly why or how it had come about, the poet felt himself to be a "nature-mystic." A mere two years later, in the spring of 1956, he finished the manuscript for *Myths & Texts,* began work on his new long poem, and embarked for Japan to take up formal Zen studies.

As a finished artifact, *Mountains and Rivers Without End* was to become a veritable river of knowledge, a flowing landscape packed with information on ecology, geology, travel, painting theory, Buddhist philosophy, and food chains, to name a few of its more obvious topics. In the years between the setting forth and the accomplishment, from the evidence of letters, interviews, and public statements, we know that Snyder often thought, mistakenly so, that he was only a few months away from completing his masterpiece. Clearly, the only certitude among these multiple interweavings is that Gary Snyder, as a young man in his mid-twenties, never envisioned spending forty years of his life on the making of *Mountains and Rivers Without End,* but dammit, that's sure what he went and did.

Opening the Poem

On October 22, 1965, Snyder, Philip Whalen, and Allen Ginsberg ritually hiked around Mount Tamalpais, just north of San Francisco, in accord with an ancient Hindu-Buddhist practice known as *pradakshina.* The event is commemorated in "The Circumambulation of Mt. Tamalpais," a prominent section of Snyder's *Mountains and Rivers Without End.* In a note to the poem, as first published in journal form, Snyder tells us that *pradakshina* is performed as a way of "opening the mountain":

> You circumambulate (always clockwise) a stupa, a tree, a person you wish to show respect to, or a mountain. On Mt. Hiei some of the practicers of the Tendai sect go around the mountain every day for 100 or 1000 days, as a magical and meditative exercise. (*Coyote's Journal* 5-6: 5)[2]

Similarly, "circumambulation" is a fitting term to describe each reader's exploration of *Mountains and Rivers Without End.* To "open" the resonant energies of Snyder's poem, one must integrate an attentive step-by-step passage along the spiraling pathways of its verbal panorama with an inspired consciousness of what lies just off its virtual trails. Still, as a mountain has a way of just "being mountain" regardless of how many times one walks around it, a complete grasp of Snyder's long poem will always exist beyond any single description, analysis, interpretation, or evaluation of it. Despite the fixity of words and images on the page, Snyder's virtual streams and mountains, like their counterparts in our "real" world, will "never stay the same." Each attentive "walking" of this poetic landscape produces new interconnections, new inspirations, new insights. Simultaneously enticing and resistant, *Mountains and Rivers Without End* ultimately has a way of just "being poem," always simply *there,* awaiting yet another critical circumambulation. Forty years in the making, Snyder's poem, a landmark work engendered by a life lived with commitment and significance, plainly merits respect.

Snyder once expressed a wish that his poem would be "self-informing" (Faas 132), but it is obvious that the journey through *Mountains and Rivers Without End* is not a trip to be taken lightly. The poet's unusual blend of materials—mythological references, East Asian landscape painting, Buddhist philosophy and ritual, the Japanese Nō theater, Native American customs and folkways, planetary hydrology and geology, to name just a few—and his unique way of interweaving that content into a whole comprising distinct parts and sections make his poem challenging even for well-educated readers. Yet it is equally clear that Snyder is a poet who wishes to be read by a wider audience than the allusiveness of *Mountains and Rivers Without End* might imply. His reputation first took shape in the so-called "beatnik era," a time of social activism and populist revolutionary expectations; forty years later, he continues to espouse those concerns, although his focus has shifted toward psychological and spiritual change as he talks of "Finding the Space in the Heart." Writers like Allen Ginsberg and Jack Kerouac who also emerged out of that narrowly defined beatnik milieu may have sought and received more public attention, but Snyder's *Mountains and Rivers Without End* positions him to become the still point of the turning circle of his times. Like T. S. Eliot's *Four Quartets, Mountains and Rivers Without End* is a long meditative poem involving personal and cultural survival, yet Snyder's major frame of reference is Buddhist whereas Eliot's is Christian, and Snyder's concerns are with the planet and all beings whereas Eliot notably fixes on the human species and Western traditions. As a sage for our times, with a reputation and expertise that extends well beyond the confines of academia, clearly Snyder wishes to have his poem read by a broad spectrum of people: among others, readers caught up in cultural studies, anthropology, religion, comparative poetry, and environmental studies.

In the process of providing an account of the poem's historical development and readings for individual sections, I hope to demonstrate conclusively that *Mountains and Rivers Without End* is no mere random gathering of thirty-nine individual poems, but a carefully constructed interweaving of sound, image, and sense, the result of both intuition and conscious intention. The formal constraints of both the East Asian landscape scroll and the Japanese Nō play have profoundly affected the arrangement of sections within the four parts of the larger poem, the linear order of the thirty-nine sections, and even the composition of lines within individual sections. Additionally, the underlying "story" of *Mountains and Rivers Without End* is associated with a particular kind of Nō play wherein a wandering monk or lay pilgrim encounters a spirit, first in the guise of an ordinary person (a woodchopper, a woman by a well, etc.) and later as an awesome, whether beatific or horrific, spirit of the place. That encounter normally becomes "enlightening" in the Buddhist sense of the word. Snyder's long poem contains a series of such meetings between the narrator (typically Snyder as a character in his own poem) and, more often than not, a feminine "Other"; these confrontations grow in intensity as the poem moves linearly through its sections, culminating in the climactic section, "The Mountain Spirit." Significantly, Snyder's attention to this well-known archetypal pattern predates his acquaintance with the Nō play in Japan. As an undergraduate student at Reed he read widely in the scholarly work of writers such as C. G. Jung, Erich Neumann, Joseph Campbell, and the poet Robert Graves. In *Mountains and Rivers Without End,* this "Meeting with The Goddess" is easy to misread as a case of gendered duality, but, as always in this poem, Snyder's focus is on the enlightenment that results from the eternal dance of opposed forces and not on one, the other, or even both in their particularity.

As a teacher I have struggled to bring meaningful texts into close proximity with truly curious minds in order to allow those minds to "see" that there is more to life than the evening news, video games, and fast-food restaurants, although those too are part of the web of existence. I do not see my book as a "Reader's Guide" to *Mountains and Rivers Without End,* a key to allusive words, phrases, or meanings; nor do I have any desire to rob readers of the illuminating joy of personal discovery. In a perfect world readers would indeed discover meanings by themselves, and teachers, like myself, would be unnecessary. Nevertheless, as I have spent over twenty years in researching, thinking, and writing about Snyder's poem, I would like to share with my readers what I hope is a graceful reading of an important, yet difficult poem. In doing so I hope readers will come away with a greater appreciation of Snyder's wisdom and poetic artistry as they willingly succumb to the art of reading poetry, especially long poems, especially *Mountains and Rivers Without End.* A thousand times I have asked myself: "Why have I written this book?" My answer always turns upon Susan Sontag's words in *Against Interpretation* (1964), which I first read as a graduate student just setting forth to engage with his profession:

> The aim of all commentary on art now should be to make works of art—and, by analogy, our own experience—more, rather than less, real to us. The function of criticism should be to show *how it is what it is,* even *that it is what it is,* rather than to show *what it means.* . . . In place of a hermeneutics we need an erotics of art. (14)

Walking the winding paths—some virtual and some real—of *Mountains and Rivers Without End,* sitting quietly by rivers or standing on peaks, immersed in archival artifacts or losing myself in the empty spaces of being, my adventure with this poem has been both prolonged and deeply satisfying, one that has profoundly affected my own intellectual and experiential development, not to mention the lives of those close to me. There was no small measure of personal enlightenment on the path, a bounty that I trust awaits all those who make the trip with commitment and a good heart.

2

Composing the Space

Genesis and Development of the Poem

> I started working on *Mountains and Rivers* almost as soon as *Myths & Texts* was finished. Then in 1965 I decided that six sections from the poem stood strongly enough by themselves that we would publish them. With the publication of *Six Sections . . . Plus One,* I decided not to publish any more selections in books [except for "The California Water Plan" in the *Fudo Trilogy*], only in magazines, until I finished the whole thing, and I'm still working on it. I have no idea when it will appear.
>
> "Mountains and Rivers" is a title for a number of Chinese landscape paintings. One is by the Yüan Dynasty painter, Hsü-Pen, whose work inspired me. I'm writing about the complementarity of mountains and rivers, but that's really the planet, taking that on.
>
> (McNeil 23, bracketed material in original)

Over the intervening years—according to Snyder at a rate of once a year—he quietly published sections of his long poem in various books and literary magazines. Much like the paths in a Chinese landscape painting that take several unforeseen turns, the poem's present form was arrived at by an oblique route. As a model on which to build a poem, Hsü Pen's painting was ultimately superseded by the work of another landscape painter. Snyder's identification of sections was sporadic. In literary magazines, he sometimes specified a *Mountains and Rivers* poem by appending a tag line, most often "from Mts. & Rivers," as a header or footer to the poem. A section was sometimes identified as "work in progress" before he read it to an audience, as taped recordings reveal. His correspondence occasionally identifies a poem as a section even though it was published *without* the identifying tag line. Conversely, some sections—like "The California Water Plan" mentioned by McNeil—were published *with* the tag line yet were not incorporated into the final version. The making of *Mountains and Rivers Without End* was a dynamic process of continual give-and-take, vision-and-revision, inspiration and perspiration. For whatever reasons—the call of personal obligations, a commitment to other projects, patient waiting for moments of poetic inspiration—there were lean years in which few sections, or none, were published. Equally, there were years of active production as groups of poems appeared. Normally these bursts of poetic energy clustered around landscapes Snyder had newly visited or abstract ideas he had clarified. The sections of Snyder's poem developed both persistently and randomly. If, at times, the engendering of *Mountains and Rivers* was a reflection of Snyder's conscious choices, at other times it followed mysterious pathways into a Zen-inspired silken void where clarity of vision and no-mind intermingle.

The fall of 1955 was a grand moment for the poet Gary Snyder. Not only did he complete the manuscript that would eventually be published as *Myths & Texts,* he also had an insight into composing a "new" kind of lyric poetry that would become *Riprap.* Additionally, as a major participant in the Six Gallery reading (October 7, 1955) that launched the Beat movement, his public recognition was on the rise. And, silently, he began work on *Mountains and Rivers Without End.* Yet shortly afterward, in May of 1956, just as the San Francisco movement began to flourish, Snyder seemingly turned his back on it by leaving the United States for Japan on his first attempt to undergo rigorous training as a Zen Buddhist. Nevertheless, as voluminous correspondence among the Gary Snyder Papers at the University of California at Davis reveals, he was an energetic letter writer, never really out of touch with the poetry scene in the United States. He continued to keep detailed journals, write poems, and pursue—with the help of friends and associates like Philip Whalen, Cid Corman, and Donald Allen—the publication of his own poetry.

On February 8, 1957, approximately seven months after Snyder had arrived in Japan, Philip Whalen wrote to him: "Everybody asks me, How is Gary? I say you're happy & let it go at that. I hope your makemono poem is going ahead, flinging sparks" (GSP B89:F73). Snyder responded a week later:

> The makemono poem awaits some further research at the moment into geomorphology, Parkman's Oregon Trail, Hsuan Tsung's travels, & the U.S. Dept. of Agriculture Annual Reports on Trees, Grasses, & Water. Also must look at more paintings. . . . Am playing with idea of sort of *joruri* poetry-reading, i.e., accompaniment of occasional clacker, drum, pipe, & shamisen music effect. Like at kabuki & nō. maybe long poem I do with that in mind. ho ho. Gary. (16 Feb. 1957. Reed–PWP)

The Japanese word *makemono* refers to a handscroll painted in a horizontal format. *Kakemono* scrolls hang vertically and are normally viewed at a single glance. In contrast, the horizontal handscroll is normally perceived a section at a time. Viewers observe the scenes sequentially: noting the foreground and background, stopping to check the smallest of details, finding paths in the wilderness, following tiny travelers who wind their way along the trails. There are stopping places: a temple in the woods, a log to sit on, a small group of village huts. Boats float silently on foregrounded lakes. Mysterious rivers fall over the rocks, flow among trees. Mountain peaks vanish into the haze of distant clouds, which in turn fade into the white unpainted space. With each turning of the scroll there are new scenes to take in. Mirrored in the virtual world of these horizontal scrolls are Snyder's own early wanderings as hitchhiker, seaman, trail crewman, Zen meditator, and world traveler. His affinity for the *makemono* scroll seems a logical extension of the Beat generation desire to live life "on the road."

Joruri, a form of Japanese puppet theater that "would have been impossible without the Nō before it," depends on "a chanter delivering lines for voiceless puppets" (Keene 58). Snyder evidently envisioned his poem from the outset as a performance involving public reading, ritualized chanting, and literal poetic song. "Fascinated" by the Japanese Nō and Kabuki plays he was seeing in Kyoto, in March he wrote again to Whalen recalling William Butler Yeats's use of the Nō and describing recitation techniques that involved half-singing and half-chanting, accompanied by shamisen twangers, wooden clackers, drums, and flute music. Undoubtedly, Snyder's focus was not on Yeats's drama but on *Mountains and Rivers.* He told Whalen that he could "imagine a very jolly creative sort of modern poetry-modern-dance-music shot built around the reading of one long dramatic-type poem with musicians and possibly a dancer" (8 Mar. 1957. Reed–PWP).

The Snyder-Whalen correspondence of early 1957 about Snyder's "*makemono* poem" is the earliest documented indication that the poet had distinct ideas about the form his long poem might take. Given the success of the dramatic poetry readings begun by the Beats, Snyder's desire to utilize chanting and musical instruments is not surprising. Beat poetry often relied on jazz rhythms, and the term "beat" was as likely to refer to a musical measure as it was to mean "sad" or "beaten down." When Allen Ginsberg read the infamous inaugural poem of the Beat movement, "Howl," surely the title of his poem was a reminder that it was meant to be heard with the ear as well as felt in the gut. The Beats, whether in San Francisco or New York, created a new consciousness for public poetry readings from coast to coast. As Snyder pointed out to Bill Moyers years later,

> from the night when Allen and I and others first read our works at the Sixth [*sic*] Gallery in October of 1955, there has not been a night without a poetry reading in the Bay Area. It started just like *that,* and then it moved out across the whole country, to coffeehouses and cultural centers and then into the academy. (*Language of Life* 357)

Snyder's first encounter with Japan and the First Zen Institute of America, which had sponsored his trip, was not, however, what he had hoped. By late August of 1957 he had left Kyoto behind, signing on as a crewman on the *Sappa Creek,* a T-2 tanker that would take him from the ports of Southeast Asia, the Persian Gulf, and the Arabian Sea through Suez to Istanbul and various Mediterranean destinations before backtracking across the South Pacific via Samoa to finally leave him once more in California by mid-April of 1958. Journal entries and letters from these travels attest to Snyder's continuing work on what would become *Mountains and Rivers Without End.* Throughout these months, Snyder became one of those tiny people traversing a seemingly endless landscape of fact and imagination as it coiled about him.

While Snyder was voyaging, Jack Kerouac's *The Dharma Bums* (1958) was published. In this novel, a well-known roman à clef, Japhy Ryder (Snyder) reveals his plans to Ray Smith (Kerouac) for using the horizontal landscape scroll as a structure for his "new long poem":

> Know what I'm gonna do? I'll do a new long poem called "Rivers and Mountains Without End" and just write it on and on on a scroll and unfold on and on with new surprises and always what went before forgotten, see, like a river, or like one of them real long Chinese silk paintings that show two little men hiking in an endless landscape of gnarled old trees and mountains so high they merge with the fog in the upper silk void. I'll spend three thousand years writing it, it'll be packed full of information on soil conservation, the Tennessee Valley Authority, astronomy, geology, Hsuan Tsung's travels, Chinese painting theory, reforestation, Oceanic ecology and food chains. (157)

The actual events behind Kerouac's fictional paragraph took place as he and Snyder hiked together on Mount Tamalpais on May 1–2, 1956, just before Snyder left for Japan on the *Arita Maru* (Robertson, "Real Matter" 220–21). Since no "Mountains and Rivers" poem about the Tennessee Valley Authority has surfaced, we are left to wonder which words belong to Gary Snyder and which to Jack Kerouac's imaginative recollection. Snyder himself said, in a late 1959 letter to Joanne Kyger, that the "Dharma Bums is indeed not about me. All out of context" (GSP B104:F12). Yet, although no factual paper trail in 1956 exists, it is evident from the general correspondence of Snyder's actual long poem with Kerouac's fiction that Snyder had given a good deal of thought to the details of his poem—both in form and content—before he left for Japan.

Returning to the Bay Area by late April of 1958, Snyder stayed briefly with his father in Corte Madera, then moved into the cabin known as "Marin-an" on the slopes of Mount Tamalpais. The name given to the cabin is a good indication of Snyder's multilingual playfulness. In Chinese, *ma* is the equivalent of "horse" and *rin* means "grove," but the suffix *an* is a Japanese designation for a hermitage. The cabin was thus named both for its physical location in Marin County, California, and its purpose as a "horse-grove hermitage," a Zen-like retreat named for the horses that did indeed graze on the hillsides. During the next few months there were parties and poetry readings in the Bay Area, and there were hiking excursions. In mid-June he met Joanne Kyger, who would eventually follow him to Japan to become his second wife. There was a short trip to visit Philip Whalen in Oregon. But there wasn't much in the way of new writing. He wrote to Whalen in the fall that he hadn't written poems "for several months" ([19?] Oct. 1958. Reed–PWP). By January 1959, nine months after he had gotten off the *Sappa Creek* in San Pedro, he was on board ship for a "second time around" with formal Zen study in Kyoto.

Mountains and Rivers was never far from his thought. Donald Allen's influential anthology *The New American Poetry* (1960) includes no *Mountains and Rivers* poems among an otherwise representative selection of Snyder's poetry, but in a section of the anthology titled "Statements on Poetics" Snyder updates his ongoing project:

> Since 1956 I've been working on a long poem I'm calling "Mountains and Rivers without End" after a Chinese sidewise scroll painting. It threatens to be like its title. Travel, the sense of journey in space that modern people have lost (it takes as long to go from Cedar Grove to the Bighorn Plateau in the Sierras as it does to cross America by train), and rise and fall of rock and water. The naked burning rocks of Oman after thirty days at sea. History and its vengeful ghosts. The dramatic structure follows a certain type of Nō play. [1959] (421, bracketed date in original.)[1]

Snyder's poem is beginning to have a life of its own as "it threatens" to be without end. Once more he emphasizes the idea of time spent moving through space. If the earlier Japhy Ryder mentions hiking in an "endless landscape," Gary Snyder speaks here of specific Sierra Nevada trails that he had walked and factual travel that he had undertaken along the waterways of the Middle East on the *Sappa Creek*. Like the earlier *Myths & Texts*, an archetypal journey merges with a personal path. In "rock and water" we hear an echo of the phrase "mountains and rivers." Moreover, the dynamism of this landscape that changes over geological time is mirrored by a historical journey of human beings out of a distant past and into an unknown future, a journey made alongside "vengeful ghosts" who refuse to disappear. Snyder's allusion to "a certain type of Nō play" calls forth the paradigm in which travelers encounter ghosts in settings that appear as magical as they are ordinary. Both the East Asian horizontal landscape scroll and the Nō play involve journeying, and both hold the promise of spiritual revelation and illumination. If there is to be enlightenment in these encounters, Snyder probably has in mind ghostly figures from the relatively recent political history of Native America or, further back, representative spirits of the Paleolithic way of life that the modern world has forgotten. At one stroke Snyder merges several topics that will bind *Mountains and Rivers Without End* into a harmonious sequence.

A letter written to Allen Ginsberg in January 1959 is similar in tone and content to the statement he gave Donald Allen:

> 21.1.59
> I had a big dream last night exposing & revealing the necessary plan of "Mountains & Rivers Without End" which has been growing but without design; it is going to be the first complete poem of SPACE and questions of time in space; sense of distance, heart of journey, 6 hours to fly to New York or walk from a creek to a certain lake; things like Aden or Oman seen from afar; the falling-back-in-time of a striped.lateen sail on the Red sea, what happened in certain towns, the kinds of cheap wines, gradual lowering of the north star as you travel south . . . Gary. (*Origin* 2nd ser. 2: 63.)

The thematic motifs of "time in space, sense of distance, heart of journey" are paralleled in the Allen anthology quote, and Snyder's complaint that his long poem had been "growing but without design" was repeated to other correspondents and interviewers at later dates. If indeed the Muse had revealed "the necessary plan" for the poem, hindsight reveals that it would undergo many changes even as the poet held onto a steady vision of its totality. What is new here is Snyder's emphasis on SPACE in-and-for-itself and the notion that "dream" has a role to play in the making of *Mountains and Rivers Without End.*

The truth is that by mid-1959, with the poet once more engaged in full-time Zen study in Kyoto, the public had not actually seen much of Snyder's poetry on the printed page, certainly not in book form. There was a great deal of general hoopla about the Beats, and Snyder's name was usually included in articles about the "movement." However, neither *Myths & Texts* nor *Riprap,* Snyder's gathering of short poems written between 1953 and 1958, had yet been published. The "Cold Mountain" translations of Han Shan's poetry appeared in *Evergreen Review* in mid-1958, the timing of which probably reinforced Kerouac's image of Japhy Ryder-Snyder as a mountain ascetic. It is not surprising to hear Snyder complaining about his poetry, as he does to Whalen in a letter from Kyoto on August 14, 1959:

> I have created heaps of fragmental poems lately, but can see no order or development in them as a whole, & have no specific sense of line at the moment. Rather frustrating. All of the "Mountains & Rivers Without End" material awaits a few inspired weeks of work & it will be complete. But I've been waiting almost 2 years to get that finished. I think part of it is that zazen, at this stage for me at least, de-verbalizes me. I hate to talk to people, I don't like to read, & it's difficult to write letters. (Reed–PWP)

Now studying Zen intensively under the guidance of Oda Sessō at Daitoku-ji, a Rinzai temple in Kyoto, Snyder seemed unable to find the time he needed to meditate on his long poem. Despite his naive optimistic note that "a few inspired weeks of work & it will be complete," his need to stay focused on Zen and its practice of sitting meditation (*zazen*) and his desire to find some "development" or "order" or "specific sense of line" for his poem kept him from putting the "all" of it together. Surely his conception of the whole poem at that time must have been markedly different from what the poem has turned out to be, but whatever design he had in his mind, it is clear that he *did* have some plan or there would have been no "all."

In contemplating a horizontal landscape painting, one wonders if an artist knows from the first turn of the scroll how the work will develop and where it will all end. It is, of course, possible to begin in a spatial middle and paint in panels as one conceives of them. Yet how much comprehension of the whole is necessary to allow an artist to fill in (or leave blank) the spaces? In good Zen fashion, once begun in earnest there is no stopping; the ink continues to flow and the blank spaces call forth the painting. Time and progress become relative. A year may be a moment; an achievement, however small or large, may be significant or insignificant.

By "waiting almost 2 years" to create whatever sections he had in hand, Snyder may have paused in his composition, but he continued to believe he had something new and different to say. Still mourning his slow progress, he wrote to Joanne Kyger in December of 1959: "I have rumblings of a vast new poetry inside me but it is slow borning—like I'm waiting almost 2 years now" (29 Dec. 1959. GSP B104:F12). His tension is palpable; the poem won't go away, but it won't come together either.

In January, as Kyger was making preparations to sail for Japan to join him, Snyder wrote to Whalen: "Am working on the *Sophia* section of Mountains & Rivers by fits and starts. Another section in lagging progress is called *Night Highway Ninety-Nine.* But all in all I must say this past year has been signally unproductive" (13 Jan. 1960. Reed–PWP). Complain though he might, there is dramatic evidence here of the impressive scope of *Mountains and Rivers Without End.* "Night Highway 99," a journey poem that readily suggests the little travelers of the Chinese landscape scroll, eventually became an integral section of the final poem, but the "Sophia" section of the poem has failed to materialize. During his visit to Istanbul a little over two years earlier, Snyder had been immensely impressed by the huge dome of the Hagia Sophia, sometimes referred to as Santa Sophia. He wrote to Allen Ginsberg that he "went walking alone on Christmas to Blue Mosque & SANTA SOPHIA where I was completely translated & rendered new & different by INSIDE EMPTINESS OF HOLY DOME" (22 Apr. [1958]. "Letter to Allen Ginsberg," *Unspeakable Visions of the Individual* 4: 114). Several years later, writing to Whalen, Snyder compares the Santa Sophia dome to the enormous wooden structure covering the statue of the Buddha at Todaiji, acknowledging that although the Buddhist building is "a magnificent structure," somehow the "Santa Sophia is a more 'Buddhist' temple. More presence of the Void. Maybe because of that great empty dome. The empty dome or the big bronze Buddha. Well" (9 Jan. 1961. Reed–PWP). Never published, the existence of even a partial "Sophia" section reveals the importance of the "presence of the Void" to Snyder's evolving conception of his poem. Metaphorically his terms "SPACE" and "EMPTINESS" take on the weight of the Mahāyāna Buddhist metaphysical concept of *shūnyatā:*

> *Shūnyatā* [Sanskrit] . . . lit. "emptiness, void"; central notion of Buddhism. . . . in the Mahāyāna . . . all things are regarded as without essence, i.e., empty of self-nature. . . . All dharmas are fundamentally nothing more than mere appearances. They do not exist outside of emptiness. . . . It does not mean that things do not exist but rather that they are nothing besides appearances. ("Shūnyatā" *Shambhala Dictionary*)

The *Heart Sūtra,* a centerpiece of Mahāyāna Buddhist thought, contains the most succinct statement of the emptiness doctrine, so significant that it is chanted daily by practitioners of Zen: "form is no other than emptiness; emptiness is no other than form."[2] Since, at the time of his comments to Whalen and Ginsberg, Snyder had not yet discovered the empty "silvery flats" of the Black Rock Desert, it is certain that he had not yet conceived of "Finding the Space in the Heart" as the final section of his long poem. There is little doubt, however, that he imagined "emptiness" to be "at the heart" of his long poem.

On the 23rd of February, 1960, three days after Joanne Kyger disembarked in Japan, she and Gary Snyder were married in the American Consulate in Kobe. By April, as we know from the "20. iv.60" date printed at the end of "Bubbs Creek Haircut," Snyder had completed another section. He was delighted with his accomplishment and wrote to Whalen to tell him so: "I have written a new poem which is possibly the best thing I've done in 2 or 3 or more years; which I am calling 'Bubbs Creek Haircut' & with another rewriting or so, will send you a copy to see" (3 May 1960. Reed–PWP). True to his word, a month later he sent a draft of "Bubbs Creek Haircut" for Whalen to criticize, calling it "an installment of *Rivers & Mountains sans souci*" and saying that he "wrote it all down in one draft in 20 minutes by hand—the Muse really had me by the balls there" (13 June 1960. Reed–PWP). Continuing to assess his relationship with "the Muse," by September of that year Snyder's comments show that the actual process of composition was much on his mind: "This long poem grows on me, the conception of it, only it's too intellectual still, apparently I work by getting a sort of overall intellectual structure & then sort of forgetting it a long time & then beginning to fairly spontaneously write into it" (23 Sept. 1960. Reed–PWP). Snyder's desire for spontaneity is in keeping with the general predilection for the rhythms of impromptu jazz, the "spontaneous prose" that Kerouac was writing, or the idea of "projective verse" as put forth by Charles Olson, to name only a few examples.[3] In addition, Snyder's ability to write "fairly spontaneously" after long periods of nonattention may be related to the very practice of *zazen* that he felt, at first, was "deverbalizing" him. Then again, the delights and tensions of his marriage to Kyger, a strong personality and poet in her own right, may have helped the flow of his poetic activity in 1960. By January of 1961 he tells Whalen that he is "happy because I've done a lot of work the past 2 weeks, typed notes I've had laying around 2 or 3 years, gotten a lot of notions cleared up about some poems, & wrote some new other ones, & have plans for some steady work projects this month on—making the time to do it" (9 Jan. 1961. Reed–PWP).

Although it would be several years before a book with the title of *Mountains and Rivers Without End* would appear, 1961 was a very good year for the poem. As the first sections began to appear in print, it began to take shape in the minds of its readers. During this time, Snyder was listening attentively to Will Petersen (Pete), his colleague in Zen, fellow hiking enthusiast, artist, and intense student of the Nō drama. They had met in Berkeley when Petersen was the art editor for the (Berkeley Buddhist) *Bussei.* After Snyder left for Japan the first time, they continued to correspond, and Petersen requested some poems from Snyder for publication in the *Bussei.* Shortly thereafter, Petersen himself moved to Japan—he had lived there previously—and their friendship grew stronger. When Snyder left Japan on the *Sappa Creek,* Petersen remained in Kyoto, and they kept up an extensive correspondence. He was still in Kyoto when Snyder returned in early 1959. When *Myths & Texts* was published in 1960, it was Petersen who provided the cover and the drawings for the book. As an artist, Petersen had also fallen under the spell of Nō; so much so that he was taking *shimai* (dance) lessons from a Nō teacher. Nō had become a kind of "walking zazen" for him, an extension of his studies in Zen. Snyder attended Nō performances on a regular basis and, in conversations with Petersen, continued to refine his ideas about the structure and rhythm of Nō as they might apply to *Mountains and Rivers.* In February 1961 Snyder told Whalen that Petersen had "gotten into No deeper than any other westerner" and that he had given Snyder "some excellent ideas for poetry structures and relationships of voice to dance & music" (10 Feb. 1961. Reed–PWP).

In the meantime, curiosity about Snyder and his *makemono* poem was growing in the United States. Dan Welch, a Snyder correspondent who later joined the Tassajara Zen Center in California, wrote to him to ask about the progress of his poem: "Say didn't you write a poem 'Mountains and Rivers Without End'? If so when published & by whom or if not would you send a copy? I have asked at City Lights in S. F. and nobody there knows anything about it" (28 Mar. 1961. GSP B88:F58). That no sections had actually been published at the time Welch requested information about the poem is proof of the mystique that had begun to surround Snyder. Welch must have had in mind the Japhy Ryder quotation in *The Dharma Bums* or the published statement in the Grove Press anthology. It is also possible he heard Snyder read from his "work in progress" during poetry readings in the Bay Area between April 1958 and January 1959. If so, his regard for Snyder's work is a testament to the impact of the Beats on their listeners (as opposed to readers). Welch's curious questioning marks the moment of a major shift in the state of Snyder's poem. In June of 1961, shortly after Snyder became an honorary member of the Yamabushi (Japanese mountain climbing sect), we find the poet hard at work on "Night Highway 99," with the expectation that it will soon be published.

> I wrote another section of . . . Mts & Rivers—called "Night Highway 99"—I lose all semblance of literacy—but Corman says he'll put it in *Origin 3* or *4*—look out. Pete's translation of *Yashima* [a Noh play] to be in *Origin 3*. . . . [I] was initiated a Yamabushi and get to do magic on mountaintops (branch of Shingon) lookout lookout! I'll sacredize Tamalpais. (letter to Philip Whalen, 17 June 1961. Reed–PWP; my brackets)

Cid Corman was the publisher for Snyder's first book, *Riprap,* and his *Origin* was recognized as one of the defining "little magazines" of the times. Two weeks after Snyder's letter to Whalen, Corman printed "Bubbs Creek Haircut" in *Origin 2*. As published, it was not directly identified as a section; nevertheless, whether the public knew it or not, a section from *Mountains and Rivers Without End* had finally been set before its eyes. Furthermore, Snyder's comment about sacredizing Tamalpais surely indicates that he had already had an inspiration, if not the words, for another section involving San Francisco's most famous mountain.

Shortly after this productive burst of poetic activity, Snyder seemed, temporarily, to be running out of inspiration. At the end of July he wrote Whalen that he hadn't "written a line in weeks" (24 July 1961. Reed–PWP). There were probably external reasons. Not only had he just resigned from his official duties at the First Zen Institute (though not from Zen studies), he and Joanne were about to take an extended motorcycle trip in Japan. After that, they journeyed to India where they met, as planned, with Allen Ginsberg. The India trip began with a train to Tokyo on December 10, 1961; it was approximately five months before they returned to Kyoto (on May 8, 1962).[4] Significantly, if at first these adventures got in the way of writing poems, ultimately their travels generated an abundance of raw material for new sections of *Mountains and Rivers.*

As he had promised, in early 1962 Corman published "Night Highway 99" in *Origin 4*. Because it was printed with a line that said "from mountains and rivers without end," readers finally knew they were reading a piece of Snyder's long poem. When the first edition of *Mountains and Rivers Without End* was printed, this poem was the third section in the sequence, the same position that it keeps in the final version of the long poem. The epigraph was a quote from a letter written to Snyder by Lew Welch, a good friend:

> only the very poor, or eccentric, can surround themselves with shapes of elegance (soon to be demolished) in which they are forced by poverty to move

> with leisurely grace. We remain alert so as not to get run down, but it turns out you only have to hop a few feet, to one side, and the whole huge machinery rolls by, not seeing you at all. (5 Nov. 1960. GSP B88:F84)

Shortly after the poem was published, Welch wrote to say: "saw *Origin* with yr. fine Hiway poem. Most flattered by dedication" (13 Feb. 1962. GSP B88:F87). Snyder identified the epigraph as the words of "Lew Welch," but such is not always the case with quoted fragments in *Mountains and Rivers.* Normally a reader must be satisfied with quotation marks that signify the presence of a textual allusion. The punctuation is a waggling finger, a reminder to readers that there is something they do not know, something they may, if they like, discover on their own. As a scholar himself, Snyder is aware of the delicate balance between a need to satisfy the curiosity of readers—to allow them the poetic pleasure of "aha, I understand the connection"—and a fear that footnoted or intratextual explanations will draw attention away from the direct effect to be conveyed by the raw fact of the quotation. Footnotes bring on the danger of overintellectualizing the poem, yet, ironically, these fragments surrounded by their quotation marks also inspire a search for interconnectedness, a major structural strategy of *Mountains and Rivers Without End.*

From the evidence of correspondence available in archives, almost a year seems to have passed before Snyder reentered the world of *Mountains and Rivers* with intensity. In September of 1963 he wrote to Whalen that he had just "raved off ten or twelve pages with long lines of Mountains and Rivers. Maybe I should have been a novelist myself" (10 Sept. [1963]. Reed–PWP). Snyder may have been referring to "The Market"—published in Corman's *Origin* in January of 1964—a poem that could only have been written after the India trip since three of the markets mentioned in the poem were encountered for the first time on that trip. Yet given the large number of pages mentioned, a stronger case might be made for "Hymn to the Goddess San Francisco in Paradise," a section printed in the first two editions of *Mountains and Rivers Without End.* Since "Hymn" touches on the use of drugs and/or being "high," Snyder's use of the word "raved" seems appropriate for referring to this section. As published in *Fuck You / A Magazine of the Arts,* it carried composition dates of "Summer 1963–January 1964." The latter date can be roughly corroborated by a whimsical postcard sent to Whalen in February 1964: "I sent a long-poem to F.You. You too" (24 Feb. 1964. Reed–PWP). Several draft versions of this poem exist in the UC-Davis archives; one of them carries the initial date of "Summer 1963" ("Draft D," GSP B4:F60).

This was a difficult period in the personal lives of Joanne Kyger and Gary Snyder. By the time "The Market" was published, they had decided to separate. Kyger was making plans to return to the States. On January 20, 1964, as her published journal records, she had a beer with Gary on the boat in Kobe harbor and left (*Japan and In-*

dia Journals). A few months later, in April, Snyder also boarded a ship for the States. Several months later they were officially divorced. It appears that Snyder worked on at least one *Mountains and Rivers* section during this period. "The Elwha River," as printed in *Six Sections from "Mountains and Rivers Without End"* (1965), originally comprised three distinct parts. The first is dated "21.x.1958," making it the earliest part of *Mountains and Rivers* to have been written. The concluding third part ends with the date "21.VIII.1964," suggesting that it was probably composed as Snyder traveled in the Southwest taking notes for, or actually writing, many poems, several of which appear with timely dates in *The Back Country*. Part two of the original version of "The Elwha River" is undated, but thematic links suggest that it was written at the same time as the third part. Of the three original parts, only the first has been retained—with alterations—in the final book version of the long poem. Curiously, "The Elwha River" appears to have been the only poem of the original *Six Sections* not to have been published first in a journal.

Living again in the United States, Snyder became closely involved with the "business" of poetry. In September 1964 he began teaching two freshman composition courses and a creative writing course for the University of California at Berkeley. Among other things, he was at work with Donald Allen to reissue *Riprap* and *Cold Mountain Poems* as a composite book, and arrangements were being made for the publication of "Journeys," another *Mountains and Rivers* section (*Wild Dog* June 1965). In July 1965, *Six Sections from "Mountains and Rivers Without End,"* the first book edition, was published by Donald Allen's Four Seasons Foundation. Having heard about this long poem for just under a decade, the reading public finally had a real glimpse of it. As it was issued, Snyder was hiking in Kings Canyon with Philip Whalen and Drum Hadley. In September he returned to the mountaintops of the North Cascades, the locale of his "lookout days" during the summers of 1952–53. With Allen Ginsberg and a female companion, "Justine," the small group hiked for eight days in the Glacier Peak Wilderness (*EHH* 94ff.). Here, and just across the Straits of Juan de Fuca where the peaks of the Olympic Range poke through the clouds, were the original tangible spaces that served as the physical inspiration for the "mountains" of *Mountains and Rivers Without End.* How fitting that Snyder should be encircled by mountains as the first edition of his book emerged. Even more intriguing, in retrospect, is the probability that his first encounter with the Black Rock Desert took place "in the Sixties" as he returned with "a fierce gay poet" (Ginsberg) and "a / lovely but dangerous girl with a husky voice" ("Justine") from their trip north (*MRWE* 149). The ultimate setting for his long poem was gathered into his data bank of experiences.

A month later, in October, he was on his way back to Japan for further studies, this time funded by a Bollingen Foundation grant. By January 1966 Snyder was feeling extremely confident about his poetry. He wrote from Kyoto to Donald Carpenter:

> Man I'm in great shape. Having three months & nothing but time was just what I needed. I've now finished another book of poems (*Kali*) which Coyote has and will print; and another book of poems (*Six Years*) which somebody will print; written 8 or 10 new poems, including 2 more sections of Mountains & Rivers Without End; & blocked out 14 advance sections of Mountains and Rivers. In my spare time managed to read again, or anew, historical surveys of China and Japan, van Gulik on sexual customs of the ancient Chinese, Confucius etc. etc. (letter to Donald Carpenter, 27 Jan. 1966)

His three months of productivity were a time when he was, once again, alone. The two sections of *Mountains and Rivers* that he speaks about are most probably "The Circumambulation of Mt. Tamalpais," which was dated internally as "22.x.1965" and identified as "from Mountains and Rivers" when published, and the six-part "Three Worlds / Three Realms / Six Roads," which was printed in *Poetry* (Chicago) toward the end of 1966 and carried the tag line: "From *Mountains and Rivers Without End.*" The "circumambulation" poem commemorates Snyder's fulfillment of the promise made to Whalen in 1961 that he would "sacredize" Mount Tamalpais. As to the other "14 advance sections of Mountains and Rivers," there is no way to confirm with accuracy which poems Snyder had "blocked out."

In the meantime, other Snyder books were being published and other significant events were taking place. An early version of *The Back Country* was published in London as *A Range of Poems,* and an enlarged U.S. edition was to be published the following year. Snyder returned briefly to the United States to join Allen Ginsberg and thousands more for the Great Human Be-In that was held in San Francisco's Golden Gate Park in February of 1967. On his return to Japan he met Masa Uehara, whom he married in the summer of that year. By the spring of 1968 their son, Kai, was born in Japan, and by the end of that year the Snyders had returned to take up permanent residence in the United States. With the single exception of a little known poem, "A Lion Dream," which Snyder once referred to as a section of *Mountains and Rivers,* there was little outward evidence of work on his long poem during this period. Indeed, as Bob Steuding says of *Mountains and Rivers* in his 1976 book on Snyder: "Two phases can be seen in the development of this work: the first, which runs from 1956 to about 1966, includes seven sections; the second, from 1968 to mid-1976, covers so far six sections" (93).[5]

The year 1968 saw the introduction of two poems that Snyder would keep for the final manuscript. "The Rabbit," to be known in the final book version as "The Black-tailed Hare," was the first of "Eight Songs of Clouds and Water" published in *Poetry* (Chicago). The second section to be published that year was "The Blue Sky," destined to become the "Plus One" poem of *"Mountains and Rivers Without End" Plus One* (1970).

In 1969 "Kumarajiva's Mother" was printed with the tag line "From *Mountains*

& Rivers," but this short poem was not, finally, included as part of the finished sequence. Nor did "Down," printed in the *Iowa Review* in 1970 and also identified as a *Mountains and Rivers* section, make the final cut. Thus, of the five potential *Mountains and Rivers* poems published between 1967 and 1970, only "The Blue Sky" and "The Black-Tailed Hare" ("The Rabbit") have survived as part of the final poem.

Donald Allen wrote to Snyder in November of 1967 to ask him what he would like to do about a future edition of his long poem:

> only 550 copies of *Six Sections* left. And I wonder if it would not be better to add other sections and reset the whole thing for a new edition. What do you think? Or would you rather have the Six reprinted and then plan to bring out another book of other sections? All in all, I believe the enlarged and reset volume would work better. (27 Nov. 1967. DAC B38:F7)

Snyder replied a month later:

> As for Six Sections, my feeling at the moment is that I'd prefer not to add anything to it—the next publication of Mts. & Rivers stuff I'd like to be the WHOLE THING which will be very different in total effect from Six Sections. I'm coming back to the US next fall primarily to finish Mts. & Rivers. So, I'd say offhand, let it sell out. If demand seems to really justify it, reprint as it is. (19 Dec. 1967. DAC B38:F7).

Snyder's compromise, as readers know, was to add a single poem, "The Blue Sky," to the new edition, calling it *Six Sections from "Mountains and Rivers Without End" Plus One.* Perhaps Snyder truly thought he would return to the United States in 1968 to "finish Mts. & Rivers," but he would find himself diverted once more from realizing his wish. It would be 1993 before another book containing *Mountains and Rivers* sections would be published. Not long after his return to the Bay Area, he became preoccupied with commitments to family and community. There was "real work" to do: the building of Kitkitdizze, his new home on the western slope of the Sierra Nevada, and the establishment of a working American Buddhist community, an aspiration that involved building a spiritual, psychological, and physical network, starting with the construction of a Zendo (a large room—often a separate building—for the communal practice of *zazen*) on his property. Perhaps Snyder found some time to work on *Mountains and Rivers,* but the "WHOLE THING" was nowhere in sight. Most interesting about his comment to Allen is his feeling that he had to return to the States to finish his long poem. Indeed, the landscape of Snyder's long poem would reflect a change in focus as the poet began his own reinhabitation of Turtle Island.

In the next four or five years (1970–75) five sections of *Mountains and Rivers* were published. In 1971, Snyder published an outstanding poem from the sequence:

"The Hump-backed Flute Player." The setting of this poem, like that of "The Blue Sky" before it, clearly interconnects the landscapes of Asia and North America, yet Snyder's strong sense of regional landscape provides this poem with a feeling of "settling in" to the Great Basin of the American Southwest. He told an interviewer from Reed College that he was "dealing *from*, not *with*, the West Coast and the Great Basin so that locality is very important to me as far as the specifics go, but the specifics do get translated also into an interior landscape." Still, even while admitting the subjective quality of his landscapes, he reemphasized that "the power of region is very important. The smaller and more deeply noted the region is, the better" (Snyder, "Conversation with Gary Snyder" 6-9. GSP B19:F5). These thoughts, expressed about the poetic landscapes of *Mountains and Rivers Without End*, reflect Snyder's growing interest in "bioregionalism" and "reinhabitation," concepts embodied in much of his subsequent writing, prose or poetry.

By November 1971 "The California Water Plan" had been published. It later became part of *The Fudō Trilogy*, which included "Smokey the Bear Sūtra" and "Spel Against Demons." All three poems contain references to the Japanese Buddhist figure Fudō Myō-ō, whose diamond sword and mantra are called on to exorcise specific social evils. Although the poem was included on Steuding's list of *Mountains and Rivers* sections, Snyder chose not to include it in the final book.

It was two years before another *Mountains and Rivers* poem surfaced. In June of 1973 *Caterpillar* published a facing-page selection entitled "Gary Snyder: 2 Poems." The left-hand page contains "Greasy Boy"; the lines on the right-hand page—beginning with "I saw the Mother once"—are not titled. The two poems are disconnected imagistically, yet they are linked by the fact that one is about a "boy" and the other a "mother," a prevalent theme in Snyder's poetry, especially in *Mountains and Rivers*. Neither poem was identified on the page as a *Mountains and Rivers* poem, yet when Snyder subsequently gave public readings of "Greasy Boy" he referred to it as a section, and it was reprinted as part of *North Pacific Lands & Waters: A Further Six Sections* (1993). It was not, however, among the final thirty-nine sections.

The year 1974 saw two sections published: "Ma" and "The Flowing." For Steuding, "Ma" speaks with "the voice of the Indian" and is, therefore, another indicator of Snyder's return to motifs of the American West (104). "The Flowing," which has undergone some revision over the years, was first published in the journal *Kyoi Kuksu*. When first published it was divided into four parts—"1. Watershed," "2. Riverbed," "3. Floods," "4. Mouth"—and there was no subsection entitled "Falls." A subsequent publication of "The Flowing" in *Conjunctions* (1981) carried the "Mountains and Rivers" tag line and substituted the present "Falls" subsection for the former part "3. Floods." "Falls" itself was published as a distinct poem several times, once as an identified section of *Mountains and Rivers* (*Sierra* 73 [May–June 1988]: 46–47).

Apart from "The Canyon Wren," a poem that was not originally conceived of as a part of *Mountains and Rivers*, approximately a decade passed before another section of the poem was published. In the meantime, Snyder's influence, as poet, environmentalist, and key figure in the spread of American Buddhism, continued to grow. He lectured and gave interviews widely; when he had time he worked on some prose. He had published *Earth House Hold* at the end of the '60s; *The Old Ways* followed in 1977; his Reed College thesis, *He Who Hunted Birds in His Father's Village*, was released in 1979. Although he was extremely active in writing and publishing books of poetry during this period, even winning the Pulitzer Prize for *Turtle Island* in 1975, evidently he put aside his work on *Mountains and Rivers*. He admitted as much to Hank Fincken in 1979 when he told him that he had temporarily stopped working on the poem. (interview, *Indiana Writes* 3.2: 42. GSP B26:F9).

In 1986, I wrote to Snyder about my continuing interest in *Mountains and Rivers*. In reply he enclosed a copy of Dōgen's *Mountains and Waters Sūtra*, a work he said had helped him to "clarify" his thinking about *Mountains and Rivers*. His response indicated he had returned to thinking actively about his long poem. Indeed another section—"Night Song of the Los Angeles Basin"—appeared in the summer of that year, and its city landscape clearly signaled a broadening of Snyder's focus. A rush of poems soon followed; most were grounded in landscapes that Snyder had not previously experienced: Australia; the far reaches of the Pacific Northwest, including Alaska and the Queen Charlotte Islands; the Western Tibetan Plateau; and Taiwan, to name the most prominent. From this point on, he never let up, driving steadily and surely toward a point where he could let his long poem go into the world of its readers.

In the fall of 1986 Snyder published *Left Out in the Rain: New Poems 1947–1984*, a diverse assortment of previously unpublished poems that helped to fill in the poetic spaces of his life. Shortly thereafter, in the winter edition of *Zyzzyva*, a *Mountains and Rivers* poem with one of the longest titles in modern poetic history appeared: "Daylight All Day / Cool North Breeze with Low Clouds / Midnight Twilight / Steep Rock Slope Mountain Sheep / Green Summer Slopes Song." This Arctic poem is both end-dated—"VIII 40085 [1985]"—and located—"Headwaters of the Koyukuk, Brooks Range, Alaska." Snyder sent me a typescript of the poem, marked as "from *Mountains and Rivers Without End*," in March of 1987. With a change of title it would appear as one of the "Six Further Sections" in the 1993 *North Pacific Lands & Waters*.

Continuing his exploration of city landscapes, "Walking the New York Bedrock / Alive in the Sea of Information" appeared in the fall of 1987. Internally dated as "V:85-III:87," it was obviously written in the same time frame as the Los Angeles poem. Both of these "city poems" concentrate on the wilderness to be found within the heart of the megalopolis. Together they conveniently mark off the opposite shorelines of Turtle Island. Although "Night Song of the Los Angeles Basin" was not published with a tag line, Snyder sent me a copy of the poem in November 1991, marking it as "from 'Mountains & Rivers Without End.'" "Walking the New York Bedrock" was identified as a section from the outset.

"The Bear Mother," "Jackrabbit," and "Raven's Beak River / At the End" appeared, along with two other poems, in the spring 1988 issue of *Sulfur.* "The Bear Mother" is internally place-dated as "Brooks Range / VIII:86"; "Jackrabbit" carries a date of "V:87"; and "Raven's Beak River" is place-dated "Tatshenshini/Alsek Lake—July 86." Thus "Jackrabbit," which has no reference to a specific place, appears to have been written shortly after "Walking the New York Bedrock." On the other hand, both "The Bear Mother" and "Daylight All Day" derive from experiences in the "Brooks Range," while compositionally or experientially they are separated by a year.

The next poem in order of publication, "Haida Gwai North Coast, Naikoon Beach, / Hiellen River Raven Croaks," appeared in 1989, but it too is dated from the 1985–87 period. As printed it was dated "Fall of '86–Summer of '87," but a typescript copy, sent to me by Snyder, is more specifically dated as "from Mts. & Rivers / 24:IX:86." The poem has its origins in a trip the poet took to the Queen Charlotte Islands to visit the sacred sites of the Haida Nation. It must have been a significant moment for him. Snyder's early work on Haida mythology at Reed College was surely an impetus for his poetic odyssey, and now, once again, his travels along the pathways of the Pacific Northwest intertwined with, and inspired, the making of his long poem.

In November 1991 Snyder sent me a letter that included a list of poems that were to be incorporated into the final manuscript of *Mountains and Rivers Without End.* There were several surprises. "A Lion Dream," "Kumarajiva's Mother," and "Down" were not listed; "Smokey the Bear Sūtra," an early favorite of Snyder's readers, was. "Greasy Boy," attributed earlier only by a comment on a taped recording, was confirmed as a section and, indeed, would appear as such in the soon-to-be-published *North Pacific Lands & Waters: A Further Six Sections.* Several poems on the list—"Old Bones," "Afloat," and "Earrings Dangling and Miles of Desert"—had not yet been published. The poet enclosed typescripts of the latter two poems. Their antithetical landscapes made them a surprising pair: one floats on a sea of water; the other is rooted in the sand and shrubbery of a desert location. "Afloat," set in Glacier Bay, has obvious links with other Pacific Northwest poems like "Haida Gwai North Coast" and "Raven's Beak River." The introduction of a desert locale was a new turn for the poem.

"Macaques in the Sky" (*Wild Earth* Winter 1991) grew out of a trip Snyder had taken to southern Taiwan in September of 1990. "Earrings Dangling and Miles of Desert" was printed in the *Yale Review* (Spring 1992), and "Afloat" appeared a year later in the spring of 1993. Six months later, in the fall of 1993, "Under the Hills Near the Morava River," a poem with a European location (the Czech Republic), was printed in *Sulfur.* Despite its geographical title, Snyder's emphasis is on an imagistic connection with the Upper Paleolithic rather than on the "landscape."

Remarkably, in the next two and a half years, fourteen more sections and two small *Mountains and Rivers* books would be issued. As 1993 came to an end, Snyder was reading in public from his recently published *No Nature: New and Selected Poems* and simultaneously working diligently to wrap up *Mountains and Rivers Without End.* Two new poems surfaced just before 1994 began. Snyder sent me a typescript copy of "Covers the Ground," a poem to be published the following summer in *The Threepenny Review.* According to a handwritten note on my copy, Snyder had worked on the section from the "Spring of '88" to mid-November 1993. Its generic setting in California's Central Valley was noted specifically as "Down highway 99 toward Merced," providing an echo with the earlier "Night Highway 99." In late December, Snyder sent me a copy of "An Offering for Tārā," a section based on a September 1992 trip he made to Leh in northern India to speak at a conference sponsored by the Ladakh Ecological Development Group. The leap from California to the Western Tibetan Plateau was not the only contrast; the spirit of John Muir hovers over "Covers the Ground," while the Tārā poem is overtly filled with Buddhist and East Asian symbology.

The most significant event to take place before the turn of the year, however, was a new gathering of selected *Mountains and Rivers* sections in a book, the first to be issued since 1970. *North Pacific Lands & Waters: A Further Six Sections,* published by Brooding Heron Press, assembled "Afloat," "Haida Gwai North Coast," "Greasy Boy," "Raven's Beak River / At the End," "Arctic Midnight Twilight . . . " (formerly titled "Daylight All Day . . . "), and "The Bear Mother." A collector's item, the book is beautifully illustrated by Bill Holm, a professional artist and authority on Haida art. The interaction of the poems with Holm's carefully drawn totem animals—frog, sea wolf, seal, eagle, shark, raven, thunderbird, grizzly bear, orca—connects the book visually and verbally to the narrative culture of the native peoples who inhabit the lands and waters of the Pacific Northwest. Curiously, "mountains" and "rivers" became "lands" and "waters," signaling a distinctive change in Snyder's perception of his long poem.

In May 1994, the poet gave me copies of "Old Bones," "Reeds," "Cross Legg'd," and "Endless Streams and Mountains." Both "Reeds," inspired by a visit to Baja California, and "Cross Legg'd" were published in the fall of 1994. Taken together their focus seemed unrelated to sections that had recently been published. Unlike the wild and misty oceanic scenes of the Pacific Northwest, both the Baja poem, retitled as "With This Flesh" in the final book, and "Cross Legg'd," an intimate lyrical poem, take place in arid settings.

In March of 1995, shortly after "An Offering for Tārā" was printed in the *Yale Review,* the poet sent me a spiral-bound, first-draft copy of the final book. In it were, as there are in the final book, thirty-nine poems, but the draft copy contained surprises, and, in retrospect, many changes were still to come. The manuscript began with "Endless Streams and Mountains" and ended with a new poem "Finding the Space in the Heart." Also surfacing for the first time in this early draft version were "Mountains Walk on Water," "Musgrave Mountains Gatha," "Instructions," "New Moon Tongue," "Boat of a Million Years," "Old Woodrat's Stinky House," "The Mountain Spirit," and "We Wash Our Bowls in This Water." "Greasy Boy," which had appeared among the six poems of *North Pacific Lands & Waters,* was included, yet "The Circumambulation of Mt. Tamalpais" was conspicuous by its absence. Two poems that would become part of the final book—"The Canyon Wren" and "The Dance"—were not included, and two that were—"Greasy Boy" and the new "Mountains Walk on Water"—would ultimately be dropped from the published book. Several of the "new" poems contain internal references to earlier times and places in Snyder's life, but there is no way to tell when they were actually composed. "Boat of a Million Years," with its obvious references to Snyder's experience on the *Sappa Creek* in 1957–58, may have been written at that time. "Musgrave Mountains Gatha," eventually retitled as "Earth Verse," was probably published in an Australian journal as far back as 1981 when Snyder visited sites in the Central Australian Desert with his good friend Nanao Sakaki. "Finding the Space in the Heart," with its references to several visits to the same Great Basin Desert landscape over three decades, was obviously conceived and reconceived over a span of many years. Allusions in "The Mountain Spirit" hearken backward to Snyder's earliest days attending Nō drama in Kyoto and to a moment of creative inspiration on the peaks of the White Mountains that belongs to the same time frame as "The Hump-backed Flute Player." With the exception of "Mountains Walk on Water," all the new poems in this first draft were published apart from their appearance in *Mountains and Rivers Without End.* "Endless Streams and Mountains," "Instructions," and "Old Bones" saw print in 1995.

In February 1996 I received a second spiral-bound draft version of the completed book manuscript. Although the long poem still began with "Endless Streams and Mountains" and ended with "Finding the Space in the Heart," it now comprised only thirty-seven poems. "Hymn to the Goddess San Francisco," "Mountains Walk on Water" and "Greasy Boy" were no longer part of the long poem, but "The Circumambulation of Mt. Tamalpais" had been reincorporated. Several sections had been shifted to different locations within the longer poem, and all the sections were now grouped into four distinct parts. The number of poems grew to thirty-eight when, shortly after receiving this second draft, I received a note from the poet indicating that he had added "The Canyon Wren," a river-rafting poem from the '80s. Early draft versions of that poem in the Gary Snyder Papers at UC-Davis date Snyder's original notes for the poem as April 22, 1981; printed versions of the poem invariably locate the site of the raft trip as "Stanislaus River / Camp 9 to Parrott's Ferry"

(GSP B2:F28–32). Both "Boat of a Million Years" and "The Mountain Spirit" were published in the spring of 1996. While there is no reason to consider the two sections as a deliberate poetic pair, they nevertheless represent significant moments in the poet's life. "Boat of a Million Years" represents a fruitful moment at the outset of *Mountains and Rivers Without End.* As his correspondence reveals, Snyder's poetic imagination experienced great leaps forward as he perched meditatively on the bow of the *Sappa Creek* feeling the waves of the planet move under him. On the other hand, "The Mountain Spirit" is clearly a poem of closure in which Snyder's alter ego finally comes face to face with The Goddess; it is the meeting with this energizing spirit that drives the poem forward.

There was still one more gathering of *Mountains and Rivers* poems for a special edition. In deliberate contrast with the cold, wet poems of *North Pacific Lands & Waters,* Snyder now published a desert tetralogy celebrating the landscape of the Great Basin and the ranges surrounding it. *Finding the Space* (1996), like the earlier special edition, was a work of art. Enclosed in black wrappers and printed on buff-colored handmade paper, the poems in the book are beautifully enhanced by relief engravings of desert images. Three of the poems—"Earrings Dangling and Miles of Desert," "Old Woodrat's Stinky House," and "Finding the Space in the Heart"—are quite obviously poems with a desert locale; "Cross Legg'd," although less specifically set, nevertheless speaks of the "dry old west" and a "scratchy breeze."

The last poem to be written for the final book was "The Dance." During the spring semester at UC-Davis Snyder taught a graduate seminar that focused on the place of *Mountains and Rivers* within the tradition of long poems. In May Snyder sent me a copy of "The Dance" with a short note explaining that he felt his long poem needed to have a section commemorating "the founding of Nō and traditional performance in general." He was careful to add that most of the poem had been worked up much earlier and that its inclusion had only been a matter of making some final revisions. Once again there were thirty-nine poems in the book. By the middle of the summer of 1996, "We Wash Our Bowls in This Water" had been printed in a journal, and arrangements had been made for "New Moon Tongue" to appear at the end of the year in *Wild Earth.* As far as I know, "The Dance" was never issued in periodical form, certainly not before the book appeared.

In September of 1996, after forty years of inspired and thoughtful composition, Snyder's *makemono* poem, *Mountains and Rivers Without End,* was published by Counterpoint.

The Landscape Scroll

Mountains and Rivers Without End is, quite literally, a verbal landscape painting. To read its pages poem by poem—either front to back or back to front—is to travel through thirty-nine sections with distinct settings and a strong sense of space. The illustrations accompanying the book are reproductions of a well-known Chinese horizontal handscroll—*Ch'i-shan wu-chin* (*Streams and Mountains Without End*)—found in the Cleveland Museum of Art.

Dan McLeod believes that Chinese landscape painting may well be the "aspect of the Chinese imagination with the longest influence on Snyder's poetry" (378). The poet told McLeod that his first encounter with the world of Chinese landscape painting came before he was a teenager:

> The cascades [*sic*] of Washington, and the Olympics, are wet, rugged, densely forested mountains that are hidden in cloud and mist much of the year. When I was a boy of nine or ten I was taken to the Seattle Art Museum, and was struck more by Chinese landscape paintings than anything I'd seen before, or maybe since. I saw first that they looked like real mountains, and mountains of an order close to my heart; second that they were different mountains of another place and true to those mountains as well; and third that they were mountains of the spirit and that these paintings pierced into another reality which both was and was not the same reality as "the mountains." (McLeod 378)

Snyder's recall of these painted mountains reminds one of Dōgen's observations: "If you say the painting is not real, then the material phenomenal world is not real, the Dharma is not real. / Unsurpassed enlightenment is a painting. The entire phenomenal universe and the empty sky are nothing but a painting" (*MRWE* ix). The misty painted Chinese mountains seen by the young Snyder in Seattle are "real" on several levels: in a generic sense they appeared to him as a true, or "real," reflection of the verifiable Cascade and Olympic Ranges that surrounded him. Yet the mountains painted by the Asian artists obviously were not drawn from these mountains of the Pacific Northwest; they mirrored mountains to be found in China, and in their carefully drawn verisimilitude they are a "real" image of those Chinese mountains, not some "unreal" or falsely drawn depiction. Lastly, these painted landscapes are "real" in that they capture the essence of what a mountain range is for Snyder, an animated and animating spirit that could not exist without correspondence to the physical mountains. Undoubtedly, such sophisticated observations about mountains (and rivers) developed at a later stage in Snyder's thinking, but their origin may be traced to that insightful moment impressed on the mind of a ten-year-old boy.

The genesis of the poem's title—and consequently much of its structure—came when Snyder was a student in Oriental languages at the University of California at Berkeley. While he practiced *sumi* painting under the tutelage of Chiura Obata, whose *Evening Glow at Yosemite Waterfall* (1930) illuminates the book's cover, the poet was immersed in understanding the spirit and mind of East Asian aesthetics. "In museums and through books," he says, "I became aware of how the energies of mist, white water, rock formations, air swirls—a chaotic universe where everything is in place—are so much a part of the East Asian painter's world. In one book I came upon a reference to a hand scroll (*shou-chuan*) called *Mountains and Rivers Without End.* The name stuck in my mind" (Snyder, "Making" 153). According to Chiang Yee, the Chinese term for landscape painting is "'*Shan-shui*' . . . 'Mountain and Stream'" (134). Although *shui* in Chinese literally translates as "water," depending on the writer the Chinese ideograms are variously translated as "mountain-stream," "mountain-river," or "mountain-water." Whichever way the phrase is translated, Chinese landscape painting, a reflection of actual mountains and waters, attempts to capture life in its essential complementarity. As François Cheng explains: "Mountain and water constitute, in the eyes of the Chinese, the two poles of nature, and they are charged with rich meaning" (84). In terms of their "relationship of contrast and complementarity" they "become the principal figures in the universal process of transformation" and "have a relationship of reciprocal becoming. Each one is perceived as a state that is constantly attracted to and complemented by the other. Just like yang, which contains yin, and yin, which contains yang, mountain, which is characterized by yang, is virtually water, and water, characterized by yin, is virtually mountain" (84–85).

Snyder's long poem unquestionably deals with these relationships and correspondences, the "universal process of transformation," the same "reciprocal becoming" of the mountains-rivers dyad. In 1964, he told Gene Fowler that "more and more I am aware of very close correspondences between the external and internal landscape. In my long poem, *Mountains and Rivers Without End,* I'm dealing with these correspondences, moving back and forth" (Snyder, "The Landscape of Consciousness" [Fowler] 5). Many years later, he told Katherine McNeil he was "writing about the complementarity of mountains and rivers, but that's really the planet, taking that on" (McNeil 23). When he first went to Japan, as he tells us in "The Making of *Mountains and Rivers Without End,*" he "read geology and geomorphology" and "came to see the yogic implications of 'mountains' and 'rivers' as the play between the tough spirit of willed self-discipline and the generous and loving spirit of concern for all beings" ("Making" 155). In Buddhist iconography this "dyad" of "the dynamics of mountain uplift, subduction, erosion, and the planetary water cycle" is represented by Mañjushrī, who embodies "transcendent insight" and "Tārā, the embodiment of compassion" (155). The overarching dyadic correspondences are evident: on the one hand we have a combination of mountain dynamics / self-discipline / Mañjushrī / transcendent insight, while on the other we find an interweaving of planetary water cycle / loving concern for all / Tārā / compassion. Keeping in mind that it is the dance of the dyad that counts, one must add that the former set is seen as masculine while the latter is feminine. A reader's clear perception of these interrelationships is essential for an understanding of *Mountains and Rivers Without End.*

Much of Snyder's thinking about the aesthetics and history of Chinese landscape painting is captured in the manuscript he shared with McLeod. T'ang landscapes, for example, are said by Snyder to be "still half-tied to journeys, topographies or poems," but with the Sung dynasty, the landscape artists "opened out to great space: with the rock formations, plants and trees, seasons, ways of appearance and disappearance . . . [and how] vast scenes . . . become visionary timeless lands of mountain rocks and air-mist-breath and far calm vistas; in which people are small, but lovingly rendered, doing righteous tasks, or reclining and enjoying their world" (McLeod 379). Snyder speaks of those Sung landscape painters who "didn't always walk the hills they portrayed," but who "could invent mountains that . . . seemed to float in mist." Their "vision of earth" was as an "organism, in which water, cloud, rock, and plant growth all stream through each other." The Sung landscapes contain mountains that Snyder feels are "magical and difficult, the routes are not clear. Yet they are passable." After the Yüan dynasty, he theorizes, "painting kept love of nature alive" for a civilization that was "living more in cities and farther from the hills." These were paintings "done by people who had never walked the wild, for people who would never see it." Nevertheless, he singles out a painting from the 1700s (Wang Hui's *Landscape in the Style of Chu-jan and Yen Wen-Kuei*) that "does one more turn": "it draws out to sea at the end, where the sea-fog is twisting into scrolls that take us back to the very beginning. Fine. Mountains were meant to be deeply entered, on foot, where the naked energy can be touched anew" (379).

Among these comments one sees the workings of Gary Snyder's imagination. At times the trails of the painting are maplike in his mind, yet sometimes he "walks" the spaces of the landscape painting as if they were actually under his feet. At other times his understanding moves "outside the painting" as he coolly becomes critical of its style or of the civilization revealed by that style. And then there are moments when he clearly imagines going "beyond," into spaces farther than the spaces of the painting, into "visionary timeless lands of mountain rocks and air-mist-breath and far calm vistas." The interweaving of Snyder's multiple perceptions is a natural outcome for an ecological vision of planetary interdependence.

Early in the development of his long poem Snyder spoke of being inspired by a scroll located in the Freer Gallery in Washington, DC, entitled *Mountains and Rivers Without End*, painted "by the Yüan Dynasty painter, Hsü-Pen" (McNeil 23). Yet as the Freer scroll became problematic on several levels, Snyder began to allude to a scroll with a similar title in the Cleveland Museum of Art (Snyder, "Making" 156). Scholars had discovered that Lu Yüan of the Ch'ing dynasty—and not Hsü Pen—was the painter of the Freer handscroll. On the other hand, although it was anonymously painted, the Cleveland handscroll had accumulated a full-length monograph, several scholarly articles, photographs, and slides for study (S. Lee; Lee and Fong; Bush). Snyder also felt that the Freer scroll—approximately sixteen feet long with multitudes of patterns and objects to contemplate—was just "too rich."[6] In contrast, the Cleveland scroll is both comprehensive and elemental, easier to take in at a single glance.

In using the horizontal handscroll as a structural model for his long poem, in one stroke Snyder had access to the aesthetics and the content that he desired. It is fairly obvious, even to one with little expertise as an art critic, that the Cleveland scroll may be divided into distinctly different sections, providing, at the outset, a viable comparison: a complete scroll with discrete parts; a long poem composed of separate sections. Further analysis of the scroll reveals that

> it is a somewhat eclectic picture . . . and [it] recapitulates much of the previous development [i.e., of the historical progression of landscape painting in China]. It begins with a small, low, intimate landscape in the then up-to-date and fashionable style of Zhao Lingran, goes on to a mountain-encircled space recalling *Wang Chuan Villa*, then proceeds to a style of painting rather like Dong Yuan's, rolling and resonant in its form, followed by a crystalline style based upon another Northern Song [Sung] master, Yan Wengui, then moves to a climactic mountain unit painted very much in the towering style of Fan Kuan, and finally ends with a forest and distant mountain area, perhaps close in style to Guo Xi. (S. Lee 351–52)

Sherman Lee here characterizes different parts of the scroll as it unrolls from right to left in terms that are, for the most part, easily perceived by the viewer: a "small, low, intimate landscape," a "mountain-encircled space," a "rolling and resonant" form, a "climactic mountain unit," and finally a "forest and distant mountain area" to end it. Lee comments that such handscrolls not only allow for the "development of pictorial structure within a frame formed by the beginning and end of the painting," they also require "organization in time and space":

> one can vary the frame by rolling either end, or both, thus creating innumerable small pictures at will. At the same time, in moving along the composition from right to left, viewing a few feet at a time, one passes in time through a landscape, something not possible in the hanging scroll or album painting. (S. Lee 352)

Lee's "reading" of the scroll provides a model for readers of Snyder's *Mountains and Rivers Without End*. Various sections of the poem can be read in and for themselves, as "innumerable small pictures," or the entire poem may be read from beginning to end as a singular long poem, a linear journey. In addition, selected sections have been gathered into four larger units, each of which may be appreciated as an integrated module. Finally, one can demonstrate that the poet's close study of the handscroll has influenced the placement of certain sections. For example, as the last section of the scroll levels out visually, so "Finding the Space in the Heart," the final section of

Mountains and Rivers, drops down from the peaks of the White Mountains to the flattened spaces of a Great Basin playa and becomes less intense, poetically speaking. After the enraptured dialogue among the voices of "The Mountain Spirit" and the compressed lyricism of "Earth Verse," the reader senses a lower key, a plainer style, in the last section. Still, as one finds with the fractal rhythms of the Nō drama, even this "flatter" final section has modulations among its internal cadences. Beginning rather prosaically, it pulses toward a highly charged and poetic verbalization of the desert's "emptiness" before subsiding, as the poet's words recede, like the "wet black brush" and the lingering sound of the Nō actor's foot stamp, into the distance of the "space" that "goes on."

Lee goes so far as to posit a musical quality to the Cleveland handscroll:

> Sequence and spacing can be used to create "movements," as in music. *Streams and Mountains Without End,* for example, begins with a gentle, quiet theme, then gradually shifts to a first climactic theme of mountain peaks and village. This alters to a strong and rolling but quieter passage, ending in a second climactic variation of the mountain theme, which recalls the recent past and hints at things to come. Here a new, staccato motif begins, of vertical mountains with an almost crystalline structure. This ends, and a rocky variation prepares us for the final great climactic mountain theme. . . . Finally, the scroll ends with a variation on the quiet opening passage, incorporating mountain elements that have occurred throughout most of the picture. This coda, though not dramatically as powerful as some earlier passages, summarizes the whole. (S. Lee 352)

Focusing on merely one example, we might say that if "The Mountain Spirit" is the "final great climactic mountain theme" of Snyder's poem, then "Finding the Space in the Heart" is its ending element, "a variation on the quiet opening passage," a "coda, though not dramatically as powerful as some earlier passages, [which] summarizes the whole." The end of Snyder's poem, as Lee states of the painting, is a "variation" on the beginning as the poet returns to "*[w]alking on walking*" and "lifts away" the wet black brush tip that was set down in the first section. The harmony between the two artistic forms, while hardly programmatic, is tantalizing. Because they are works of art, exact aesthetic parallels will never be found, but there is little doubt that Snyder has attended to the felt rhythms of the Cleveland handscroll as he composed *Mountains and Rivers Without End.*

In an interview from the early '70s, Snyder discussed the possibility of finding a different "fluidity in form" and "formal patterning" as one extended measurement over a sustained period. He spoke specifically of the music of India with its interplay of *raga* (melodic mode) and *tala* (rhythmic mode) that had given him a model for "a longer range sense of structuring with improvisatory possibilities taking place on a foundation of a certain steadiness that runs through it" (Snyder, interview [Jacoby] 38–39). The longer range that he speaks of may easily be applied either to his poem or to the handscroll if one "steps back" to view the whole. Dramatic evidence of this structural patterning in the Cleveland scroll may be found by glancing at the miniaturized photo of it that has been reproduced across a two-page spread in Sherman Lee's *A History of Far Eastern Art* (352–53). There, displayed horizontally and seen with a single glance, the planes of the opening and closing units, the lifting and dropping of various ridgelines, the triangular peaks and intermittent valleys, the misty places set off by those settings that are precisely drawn, all unfold into a unified gestalt, a rhythmic patterning. If this "reading" of the scroll's rhythm seems farfetched, it would be good to remember that Snyder has spoken of observing "real" ranges of mountains in a similar manner. In his interview with Jacoby, Snyder explains his "evolving ability to visualize the whole of the landscape of the Sierra Nevada, to sort of feel it all moving underneath me." He speaks of the "periodicity of ridge, gorge, ridge, gorge, ridge . . . an interlacing network of, oh, 115-million-year-old geological formation rhythms" (44). When Jacoby asks Snyder how to do that in poetry, Snyder asks him if he has "ever tried singing a range of mountains" and then proceeds to tell him how to do it:

> Well, you sit down somewhere where you're looking at a long mountain horizon. Then you sing up and down all the way along like that. . . . I tried it on the mountains up above Death Valley, the Panamint range, one time. I tried it many times until I got it right. . . . I got to know that skyline so well that I knew when I was following the melody that the mountains were making. . . . [Y]ou get so that it's a kind of source of form, right? (44)

Evidently, Snyder is able to sing the rhythm of actual mountains as well as those that are painted on silk or printed on paper. As Dōgen says, "If you say the painting is not real, then the material phenomenal world is not real" (*MRWE* ix). The sung rhythms of the Sierra Nevada may be heard just as surely as the periodicity of the ridges and gorges of the Cleveland scroll; the sections of *Mountains and Rivers Without End* also lead toward an observable rhythm. Some sections are short; some are average length; some are extended. Some sections are prosaic; others are intensely poetic; others combine these modes of presentation. Within sections some lines are factual and flat, encyclopedia and dictionary entries; others rise to moments of heightened emotion. However one chooses to measure the beat, it is clear that a cadence does exist and that it exists on several levels. The rhythm of the eye often corresponds to the rhythm of the ear, and both are grounded in actuality. Tracing the measure in the units of the poem develops one's sense of its longer form; stepping back to observe the totality serves to underscore the periodicity of the units. Any way one looks at it or hears it, rhythm is a primary way into the poem.

With regard to content, as Lee states, the "representational organization is fully as important as the aesthetic one" (S. Lee 352). From the very beginning, if it was nothing else, *Mountains and Rivers* was a poem replete with travelers seen against a background of the planet's rocks, soil, and waterways, especially—though not exclusively—those of Asia and the American West. Turning from section to section as the poem unrolls, hundreds of mountains and rivers are encountered on the reader's journey, their names flowing off the tongue with ease:

Of mountains and mountain ranges, to select only some of the most prominent: the Olympics and the Cascades ("Night Highway 99," "Three Worlds, Three Realms, Six Roads"), the Sierra Nevada (Mount Whitney—"Bubbs Creek Haircut"), the Brooks Range of Alaska (Doonerak—"Arctic Midnight Twilight"), the White Mountains of California/Nevada ("The Hump-backed Flute Player" and "The Mountain Spirit"), the sacred Mount Tamalpais, the Central Asian Pamir ("The Hump-backed Flute Player"), the Western Himalaya ("An Offering for Tārā"), and King Lear Peak ("Finding the Space in the Heart").

Of rivers and watercourses to name only a few: the Elwha River, the profusion of rivers found in "The Hump-backed Flute Player" (Sweetwater, Quileute, Hoh, Amur, Tanana, Mackenzie, Old Man, Bighorn, Platte, San Juan), the Ganges in "The Market," the Kamo and Columbia Rivers in "The Flowing," the Hiellen River of the Queen Charlotte Islands, the Tatshenshini (or Raven's Beak) River in British Columbia, the Morava River of the Czech Republic, the unnamed watery location (actually Adams Inlet, Glacier Bay) of "Afloat," the ancient geological Tethys Sea and the present Indus River in "An Offering for Tārā," and the prehistoric Lake Lahontan of "Finding the Space in the Heart." Nor should we forget the metaphorical "Sea of Economy" in "Walking the New York Bedrock." We earthlings truly wash our bowls in this water.

In the mid-'80s Snyder seems to have come to terms with the city landscape as a part of his poem. Two sections of the final poem—"Night Song of the Los Angeles Basin" and "Walking the New York Bedrock"—explore the wilderness in the city landscape. It is not that "the city" did not exist beforehand; very early sections of the poem, including "Night Highway 99," "Three Worlds, Three Realms, Six Roads," and the displaced section "Hymn to the Goddess San Francisco," all dealt with a cityscape. Yet the tone of these early sections inclines toward rejection rather than the accommodation to the city that one finds in the later "city poems."[7]

There was, however, a notable change in Snyder's poetic landscape. Somewhere in his imagining of the poem, whether it came from exploring the rhythms of Chinese handscrolls, Dōgen's philosophy, or from other developments in his life, Snyder lowered the heights and broadened the rivers. In the mid-'80s as he began writing into his poem again after almost a decade of having set it aside for other projects, the poet began to de-emphasize the linear rivers and vertical peaks. When, in 1993, he quietly published *North Pacific Lands & Waters: A Further Six Sections,* the mountains became "lands" and the rivers had become "waters." The Hiellen River of "Haida Gwai North Coast" and the Tatshenshini River of "Raven's Beak River" both eventuate in unique "doabs" (a confluence of rivers): In the former the setting depicts the meeting place of river and ocean; in the latter, under the watchful eyes of the glaciers, the river flows into Alsek Lake. "Afloat" takes place in an ocean bay. "Arctic Midnight Twilight" is the *only* poem of the six to describe a mountain setting, and even then the peaks of Doonerak and Midnight Mountain are made subservient to both the clouds that surround them and the sheep that take to their slopes. The landscape, such as it is, of "Greasy Boy" speaks of "dirt . . . sand blown . . . dirt bits—down the wind. / across scab land." Clearly not a mountain setting, this flat dusty landscape may have been an early instance of what would become explicit desert scenes in the later "Earrings Dangling and Miles of Desert" and "Finding the Space in the Heart."

Snyder has painted numberless little travelers across the scroll of his poetic landscape. Some are historical and some are mythical or legendary; some are ghostly; many are human, and many more are animal. In addition to Snyder's own persona and those of his personal friends and acquaintances, we find Hsüan-tsang, Wovoka, and Kokop'ele; Coyote, Bear, Rabbit, and Raven; wild monkeys and sheep; a host of women from Mā to Artemis to Tārā; the poet Su Shih and the philosopher Dōgen; and a cast of what seems like hundreds more. Nor should we forget that the journey undertaken here is as much an act of the land as it is of the beings upon it. In some of the sections—"Arctic Midnight Twilight" is a good example—the landscape itself "calls forth" the beings, sheep in this case. Indeed, the spacing of the quintessential lines of the poem—"*Walking on walking / under foot   earth turns*"—leave readers wondering whether it is the walking foot that turns the planet or the turning planet that has taught the foot to walk. In the immense landscape of *Mountains and Rivers Without End*, the very mountains and rivers *are* travelers, always in motion, always flowing. Continents drift and volcanoes provide uplift; entire "seas" come and go, destined to come again with some future turning of the universe. Historical, legendary, and mythical movements take place from the Paleolithic era via migrations of the Ice Age(s) to the present moment. In all, it is a vast dance of all beings interrelated with the ongoing rhythms of the universe. Yet, at the heart of this space, in the midst of these enormous movements implied and activated by the poem, sits a listener, an attentive reader, who hears the rhythms. There, with the melody of flute players like Krishna, the Nō musician, and Kokop'ele in the background, in a space that can and cannot be defined, sitting quietly, cross legg'd in the emptiness, one meditates with Snyder on the curl in the horns of sheep or on the twisted branches of the oldest living being on the planet, the Bristlecone Pine. We listen for the rhythm in the whorl.

Snyder's poems commemorate no mere picaresque wandering in linear time. The horizontal dimension of the scroll may be seen as a symbol for Snyder's personal journey in time and space and for humanity's general historical and cultural journey starting from some dim recess of time in the Paleolithic era and continuing into the present of our so-called civilized eras and places, but it coexists with a vertical dimension that disappears into the recesses of our minds even as our eyes begin to perceive it. Journeys that begin as if they were rooted in the physical wander into a different dimension of SPACE; the path winds up into the "upper silk void" represented by the cloud-air-mist-white space in the Chinese landscape paintings. As Chiang Yee states:

> It is illuminating to see the later Sung masterpieces with large areas of empty space occurring as part of the composition, while only the topmost peaks of a few mountains are limned in, or a single leafy spray of peach blossom or other flower. Ever since [the later Sung period], SPACE has been the most outstanding characteristic of our landscape painting. (157)

The merger with empty space is as important as the journey that follows the path; yet one way does not negate the other. The onward-and-forward trip in time is truly a journey "without end" because the road *does* loop back on itself; the traveler follows an endlessly turning wheel of life. This journey is the same interminable trip that the Nō play's Yamamba or Snyder's Mountain Spirit or the planet itself takes on our behalf in the poem: "*Walking on walking / under foot earth turns.*"

Snyder's concept of space always includes the possibility of Buddhist "enlightenment," a moment when one "awakens" to "a nowness of emptiness (. . . *shūnyatā*)" wherein one comprehends "the true nature of things" by knowing that "the entire universe is emptiness," including oneself ("Enlightenment" *Shambhala Dictionary*). This "consciousness," or *prajñā,* is not the result of logical reasoning, but a moment of "immediately experienced intuitive wisdom" ("Prajñā" *Shambhala Dictionary*). The Buddhist concept of the "void" or "emptiness" is not nihilistic; the world of emptiness is not separate from the world of phenomena but inheres in it. It is not that "things do not exist but rather that they are nothing beside appearances" ("Shūnyatā" *Shambhala Dictionary*). In "Night Highway 99" in the midst of describing thousands of miles of journeys taken at various times over the same highway running south from Washington State to California (and back again), the poet speaks of a "Chinese scene of winter hills and trees / us 'little travelers' in the bitter cold" (*MRWE* 21). These might well be the same travelers described in *The Dharma Bums:* "little men hiking in an endless landscape of gnarled old trees and mountains so high they merge with the fog in the upper silk void" (Kerouac 157). Indeed, five lines later Snyder alludes to a metaphorical merger with emptiness: "The road that's followed goes forever; / in half a minute crossed and left behind" (*MRWE* 21). Ultimately, all talk of "the void" can be couched only in metaphorical terms. Even words are dyadic; they are, themselves, "empty." Yet these words, these forms, these metaphors are the only ones we have; they are what we cling to. The white spaces of the scroll, whether left empty by the artist, or imaged as tangible cloud-mist-air, remain metaphors for the indescribable. Still, as humans hope and pray to be transported somewhere "beyond," the Mahāyāna Zen masters bring them back down to earth with a reminder that all such wisdom gained is ultimately nothing special; the wisdom of beyond is rooted in the earth. Attentive readers may detect analogues to the "upper silk void" in Snyder's poem. At such moments, often with only slight poetic slippage in time or space or customary logic, the poet endeavors to alter the reader's perception in a profound way.

So, in "Journeys," the reader struggles with the reality of Snyder's dream visions, visions that conclude with a deadly falling over a cliff that opens up "the way to the back country." In "Bubbs Creek Haircut," the mountain-climbing narrator has his consciousness altered as he meditates on the slippery solidity of our world during his ritualized haircut. The "Blue Sky" attempts to cut across the normal sense of time and language, to make things whole under a single, curving, turquoise-blue sky of consciousness. When the eagle of that section "flies," it flies into the same metaphorical *beyond* reached by travelers who cross a road in half a minute, leaving it behind, rather than following it forever. It flies into the wild or it falls into the back-country; that is, it encounters the wisdom of the void beyond. In "The Hump-backed Flute Player" it is the wisdom we find in the prophet Wovoka's hat where, like Black Coyote, we see the "whole world" when there seemed to be only emptiness an instant before. It is woven into the very fabric of *Mountains and Rivers Without End*, although it culminates, momentarily, in the nondual space described in the final section, "Finding the Space in the Heart." The wisdom to be gained when one steps back at the end of this long poem, a wisdom hinted at in encounters in earlier sections along the path of our reading, is the realization of the dynamic itself: that the universe, be it mental or physical, up or down, poet's or reader's, is a vast network of interrelationships that we perceive only in glimpses and guesses in any given time span. The trick, if it may be called that, is to realize ourselves as integral with the entire landscape we inhabit even as we stand apart from it musing on the paths we have already traversed and those we may yet explore. With the scroll unrolled and laid out before us, we may see in the distance, and perhaps even hear, the rhythms of its drawn dimensions. As we come closer to its representational world, we note the travelers on their journeys among the mountains, the tiny boats floating on the rivers, the small birds in the chinquapin or liquidambar trees.

Finding oneself in the mystical space, "[a]t the still point of the turning world," as T. S. Eliot phrased it in yet another impressive long poem of religious intent, one can say "*there* we have been," but one "cannot say where" one has been physically located ("Burnt Norton" *Four Quartets*). This "place" is out of time and beyond the processes of the natural world as we know them, yet both Eliot and Snyder suggest that such places can *only* be reached in and through time. A fundamental paradox of Buddhist logic, this tangible "empty" world, the only one we will ever have, is not only the path to enlightenment; it *is* enlightenment. For Snyder there is no other world. What a marvelous painting-poem it is; what mountains, what rivers, what vistas of open space, what tiny trails we humans have walked on for thousands upon thousands of years! What flora and fauna reside there! It slips by—all of it—in each moment of time, all unrolling forever, always here.

The Nō Play

Knowing the work of both Ezra Pound and Arthur Waley, Snyder was intellectually familiar with the Nō before he arrived in Japan, but seeing actual performances left a profound impression on him. His fascination was such that he purchased season tickets for the plays performed in Kyoto throughout the years he lived there. In June of 1956, barely a month after his arrival, he wrote to Will Petersen that he was about to attend his first performance of Nō (Halper 77). Nine months later he wrote to Whalen:

> I am fascinated by the kabuki and noh recitation technique—at kabuki one man half-sings half-chants the narrative (in a sort of poem form, alternating 7-5-7 syllable lines) with one or two samisen twangers, occasional wooden clackers & drum. At noh, a flute, a big drum & a little drum, sometimes clackers, are used. Very sparingly. Sometimes the man on the small hand-drum sort of yowls as he hits it. . . .
>
> . . . I can imagine a very jolly creative sort of modern poetry-modern-dance-music shot built around the reading of one long dramatic-type poem with musicians and possibly a dancer. (8 Mar. 1957. Reed–PWP)

Whalen wrote back: "I wish I could come over to hear the Noh scene you tell about. I think the only possible music to go with poetry is something on the order you describe, monodic, twangy, percussive. . . . I'm uncertain about having dancing [in it]" (23 Mar. 1957. GSP B89:F75). Both writers were unquestionably interested in developing a new form of poetry, one utilizing music and, perhaps, dancing. Additionally, Snyder envisioned a "long dramatic-type poem," especially as influenced by the rhythms and dance motion of the Nō.

In August 1957, Snyder broke away from the rigors of his first year of Zen study to embark on the *Sappa Creek*, but he didn't leave behind the influence of either Buddhism or Nō. Will Petersen, now living in Kyoto, wrote him several letters during this period, often including comments on the aesthetics of the Nō. Toward the end of 1957, Petersen spoke of the "whiteness of Noh," the "interrelatedness of objects," and the "instant" of "persons in movement-nonmovement" (4 Dec. 1957. GSP B77:F14). Two days later, he wrote again: The best actors in Nō don't become "characters," "they become 'nobody'; and the best Nō players see the other people but are not aware of them" (6 Dec. 1957. GSP B77:F14). Lew Welch also wrote to comment that using "music, masks, and everything" is an "excellent far-out, long-range, thing" (6 Dec. 1957. GSP B88:F74). Strongly under the influence of the classical Japanese Nō play, Snyder was evidently sharing his vision of poetry as an artistic performance combining lyric, narrative, and dramatic modes.

By February 1959 Snyder was back in Japan to take up his studies at the Zen Institute under Oda Sessō Rōshi. From letters written to Joanne Kyger during the next year, it is clear that he was fully absorbed in Zen thought and practice and equally preoccupied with the positive and negative aspects of his growing relationship with her. Although he was working on his poetry—*Riprap,* financed by Ferlinghetti and published by Cid Corman's Origin press, was sent to the printers in August 1959—in general this was a time of input, not output. On April 1 he wrote to Kyger that he didn't care "if I ever write poetry again or read anything or go anywhere. The 1st thing is to get at the *root* of the mind. Fuck the Beat Generation, etc." (GSP B104:F10). Obviously in a dour mood, a few days later he sent a second letter filled with negative worries about the prospects of Joanne joining him in Japan. Then, on April 11, he wrote again, apologizing for his intemperate words and mentioning that he would be attending an entire day's performance (10 A.M. to 6 P.M.) of Nō plays with Cid Corman and Will Petersen (GSP B104:F10). In July he spoke of "a weird consciousness constantly of every movement—a continuous slow dance" (7 July 1959. GSP B104:F10), a comment that reveals a deepening Zen mind, possibly influenced by an awareness of movement in the Nō. By late August he was speaking of a "poetical inspiration" that for him "is secured in the female spirit of the universe & the play of creatures (like mountains too) in the world" (28 Aug. 1959. GSP B104:F10). Snyder's consciousness of a female presence at play both in the world and in his poetry is evident here; one wonders if he has already attended the Nō play *Yamamba,* the story of the Old Woman of the Mountains, the Mountain Spirit that will become central to *Mountains and Rivers Without End.* That he is writing to Joanne Kyger, a woman he now perceived to be both his *devi* and prospective wife, is not without significance. By September, as their correspondence shows, she has decided to join him in Japan, and Snyder began to provide her with practical advice on making the trip. Still, as much as he looked forward to her coming, he was ambiguous about having constant companionship. On September 3 he told her of the benefit of quiet time:

> [C]reatively and every which way I can only take so much social company & moving about. My mind gets cluttered. The last few quiet days working on poems & reading . . . has gotten me real high, can see what I'm doing & how the poetry shapes up. (GSP B104:F11)

A letter written a week and a half later is more social; among talk of some wild partying, he speaks positively of the ferment caused by the Beat movement and reports that some Japanese magazines have asked him to contribute something as a member of the movement (12 Sept. 1959. GSP B104:F11).[8] Living alone in search of the "root of the mind," Snyder constantly wavers between his quest for an uncluttered creative silence and his desire to be a member of a larger community, be it a partnership with Joanne Kyger or part of the growing Beat movement.

In mid-December Snyder excitedly tells Kyger that he has seen a Nō play called *Eguchi* with Corman and Petersen. He sums up the story as one "about [a] prostitute who is actually Samantabhadra (Infinite Love) in disguise" (15 Dec. 1959. GSP B104:F11). On the 29th he speaks of "rumblings of a vast new poetry inside me" (GSP B104:F11). A letter written to her a month later is more specific: "I've been working on Mts. and Rivers lately. A section called 'Sophia' and a section called 'Night Highway Ninety-Nine'" (13 Jan. 1960. GSP B104:F11). Evidently Whalen received a similar letter, for he wrote back to tell Snyder: "I'm glad to hear that *Mountains and Rivers Without End* is still in the works & hasn't bogged down. I'm looking forward to seeing it, so you can't quit now" (19 Jan. 1960. GSP B90:F33). The Nō appears as a backdrop for much of this correspondence. The letters at the turn of the year, in particular, seem to mingle Snyder's interest in the Nō with a rekindling of poetic energy. A year that seems to have started in poetic despair and enforced loneliness has culminated in literal reanimation as the female spirit of the universe, assisted by the magical power of the Nō plays and the expectation of Joanne Kyger's arrival, invades his being to inspire rumblings of a vast new poetry, rumblings that just happen to coincide with the writing of sections of *Mountains and Rivers.*

Snyder's letters continue to show his interest in the classical Japanese Nō. In early 1961, he enthusiastically writes to Whalen about Will Petersen's knowledge of the Nō (10 Feb. 1961. Reed–PWP). At the same moment he is writing sections of *Mountains and Rivers,* he is absorbing the spirit and technique of the Nō, often with Petersen's help. Petersen was undergoing formal instruction in both chanting (*utai*) and movement (*shimai*) as well as working on a way to translate Nō plays more completely by incorporating the rhythm and movement that attends the words. His letters often provide insight into the concepts that interested Snyder:

> EGUCHI and YAMAUBA both seem to lend themselves to what you seem to be up to. I've worked on neither, and know little about them—but one of these days will check into the texts and see what I can come up with. None of the existing translations reveal the structure of noh, at least not with the clarity that *is* there. YASHIMA, which I've about finished—it needs a few minor alterations—may be a stimulus, and suggest ways of approach. What I'll do, as soon as possible, is to send you some notes on structure: groundwork for discussion when we meet.

I also have been keeping SHIMAI NOTES, which will interest you—not in relation to MOUNTAINS & RIVERS, but in relation to . . zazen? let's say, breath, life in general.

No more now—all else takes time to say.

(I'll let you know whenever EGUCHI or YAMAUBA are being performed around town.)

How about: old mountain woman / young river gal? YAMAUBA, by the way, is also pronounced "Yamamba": an alternative reading you may have occasion to use. (Jan. [1960?/61?]. GSP B77:F19)

Evidently Snyder has asked Petersen for advice about the general structure of the Nō and information about two plays that have caught his attention: *Yamauba* (*Yamamba*) and *Eguchi*. While the direct influence of a "young river girl" (*Eguchi*) in *Mountains and Rivers Without End* remains conjectural, that of the "old mountain woman" on "The Mountain Spirit" has been identified by the poet himself (*MRWE* 162). In June 1961, Whalen received a letter from Snyder that combined talk of *Mountains and Rivers,* Petersen's work on the Nō play *Yashima,* and Snyder's own initiation into the rites of the Yamabushi, a Japanese mountaineering cult whose physical hiking is identified with spiritual activity. All these activities interconnect. Like Petersen's description of *shimai* practice as a form of "walking zazen," the physical hiking of the Yamabushi is a spiritual event. When Snyder warns Whalen, in the same letter, that he will "sacredize Tamalpais," he not only reveals his intent to bring all this "home" to California but discloses the religious impulse of his intentions (17 June 1961. Reed–PWP). The ritualistic walking of Tamalpais will be a sacred action, bringing Buddhist attitudes toward space-time-being back to America. For those who cannot hike the mountain, a reading of the Mount Tamalpais section in *Mountains and Rivers Without End* will allow them to "walk" the sacred spaces of the mountain in the poem. In its religious dimension, *Mountains and Rivers Without End* is a vehicle for promoting psychic and spiritual healing of an overly egotistical and consumer-oriented society, one that the early Beats typically labeled "Amerika." Similarly, for Snyder, full participation in the experience of the Nō involves psychic or spiritual healing. According to the poet, the confrontation staged by its participants is an "encounter that resolves karmic knots, the dance of release" (letter to Dan McLeod, 6 Nov. 1983).

The Nō play, steeped in Zen religious thought and practice, is usually ascribed to a system of performance worked out by the famous *sarugaku* actor Kan'ami [Kwannami] Kiyotsugu (1333–84) and his son Zeami Motokiyo (1363–1443). Zeami, both an actor and composer of Nō plays, set down much of the traditional aesthetic of the Nō even as it is performed to this day. Snyder, in his drive to connect with the roots of things, traces the beginnings of the Nō even further back by going to its folkloric source in the *Kojiki* (A.D. 712), the first record of Japan's history. Snyder's version is retold in the *Mountains and Rivers* section entitled "The Dance" where the erotic dance of the goddess Ame-no-uzume lures the Sun Goddess Amaterasu out of her dark cave. In the roots of the Nō, myth, history, and culture are interwoven as imported and adapted dance forms from China combine with local fertility rituals and entertainment dances involving, among other things, music, puppets, costumes, and masks. All these were precursors to the form known as *sarugaku,* which developed into Nō starting with Kan'ami. As Nō became associated with the ruling class, it was refined into an elegant and artistic form. In Nō, as projected by Zeami,

> [t]he significance of the action, the beauty of the verse, and the excellence of the music and singing . . . are purposely designed to "open the ear" of the mind, while the miming (*monomane*) and the dancing (*mai*) awaken the emotions of the spectator and "open his eyes" to that supreme form of beauty denoted by the word *yūgen,* which is the ultimate goal and the essential element of all aesthetic expression, be it dramatic or lyrical. The term *yūgen* has no exact equivalent in English; literally it means "obscure and dark," but, as used by Zeami, it carries the connotation of half-revealed or suggested beauty, at once elusive and meaningful, tinged with wistful sadness. (NGS, *Noh Drama* ix-x)

Words are no substitute for the experience of a Nō performance. Yet since even the basic principles of the Nō are not well known outside of Japan, some words of explanation must be provided. Its music and rhythm, including silence and nonmovement, are particularly mysterious:

> The Noh creates its own time, its own reality. . . . The Noh makes its concept of time clear in its production, where the music is of greatest aid. Each moment, disconnected or discontinuous, aims at being self-contained and independent. The personality of a character, a note of music, or a gesture in movement exist for the moment in which the audience senses their existence. And yet each of these moments is made possible not so much through their own power as through the generative power of each moment acting on the next. . . . The striking features of this music are its sense of tension, of silence, of discontinuity. The use of the pause, or break, is characteristic of this music, though the Japanese concept should perhaps best be translated as "silence," to avoid the more limiting connotation of the "pause" or "rest" in Western music. This "silence" should have a positive meaning and should enable one to feel immense depth and a sense of infinity just as space does in Far Eastern painting. Moreover, the use of "silence" and of percussion instruments in music and of shouted interjections serves to separate one moment from the other in a sharp manner and to enhance the rhythmic power of the music. (Ishibashi 138–39)

The silent tangibility of space is a common element in the Nō and "Far Eastern painting." Snyder's interest in commingling the two Asian art forms in his poem is yet another way to embody the "emptiness," the music of silence, that is at the tangible heart of Zen thought.

The music heard (or not heard) during a performance belongs to a flute player and three drummers; each percussion instrument produces a different sound. Unlike the classical Greek chorus, the chorus of eight to ten persons sits to one side of the stage and normally has no part in the action of the play. The chorus may speak the words of the main actor as he dances, or it may comment impersonally on the events or carry on a dialogue with the actors. The primary actor is called the *shité,* and he may have one or more attendants called *tsure.* The supporting role belongs to the *waki,* who may also have one or more attendants known as *waki-zure.* Generally, the main actors are masked, wear extravagant costumes, and move with measured step and deliberate gesture. The main playing or dancing area of the stage is square and raised about two and a half feet above the floor of the auditorium. A long wooden walkway in full view of the audience serves as a "bridge" that connects the main platform stage with a curtained "mirror room" off to their left. The actors emerge from the mirror room, entering the stage area with measured steps along the bridgeway toward the main playing area. The stage has little decoration: an ancient pine tree painted on a panel at the back of the stage, several important pillars that mark special sites for the actors, and three sapling pines that are placed at intervals along the bridgeway. The chorus sits to the right of the stage; the musicians sit on stage at the back. The action of the play begins and ends with the reverberating sound of a foot stamp on the wooden boards.

When Snyder said, in 1959, that the "dramatic structure" of his poem followed "a certain type of Noh play" (D. Allen, *New American Poetry* 421), he was thinking of a two-part or double Nō, which is based on two appearances on stage by the *shité.* Typically, such plays begin with the entrance of the *waki,* who is traveling to a shrine or through some culturally important landscape. The *shité*'s first appearance is "in the guise of a quite ordinary contemporary of the *waki.*" In fact "the *shite* of the earlier part . . . is the ghost or specter of a person involved in events long ago at the imagined site of the action." In the ensuing conversation with the *waki,* the *shité* usually reveals what events occurred in this place in the past. Then the *shité* retires. Many plays inject an "interlude" at this point. The second part begins with the *waki*'s expectant waiting. Soon "the *shite* of the later part . . . reappears as a vision in a dream to the *waki* and, now in the proper role of the *shite,* revives from the past the circumstances of the older time" (Miner, Odagiri, and Morrell 308). A major distinction between the two appearances of the *shité* has to do with the type of performance: in the first part the past events are narrated; in the second, they are enacted through movement, mime, and dance.

The Nō cannot be understood without some familiarity with the structural principle known as *jo-ha-kyū*. It is, as Hiro Ishibashi calls it, the "essential rule" of composition in the Nō, and it dominates everything that is "concerned with timing—from the making up of a programme to the way of pronouncing a single word":

> *Jo* (or Introduction): The ideogram for *Jo* means "Beginning." This part is straightforward, and rather slow in tempo.
>
> *Ha* (or Development): The ideogram for *Ha* means "Breaking." The *Jo* part is broken up and developed into a more elaborate stage. There is a change in tempo.
>
> *Kyū* (or Conclusion): The ideogram for *Kyū* means "Rapidity." As a rule this part is quicker than the *Ha*, vigorous in some pieces, and gives an impression of conclusion. (191)

The *jo-ha-kyū* rhythm is applied to every aspect of the Nō, and it is easily detected in the structural breakdown of the two-part Nō play. The *waki*'s first entrance, in which he gives information about his journey, is regarded as introductory. The development begins as the *shité* enters and, in a chanting voice, gives hints about his character. It continues through the dialogue between the *waki* and *shité*, and ends with the *shité*'s narration. The speedy exit of the *shité* serves as a rapid conclusion to the first part. In terms of an entire two-part Nō play, the first part may be viewed as a combined *jo* and *ha* while the relatively speedy second part is a *kyū*. Nevertheless, the second part of the play may also be broken down into its *jo, ha,* and *kyū* elements. The introductory note is sounded again by the waiting of the *waki*. The reappearance of the *shité* signals the beginning of the *ha* stage. Again there is an encounter between the two as the intensity develops. The climax of the play—the high point of the *ha*—occurs with the dance of the *shité*, as he reenacts the past events. The *kyū* of the second part then takes place with a quick final dance of the *shité*. With a stamp of the foot, the *shité* retreats. "The end of the second appearance repeats the disappearance of the *shité* at the end of the first" (Miner, Odagiri, and Morrell 312–13).

Not only does the *jo-ha-kyū* govern the order of action within plays, it controls which plays will be performed in a season, and which ones on a certain day, and in which order they will be presented on that day. It influences the presentation of masks, costumes, music, poetry, and motion—as well as their various combinations.

> [I]t is further held that the *jo*, the *ha*, and the *kyū* themselves each have their *jo, ha*, and *kyū*. Ideally speaking, all else is so governed. A given subpart (*mondō, ageuta, rongi*, and so on) should be governed by the same three-part rhythm. Even a given gesture—for example, the *shite*'s raising the right hand slowly toward the eyes of the downward inclined face as a gesture of weeping—should be governed by the *jo-ha-kyū* rhythm. In considering such details, we perhaps

> do best by considering the rhythm an ideal with which the actor imbues his art, having made—through his practice and interpretation of a given work—the rhythm second nature and a feature of aesthetic habit in performance of parts and the whole. (Miner, Odagiri, and Morrell 311)

No rigidly formulaic method has been imposed on the composition of *Mountains and Rivers Without End;* however, as an exemplary pattern capable of many variations, the fractal character of the *jo-ha-kyū* rhythm has plainly influenced the composition of Snyder's poem. Given his years of attending to matters of the Nō, its aesthetic rhythms have become ingrained, "a feature of aesthetic habit," in his own writing. As an ideal the pattern has influenced his gathering of sections into four parts, the arrangement of those parts, the position of selected sections within the parts, and the placement and rhythm of units of prose, poetry, image, and idea within sections.

All Nō plays are envisioned as modular structures with smaller segments (*shodan*) named and classified according to the kind of event taking place or to the type of language used or mode of performance, to name a few of the major categories.

> Following the entrance music (*shidai*), the play generally opens with a *shidai* sung by the *waki* alone or in unison with his attendants (*waki-zure*) accompanied by a few notes of the flute and drum taps, subsequently repeated (*jidori*) by the chorus. It is followed by the *michi-yuki* (travel song) also executed by the *waki.* The entrance music of the *shite,* called *issei,* is usually followed by a song of the same name executed by the *shite.* The *sashi* somewhat resembles a recitatif and precedes the songs proper (*uta*) or takes the form of a dialogue. . . . The *uta* . . . are sung by the *shite,* the chorus or the *waki,* and are divided into *age-uta* (high-pitched singing) and *sage-uta* (low-pitched singing). . . . To these should be added the *kiri* (finale) sung by the chorus at the end of the play. The spoken portions (*kotoba*) written in prose are classified into *nanori* (name-introducing) delivered by the *waki, mondō* (dialogue), and *katari* (narration) delivered in a somewhat monotonous rhythm. (NGS, *Noh Drama* xii)

The meticulous care that goes into the nuanced composition and performance of a Nō drama has its parallels in Snyder's *Mountains and Rivers Without End.* There is a journeying *waki*—more often than not, Gary Snyder's invented self. The traveler's role enlarges to include multitudes if we consider ourselves and all other beings who "walk" the endless paths on earth's turning globe as performers. Insofar as the *shité* in *Mountains and Rivers* makes more than one appearance, Snyder is generally faithful to the design of a traditional two-part Nō play. Yet the poet goes further by evoking multiple appearances of the protagonist. The awesome "Mountain Spirit" met by Snyder's alter ego in a dream-vision on the high ridges of the White Mountains may be glimpsed earlier in the poem wearing different "costumes" or "masks." Mostly "feminine" in form, some of those entities who appear in disguise are Jackrabbit, the strange teacher in "The Elwha River," Mā, the "Goddess in tall rain dress" from "Night Song of the Los Angeles Basin," the flowing river goddess of "The Flowing," the "she" who lies "Under the Hills Near the Morava River," Tārā, the Bear Mother, the mother monkey in "Macaques in the Sky," Artemis in "Earrings Dangling and Miles of Desert," the woman—Carole Koda—in "Cross Legg'd," and Yamamba, the "Mountain Spirit" herself. There are others, all reflections of the spirit embodied in a feminine Other. To dance with her is to be transformed beyond gender and species, time and space.

Snyder's story of an encounter with a magical mountain woman—often seen naked by a river or lake—one who literally engages a man with a dance, often erotic, is a type of the Swan Maiden story, an ancient tale whose tracks disappear into prehistory. Deep in the forest, discovered bathing by a man, the swan maiden entreats him to return her "clothes" that he has taken. To induce him to do so, she dances. Her dance revitalizes him even as she, swan maiden that she is, having regained her feathered robe, flies off into the distance, leaving him behind. This folkloric motif underlies Snyder's 1951 senior thesis at Reed College, *He Who Hunted Birds in His Father's Village.* As a student of anthropology and linguistics, he explored the dimensions of a Haida myth about a goose-girl, seeing it ultimately as a type of the universal Swan Maiden story. The Nō play *Hagoromo* and a poem Snyder derived from it—"The Feathered Robe"—are both versions of this myth. There are echoes of it in the enticing dances of Ame-no-uzume and Pārvāti, among others, and it may be that Snyder has wrapped the young river gal (Eguchi) and the old mountain woman (Yamamba) into one dancing figure. The theme can be spotted in several of his early poems, most obviously in "For the Boy Who Was Dodger Point Lookout Fifteen Years Ago," where Snyder's first wife, Alison Gass, is the "Swan Maiden" (*Back Country* 34). There are also, in letters and journals, both published and unpublished, many glimpses of actual women found in similar circumstances, usually while on back-country trips with the poet. Snyder retells the story one more time, and grandly so, in his Nō-inspired *Mountains and Rivers Without End.*

Serving as a reminder of the formal "foot stamp" that opens and concludes a Nō play, the echoing sound of "[w]*alking on walking*" begins and ends the action of Snyder's poem. In the first section, "Endless Streams and Mountains," Snyder points the way toward this ritual movement with the line "stamp the foot, walk with it, clap! turn." As the action draws to a close in "Finding the Space in the Heart," the "[w]*alking on walking*" phrase appears again on the last page of the long poem. Several sections appear as enlarged segments of the Nō: for example, "Night Highway 99" may be compared to a *waki*'s "travel song" (*michi-yuki*) and "Three Worlds, Three Realms, Six Roads" may be seen as a *nanori,* or "name-introducing" section. Snyder's placement of unmistakable prose passages alongside those of obviously poetic—imagistic or rhythmic—intensity is the mark of an ear attuned to the rhythms of the Nō. "Earrings Dangling and Miles of Desert"—which begins with scientific and encyclopedic description and ends in lyricism—provides one easily perceived example of this intentional stylistic juxtaposition. The poet has, in fact, given public performances in which he has chanted, sung, and spoken the entire script of *Yamamba* in an English-language version. Some passages within sections are narrative, others are intensely lyrical, and some function as dialogue. Impersonally delivered shorter sections not only provide rhythmical variations among the various sections of the long poem, at times they have the feel of a chorus.

Snyder deliberately utilizes indention and spacing to convey kinesthetic and/or musical effects. A headnote to the original 1960 printing of "The Feathered Robe" in *Poetry Score* said as much: "The poem is a statement of the action of the Nō play *Hagoromo* (*The Feathered Robe*) and in the short lines and stanza-insets the poet [i.e., Snyder] is trying to get the feel of it as he saw it danced" (GSP B14:F3, my brackets). If, in 1960, Snyder was attempting to capture the dancing and chanted rhythms of the Nō by printing poems with "short lines and stanza-insets," then what appear to be idiosyncratic indentions, line breaks, pauses, alternations of prose and poetry, white spaces, and compression and expansion of images in *Mountains and Rivers* are likely to be derived from the same influence. Even though Japanese and English methods for syllabication are radically different from each other, it is quite possible to find occasional English imitations of recognizable Japanese poetic forms involving five and seven syllables or a regularized pattern of stresses. Still, syllable counting is not Snyder's normal approach to metrics. Rhythm is more a function of his kinesthetic imagination, and breath becomes the final measure of the line, as it is with so many of the poets who began writing in the early '50s. Without actually hearing the poet speak (or sing or chant) lines, it is difficult for readers to make valid judgments about the oral-aural quality of Snyder's long poem, but there are evident places in his poem where he intuitively or consciously follows the model of the Nō play that has so entranced him.

Additional structural parallels exist between the two-part Nō and Snyder's poem; most will be discussed in the commentaries on individual sections. At a most basic level, in accordance with the *jo-ha-kyū* principle, there is a perceivable introduction, development, and close to the entire sequence as well as in each of its four parts. Although the overall *jo-ha-kyū* rhythm normally calls for a five-part structure with three subparts to the middle *ha* unit (a *jo-ha-kyū* within the *ha*), Snyder openly stated to his graduate class at the University of California at Davis that his poem had been adapted to a four-part rhythm with part I as a *jo*, parts II and III a double *ha*, and part IV as the *kyū* (May 1, 1996 seminar discussion).[9] Realistically, as the entry on Nō in the *Princeton Companion to Classical Japanese Literature* states: "There are not many works that provide complete examples [of the ideal pattern]. . . . [M]ost nō lack one part or another" (Miner, Odagiri, and Morrell 315). Individual readers vary, but most will sense a growing complexity in each of the four parts of the poem and a rough parallel with the *jo-ha-kyū* principle. Each formal part of the long poem begins with an introductory section or sections, often a poem of statement with a formal or ritual tone to it: "Endless Streams and Mountains" and "Old Bones," "The Market," "The Circumambulation of Mt. Tamalpais," "Old Woodrat's Stinky House." Compared with the rest of the poem, *all* the sections of part I seem in the *jo* mode, if for no other reason than that they introduce us to the early life of the primary *waki,* Gary Snyder. Five of the original seven sections of *"Mountains and Rivers Without End" Plus One* occur in this part. In each of the four parts there is a noticeable increase in poetic intensity and a cumulative effect as each part climbs toward a major section: "The Blue Sky" (part I), "The Hump-backed Flute Player" (part II), "An Offering for Tārā" (part III), "The Mountain Spirit" (part IV). Finally, although neither "The Blue Sky" nor "The Hump-backed Flute Player" are followed by a section one might term a *kyū* section, both "The Bear Mother" and "Macaques in the Sky" of part III and "Earth Verse" and "Finding the Space in the Heart" of part IV have the feel of closure, including a quieter tone. In some ways, "Endless Streams and Mountains" and "Finding the Space in the Heart" bracket the entire sequence, and one might speculate that the true opening and closing sections of *Mountains and Rivers* are "Old Bones" and "Earth Verse," both short poems that are formally wrought in a poetic sense. It is not a matter of great importance; there are many paths, some of them off the trail, to comprehending this poem.

Thematically, Snyder's early phrase about "history and its vengeful ghosts" (D. Allen, *New American Poetry* 421) points far beyond a meeting by an individual poet with his female "Mountain Spirit." No mere personal journey, *Mountains and Rivers Without End* is a "dance of release," a model for the resolution of "karmic knots" that plague contemporary society. The spirits that inhabit the imagination of Snyder are global and planetary: air, rock, water, plants, trees. All beings have a story that demands repeated, if not endless, attentive listening. Sheep provide models for how to live "at home." "The Bear Mother" resides mythically in the human imagination. Just below the skin of our dusty world are Paleolithic skeletons from "Old Bones" and "Under the Hills Near the Morava River." Hordes of animals are called forth in "The Hump-backed Flute Player": "ghost bison, ghost bears, ghost bighorns, ghost lynx . . . ." On a larger scale their ghostliness brings the fear of lost species, a reduction in biological diversity. Moreover, this vast "ghost dance" should remind North Americans of Snyder's statement in *Earth House Hold* that "the American Indian is the vengeful ghost lurking in the back of the troubled American mind" (*EHH* 112). Snyder once intended to use that "ghost" as a "kick-off" for the "final version" of *Mountains and Rivers* (Snyder, "From Anthropologist" [Tarn interview] 112). The old ways embodied in the spirit of Native America are, as a rule, invisible to present-day citizens of the "New World." Yet that selfsame ghost lingers in the background prophesying a day of reckoning, if not one of violence then at least of awareness.

Like the revisitation of spirits in the No play, in the midst of rather ordinary proceedings, when one is least expecting it, one may experience a frightening, and illuminating, instant of true vision, a moment when the ghosts of the past catch up with the present. When what has formerly been unacknowledged, a seeming emptiness, is accepted and fully embraced in a dance of release, new worlds of possibility may indeed open up. *Mountains and Rivers Without End* contains many such moments. Whole sections, or lines within sections, capture the reader's attention, give the reader "pause." The stated intent of "The Blue Sky," a shamanistic poem based as much on folklore as on linguistics, is to exorcise ghosts and to bring a healing wholeness to the living. Among other things, "An Offering for Tārā" instructs us that we all eat at the same table. We all "Wash Our Bowls . . ." in the same water cycle. Reading *Mountains and Rivers*—a song of interconnectedness—we join Snyder as little travelers engaged in an ongoing dance with the planet we live on, hopefully poised to leap beyond the particulars of our divided worlds and selves in order to reinhabit this planet we call Earth, these actual places we call our various homes.

The final intent of following the dramatic structure of "a certain type of Nō play" is not substantially different from using the Chinese horizontal landscape scroll as a compositional tool. The two-part Nō play describes a journey whose climax is an awesome and enlightening moment of confrontation with the *shité*'s symbolic shape-shifting presence. Similarly, painted scrolls depict a dynamic merger of the meticulously drawn "realistic" landscapes and paths with the amorphous "upper silk void" that both looms above and floats down on them. Each structural model serves to move the reader's mind "beyond" while never allowing us to forget where we "really" are. Snyder's canvas begins with mountains and unrolls among hills, rivers, oceans, cities, and deserts to show us encounters with animals, mythological and legendary beings, humans past and present, spirits, and the Other in "her" many guises. At the end of this scroll-play, we finally come to a breathing space on a playa—a landscape of "emptiness" where all things are possible. Here, finding that all things have value, the *shité* stamps his foot for the last time, the players retreat, the music dies down, and "the space goes on" in the reader's mind.

The Goddess and Her Companion(s)

Unquestionably, there is a major narrative thread—a series of encounters with incarnations of what I have labeled "The Goddess"—woven through *Mountains and Rivers Without End*. The story culminates in the dynamic meeting of the poet's alter ego with the "Mountain Spirit," whose interminable "[w]*alking on walking*" is matched only by his ongoing pilgrimage in search of her on behalf of all beings. However, to speak of "The Goddess" in the work of Gary Snyder is to speak of a multivalent, and controversial, symbol. At times his reference is to anthropological evidence that suggests a so-called Paleolithic Magna Mater, but the multiplicity of feminine images that he draws on, both modern and ancient, from Asian, European, and New World cultures, more strongly suggests his reliance on a highly poeticized, archetypal goddess figure. Buddhism, in particular, has supplied Snyder with notable female symbols, but the natural world, especially the animal kingdom, and his personal life have also furnished feminine icons for the shaping of *Mountains and Rivers Without End.*

Archetypally, this meeting of male and female is an ancient verbal dance. The geomorphological story of the interplay of mountain and water begins in the distances of barely imaginable time, but the human tale, in Snyder's mind, begins with the dance of a primitive dyad: the antlered shamanistic "Sorcerer" of Troís Frères and The Mistress of the Animals. According to some scholars, "some 20,000 years ago and more," there was an "image of a goddess" that

> appeared across a vast expanse of land stretching from the Pyrenees to Lake Baikal in Siberia. Statues in stone, bone and ivory, tiny figures with long bodies and falling breasts, rounded motherly figures pregnant with birth, figures with signs scratched upon them—lines, triangles, zigzags, circles, nets, leaves, spirals, holes—graceful figures rising out of rock and painted with red ochre—all these have survived through the unrecorded generations of human beings who compose the history of the race. (Baring and Cashford 3)

Some figurines, identifiably feminine, are known only by generic names such as "goddess figure." A well-known example is a stick figurine with defined arms, breasts, legs, and head carved from mammoth ivory, found in Mal'ta, Siberia (16,000–13,000 B.C.). Others, while not naturalistic, are shaped so expressively that they have been given individualized names like the "Venus of Laussel" (rock carving, c. 22,000–18,000 B.C., Dordogne, France) or the "Venus of Lespugue" (mammoth-ivory statue, c. 20,000–18,000 B.C., Pyrenees), or the "Venus of Willendorf" (limestone, 20,000–18,000 B.C., Austria). Often found deep inside caves that have been described as "sacred caverns" where one may have "an experience of divinity," as Joseph Campbell tells us, the expressionistic nature of most of these statues, which generally exaggerates the breasts, vulva, and/or buttocks, leads to conclusions about them that are much broader than that suggested by the name "Venus," the Roman goddess of love (*Primitive* 300). Their widespread presence "from France to Russia" has led some scholars to a controversial interpretation that there was a "continuity of religious structure stretching from Europe to Siberia" (Baring and Cashford 13). No mere fertility idols, these so-called goddess figures call forth a world of numinous religious experience because "the mystery of the female body is the mystery of birth, which is also the mystery of the unmanifest becoming manifest in the whole of nature. . . . [T]he body of the female of any species leads through the mystery of birth to the mystery of life itself" (Baring and Cashford 8). Joseph Campbell has no doubt that the female figurines are "the earliest examples of the 'graven image' that we possess, . . . apparently, the first objects of worship of the species Homo sapiens" (*Primitive* 325). Along with the Paleolithic cave paintings of roughly the same time frame, the figurines are said to form the basis for a continuous expressive language "present to this day in Western culture" that draws on the creative wellsprings of art and devotion. "[T]hese images of the goddess appear throughout human history" because "they all express a similar vision of life on Earth, one where the creative source of life is conceived in the image of a Mother and where humanity feels itself and the rest of creation to be the Mother's children" (Baring and Cashford 9–10). To celebrate "The Goddess" is to celebrate the "mystery of birth and death and the renewal of life, not only human but all life on earth and indeed in the whole cosmos" (Gimbutas xix).

Nothing could be simpler and yet more complex than this symbology. Descending from a time in which human beings were in awe of the animal world, when "animals were sacred beings, teachers of fundamental laws within which both human and animal were bound" (Baring and Cashford 26), the goddess figure is sometimes referred to as a "Mistress of the Animals." As a Mother Goddess she is "linked with primeval mothers in animal form such as the bear, deer/doe, elk/doe, and in the Upper Paleolithic with the she-bison and mare" (Gimbutas xxii). She is associated in early mythological times, perhaps because of her nurturing breasts, with cows. She is frequently connected with a moon symbol, possibly because of the fit between her menstrual cycle and the moon's "magical" power of waxing and waning. Others suggest that her representation as (or with) the crescent horn of the moon is due to congruence of that shape with the horns of the bull; hence there are stories relating her to a moon-bull-child. As a "Life and Birth Giver" she may be seen as "a frightening image of death," especially when "ornithomorphic features of her mask and her vulture's feet betray her connection with the bird of prey" or her "ophidian features—long mouth, fangs, and small round eyes—link her with the poisonous snake" (Gimbutas xxiii). In sum, she is seen as a "parthenogenetic Goddess" whose basic functions encompass totality; she is a "Giver of Life," "Wielder of Death," and "Regeneratrix," yet she is also "Earth Mother" and "Fertility Goddess." During her presumed reign in this time before the "father gods" take over, "The Goddess" is the "single source of all life" who takes "her energy from the springs and wells, from the sun, moon, and moist earth," and her "symbolic system represents cyclical, not linear, mythical time" (Gimbutas xix).

Assuming that there was a harmonious "Old European" world of The Goddess, Gimbutas suggests that it was supplanted by the Neolithic, male-dominated, Indo-European world system that eventually replaced it in the fourth millennium B.C. "with its horse-riding warrior gods of thundering and shining sky or of the swampy underworld, the ideology in which female goddesses are not creatrixes but beauties—'Venuses,' brides of the sky-gods" (xx). Successive invasions of the warlike, patriarchal Proto-Indo-European "Kurgan people" (as Gimbutas names them) who came from the Volga basin of South Russia "put an end to the Old European culture roughly between 4300 and 2800 B.C." Because it took a while for "Aegean and Mediterranean regions and western Europe" to succumb, in those areas, especially on islands of the Mediterranean like Crete—where we may find traces of Artemis—the matriarchal "Old European culture flourished in an enviably peaceful and creative civilization until 1500 B.C." (Gimbutas xx–xxi).

More recent scholarship, based on additional archaeological evidence and further study, is much less given to this picture of widespread goddess worship in the Paleolithic era. Some scholars have called into question the interpretation of artifacts as "necessarily depicting goddesses or genitalia" and have strongly expressed doubts that "these ancient cultures were necessarily matriarchal or even woman-focused" (C. Allen 22). Yet these scholarly disagreements, still unresolved, are not poetic issues. One may reject the notion of an "Old European" religion honoring The Goddess, and still concur with Gimbutas that "many of these symbols are still present as images in our art and literature, powerful motifs in our myths and archetypes in our dreams" (xxi). Certainly these feminine symbols figure prominently in Snyder's work. Moreover, his storehouse of myths and images is not limited to the history and culture of Old Europe; it embraces the archetypal feminine spirits of Asia and North America. In the final analysis his long poem is rooted in the larger landscape of Gaia, the planet itself, the encompassing sphere of all cultures.

Notwithstanding the relish with which Snyder speaks the language of tools with the tongues of men at work (trail crewmen, truck drivers, and seamen), he is never far from the feminine Other. In her most tangible aspect, The Goddess is, and always has been, there among the shapes and sounds of numerous women caught in his poems, some named, some nameless, all flowing into and out of his life, some lingering longer than others. In real life, to name only a few of the more significant ones, there is his mother, Lois Snyder Hennessy, to whom he dedicated *Turtle Island;* his sister, Thea, the recipient of a ninety-page letter that later became *Passage Through India;* four wives—Alison Gass, Joanne Kyger, Masa Uehara, and Carole Koda—each one important as inspiration for an aspect played out in Snyder's life and poems; and the shadowy figure of Robin Collins, who haunts his early poems and is probably the referent in Snyder's cryptic statement that "He Who Hunted Birds in His Father's Village" is "a story of lost love."[10] So much of Snyder's work is bound up with "finding the space in the heart," that it is not surprising to find women, whether representative of lost or found loves, whether in mythic or actual bodies, at the core of *Mountains and Rivers.* The list is long: the Paleolithic Magna Mater, "she" whose bones are found "Under the Hills Near the Morava River" or among the "Old Bones"; Artemis, with her "Earrings Dangling," the Mistress or Lady of the Animals; Earth Mother Gaia; Isis, Mother-Lover-Regeneratrix; the Moon Goddess in her associations with the Rabbit, the Owl, Mother *Bos* (Bossy the Cow); the Bear

Mother; Rhesus Macaque as Mother; Sarasvatī, the River Goddess; Vak of the flowing voice; the ecstatic dancing Pārvāti or the erotic Ame-no-uzume; horrific Kali; merciful Kuan-yin/Kwannon/Avalokiteshvara; Tārā, Mother of the Heavens, Joy of Starlight; the Milky Way; Prajñāpāramitā, the Perfection of All Wisdom; Māyā, the Mother of Illusion, Mother of All the Living Things; Mā; Yamamba, the Old Woman of the Mountains; the awesome "Mountain Spirit." Some published sections not included with the final poem, like "Kumarajiva's Mother" and "Hymn to the Goddess San Francisco," have a strong feminine presence. Finally, the unpublished early section known as "Sophia" was surely intended to refer to the universal Goddess of Wisdom as well as the empty dome of Hagia Sophia in Istanbul.

Snyder's references to Tārā deserve special mention, especially since an entire section alludes to her. A Tibetan goddess, Tārā is closely connected to Buddhist Shaktism and Hindu Shivaism. Edward Conze defines a "Shakti" as

> the creative energy, or "potency," of a deity, personified as his wife, or consort. In Shivaism Shakti-worship is directed toward Shiva's wife—Parvati or Uma—also known as *The great goddess*, and the *Great Mother.* It is a peculiarity of Shaktism that many deities exist both in a benign and a terrible form. The terrible form of Parvati is Durga, *The Unapproachable*, or Kali, *The Black.* (Conze 177)

Snyder's image of Pārvāti dancing before Shiva in "Bubbs Creek Haircut" is an example of Shivaism; more subtly, there may be an implication of Kali worship among the bones of "Under the Hills Near the Morava River." Sounding much like Gimbutas in reverse, Conze points out that the newer Mahāyāna system was in sharp contrast with the "severely masculine system" of "old Buddhism" to which "only a few quite subordinate feminine deities were admitted. The higher gods are sexless. . . . A woman cannot possibly become a Buddha" (192). When we discover that the two Mahāyāna goddesses, Prajñāpāramitā and Tārā, were "the first autonomous Buddhist deities" (192), it seems suddenly relevant that these two goddesses are at the heart of Snyder's long poem. "Tārā," from the Sanskrit *tārayati*, literally means "savior" ("Tārā" *Shambhala Dictionary*). She is, as Conze tells us, "the saviouress who helps us to 'cross' to the other shore, who removes fear and dread and who grants the fulfillment of all our wishes" (192). The name "Prajñāpāramitā" conveys almost exactly the same idea. She is a personification of the wisdom (*prajñā*) "that reaches the other shore" ("Prajñāpāramitā-sūtra" *Shambhala Dictionary*). In other words, devotion to either of these two goddesses puts one on the path to enlightenment. Snyder's Shaktism is obvious; time and again in *Mountains and Rivers Without End* he calls forth "the creative energy or 'potency,' of a deity, personified as his wife, or consort." Sitting "cross legg'd" with a feminine embodiment of Prajñāpāramitā or Tārā is at once meditative, sexual, and spiritual; it arouses the pure energy dance of wisdom and compassion combined. If, on the other hand, the dyadic relationship appears to be maternal, we may imagine the "savior" aspect of Tārā to predominate. In a culminating statement Conze brings it all together:

> Almost everywhere in ancient thought we find the notion of a principle which represents both wisdom and femininity, and which combined motherhood with virginity. In the Mediterranean world, we meet, at the same period, with a *Sophia,* who is modelled on Ishtar, Isis, and Athene; she represents a fusion between the idea of wisdom and the idea of the Magna Mater, and is placed by the side of the supreme male being. Like Ishtar and the Virgin Mary, the Prajñaparamita was in essence both mother and virgin. She is the "Mother of all the Buddhas," i.e., she is not barren but fertile, fruitful of many good deeds, and her images lay great stress on her full breasts. Like a virgin, on the other hand, she remains '*unaffected, untouched,*' and the Scriptures emphasise her elusiveness more than anything else. (193)

These goddesses, whether maternal, sexual, or virginal, and many more like them, are the feminine spirits we encounter in *Mountains and Rivers Without End.* Many-breasted, they nurture, entice, or inspire.

Snyder's scholarly inquiry into goddess mythology probably begins with Robert Graves's intriguing book *The White Goddess,* a reference point that can be traced to Snyder's Reed thesis where it appears in the bibliography. Graves's central idea is that

> the language of poetic myth anciently current in the Mediterranean and Northern Europe was a magical language bound up with popular religious ceremonies in honour of the Moon-goddess, or Muse, some of them dating from the Old Stone Age, and that this remains the language of true poetry—"true" in the nostalgic modern sense of 'the unimprovable original, not a synthetic substitute.' The language was tampered with in late Minoan times when invaders from Central Asia began to substitute patrilinear for matrilinear institutions and remodel or falsify the myths to justify the social changes. (9–10)

Once again we see the Old Stone Age linked with the Muse-Goddess, a link Graves—and Snyder after him—champions in poetry in order to resurrect a world of mythic truth and thereby bring modern civilization once more into active contact with its own inner vitality. Much later, in a 1980 foreword to Edward Schafer's book on the presence of the "Divine Woman" in T'ang literature, Snyder refers again to the centrality of Graves's work for its "recovery of a deeper sense of what 'Muse' means, and the male-female play in our own hearts." He commends Graves's "poetic essay, *The White Goddess*" for being "pivotal in disclosing the continuity of a muse-magic tradition" and points out that "the post/muse relationship is seen from the male side only for we live in cultures, both east and west, which have been dominated by men for several thousand years." He concludes:

> Of all males through those patriarchal years, the poets and artists were most apt to go beyond the one-sided masculine ethos and draw power from that other place, which the Chinese would call the Yin side of things. It is likely that men become creative when they touch the woman in themselves, and women become creative when they touch the woman in the man in themselves. (Snyder, foreword xi)

Snyder establishes several dyadic links here: the Muse and the poet, female and male, myth and historical fact. Modern poets, whether male or female, Western or Eastern, have been entrusted with an act of recovery. Buried under "several thousand years" of patriarchy is a creative energy that exists in "our own hearts," a force waiting to be encountered. In myth and poetry that something may be called "the Muse"; in gendered psychological terms Snyder refers to it as "the male-female play." The hyphen between the terms tells us he means their interplay, not the narrow one-sidedness of gender. To recover the Muse—or better yet, to prepare to be found by the Muse—Snyder suggests, as does Graves, that both men and women must look to "the woman in themselves." While both poets insist again and again on the importance of the feminine, neither suggests that we move from one-sided masculinity to a one-sided femininity. It is, instead, a recovery of harmonious creative balance. Snyder's use of the yin symbol always implies the presence of its opposite yang. His Buddhist thought continually directs him "beyond" either one or the other, into a tangible void, a dynamic interconnectedness that will always be "two places. Forever, // or, not even one" ("Instructions," *MRWE* 61).

The spiral is one of Snyder's favorite images, especially the coiling Kundalini "dragon in the spine" that is rooted in sexuality as it winds its way toward heart and spirit. Similarly, to know The Goddess creatively is to become intertwined with her presence whether the referent is sexual, poetic, or planetary:

> In the belly of the furnace of creativity is a sexual fire; the flames twine about each other in fear and delight. The same sort of coiling, at a cooler slower pace, is what the life of this planet looks like. The enormous spirals of typhoons, the twists and turns of mountain ranges and gorges, the waves and the deep ocean currents—a dragon-like writhing. (foreword xi)

In his book, Graves asks rhetorically: "What is the use or function of poetry nowadays?" With no apologies he turns to religion for an answer: "The function of poetry is religious invocation of the Muse; its use is the experience of mixed exaltation and horror that her presence excites." Angry with the "stupid people" of his time who might label poetry as useless, Graves argues that the experience of the Muse is necessary, but that we have lost contact with her. The confrontation with her "exaltation and horror" was "once a warning" for humans to "keep in harmony with the family of living creatures" by "obedience to the lady of the house." Now, however, it is "a reminder" that humans have "disregarded the warning, turned the house upside down by capricious experiments in philosophy, science and industry" (14). These words might well have been said by Snyder. *Mountains and Rivers* often calls modern civilization to task for having turned the house upside down, especially in terms of its failure to use the planet's energy resourcefully. Yet the poem is equally a statement of the human need to "keep in harmony with the family of living creatures." Like Graves, Snyder believes that the function of poetry is to present the whole harmonious picture, one that is best presented in and through mythical time. A poem communicates through its tangible words or its audible sounds, yet its final transaction takes place in the give and take it establishes with its readers. The experience of *Mountains and Rivers Without End* is rooted in the concrete swirl of its sound-image-idea strata, but its meaning is consummated only when readers "touch the woman in themselves" and fully realize their encounter with the "lady of the house," Gaia, both Earth Goddess and living biosphere, who speaks to us through the words of the poet as she does through the planet itself.

> We work with the faint facts of a Neolithic past and the actual facts of a planet-wide interconnected web of living beings. The totality of this biosphere is called by some Gaia after the ancient Greek Earth Goddess. It should be no surprise that one singer will be inspired by the heavy breast of a slender girl and another by the wind whipping though a col plastering the cliffs with gleaming rain. (foreword xii)

As a singer in service to the Muse-Goddess, Snyder's inspiration comes from both forms named here . . . and many more. She is never fully perceived, only glimpsed; there is always another vision, another encounter, ahead. She can be touched, but no one is capable of lifting her veil completely.

3

Inhabiting the Landscape

Milarepa

The notion of Emptiness engenders Compassion

Milarepa (*MRWE* ix)

Milarepa ("Mila who wears the cotton cloth of an ascetic") is a renowned figure of Tibetan Buddhism who lived roughly from 1025 to 1135. Warmed only by "inner heat," he lived for many years in total solitude in ice caves high in the Himalayas, wearing only a cotton cloth. When his father died, Milarepa, then seven years old, watched helplessly as his mother suffered and the family property was taken away. He swore vengeance and later, with great violence, did indeed redeem the wrongs enacted upon his family. The consequence of his violent action, however, was shame at his own behavior. Seeking atonement for his deeds, at the age of 38, he found himself under the guidance of Marpa (1012–97), a famous translator and yogi who was responsible for bringing Buddhist scriptures from India to Tibet. Marpa's own teacher had been Nāropa (1016–1100), a scholar at Nalanda, whose thought, once codified, became the central doctrine of the Kagyüpa school of Tibetan Buddhism. Marpa subjected Milarepa to great trials and immense suffering, bringing him to the point of suicide. Enlightened by these humbling activities, Milarepa became a major figure in the transmission of the teachings of Marpa and Nāropa ("Milarepa," "Marpa," "Nāropa" *Shambhala Dictionary*).

Both the epigraph and Milarepa's biography lead literally and figuratively toward the final section of the sequence: "Finding the Space in the Heart." The locale for the last poem is a vast geological playa in northwestern Nevada known as the Black Rock Desert. Immersed in this seemingly "empty" space in the Great Basin, imaginative readers of *Mountains and Rivers*—those who have heard intimations of spirituality within the poem—will find themselves simultaneously at the last unrolling of this poetic landscape and at the beginning of insight into the need for global and regional community. Milarepa's story, like that of Job's in the Old Testament, is a confirmation of the importance of having nothing, a renunciation of the things of the world, including the significance of the self. Accepting loss leads to both humility and gratitude. For some, renunciation points toward the reclusive path of the ascetic, but Snyder's vision leads in the opposite direction: to recognize one's own "emptiness" is to become aware of one's ongoing dynamic interconnection with the Other. Each of us is a piece of the continent. As Snyder reminds us in sections like "An Offering for Tārā," "The Mountain Spirit," and "Finding the Space in the Heart," our interconnectedness and dynamism is literally geological. Floating on the same molten liquid at the core of a single globe, our drifting continents continually break away from one another over eons of time only to reattach themselves later on in differing shapes. To recognize how completely interconnected all beings are in time and space is to know the true meaning of emptiness: nothing, no thing, no species, exists in and for itself. The human species, in particular, has no right to be arrogant about its status; we share the turning world with other beings.

For Buddhists, the "heart" of the final section's title has immediate associations with the *Heart Sūtra* where the play of "emptiness" and "form" conveys the philosophical notion of interbeing. For most readers of *Mountains and Rivers* it is enough to see the analogy between Milarepa's epigraph and that of "Finding the Space in the Heart": in the emptiness associated with the vast spaces of the desert and the meditative heart, there is unlimited room for compassion.

Dōgen

An ancient Buddha said "A painted rice cake does not satisfy hunger." Dōgen comments:

"There are few who have even seen this 'painting of a rice cake' and none of them has thoroughly understood it.

"The paints for painting rice-cakes are the same as those used for painting mountains and waters.

"If you say the painting is not real, then the material phenomenal world is not real, the Dharma is not real.

"Unsurpassed enlightenment is a painting. The entire phenomenal universe and the empty sky are nothing but a painting.

"Since this is so, there is no remedy for satisfying hunger other than a painted rice cake. Without painted hunger you never become a true person."

(*MRWE* ix)

This epigraph, adapted by Snyder from Dōgen's essay "Painting of a Rice-Cake," discourses on the nature of enlightenment, using painting as a central metaphor for understanding. Some earlier Zen commentators had suggested that the reading of sūtras was superficial, like painting rice cakes. Curiously, since his thought normally underscores the need for *zazen,* Dōgen Zenji (1200–53), the eminent Japanese founder of the Sōtō school of Zen, here argues in favor of the "painted rice cake," that is, the relative value of reading sūtras. In fact, for Dōgen enlightenment is a lifelong commitment, a crucial issue that actually resolves the paradox, for in his opposition to those who favor sudden enlightenment, Dōgen accepts the reading of sūtras as an appropriate gradual means of fulfilling that lifelong practice. Since Snyder's initial connection with Buddhism was with the Rinzai school of Zen (i.e., sudden enlightenment based on kōan practice), it is equally curious that he has given Dōgen's thinking such prominence in his life and poem. Yet Snyder's Buddhism draws on multiple techniques and concepts, and *Mountains and Rivers Without End* is eclectic in its representation of Buddhist schools. Several distinct associations with Buddhist practices are easily recognizable: the Pure Land school is represented by "The Blue Sky"; the contradictory logic of "The Elwha River" has the feel of a kōan; *zazen* is represented in "Raven's Beak River"; the Tibetan practice of *yab-yum* is noticeable in "Cross Legg'd"; "The Hump-backed Flute Player" is indebted to the Yogāchāra school as transmitted from India to China by Hsüan-tsang; and the entire poem is seen as a sūtra in honor of the Tibetan female Buddha, Tārā. It is not unfair to say that *Mountains and Rivers* is a compendium of essential Buddhist thinking and that Snyder's poem is, in part, his contribution to the transmission of this ancient wisdom.

"Unsurpassed enlightenment is a painting. The entire phenomenal universe and the empty sky are nothing but a painting." The essence of the epigraph from Dōgen points the way toward two major ideas embodied in Snyder's *Mountains and Rivers:* one, the essential truth of Mahāyāna Buddhism that enlightenment itself is "empty"; and two, that a major structural device of this poem will be that of a painting, even though a painting may be "nothing but a painting." In the world of rational logic—not necessarily in that of Buddhist metaphysics—a simple algebraic equation tells us that if "a = c" and "b = c," then it follows that "a = b." Therefore, if "unsurpassed enlightenment" = "painting" and if "the entire phenomenal universe and the empty sky" = "painting," then it follows that "unsurpassed enlightenment" = "the entire phenomenal universe and the empty sky." In other words enlightenment will come, if and when it comes, from this world we live in, this "thusness," as Buddhists say. There is no other world; this is it, even if it is illusory like a painting that rolls on and on endlessly.

"Enlightenment" (Sanskrit *bodhi;* Japanese *satori*) is an "awakening" to a "nowness of emptiness" (*shūnyatā*) ("Enlightenment" *Shambhala Dictionary*). Yet "emptiness" should not be construed in a negative manner, as in "meaninglessness" or "of no value." Nor should or can one "escape" into an empty void called "enlightenment." It exists, if one could use the word "exists," in one's full awareness of the eternal interplay of this world, this world of *tathata,* or suchness, with *shūnyatā.* Like the site of Eliot's "dance" that takes place where "the still point" intersects with the "turning world," one is not able to say "where" one is or has been, only that one has been "*there*" ("Burnt Norton" *Four Quartets*). In the paradoxical twists of Buddhist logic, the "empty" world is the "way in" to "enlightenment," even though the world itself is referred to as *māyā*, or illusion. In the quote from Dōgen the world we know is compared to an illusionary yet tangible painting. A painting, as we know, is one of many appearances of reality. We may speak of it as if it were a representation of reality; and so it is, even as it is a reality in and for its tangible self. Here, in this epigraph, the entire phenomenal universe and the empty sky in which it resides—everything that we might possibly see, touch, taste, hear, and smell—is reduced to nothing more than a painting. Yet only in, and through, this "painted" world will we discover "unsurpassed enlightenment."

Dōgen's words lead us directly into the first section of *Mountains and Rivers Without End*, "Endless Streams and Mountains," a section based on a Chinese horizontal landscape scroll. We begin our journey through this poem like travelers in a scroll, at the edge of the canvas, at the start of the trail, as it is about to be unrolled by us and through us and for us, a canvas, once empty itself, about to be filled with another kind of emptiness.

Part I

ENDLESS STREAMS AND MOUNTAINS

"Endless Streams and Mountains," the opening section of *Mountains and Rivers Without End*, is based on an anonymously painted Sung dynasty horizontal handscroll (*MRWE* 9).

> The physical aspects of the Cleveland landscape are as well known as those of any early Chinese painting. It is an unsigned handscroll (35.1 by 213 cm) done in ink and slight coloring on silk with nine colophons that provide information about the work's early history. Forty-eight seals of collectors, including eight belonging to Liang Ch'ing-piao (1620–1691), give further evidence of the transmission of the scroll from the 1340s on. (Bush 197)

Known in Chinese as *Ch'i-shan wu-chin*, the handscroll currently resides in the Cleveland Museum of Art where it is occasionally on display. It has been meticulously described in a monograph written by Sherman Lee and Wen Fong, a book Snyder refers to in the endnotes he published with his long poem (*MRWE* 159). The date of the scroll has become controversial in recent years. Susan Bush points out that it was "originally placed in the first quarter of the twelfth century (late Northern Sung), [but] it is now thought by several eminent authorities in the field to be more likely to date around 1150 (early Chin)" (Bush 197). In addition to its dating, the scroll has received critical attention from art historians because it appears to be a composite of several landscape styles. With its "shifting points of view or arbitrary spatial juxtapositions, and the relatively abbreviated depictions of motifs," it is, suggests Susan Bush, an intentional review of earlier landscape styles: "an *hommage à* five early masters of monochrome landscape painting." Her theory is that a viewer who looks at the complete scroll from left to right will see in its "compressed mountainscapes" a reference in "historical sequence to the styles of the five founders of monumental ink landscape traditions, the tenth-century masters Ching Hao, Kuan T'ung, Li Ch'eng, Yen Wen-Kuei, and Fan K'uan" (Bush 199–200).

Up to the early 1980s Snyder often referred to a scroll with a similar title at the Freer Gallery in Washington, DC (McNeil 23). However, since the *Orion* publication of "Endless Streams and Mountains" indicates that the poet saw the Cleveland scroll "in the Seventies" (Summer 1995: 40), he obviously had already been studying it, and most likely many others, at the time that he was making references to the Freer handscroll. The Cleveland scroll may have drawn Snyder's attention by the very fact of its creator's anonymity, the uncertainty about its dating, and its multiplicity of styles. Susan Bush associates the five prominent styles of the Cleveland landscape with the "five schools of Ch'an [Zen] Buddhism" (202), a connection that would surely not be missed by Gary Snyder. Nonetheless, it is more probable that Snyder is responding intuitively to the scroll's observable distinction among its landscape styles, a technique he emulates in depicting varied landscapes in *Mountains and Rivers.* To Bush, some sections of the scroll have "the overdramatized quality of cardboard stage sets," while others, like "the misty, level reaches or layered stretches that open and close the painting" are "signs of a contemporary realism" (202). Portions of the painting emphasize the human in the midst of nature, while other scenes, reminiscent of other styles, depict an elemental landscape of hard-edged rock and water, the veritable "wild." Overall, it is a remarkable painting to view, even in reproductions and slides.

As the opening section of *Mountains and Rivers Without End,* "Endless Streams and Mountains" both introduces and mirrors the whole work. It is symbolic of the poetic trip that Snyder is about to take us on, the lifetime journey that he himself has made, the journey of the world itself as it whirls its way down the corridors of time in the vastness of space. At times the reader is merged with Snyder's traveling persona. On the road with Snyder, his eyes become our eyes and we see as if inside his perceptions. At other times our viewpoint broadens, shifting to a seemingly more objective mode as we see, in the words of the poem, "this land from a boat on a lake / or a broad slow river, / coasting by." Knowing Snyder's appreciation for Ezra Pound, one is reminded of the perspective described in Canto LIX of Pound's *Cantos:* "periplum, not as land looks on a map / but as sea bord seen by men sailing" (324). Daniel Pearlman explains "periplum" further: "the word implies not only a voyage of discovery . . . , but in the case of a poet, a voyage of spiritual discovery. As a narrative device, the 'periplum' image binds the disparate elements of the *Pisan Cantos* into a pattern of continuity" (239). Snyder's intentional use of the boat image in

"Endless Streams and Mountains" points toward the same effect. Unquestionably, there is discovery here: the reader is simultaneously asked to participate in and to reflect on the nature of spiritual revelation in several of the long poem's poetic journeys. Further, the perspective imposed by the painted boat image on the reader's mind and eye (and on the author's as he too "views" his own "painting") serves as a device to "coast" one's way across the unrolling landscapes of the scroll and the various sections of the long poem. A perfectly valid way of perceiving the complex interconnected structure of *Mountains and Rivers* is to see the entire poem as a sequence of *periploi,* each section a distinct voyage of discovery yet all bound together in a "pattern of continuity."

Returning to the verbalized scroll before us, we proceed along the edge of the painting, looking into the landscape of the unrolling scroll, floating along in front of it as it unrolls. We turn the pages of the poem from front to back. We become both observer and participant. Even as we remain external viewers—readers of a scroll-poem that "goes by" in sections (and subsets of sections)—we also see ourselves among the tiny people found in the scroll-poem; at times we imaginatively become those people. We are in and out of this poem-painting simultaneously! In his notes to the *Orion* publication, Snyder makes several of these points directly. In remarking on a line from K'ang-li Kuei-kuei's 1332 colophon—"In the *Streams and Mountains Without End* a single look causes one to have thoughts of mists and clouds"—Snyder observes:

> The remark leads a viewer to turn the handscroll slowly and to journey through the streams and mountains and into the mists and clouds. The scroll is read from right to left and one is affected by the nature as if actually there. The journey a viewer makes through the canvas is marked clearly: There is a path that can be followed even if, at times, there are alternate paths to create variety, and always along a passage, a reader experiences a harmony with nature. ("Endless Streams," *Orion* 40)

As with the landscape, so with the poet-traveler; we begin with the poet just as surely as we remain distanced from him. When he describes the landscape and figures of the unrolling scroll, we see with the guidance of his eyes; yet we are encouraged to see it on our own. Snyder authenticates the scroll by naming it in Chinese—*"Ch'i Shan Wu Chin"*—and placing it in the factual "Cleveland Art Museum, which sits on a rise that looks out toward the waters of Lake Erie" (*MRWE* 8). Reproductions of the painting are not hard to come by; no mere poetic fiction, it really exists. Still, like the painting, this section—and the entire long poem it introduces—is a composite of realities composed by an uncertain Creator. Just as the handscroll's creator is anonymous, so this *Mountains and Rivers Without End* may have more than one maker. Although attributed to Gary Snyder; Snyder himself would say his poem has been brought into being by the energy-mind-dance of the planet itself.

The opening lines of "Endless Streams and Mountains" focus attention on the larger scroll-poem as a matrix of places.[1] Immediately in "that created space" we find "a web of waters streaming over rocks," a phrase that points to an interconnected "web," a "streaming" energy dance, and an artistic reflection of the titles of both section and long poem in the water-rock dyad. On a path that twists and turns in the landscape of boulders and trees, we realize that there is no "we," no "I," only eyes. The locale is neither urban nor agricultural, but it is well kept. There must be people here somewhere, although they are not yet in evidence. Seeing with the eyes of the poet, we create the landscape together as we go along. The trail leads, as we might have suspected, up. Layer beyond layer, it climbs until the mind's eye roams the "[b]ig ranges" beyond the foregrounded "outcrops," "rocky uplifts" and "brushy cliffs." Finally we encounter the distant "peaks" whose tangible vagueness is surely representative of the emptiness that intermingles with the perceptible objects and defined shapes below.

Then, just as swiftly, the eye turns again, this time to people: three on land and two more in a boat offshore. These people, like the path described before them, are "real"; they have been painted into existence on the actual scroll. Yet, uncertain of his own vision, Snyder is not sure if the third man carries a "roll of mats or a lute." Vision, like "fixed" perceptions, becomes unstable. Just when our eyes become accustomed to a distinct path, diverse paths emerge in front of us; in one moment we are on the trail; in the next we have visually stepped off to look at it from beyond.

If we unroll the scroll another turn, and then another, closing the previously opened sections as we go, different people come, and then go. The trail itself continues, sometimes up or back into the disappearing distance, only to return again with new people, different locations. Stepping back to look at the entire scroll, there is always the strong hint that these many paths and these various people are somehow connected, if only by their relation to the scroll on which they all appear. On the trail or off the path, at work or recreation, fishing, hiking, riding, perhaps just "sitting"—these people are part of a single scroll, an unrolling painted universe, and we too go with them. We watch them; we step into their shoes; we sit in their places.

From somewhere higher up in the mountains, water endlessly descends: a "frothy braided torrent," a "cascading streambed"; sometimes there are bridges in sight; sometimes we know we must enter the water to cross. Vagueness coexists with distinctness: a "*jumble* of cliffs," "ridge tops *edged with bushes*," "valley *fog* below a *hazy* canyon" (my emphasis). Yet suddenly there is specificity as we return to a named world before we drift off into emptiness. Snyder tells us that the trees are "chinquapin" or "liquidambars," and we wonder how he knows this.[2] Is this Snyder's bow to the painter's skill at depiction; can we know the exact type of tree from merely viewing the scroll? With some landscape artists, the answer is surely "yes," yet here, on this scroll, it is more likely that we are observing a poetic expansion of realities. The painted world becomes three dimensional; Snyder is now within the world he meditates on, and these painted trees have become part of his actual experience, his "real" life. This kind of interaction of realities enters and reenters *Mountains and Rivers Without End.* "Dream worlds" become "real worlds"; "real worlds" become "dreamlike." All worlds are real in a world of nonduality.

The trail's end is upon us. There are "two moored boats" and a boatman "lost in thought." The eye of perception that has carried us, as if in a boat on a lake in the foreground of the scroll across its entire unrolling length, may also feel the impulse to become moored. Yet further landscapes are located beyond: "Hills beyond rivers, willows in a swamp, / a gentle valley reaching far inland." Indeed, our journey is not over, nor does Snyder bring our vision to a distinctive ending point, a terminus. Instead he simply states that "[t]he watching boat has floated off the page." There is always another dimension, another depth, other heights and other distances, to be found in such landscape scrolls. To the artists who made them as well as to the imaginative viewer of them, they are truly "without end."

Still, the representational world of the painting has ended. The poet, momentarily using prose, unrolls the scroll one more turn bringing his readers in contact with the conventional placement of "seals and poems" on the scroll. Historically, as various people came into possession of a scroll of this type, it was commonplace for them to add their personal comments. No art work exists without some form of commentary on it. Snyder himself says that "in a way the painting is not fully realized until several centuries of poems have been added" (*MRWE* 159). Analysis, interpretation, criticism, and evaluation all become part of the work to which they are attached, increasing the significance of the artwork. Chinese artists and their patrons certainly felt no reservations about placing their comments directly on the surface of such artwork, sometimes in prose, more often in the form of a poem, sometimes with an official seal, merely to indicate that it had been in their possession. Apart from issues of quality and value, these "colophons" are a demonstration of the Chinese practice of intermingling verbal and visual art. Similarly, as the verbal *Mountains and Rivers Without End* must be understood visually as a landscape, so Snyder has said that this particular section, "Endless Streams and Mountains," is "one more colophon—commentary poem on the painting—to be added to its story" ("Endless Streams," *Orion* 38). As if to emphasize that his own poem-colophon is only part of this scroll's ongoing story, as part of the section Snyder includes quotes from five of the actual nine colophons in evidence on *Ch'i-shan wu-chin.* As he does not quote colophons in their entirety or rely on the translations printed in Lee and Fong, it is evident that his choices are not randomly made.

The opening verse by Wang Wen-wei underscores the presence of Ch'an (Zen) Buddhism that pervades so many of these Chinese landscape scrolls.[3] The "Fashioner of Things" who "has no original intentions" is a reference to the Zen condition known as "original mind." In the ordinary human realm of existence it is not possible to make (create, fashion, do) anything without having some intention, yet in an attempt to experience the raw energy of creativity and to allow oneself to be a conduit for that energy, a Zen artist works toward a state of "original mind" as the work—be it a horizontal handscroll or a long poem—is fashioned. It is in this sense that Snyder opens his poem with the phrase, "[c]learing the mind and sliding in." Wang Wen-wei seems to be marveling at the suprahuman creative ability of the anonymous painter, but it is more likely that he is attesting to the ability of the Sung artist to let the Fashioner of Things "use" him as he "lets go" of his conscious intention. In a similar manner, reminiscent of Dōgen's comment on painting, these painted "mountains and rivers" convey the "condensed spirit," the ultimate energy of the "Fashioner of Things," yet remain, after all, nothing but a painting. Who indeed has "come up with / these miraculous forests and springs"; who or what speaks to us in this "[p]ale ink / on fine white silk." Again, one is grateful for an anonymous painting. To deal with a "real" ego, a distinct person, would complicate matters. Throughout *Mountains and Rivers,* and not just this first section, readers will observe Snyder himself come and go. At times the poet seems to insist on his "real" ego, that is, "Gary Snyder," either as a character in his own poem or the author of it. At other times he either fails to put in an appearance or willfully disappears from sight. The section begins with "[c]learing the mind," but the "subject" of this phrase is never specifically identified. Whose mind is this that must be cleared? At the end of the section the "mind" speaks to us anonymously once again: "Step back and gaze again at the land," but the Snyder "I" is not mentioned until several lines later when he says: "I walk out of the museum." For most of the section we are rarely aware of Gary Snyder, either as character or as author; when he does appear it is noticeable.

Li Hui provides comic relief as he speaks of an urban "noise of dogs and chickens." This "I" that complains of his odd tastes and love for "streams and boulders" (i.e., the wilderness) reflects indirectly on Snyder, as the reader hears Snyder lightly mocking his "odd taste" for the "Mountains and Rivers" he is so associated with.[4] Considering that the last section in *Mountains and Rivers* is a desert setting, the observation takes on greater significance. The contrast of locales is startling, but less so if one remembers back to this initial observation of Li Hui's.

The interdependent dyad of mountains-rivers returns in the translation from Tien Hsieh of Wei-lo: "The water holds up the mountains, / The mountains go down in the water."[5] Anyone who has seen a mountain reflected in the surface of a lake has at least a literal insight into one way among many that water holds up mountains. Nor is it difficult to understand how minerals and soil are brought down mountain slopes by flowing rivers. Above all, one should not focus on either the mountains or the water but on their nondual, mutually interpenetrating existence. In addition to its Buddhist implications, Snyder's translation clearly underscores the importance of the planetary water cycle, a major thematic strand to be found in *Mountains and Rivers Without End.*

One cannot help but wonder why Snyder has selected the 1332 quotation from Chih-shun.[6] Like Chih-shun we may also marvel at the truly wondrous quality of the anonymous scroll; so perhaps Snyder is straightforwardly extolling its virtues and nothing more. At such moments of generalization, however, readers easily substitute Snyder's *Mountains and Rivers Without End* for the scroll. It seems out of character to think of the author egotistically saying of his own work, "this is a poem worth careful keeping"; nevertheless, it *is* a rare poem, rarer still in that it was forty years in the making and that its manuscript pages actually did survive the threat of fire during drought years at Kitkitdizze.

Wang To's comment seems amusingly aimed at readers and critics of the future; hopefully they too will be "learned," have "good taste," and write "good prose and poetry."[7] What is most interesting about this quotation is that Snyder has chosen to include only some rather mundane comments from the complete colophon. Talk about brothers and brothers-in-law brings us away from aesthetic and spiritualized planes of discussion. Unconnected to a specific subject, the quotation serves as a reminder that "enlightenment" may come from the hands of one's in-laws or neighbors. A little learning and perhaps some good taste may help to recognize it when it arrives; in any event, it is not distant and unattainable.

The final two names mentioned—Liang Ch'ing-piao and Chang Ta-ch'ien—are mentioned merely to conclude the transmission of the scroll from its anonymous beginnings in Shansi Province to its present resting place in the Cleveland Art Museum where Snyder encountered it. As next in line, Snyder's own poem-colophon will leave its mark on the scroll just as surely as those of Wang Wen-wei and the others have.

One more significant, yet subtle, step remains to be taken in this section of the poem:

> Step back and gaze again at the land:
>   it rises and subsides—
>
> ravines and cliffs like waves of blowing leaves—
>   stamp the foot, walk with it, clap! turn,
>   the creeks come in, ah!

Snyder, now a character in his own poem, stands back from this horizontal scroll he has just observed and described in detail for us. The stamp of the foot, the clap and turn, are movements, for those who recognize them, imbued with the sound and feel of the Japanese Nō. Like the *waki* at the outset of his journey, the poet-actor steps formally toward the final three lines of "Endless Streams and Mountains":

> *Walking on walking,*
>   *under foot   earth turns.*
>
> *Streams and mountains never stay the same.*

Significantly, this refrain will be heard again in "The Mountain Spirit," the climactic section of *Mountains and Rivers* based on the Nō play *Yamamba,* and yet again as the entire sequence concludes. Chanting these words here, in the introductory section, Snyder clearly invokes the muselike presence of the "Mountain Spirit" whom we are destined to meet further along the pathways.

The entire scroll may now be taken in at a single glance. Casting his eyes on it —swinging them from left to right, right to left—Snyder sees the outline of the mountains rise and fall as if the line of peaks, ridges, and valleys where the earth meets the sky were a graph plotted on a two-dimensional axis. On trails that thread their way among the mountains and along the rivers, we walk in linear fashion, rarely having the opportunity to glimpse totality. From this perspective, mountains do not appear to move; the person does the moving. However, stepping back for the total picture, one sees the dynamics of the entire range over time. The step back from the logic of self-involvement to the "geo-logic" of planetary time and space provides an opening for enlightenment; it is a view captured best in the words of Heinrich Zimmer as he depicts the Hindu sense of time:

> It was as though the mountains—permanent when considered from the standpoint of our brief human span of some seven decades—should be beheld, all at once, from the perspective of as many millenniums. They would rise and fall like waves. The permanent would be seen as fluid. Great goals would melt before the eyes. Every experience of value would be suddenly transmuted; the mind would be hard put to reorient itself, and the emotions to discover solid ground. (23–24)

Snyder may indeed be the person who steps back to gaze in this section, but, unnamed as he is, he allows readers to partake of his insight into totality much as they shared his linear view while trudging along the path or his coastal view while drifting in a boat on the "edge" of the scroll. We watch, yet feel our bodies move as we watch. The speaker stamps his foot, "walks" with "it," claps, and turns. One imagines the Nō-like stylized grace and dignity that accompanies these final actions that move the section swiftly through its concluding phase. "[T]he creeks come in, ah!" One hears the creeks flow with the extended vowel sound. As he speaks, Snyder invites himself, and his reader, to "see" through hearing; saying "ah" marks an awesome moment of relationship between the self and the planet:

> The phenomenal world experienced at certain pitches is totally living, exciting, mysterious, filling one with a trembling awe, leaving one grateful and humble. The wonder of the mystery returns direct to one's own senses and consciousness: inside and outside; the voice breathes, "Ah!"
>
> . . . In mantra chanting, the magic utterances, built of seed-syllables such as OM and AYNG and AH, repeated over and over, fold and curl on the breath

> until—when most weary and bored—a new voice enters, a voice speaks through you clearer and stronger than what you know of yourself; with a sureness and melody of its own, singing out the inner song of the self, and of the planet. (*EHH* 123)

As the creeks are "strained" by the "boulders," so the "mountains" walk "on the water" and "water ripples every hill." With this echo of the lines quoted earlier from the T'ien Hsieh colophon—"The water holds up the mountains, / The mountains go down in the water"—we are reminded once again of the interpenetration of the mountains-waters dyad. The painting becomes "real" in that the energies that it represents, those that were placed there by the "Fashioner of Things" through the anonymous artist, coalesce with the dynamic body movements of the speaker who now performs as a Nō dancer. We feel the intense energy, the dance, the sheer rhythm of spirit moving in these lines. No longer just narrated, the landscape in "Endless Streams and Mountains" becomes energized.

Instantly the scene shifts again. A moment ago one was inside, not just in the museum but "in" the world of a landscape painting. Now one is with the poet outside the museum, yet still in a landscape: "—I walk out of the museum—low gray clouds over the lake—chill March breeze." Which landscape is the painted rice cake? Acknowledging a world of shifting realities is a primary step toward the knowledge of emptiness. Here, at the end of "Endless Streams and Mountains," Snyder, a traveler in a Nō drama of his own making, *Mountains and Rivers Without End,* is about to encounter the other half of his own eternal ongoing dyad, the spirit of this Nō play, a feminine presence who walks the landscapes of the planet. The encounter will occur and recur with rising intensity and in different guises throughout the poem. These are engagements that lead to wisdom, which, in turn, leads to compassion, the "heart" that waits at the center of emptiness at the end of the poem. As with mountains and rivers, so with wisdom and compassion, so with the traveler and the spirit he must meet: it is the act of their coming together that brings enlightenment; their existence depends on their eternal interpenetration.

There will be ghosts, as indeed there are in all Nō plays of this type. The planet's "[o]ld ghost ranges, sunken rivers" hearken back to the Paleolithic and even further into the misty past. Like the blank space before the artist, be it painter or poet, the tale of the planet begins in emptiness, the "broad white space." Something makes marks on the white void. Snyder, the word-artist, impelled by the anonymous maker of "Endless Streams and Mountains," impelled by the raw spirit and energy of SPACE itself, awakened by the Fashioner of Things, begins his creative reenactment. Out comes the brush or pen that will limn the narrative of the beings of the planet, the paths they traverse. The planet turns, leaving traces of its own tale. The planet paints its own scroll: the mountains themselves "grind the ink" of their own substance; the waters "wet the brush." In the broadest sense the ranges and rivers of the veritable landscape tell these stories. The planet itself walks a path and sits the rains. Listen and watch. The performance begins; the spirit eternally approaches again; the scroll unrolls once more:

> *Walking on walking,*
> *under foot earth turns.*
>
> *Streams and mountains never stay the same.*

OLD BONES

Continuing the walking motif in the final lines of "Endless Streams and Mountains," the opening lines of "Old Bones" locate readers "out there walking round." Ambiguity of time, place, and character abound. When a "you" is mentioned in the second line we become aware of someone who can crack a seed, someone involved with "plucking, digging, snaring, snagging," who is "barely getting by." Who is this "you"? Perhaps someone from the community shared by Mā, her relatives, and friends, inhabitants of a dusty place who scratch a meager living from the earth? Or perhaps someone from further recesses in human history, from the Paleolithic, a favorite hunting ground of the poet?

> As a poet I hold the most archaic values on earth. They go back to the late Paleolithic; the fertility of the soul, the magic of animals, the power-vision in solitude, the terrifying initiation and rebirth; the love and ecstasy of the dance, the common work of the tribe. (*EHH,* back cover)

Given Snyder's outlook, it is likely that the "you" is a hunter-gatherer "looking out for food." Anything will do; he or she will dig up roots, set traps, or listen for birds that might be snared. It is difficult work, especially since there seems to be "no food out there on dusty slopes." Insofar as "dusty world" is an epithet that Buddhists use for the everyday world of circumstances, it is easy enough to interconnect the world of "Old Bones" with that of modern hardship. Contemporary societies are filled with people who are "barely getting by." On the other hand, Snyder may be encouraging readers of *Mountains and Rivers* to dig in the lines for more information, to search for some seeds of truth to be cracked open for revelation, as the gatherers opened theirs for food. Material, or spiritual, hunger is a driving force in this dusty landscape.

We carry with us what little nourishment we have as we look for more. Snyder seems to imply here that our communal search for sustenance leads to the world of myth. We make up stories to explain our lives; we compose them while we search, while we wait, while we eat together. One thinks of petroglyphs like those of the Hump-backed Flute Player, Kokop'ele, that appear scratched in stones in locales where the hunters waited, or, further back in time, of the paintings of bulls and the statues of goddesses found in the caves where the "old ones" lived and probably worshipped. We associate "old bones" with artifacts that we might hold in our hands, but there is nothing to prevent us from seeing, as Snyder does, the "tracks" of our past in the myths that remain from the past. Such stories are also "old bones" that a present-day audience may "read" and assess for truth. To read them, to listen to them properly, is to invite enlightenment, for they too are a "way in." Stories told around ancient fire rings are not substantially different from those told now: at bedtime; around the dinner table; whenever, wherever. Where there is a search for nourishment—material, psychic, or spiritual—there we hunger for dreams, and there, if we are reverent, we may find a "shrine for the old ones" among the "dust" of "old songs and tales."

This short section was written "for Paul Shepard," Avery Professor of Human Ecology Emeritus at Pitzer College and the Claremont Graduate School until his death in 1996. His book *The Others: How Animals Made Us Human* is a stimulating demonstration of how humans have learned to be what they are by interacting with animals, a theme that resounds in *Mountains and Rivers* with its multitude of instructive black-tailed hares, cows, canyon wrens, ravens, deer, Dall sheep, wood rats, and coyotes. *The Sacred Paw: The Bear in Nature, Myth, and Literature,* which Shepard co-authored with Barry Sanders, is a testimony to the importance of the bear to humans and to the planet in general. Gary Snyder has given his own testimony to the significance of the bear in his prose and poetry, and here, in *Mountains and Rivers Without End,* we will share with "The Bear Mother." In reading "Old Bones" one can create a picture of a physical anthropologist, someone similar to Shepard, searching in the dust for "old bones," so that he (or she) might tell the story of the "old ones" who may, indeed, be animals as well as humans. The anthropologist searches—plucking, digging, snaring, snagging—perhaps for "[d]eer bone, Dall sheep," looking for evidence. Archaeology and anthropology tell us the story of creatures on the earth, creatures who were here at an earlier unrolling of the planetary scroll. These "old bones" reveal the planet's story as it has turned though the ages, "walking and walking." Here we see the tracks, the trail, of the journey that has been taken so far. This story of hard factual evidence involves bits and pieces of bone that tell us where and who we have been and who has eaten whom. In "Old Woodrat's Stinky House" we examine the feces and bones of the past as it has been passed on to us through the bowels of time. As "earthy" as this matter is, it remains a story of religious dimension, a worshipping at the altar of the ancestors. This story of dust and bones, seeds, roots, and tubers interconnects with other beings, our companions, the animals, and the earth itself. It is, above all else, a story of the food chain—our interdependency. Those of us who have prevailed have done so only with the help of others, even to consuming the others. For this communion, we must be grateful.

NIGHT HIGHWAY 99

Although the time period is now relatively modern and the mode of travel has switched to hitchhiking, the third section of part I continues to locate us "[o]ut there walking round." An entry from a shirt-pocket journal dated August 4, 1957, a few weeks before he boarded the *Sappa Creek,* reveals Snyder's first inklings of what would become "Night Highway 99":

> 99 66 101 40
>
> 4 VIII 57. THE HIGHWAY—Been up and down it all my life. O Mexico!!!
> 99. b San Francisco 1930. Coast. The obscene future of this coast. Shasta Dam
> Roseburg
> honeydewmelons.
> thank you Jesus.
> the world's biggest millpond
> Sedro-Wooley
> big logs on off the road trucks
> Eugene milk trucks
> the Columbia river bridge
> strange mounds south of Olympia
> view of the mountains.
> red dirt
> —north to Blaine Washington
>
> (Journal—"30:V:1957." GSP B30:F7)

Here Snyder sketches the idea of moving north along the length of Highway 99 (in the days before Interstate 5) from San Francisco to Blaine, a small town on the border between the United States and Canada. The published poem reverses that direction, taking the reader south from Ferndale (WA) through the cities and towns of Washington, Oregon, and California, to end in San Francisco.

The cynicism in the journal entry is evident. He notes the "obscene future" of the West Coast and sandwiches a sarcastic "thank you Jesus" between "honeydewmelons" and "the world's biggest millpond." By December of that year Snyder was complaining, somewhat rhetorically, that all his poetry so far was "worthless," yet soon he would "commence great jewels of prose & unseen & unbelievable poems" (Journal—"1:XI:1957"; 3 Dec. 1957. GSP B30:F8). His hopes were probably pinned on "Night Highway 99" and his vision of the larger *Mountains and Rivers Without End.* A nearby entry, written a few days later, speaks of Goodwill stores in "Seattle, Portland, Oakland, San Francisco" and "—rivers & mountains / without end; travelling through" (6 Dec. 1957. GSP B30:F8). It would be several years before the actual poem surfaced. He was working on it in January of 1960, but it wasn't until mid-June 1961, now married and well into his second stay in Japan, that he wrote to

Philip Whalen to tell him that Cid Corman would publish a section called "Night Highway 99" (17 June 1961. Reed-PWP). Although several minor changes have been made along the way, the final Counterpoint version of "Night Highway 99" is essentially the same as the one published by Corman.

The epigraph, excerpted from a letter written by Lew Welch to Snyder on November 5, 1960, has always opened the poem (GSP B88:F84). The full letter depicts Welch living on very little money; still, that condition of poverty, he says, leads to grace and dignity. Snyder's poem, with its multitude of trucks barreling along highways, points toward commercial interests that pay little attention to how their money is made. "AIR REDUCTION," a sign glimpsed on a truck passing in the night rain outside of Tacoma, is plainly one ecologically disastrous by-product of such traffic. Highway 99 begins as a specific route—at the time of the poem the primary north-south corridor stretching from Canada to Mexico—but the echoing "highway 99" phrase, as in "go hitching down that / highway 99," soon tells us that this particular highway is a type for all such highways of commerce and travel. Drivers on this road come from, and are going to, locations far from Highway 99: "I'd like to save up all my money / . . . go down to Reno," a "[f]at man . . . [who] / wants to go back to L.A.," a "North Dakota boy," a "Waco Texas boy," a "[g]uy just back from Alaska." Multiple drivers and destinations reinforce the generalizing aspect of Snyder's highway of life. Moreover, the poet alludes to a far different set of highways with his telling parenthetical phrase: "(Six great highways; so far only one)." These six highways refer to six Buddhist dharma existences: hells, animals, humans, delightful gods and goddesses, angry warrior geniuses, and hungry ghosts. The title of the following section—"Three Worlds, Three Realms, Six Roads"—also alludes to the six existences. In "Night Highway 99" Snyder sees himself as having, "so far," traveled only the "human" road.

The Buddhist aspects of this highway can be both subtle and straightforward. Snyder explained to Ekbert Faas that the lines "Abandon really means it / the network womb stretched loose all / things slip through" refer to the *Avatamsaka Sūtra*, also known as the *Flower-Garland Sūtra*, and subsequently clarify the next lines in which Snyder wakes from his "dreaming" on a bench in Oregon to find that the newspapers he had used to cover his body have all turned to flowers (Faas 135). Such moments of "slipping through" are similar to the tangible-void visions one sees in the fog-shrouded peaks of the Chinese landscape scroll. These split-second shifts in perception result in moments of heightened awareness; they are found not just in this section but throughout the poem. Welch's letter carries the same kind of eye-opening insight: "it turns out you only have to hop a few feet to one side and the whole huge machinery rolls by, not seeing you at all." The same idea is repeated in Snyder's own comment toward the end of the poem: "The road that's followed goes forever; / in half a minute crossed and left behind." This statement is not merely about the machinery of capitalism. No[thing]ness inhabits the last lines of the section:

NO
body
gives a shit
man
who you are
or what's your car
there
IS no 99

As a visual equivalent to jazz rhythms, the spacing reminds one of the work of e. e. cummings or Ezra Pound. As with Pound's "ideograms," a reader "sees" a spatial whole alongside a logical, and linear, progression of ideas. The white space and line breaks emphasize not just the negativity of the word "NO," but the isolation of the "body" and the "man," both singularly alone on their lines and in life itself; the flat concluding statement juxtaposes the reality of a possible "there" with the stated fact of its opposite: that "there / IS no."

Why "99"? We know from the original journal entry that Snyder was considering others: "99 66 101 40." Highways 66 and 40 were east-west highways and Route 66 had already been spoken for in *On the Road*. Having spent most of his life in Seattle, Portland, and San Francisco, Snyder's choice of a north-south route in that region seems evident. Both north-south Highways 99 and 101 were well known to the poet. Mathematically both numbers have "poetic" connotations because of their proximity to the number 100, but, unlike 101, which hugs the coast, Highway 99 runs in the symbolic middle between the inland mountains and the ocean and, as a major north-south truck route, was the obvious choice to sustain a poetic lament for those suffering at the hands of consumerism. Snyder rarely relies solely on either a fact or a symbolic value; instead, he seizes on the interpenetration of the two realms as they validate each other and lead beyond one or the other. The people who speak in this section, although selected for poetic reasons, are nevertheless "real," and the poet takes great pains to capture their actual language and the harshness of their existence as if, somehow, the more strained one's circumstances are, the "more real" they seem. Given Snyder's compositional habits, somewhere there must be notebooks filled with snippets of accurately rendered actual dialogue and life stories captured in a few lines, notes taken over years of traveling highways like Highway 99. Although Snyder does not point to it, Lew Welch's letter describes the speed with which the landscape actually was changing: "Portland is sacrificing All for Freeways. No other activity. All the mansions must come down. This one [an old Victorian house in which Welch has rented a room] goes in 3 years." Interstate 5, the new freeway, was cutting its way through Portland. The irony attached to the word "freeway" in Welch's letter is obvious. In one sense, awareness of this great machinery rolling by IS a step into freedom—it is the awareness that brings about the "step aside," the move off the path and into the "the wild," as Snyder would say in later years.

On the other hand, this section does focus on the negative aspects of the highway, a signifying highway that modern life travels. Most of the stories related in short bursts of poetry or prose or dialogue carry an overwhelming note of sadness; the portraits are of poor—literally and spiritually—people caught up in the web of actuality, grinding away at their lives much like the people in T. S. Eliot's *The Waste Land.* Although the people of Snyder's all-too-real "unreal cities" are drivers or "driven," these characters, who are met up and down the highway, have the feel of Eliot's robotic people who emit short but audible sighs as they walk the city streets. One imagines Snyder, like Eliot, ruminating on the multitudes that have been reduced to a mechanistic, zombie-like existence. "Night Highway 99" is essentially about an all-too-familiar world, a "dusty world" that contributes to our obscured sight. This is the world of "trucks [that] roll by / kicking up dust   dead flowers." This world is a "state of cars," and its narrator is "sick of car exhaust." In contrast to "the view of the mountains" noted when he first thought of writing this poem, the Sierra Nevada cannot be seen in "Night Highway 99." As a nightmare vision it generally precludes more positive revelations. It is a world where a prominent lotus goddess of India, Lakshmi, becomes LASME: Los Angeles–Seattle Motor Express. Nor do animals fare well; "Little Elk" is merely the name of a roadside business, a "place on Highway 20." There is "smoke" in the speaker's brain. He tries—we imagine unsuccessfully—to "stay on the rightside of that / yellow line." Fragmentary details imply larger situations, either in the "present time" of Snyder's making of the poem or in the past time that has led up to it. The sheriff's posse persecutes the Wobblies. Because of Snyder's "red beard" the FBI harass him, as they actually did when he applied for a passport to go to Japan. Among the travelers on this path are possible suicides, shingle weavers who easily lose their fingers to saws, weary Indians, burnt-out minds, sexual predators, and more. With so much misery, it is not surprising that the hitchhiker just doesn't "feel right / without something on my back"; his backpack contains the psychic load that he always carries with him.

Still, there are moments of valuable insight and images of affirmation. "Night Highway 99" is not merely a one-sided picture of gloom. The poet takes a stand for the animal world—"I speak for hawks." Sleeping in his backyard, the narrator spends "half the night watch[ing] shooting stars." Snyder illuminates Welch's "shapes of elegance" when he describes the good life in the midst of poverty:

> On Second Street in Portland.
>   What elegance. What a life.
>   Bust my belly with a quart of
>   buttermilk

> & five dry heels of French bread
> from the market cheap
>   clean shaved, dry feet

Ah. . . . !! Thoreau would approve of this simple life, the way of the poor, the "beat," and the Zen Buddhist monk. Sokei-an is the vehicle for two illuminating Zen moments. A "little traveler" on this great highway, he meets an old man who lives alone on the banks of the Columbia River. To Sokei-an's question as to why he lives there, the old man replies: "Boy, no one ever asked me the reason why," implying that there was no rational logic to his life-decision. The old man is beyond both logic and words: "I have forgotten how to speak human words," he says.[8] In an entirely different context, a few lines later, Sokei-an irreverently grounds the legendary life of the Buddha. Referring to the story of a maid who offered Gautama Buddha a drink, Sokei-an says: "No doubt! . . . that's all it was: / plain buttermilk." In sum, in "Night Highway 99" Snyder creates a space for enlightenment in the midst of a superficial, ego-driven, commercialized wasteland. He speaks of "Creating / 'Shasta' as I go," a sophisticated piece of Buddhist, and postmodern, reasoning that declares all landscapes to be images—Dōgen's painted rice cake, so to speak. Impermanent as it is—and truly beyond sorrow, beyond joy—whichever world we create, be it positive or negative, it is *our* created world.

A complete discussion of the section's rhythms is not possible, yet some attention should be given to its sound. Whatever idiosyncratic rhythm a reader senses, it is obvious that Snyder intends some rhythm. The placement and spacing of the lines—at times reminding us of William Carlos Williams's triadic foot, at other times emphasizing the white space that surrounds a single word—are carefully crafted, giving readers the impression that they are reading a musical score. The names of cities in the margins not only function spatially, providing us with a map full of locations along the highway, but they also resonate with sound. In the early parts of the poem they are spaced out over many lines and pages. Mt. Vernon, Everett, Seattle, Tacoma, Portland, and Yreka take over four pages to traverse. Then, in a burst of a staccato-like rhythm, in the space of half a page, we read: Salem, Eugene, Sutherlin, Roseburg, Dillard, Canyonville. Another page further on, and Phoenix, Redding, and Anderson occur within three lines. The placement of these names is a way of compressing and expanding time and space. Are these rhythms intentionally placed? Snyder appears to be using the principle of *jo-ha-kyū* as a structural device within this section, but it is next to impossible to demonstrate the rhythms of the Nō drama in words alone. Dynamic movement and sound start slowly and build in successive waves to an intense moment in the poem when a medley of sounds and sights are delivered to the reader in a concentration of short bursts. The rhythms then loosen and lengthen once more, especially after we reach the rhythmic lines

"Going to San Francisco / Yeah San Francisco . . . ," after which the poem appears to have more white space and silence. Reading Snyder's letters or journal entries, written during the time he was composing this section, one finds a good deal of discussion of Nō rhythms and poetic rhythm in general. As one of Snyder's earliest major poems, "Night Highway 99" has moments that seem youthful in diction or thought, but it is a tour de force in the way it allows its fragments of sight, sound, and idea to coalesce into a performance poem.

Readers are expected to participate in this section much as they did in "Endless Streams and Mountains." We may imagine ourselves "inside" the poem, traveling up and down Highway 99 with the poet, but we are also equally on the outside looking in, as if watching other people traverse a path on a scroll. The connection with the landscape scroll is unmistakable on at least two occasions. Snyder's narrator speaks of his friends on trail crews at Glacier and Marblemount as "[t]iny men with mustaches / driving ox-teams / deep in the cedar groves." The word "tiny" reinforces the idea of figures traversing a landscape painting. The second occasion is even more direct: "Snow on the pines & firs around Lake Shasta / —Chinese scene of winter hills and trees / us 'little travellers' in the bitter cold." The framing journey for all these comings and goings is the physical and mental path that Snyder traveled over many years as he made his way both north and south between Seattle and San Francisco. If he is a *waki* setting forth on a journey to wisdom, "Night Highway 99" is his "traveling song" (*michi-yuki*), recounting the paths he has traveled to get to this place. At the end of the section, as he declares that he has had enough of car exhaust, the poem seems to capture that "real" life moment when Snyder rejected the capitalistic ways for Zen instruction. The next section, "Three Worlds, Three Realms, Six Roads," reiterates some of these journeys and takes readers through the portal of San Francisco harbor to Japan.

THREE WORLDS, THREE REALMS, SIX ROADS

The six subsections of "Three Worlds, Three Realms, Six Roads" suggest that we are who we are because of the places we have lived. Snyder has said as much about his intentions:

> What I was interested in then was a kind of oblique looking. Each one of those poems is entirely about a place; it doesn't say anything about the individual, except by implication, what an individual can do there; and it's by the arrangement of the choices that some picture of a personality and a character emerges. (McNeil 38)

If *Mountains and Rivers Without End* is to be seen as a Nō play, this section compares favorably to a *nanori*, a set of lines in which the pilgrim introduces himself to the audience and tells them "where he is from, who he is, why he is appearing, and what he aims to do" (Hoff and Flindt 227). As we listen, we are taken from Seattle to

Portland, then to a "Lookout," San Francisco, a "Ship at Sea," and, finally, to Kyoto. Overall, we are given a picture of the developing personality of an individual we have come to know as Gary Snyder. "The title," as Snyder explains, "derives from Buddhist terms."

> The "three worlds" are periods of time: past, present, and future. The "three realms," *triloka,* describe the universe in terms of desire, form, and formlessness. The "six paths" are territories of psychological passage: the hells, the animals, the humans, delightful gods and goddesses, angry warrior-geniuses, and hungry ghosts. (*MRWE* 159)

The three worlds—past, present, and future—are easy to spot. Although born in San Francisco, the poet describes the activities of his early childhood in the subsection on "Seattle" because his family moved there when he was two years old. Moving on to Portland, as the family did in 1942 when he was twelve, the activities of the "Portland" section develop from adolescence through high school and then on to college. In the six months following his graduation from Reed College in 1951 Snyder considered a career in anthropological linguistics, actually enrolling at Indiana University for a term. Dropping the idea, he returned to San Francisco in the spring of 1952, spending the next few years in that city or its immediate environs, experiencing the activities listed in the subsection "Things to Do Around San Francisco." The summer of 1952 was spent on Crater Mountain and that of 1953 on Sourdough Mountain as a lookout for the U.S. Forest Service in Mount Baker National Forest, engaged in activities that, selectively, become "Things to Do Around a Lookout." Snyder spent a summer (1948) working on board a ship out of New York City, and in May of 1956 he made the Pacific crossing to Japan, but the activities in "Things to Do Around a Ship at Sea" refer primarily to the time he spent on board the *Sappa Creek* from the end of August 1957 to mid-April 1958. The events of the Kyoto subsection are closest in time to the actual writing of the section and may even be considered as "the present time" of the poem. The "future" in "Three Worlds, Three Realms, Six Roads" occurs at the end of the Kyoto subsection: "Throwing away the things you'll never need / Stripping down / Going home." If a reader knew of Gary Snyder's life only from the activities described in these subsections, the "home" at the end of the poem would be ambiguous and the last lines would certainly point toward an unknown future.

However, another sense of "the future" and another perspective on "the present" exists. For most readers, the present is the moment of reading. Images, even though their referents are to activities that have already happened (i.e., are in "the past"), are present to the mind of the reader in the moment of engagement with them. This perceptual truth exists even for Gary Snyder, whose past it is that we are reconstituting. Every mental moment is always present at the instant of its contemplation. By virtue of this poem's manner of composition, the future may be observed as it comes to pass in a subsequent subsection, which is one reason that Snyder has arranged the subsections in a roughly chronological structure. As readers move from an "earlier" subsection to a "later" one, they are able to link the actions of the two sections in a cause-and-effect chain of circumstance. An obvious example is "[g]et married in Vancouver without the three-day wait" (Portland), which is followed by the short line "[g]et divorced" in the San Francisco subsection. The assumption is that this marriage is Snyder's, as it most likely is. He and Alison Gass were married during his first year at Reed College, but the marriage did not last a year. Following this thread, we notice one of the things to do in the Kyoto subsection is to "[w]arm up your chilly wife, her big old feet." Readers who know something about Snyder's life identify the wife here as Joanne Kyger. Still, whether or not actual names are assigned to these wives, readers are dynamically engaged in building a portrait of "Gary Snyder" and, in the process, proving the Buddhist point that our lives are impermanent, in constant flow. Chronologically we move backward and forward in the flow of time. What appeared to be past or seems to be future becomes "eternally" present to the mind that considers such moments. T. S. Eliot makes the same point in *Four Quartets* when he conflates "[t]ime present," "time past" and "time future" ("Burnt Norton").

A more generalized "future" emerges as readers build the selected details of a young boy's life into a portrait of the poet as a young man, watching those particulars "grow into" or "become" the details of a further stage in his life. We impose connections on Snyder's life that may or may not be warranted as we create the poet's personality from the quotidian list of his activities, much as, in "Night Highway 99," he created Shasta in his travels. The implication is that we do the same with our own "stories." That our lives are created in the living of them, never fixed or static, is a fundamental point of Mahāyāna Buddhism. We are conditioned by a myriad of things, so much so that we may be said to have been "caused" by any, or all, or none of them. Philosophically, it is impossible to connect one event solely to another, yet we delude ourselves into doing it all the time. The young child in Seattle "[r]eading books in the back of the University District Goodwill" (*MRWE* 25) is the same "person" who will "[w]rap up in a blanket in cold weather and just read" (26) in his lookout and later spend "[q]uiet weeks and weeks, walking and reading, talking and weeding" (30) in Kyoto.

Snyder, as we might expect, attends to the natural world throughout the subsections:

> Sway in the wind in the top of the cedar in the middle of the swamp
> Walk through the swamp and over the ridge to the pine woods,
> Picking wild blackberries all around the stumps.
>
> (25 [Seattle])

> Bird watching and plant hunting on Sauvies Island in May
>
> (26 [Portland])

Learn the names of all the peaks you see and which is highest—
there are hundreds—
Learn by heart the drainages between

(27 [Lookout])

Suck in the sea air and hold it—miles of white walls—
sunset shoots back from somebody's window high in the Piedmont Hills

(27 [San Francisco])

Dolphins and sharks.

(28 [Ship at Sea])

Tropic- and sea-bird watching

(29 [Ship at Sea])

Watching the flocks of sparrows whirling over trees on winter sunsets

(29 [Kyoto])

Thus, in piecemeal fashion, as we move from subsection to subsection, a dynamic, yet selective, portrait unrolls of Gary Snyder, drawn by the activities he chances to remember, that he chooses to record for us, and that we choose to connect from those that he lists. It is, as Robert Kern has said, a recipe style for a person who is at once unique and archetypal:

> By releasing his experience from his subjectivity and thus from its ordinary temporal limits—that is, by adopting a recipe style—the speaker maintains an ambiguity that keeps him hovering between ownership of the experience and promotion of its availability for use by others. The experience both is and is not his, and the result of this is an intersubjectivity, the creation of an intimate community of experience between writer and reader. (Kern 193)

Snyder is depicted as attentive to nature; he travels a great deal; he observes with all his senses; he intellectualizes; he "turns on"; he likes animals; he likes women; he likes tools; and so forth. The evolving picture, however, can never become a "finished portrait," in part because the reader is entangled in the drawing of it just as surely as Snyder is. The journey into the future is a linear journey of the self creating the self or of the self being created by the context in which it finds itself. The journey, of course, loops back on itself endlessly.

It is far easier to connect the "six roads" to the above six locales than to the six Buddhist "territories of psychological passage: the hells, the animals, the humans, delightful gods and goddesses, angry warrior geniuses, and hungry ghosts" (*MRWE* 159). Curiously, an undated manuscript version containing only four subsections—Seattle, Portland, San Francisco, and Ship at Sea—is entitled "Three Worlds, Four Realms, Six Roads" (GSP B8:F62). Logically, the "Six Roads" of this apparently earlier manuscript must refer to the "territories of psychological passage" since the "Four Realms" can only connect with the four named sites. Indeed, the six territories can be teased out from the lines of the section, although one should be circumspect about imposing formulaic point-by-point comparisons. Lama Anagarika Govinda's book on *Foundations of Tibetan Mysticism,* describes the six roads in psychological terms that are readily applicable.

> [C]orresponding to the nature of this world, in which the endless cycle of rebirths takes place, the six realms are represented as a wheel, whose six segments depict the six main types of worldly, i.e., unenlightened existence. These forms of existence are conditioned by the illusion of separate selfhood, which craves for all that serves to satisfy or to maintain this "ego," and which despises and hates whatever opposes this craving. (236–38)

The wheel represents contrasts among the six states:

> Conditions of heavenly joy are opposed by states of infernal tortures; the realm of titanic struggle and lust for power is opposed by the realm of animal fear and persecution; the human realm of creative activity and pride of accomplishment is opposed by the realm of "hungry spirits" . . . , in whom unsatisfied passions and unfulfilled desires lead a ghostlike existence. (238)

Snyder not only knew of Govinda's book but had met with him in India in March 1962 (*Passage* 68–70). Snyder's "delightful gods and goddesses" correspond to Govinda's godlike "*devas*" who are said to be so dedicated "to their own pleasures, they forget the true nature of life, the limitations of their existence, the sufferings of other beings as well as their own transiency" (Govinda 238). In contrast, those who suffer "infernal tortures," that is, Snyder's "hells," are in Govinda's view not punished from without by some "omnipotent god" but suffer from "the inevitable reactions of their own deeds" (239). What Snyder calls the "angry warrior-geniuses" are known as "*asuras,*" who "understand only the language of force and strife" (240). Opposed to them is the realm of "animals" who lack "articulate speech and reflective thought" and are subject to "blind destiny of natural necessities and uncontrollable instincts" (240). In "the world of man," a "realm of purposeful activity and higher aspirations," the majority are "entangled in worldly activities, in chasing after possessions and sense-pleasures, power and fame" (240). Distinguished from this "world of purposeful human activity and proud self-assertion" are Govinda's "*pretas,*" a realm of "hungry ghosts" who cling "to the objects of desire without a possibility of satisfaction" (240). At this point in his life, Gary Snyder may well have viewed himself as a "hungry ghost," a "restless spirit," one "filled with unsatisfied passions, leading a ghost-like, peaceless existence in a world of imaginary objects of . . . desire" (240). Each of these psychological modes of existence may be found among the many activities listed that constitute the portrait of the speaker as we see it in this section. More to the point, however, is the conclusion that this is a poem about a personality, endlessly in the making, an ego that exists among its joys and hells, its struggle for fame and power set alongside its animal fears, its creative energies and unsatisfied cravings. This ego is in the process of learning that all of these modes are bound to the wheel of illusion; somehow the "self" must get beyond all such stages.

As for the "Three Realms," or *triloka,* which "describe the universe in terms of desire, form, and formlessness," these interact with the six paths just discussed. The *kāmaloka,* or sphere of desire, involves "sexual and other forms of desire." In the *rūpaloka,* a "sphere of desireless corporeality or form," we find that "desire for sexuality and food falls away, but the capacity for enjoyment continues." Finally, within the sphere of bodilessness or formlessness known as the *arūpaloka,* we are in a "realm" that is "a purely spiritual continuum" ("Triloka" *Shambhala Dictionary*). Sexual, and other, desires are easily found among the activities listed in the various subsections. The lookout draws "little sexy sketches of bare girls." In San Francisco the speaker gets "drunk all the time" and finds himself "[s]leeping with strangers" as well as "[f]all[ing] in love twenty times." As with the lookout, so on the ship at sea we see the torment of sexual loneliness: "Stag, Argosy, Playboy . . ."; "[d]ream of girls, about yr girlfriend, writing letters, wanting children." In Kyoto he says he gets "buttered up" by "bar girls" and "pay[s] too much." With regard to the second realm there are moments—starting with physical facts, culminating in positive wonder, even awe—that we might describe as pure enjoyment or intense wakefulness in the implied mind of the speaker (and perhaps the reader). Such moments begin with small boys who hear the "hum" in phone poles and see the "clean red new bark" under the old bark on the madrone trees. Older boys listen to the "humming" of car tires as they sing on Hawthorne Bridge or take trolleys just to see "when cherries are in bloom." The lookout marks the sunrise and sunset well and learns the names of all the peaks and knows *by heart* all the drainages between them. This learning is pure enjoyment. In San Francisco the speaker sucks in the sea air and holds it; he observes the fog roll in across the bay as "miles of white walls," and he watches the light of the sunset shoot miles across the water, reflecting off the windows of the East Bay communities. There is a "silence and shudder" of the ship's engine that seems to imply more than just the sound and motion of the machinery; more likely it is the sheer experience of dynamic movement and nonmovement under one's feet, felt within one's body. In Kyoto the simple sensual pleasure of "[p]assing the hand around a rough cool pot" leaves an image of silent awe behind it. These are details that imply the joy of an awakened mind, an awareness of spiritual value that emanates from the things of this life. By its very nature, the third realm, the *arūpaloka,* is impossible to speak of or write about since it exists beyond form. Here we must deal with actions that are not, strictly speaking, actions. This realm points to enlightened moments immersed in the limitlessness of space and time and consciousness. It is tempting to point to phrases like "listening to looms" as a sudden appreciation of the *Avatamsaka Sūtra*'s jeweled net, or "Get lost—or / Get found" as the use of deliberate paradox to move one "beyond." These matters were surely discussed with the "Old Man," Snyder's Zen teacher Oda Sessō, at four in the morning in Kyoto. The best a reader can do is to sense a growing awareness of literal emptiness in the closing lines: "Throwing away the things you'll never need / Stripping down / Going home."

Where, one wonders, is the "home" Snyder writes of in this section? Quite literally, the answer at the time was a return to the United States, which became his permanent "home" once he left Kyoto for good. Snyder's activities thus loop around as he returns to the land that, at an earlier stage, he had viewed as obscene, but that he will now reinhabit as Turtle Island. Spiritually, that decision was a recognition that the answer is always "here," among the "things to do." There never was any "going beyond" in an escapist manner. The *Heart Sūtra* states: "form is no other than emptiness; emptiness is no other than form." The formless realm, the third realm, is right "here," at home, among the other realms.

JACKRABBIT

Further along the path, in fact "by the side of the road" we travel through this scrolling poem, we find a "Jackrabbit" who is, as it says in the second line, a "black-tailed Hare." This short poem is easily mistaken for a poem found in part II called "The Black-tailed Hare," which was originally entitled "The Rabbit." Interestingly, "The Black-tailed Hare" is, as it says in its first line, about a "grizzled black-eyed jackrabbit." The two poems, then, are about the same kind of rabbit, a jackrabbit, a black-tailed hare that Gary Snyder "knows" well. Yet the presence of two such poems raises questions about the significance we are asked to attach to this jackrabbit.

Retitling the second poem may simply be Snyder's way of saying that it was indeed a "black-tailed hare," and not some other kind of rabbit, that he factually observed at the time he wrote the poem. One should always hold on to this simple answer as at least one kind of truth about the use of the poetic imagination in Snyder's poetry. However, Snyder's definitions of "fact" and "reality" are always multileveled. Once asked why he refused to "use nature or animal symbols in his poetry unless [he had] actually seen them," Snyder responded by broadening his definition of "actual physical experience" to include mental experience:

> Maybe it is unimaginative of me, but if I don't have a ground of actual physical experience I don't make reference to it, if I can help it, in almost any area. I don't invent things out of my head unless it is an actual physical experience in my head. Like seeing a bear in a dream; this is like seeing a bear. (Snyder, "Interview" [Flaherty] 66)

Why, then, do we find this short poem, "Jackrabbit," at this point in Snyder's long poem? In the first place, the focus here is on an animal and not on a human being. The four preceding poems have dealt primarily with the perceptions of humans. Here Snyder, our narrator, stops to have an exchange with another species, and *Mountains and Rivers* immediately opens to another level of interest by becoming a poem where one talks to animals. More importantly, the implication is that one should listen to them; with patience one may hear them talk back. We have had some inkling of this in the short section "Old Bones," but here we come face to face with a "live" animal. No old bones here.

Why a "jackrabbit"? Perhaps the answer lies in the ubiquity of such rabbits; they are everywhere; there is nothing exotic about them. Mahāyāna Buddhism is non-elitist, a way of life accessible to and for all beings. Although one might say that the rabbit chose Snyder by its unavoidable omnipresence, poetically Snyder appears to have singled out the "jackrabbit," as opposed to, say, a "cottontail," for its large ears: "Great ears shining, / you know me / a little. A lot more than I / know you." The poet's focus is on the rabbit's ability to know by hopping and subsequently stopping, sitting, and listening. Of these, "listening," especially patient, silent, long-term listening, is clearly the mark of a practitioner of *zazen,* sitting meditation. Moreover, the stress on listening (or hearing) connects with the East Asian figure of Avalokiteshvara (Chinese: Kuan-yin; Japanese: Kwannon). When Katherine McNeil asked Snyder about the meaning of the title of *Regarding Wave,* Snyder responded by connecting enlightenment to hearing, to sound as a "way in":

> If you translate the Bodhisattva Avalokitesvara or Kuan Yin's name literally, it means "Regarding the Sound Waves." "*Kuan*" means "to regard intently," and "*on*" is "sound waves." That is because in this kalpa, which is under the aegis of Amitabha Buddha, with the Bodhisattva Avalokitesvara as the active manifestation of Amitabha's compassion in this universe, it is the sense of hearing by which people become enlightened most directly. This is the universe of the sense of hearing.
>
> INT: Whereas some other universe . . .
>
> GS: Different senses, yes. So that's why there's a lot of attention actually paid to sound in Buddhism. Like the sound of one hand. Or Su Tung-p'o's famous poem that Dōgen wrote a whole essay on, the poem called "The Shapes of the Mountain, the Sound of the Valley." Or the lines in the Nō play "Yamauba" about hearing "the soundless sound echo from the valleys below," which is possibly where Hakuin got the "sound of one hand" kōan. So there's a thread that runs all the way through the Far Eastern culture that has to do with enlightenment and the sense of hearing. (36–37)

The importance of these interconnections for *Mountains and Rivers*—Su Tung-p'o, Dōgen, Yamauba(*Yamamba*), and sound—is further strengthened with the knowledge that Tibetans are devoted to Avalokiteshvara in yet another form, that of Tārā, a goddess we meet in the crucial section "An Offering for Tārā." Moreover, the great "shining" ears of this jackrabbit provide a link with "The Dance," where Amaterasu, a "skinny little girl with *big* ears" becomes the sun goddess, "Shining Heavens." Further, looking ahead to the last poem in the book, "Finding the Space in the Heart," it is Avalokiteshvara, the embodiment of wisdom, who speaks the *Heart Sūtra,* which deals with the interpenetration of compassion and emptiness. No wonder the poet feels this little hopper knows him "a lot more" than Snyder can possibly know the rabbit. As in the two-part Nō play, this humble rabbit is an early embodiment of the Mountain Spirit who will not reveal her true form for many sections to come. Without realizing it, readers have actually experienced their first encounter with the feminine spirit who inhabits the pages of *Mountains and Rivers Without End.*

Still, having discovered these intellectualized bits "hidden" among the lines of this short poem, one comes back to the solid fact that this animal being met by the side of the road is a simple jackrabbit, nothing more and nothing less. How wonderful, we hear Snyder saying, if humans would just pay attention to the animals. They too have a share in the communal living space of the planet. They've been around longer, seen more, and certainly listened more intently than humans have, or do.

THE ELWHA RIVER

In Snyder's pocket-sized journal for the last four months of 1958, after some notes jotted down about a barbecue two days earlier and the comings and goings of friends, we find the following entry:

> 21:X
> mad dream:
> I am a girl waiting by the roadside for my boyfriend to come in his car; I am pregnant; I should be going to highschool. I walk up the road when he doesn't come. I walk over a bridge. I see a sleeping man. I come to the Elwha River. I see a ~~sch~~ [*sic*] grade school in session, & go sit down with the children, the teacher who is young & sad looking, homely, but w/ a good figure, assigns the class an essay to write: "What I just did"
>
> the girl (me) writes an essay: I was waiting for my boyfriend etc—the bridge was redwood, it was a fresh bridge with inner bark still clinging on some logs, it smelled good. There was a man sleeping under redwood trees he had a box of flies by his head, he was on the ground. I crossed the Elwha river by a meadow; it had a flat stony prong between two river forks . . ."[9] etc —thinking how this would please the teacher. The essays were handed in and I got mine back, it said C-. The children went home; the teacher then came to me and said "I don't like

> you" "Why?" I said—hurt and chagrinned [*sic*]—"Because I used to be a whore"
>
> —& the Elwha river, I explained, is a real river, but not the river I really crossed; I was also walking in another landscape which was a dream but for the real river; & where I just walked was real but for a dream river—actually the Elwha doesn't fork at that point (even as I write this I must remind myself that there is *another* Elwha, the real Olympic river, which was *not* the real Elwha I took pains to recall in the dream)
>
> & I was a pregnant high-school girl; the young teacher an ex-whore. We did make friends. (Journal—30 Sept. 1958. GSP B30:F11)

The entry just described is a self-contained unit in the journal. As he often did, Snyder took pains to write his dream down exactly as he remembered it, perhaps even moments after he awoke from dreaming it. With a few significant changes, the journal entry became part "I" of a tripartite poem "The Elwha River," which was first published in *Six Sections from "Mountains and Rivers Without End"* (1965). It was the only one of the original six poems that had not been previously printed in a journal, and, as published, it carried the date attached to the "mad dream" journal entry above—"21.X.1958." Part "III" was dated "21.VIII.1964," indicating that Snyder must have added that part to the poem just before he handed the manuscript material to Don Allen.[10] Certainly, given the reference in part "II" to losing a "black beret Joanne had given me for my birthday" and the 1964 closing date attached to part "III," it is obvious that the latter parts were not composed in the same time frame as part "I," nor has Snyder retained them for the final published version of his long poem.

Yet it is instructive to return to the original tripartite poem, where it seems that a feminine presence lingers in each of its segments. The first part of the poem, which focuses on the mental and physical landscape called the "Elwha River," is dated some six months after Snyder returned, via the *Sappa Creek*, from his first trip to Japan. Living in Mill Valley, California, in the cabin called Marin-an on the slopes of Mount Tamalpais, he would soon return to Japan for his "second time around." It may be helpful to remember that the "actual" Elwha River, as both the poem and an atlas tell us, is located in Washington State's Olympic Range, the magical mountains that Snyder associates with personal visionary experiences and with a romanticized portrait of his first wife, Alison, who appears as a type of the mountain Swan Maiden in Snyder's poem, "For the Boy Who Was Dodger Point Lookout." There is no directly traceable connection between the Elwha River and Robin Collins, yet her miragelike image often appears in his writing between 1950 and 1960. Not only are there poems that speak openly of eight to ten years of being haunted by her apparition, but Snyder also wrote intensely felt entries about her in his journals and letters during that period. Finally, in the time period surrounding his Elwha River dream (October 21, 1958), Snyder's personal writing attests to his involvement with poetry readings, hiking trips, visits with old friends, and current relationships with women. In June 1958 he first met Joanne Kyger. There is nothing remarkable or deep about these facts, yet there is a psychological consistency to them: his factual 1958 Elwha River dream about being a woman and meeting a woman in the Olympics occurs at a time when his daily life contains floating images of women past and present.

The second part of the original tripartite "Elwha River" is undated. In a manner of speaking, it seems to be a lesson on impermanence, a short elegy for "lost things": a hunting knife, a tobacco pouch ("left on the ground at Whiskey Bend / along the Elwha, 1950"), a sewing kit, the black beret given to him by Joanne, a Swiss Army knife, a fine italic pen, a cat (Theodora, Kitty-chan) that wandered off one night in Kyoto, a bottle of wine. All these are "things left on the sand." All have passed into the past. The "21.VIII.1964" date attached to part "III" puts its composition (and perhaps, by extension, the undated part "II") into the period just after he and Joanne Kyger had decided to end their four-year marriage. One wonders if his second wife is not another "lost thing" haunting his mind at that moment. There is a certain circularity to the poem's original structure if we consider that the final section of "The Elwha River" roughly coincides with Snyder's separation from Kyger, while the dream of the first section was recorded at the moment when he was vigorously courting her (and others). Two days before the "mad dream" entry, he writes: "ran into Joanne & went home." One reading of part "II" indicates that Joanne Kyger is one more Nō-like ghost from the past, joining lost women named Alison and Robin who, in turn, bring forth the dreamlike, misty spaces of "The Elwha River," one of Snyder's special places for meeting the Mountain Spirit. Even if we disregard such conjectures, a feminine spirit certainly resides in the one piece—part "I"—of the original "Elwha River" that the poet decided to keep for the final book. In his long meditative article on Snyder's work, Sherman Paul instinctively connected the "girl of this mysterious dream poem" with a figure "out of a Nō play" (292). Moreover, Paul recognized the important connection of Robin Collins to Snyder's early development. In discussing "Four Poems for Robin" he directly connects her to the Nō: "His [Snyder's] dreams of love are troubled by the ghostlike (Nō-like) appearance of Robin" (259).

Obvious alterations from the "mad dream" journal entry include the changing of tenses but not of content. Thus "I am a girl . . . " becomes "I was a girl . . . "; "I am pregnant . . . " becomes "I was pregnant . . . "; and "I walk up the road when he doesn't come . . . " becomes "I walked up the road when he didn't come . . . "; and so forth. The title of the essay—"What I Just Did"—remains the same. These modifications to his journal entry were made before it was printed as part of "The Elwha River" in *Six Sections from "Mountains and Rivers Without End,"* and, until the final publication of the long poem, they remained constant through subsequent printings.

Mountains and Rivers Without End (1996), however, includes a new and unusual variation among a few simple clarifications for narrative and chronological sense. In all versions the "young and sad-looking, homely" female teacher who assigns the essay tells the narrative persona: "I [just] don't like you." In earlier versions when asked "why," the teacher responds: "Because I used to be a whore." In the Counterpoint version the line is changed to: "Because I used to be a man," thereby giving the teacher a dual gender similar to the narrator's. Snyder's alter ego narrates the story as if he were a woman, just as, in the journal entry, he dreamed himself to be. Both, like Teiresias, have experienced maleness and femaleness.

Gender is not the only "reality" called into question by the poem. "The essay that the girl writes," as Steve Windham points out, "describes what she had just done all right, but at the same time it presents a totally different experience."

> The bridge is described in detail, just as everything else in the second "paragraph" is vividly described. By adding color, detail, and even qualitative judgments such as, "it smelled good," the girl has essentially created a new and distinct experience.
>
> As the girl later explains, there actually is an Elwha River, but the Elwha she described is not the real Elwha. The river of her essay was not the real Elwha because "The Elwha doesn't fork at that point," and also because in the last two lines of this section, one is given the idea that there are no redwoods at that point of the river. *She* provides the redwood bridge, the redwoods under which the man sleeps, and the fork of the river through the power of her imagination. (317–18)

Windham's hypothesis about this section, that the girl's imagination creates its own reality, is credible; it is a reality that, as he says, "is no less real despite any differences it may have with the 'real' world" (317). Yet it seems misleading to say, as he does (318), that the girl's confusion over the relationship of the river of the first paragraph ("the river as a river") to the imaginative river of the second paragraph ("the river in the essay") leads to her "ultimate enlightenment" as she reconciles her perplexity through the presence of the third river mentioned in the poem: "another Elwha, the actual Olympic peninsula river, which is not the river I took pains to recollect as real in the dream." True enough, there are at least three Elwhas in this section—the "real" Elwha where the girl walked, the dream-essay Elwha, and the actual Olympic Peninsula Elwha—but the enlightenment of the girl is somewhat beside the point. There are more significant issues at work.

For one thing, it is Snyder's narrative self who speaks the closing lines of the poem. Both with his reassumed presence as a man and in the factual tone of his "real" voice—"There are no redwoods north of southern / Curry County,

Oregon"—he contradicts everything that has gone before. Additionally, it is *his* "poet-voice" that says: "As I write this now I must remind myself that there is another Elwha"; it is *not the girl* who speaks these words. The word "now," added to the final version of the poem, makes this pinpoint in time clear. Yet another moment's thought tells us that Snyder both IS and IS NOT the girl, as, indeed, the teacher both IS and IS NOT a woman. A curious echo is heard when the girl explains to the teacher that she has written about a "dream river" in her essay and Snyder explains in the next-to-last stanza that he has taken pains "to recollect" a river that is "as real in the dream" but that is not "the actual Olympic peninsula river." The echo hearkens back to the first intuition of this poem as the *real* dream he recorded in his notebook.

Spontaneity saturated most of the art of the times; it was in music, drama, painting, prose, and poetry. Jack Kerouac, Allen Ginsberg, and others of the Beat generation often spoke of the authenticity of "spontaneous writing." The use of hallucinogenic drugs was based in part on their supposed ability to reduce the influence of the controlling mind, thereby allowing one's "true" thoughts to rise to the surface. In the psychology of the times, dreams too were (and still may be) treated as direct channels into truth and reality. Accordingly, Snyder utilizes his dream, almost verbatim, as a poem, for, at some level, there may be significance in such inspirations. As a Buddhist, however, Snyder knows that all created things are impermanent, that the dynamic flow that we perceive as fixed is only seemingly tangible. Thus a dream is no more real than the "real" thing; or, in another way, the real is no more real than the dream; it is all the stuff of illusion, *māyā-māyā*. All the Elwhas flow together; all beings, male or female, merge. One mind. This poem that playfully, yet persistently, argues that "everything is illusion" (and therefore equally real or unreal depending on one's perspective) patently contains more than the speedy enlightenment of the girl's mind.

Who is this "whore" that becomes a "man"? A plausible explanation may be found in the realm of the Nō play. At one point when Snyder and Will Petersen corresponded about the Nō, they spoke of *Yamamba* and *Eguchi* in the same breath, and Petersen referred to Eguchi as a "young river gal" (Jan. [1960–61?]. GSP B77:F19). When Snyder wrote to Joanne Kyger about attending a performance of *Eguchi*, he summed up the plot as "about [a] prostitute who is actually Samantabhadra (Infinite Love) in disguise" (15 Dec. 1959. GSP B104:F11). And, in his 1983 letter about Nō to Dan McLeod, Snyder not only mentions the two plays by name but describes the plot of *Eguchi* in some detail:

> Two plays which interest me very much . . . are Yamamba and Eguchi. . . . In the second one, an accomplished and austere mountain monk runs into a slip of a seductive girl. She dances her 19-year's old's dance, and then is astonished to realize that an old monk is vulnerable to her charms. She too is forced into a

> new recognition of the depths of the feminine, and gives him back to himself, as she becomes Prajna—and ascends into the clouds as the Bodhisattva Samantabhadra. Those are eventually thematic on several levels to Mountains and Rivers. But nothing all that literal. (letter to Dan McLeod, 6 Nov. 1983)

Indeed, as Snyder says, it is hard to find anything "literal" in these interconnections. Like the gender switching and deliberate melding of realities in the poem, so the application of the tale of *Eguchi* to the section is far from straightforward and may even be deliberately reversed. In the Nō play, a traveling monk on his way to a large Buddhist temple arrives at the town of Eguchi, which was an important crossing point on the Yodo River. The monk knows the story of the legendary Lady of Eguchi, a courtesan, who once refused lodging to a famous hermit poet, Saigyō, in order to teach him to have higher aspirations (e.g., higher than a night's stay in a house of ill repute). The twist in this story within a story is that the Lady is actually the Bodhisattva Samantabhadra and she turns Saigyō away for his own good. Remembering this legend, the traveling monk is directed to the original home of the Lady of Eguchi. A woman there, actually the ghost of the Lady of Eguchi, appears to him, tells him her version of the Saigyō story, and then vanishes. In part two of the play the Lady herself, attended by two young courtesans, returns as if on a barge by the river in a visionary dream sequence. There are graceful songs and dances that reveal that only spiritual detachment from the things of the world will result in truth. There is a dance of karmic release, and finally the Lady ascends into a white cloud as the Bodhisattva Samantabhadra. The monk is left overwhelmed with what he has seen (NGS, *Noh Drama* 109–10). At the end, then, all seems to be well or, as Snyder said of the "ex-whore" in the last line of his originally recorded dream: "We did make friends."

This scenario aligns Snyder with the position of the monk, an alignment that at first seems difficult to justify with his further dream transformation into "a girl." The opposite seems to be true of the poem's other persona. Samantabhadra, decidedly a male figure in the Buddhist pantheon, is "one of the most important bodhisattvas of Mahāyāna Buddhism. He is venerated as the protector of all those who teach the dharma and is regarded as an embodiment of the wisdom of essential sameness, i.e., insight into the unity of sameness and difference" ("Samantabhadra" *Shambhala Dictionary*). If we remember that the Lady of Eguchi is also Samantabhadra, then the "whore" in the poem's original version, or even the "man" of its final version, turns out to be an appropriate former role for the female teacher. Assuming that wise teachers give a "C" for a good reason, the "C-" that Snyder-as-girl receives from the teacher makes sense if we remember Saigyō's initial frustration when he is turned away for a night's lodging for his own good. If the "teaching" at issue here is "the unity of sameness and difference," then what difference does gender make, either for the characterization of Snyder as a girl or for the Lady Eguchi-as-

Samantabhadra figure? Is this not a poem that embodies the truth that reality—mental or physical—is one thing?

"The Elwha River" is an elliptical miniaturization of the Nō play *Eguchi.* Snyder's original dream leapt spontaneously out of the depths of his consciousness, a teaching perhaps learned from the women—all emanations of The Goddess—who had entranced him. The section describes an early meeting with the feminine spirit who pervades these poems in one of her many forms.

BUBBS CREEK HAIRCUT

From the beginning, "Bubbs Creek Haircut" was important to Snyder. Although it was not the first section of his long poem to be written, he used it as the leadoff poem for both the 1965 and 1970 editions of *Mountains and Rivers Without End.* Writing the section not only clarified important personal issues for Snyder, such as his decision to practice Buddhism "in the world" rather than in the monastery, it also renewed his confidence in himself as a poet (Hunt "Bubbs Creek Haircut"). True enough, his marriage to Joanne Kyger in February of 1960 must also have been an influence on both of these issues. By June Whalen had a typescript copy of "Bubbs Creek Haircut" in his hands, accompanied by Snyder's statement that the poem had been written down in a twenty-minute burst of poetic energy (13 June 1960. Reed–PWP). As a "beat" poet, conversant with jazz and friend of Jack Kerouac, Snyder was clearly delighted by the idea of instantaneous flowing composition, a riff coming from his subconscious mind, but he was even more pleased by the quality; a month before he had told Whalen that "Bubbs Creek Haircut" was "possibly the best thing I've done in 2 or 3 or more years" (3 May 1960. Reed–PWP).

Snyder's decision not to become a monk was matched by his resolve to be a part of the practice of Buddhism in the United States. He spoke of making a staff and doing "walking-meditation practice all over California," but he was thinking especially of focusing on Mount Tamalpais, which he called "the Hieizan of the '70s." Mount Tamalpais, which has a singular section of *Mountains and Rivers* devoted to it, is also a locus for interconnections in "Bubbs Creek Haircut." The dedication of the section to "Locke McCorkle" connects it to the cabin "up the slope from the house that Locke McCorkle rented at 370 Montford Avenue in Homestead valley, a rather steep subdivided ravine about a mile in length situated at the foot of Tamalpais in a south-southeasterly direction from East Peak" (Robertson, "Real Matter" 210–11). This cabin, often referred to as "Marin-an," was shared by Snyder and Kerouac in the spring of 1956 just before the poet left San Francisco on his first trip to the Far East. As David Robertson makes clear, Marin-an became the starting point for significant meditative hikes in and around Mount Tamalpais.

> Hiking at one and the same time frees us from a dependency on nonessential things (the products of humans) and grounds us in "rock air fire wood" (the

> products of *dharma* in another of its senses). The essential nature of things . . . does not lead to a goal. Therefore, it cannot be the object of a quest, as for the grail. Instead it goes round and round and on and on, rather like the hike that Kerouac and Snyder took and even more like the poem that Snyder projected writing and told Kerouac about as they walked [i.e., *Mountains and Rivers Without End*]. (Robertson, "Real Matter" 220)

The concept of ritualized walking is at the heart of several individual sections in *Mountains and Rivers;* it is the metaphorical point of congruence for the endless walking associated with Yamamba of the Nō theater and the dynamic unrolling of paths in the Chinese scroll.[11] In the same manner McCorkle's shack on the side of the mountain may be seen as a nexus between hiking and the making of long poems: it is where Snyder put "the final touches" on *Myths & Texts,* his "first venture into the long poem" (*MRWE* 154), just as surely as, if we are to believe Kerouac's fictionalized recording of events in *The Dharma Bums,* it is where Snyder's vision for his new long poem began to take definitive shape.

When he returned from his first sojourn in Japan and his wanderings on the *Sappa Creek,* he once again took up residence at Marin-an from late April 1958 to January 1959. In a letter to Will Petersen, dated April 22, 1958, among much talk of becoming reacquainted with the San Francisco scene, he mentions McCorkle by name: "Locke McCorkle is fine, he has a motorcycle. . . . The green hills, cherry blossoms, wildflowers blooming. Locke & I go hiking tomorrow. . . . Move into McCorkle's mountain shack before too long" (Bertholf 102). At the end of July (dated "27:VII") he writes again to Petersen: "Leaving with Locke McCorkle next week for the mountains—finally. Excitement now of food buying; weighing, ponchos & sleeping bags, nylon cord, waterproof matches, studying maps. High High Sierra—King's Canyon home" (Bertholf 106). Here then is the actual "Bubbs Creek Haircut" hike indicated by the title and referred to in some specific lines within the section:

> A few days later drove with Locke
> down San Joaquin, us barefoot in the heat
> stopping for beer and melon on the way
> the Giant Orange,
> rubber shreds of cast truck retreads on the pebble
> shoulder, highway 99.

By mid-August (August 19) Snyder described the hike in some detail to Petersen:

> Dear Pete, just back from the high Sierra countree, sitting in my foggy shack [Marin-an] & drinking coffee from a John Muir cup—I was 15 days in them hills, made a big circle from Cedar Grove on the South Fork of the Kings River (90 miles east of Fresno) around the crest of the Sierra—climbed Mt. Tyndall (14, 026) & Mt. Whitney (14,496.811) & several minor peaks, came back up the

> Kern River & crossed several divides where no trail is, rock scrambles & big snowbanks & 12,000 foot high lakes & rock meadows. It sure is a great country. Hiked about 120 miles. Now to work on poems for a week & eat fresh food & then head north to climb some REAL mountains in Washington. (Bertholf 107).

Discussing the factual basis of this particular hike is only marginally significant. The action described in "Bubbs Creek Haircut" is a composite of more than one journey into the Sierra Nevada taken by Snyder, sometimes with friends and at times alone. A trip north with A.G. (Allen Ginsberg), the mention of journeys through both Oregon and Washington, and references to hitchhiking that took place three years earlier, all convey the same deliberately jumbled sense of time and space found in "Night Highway 99."

A diversity of interconnected journeys is only one facet of the jeweled net shimmering in "Bubbs Creek Haircut"; in a larger sense, the poem is a meditation on the nature of reflections. The poem becomes clear when one understands how it literally embodies the Buddhist philosophy of interdependence set forth by the *Avatamsaka Sūtra* and carried out by the poem's emphasis on mirroring. Snyder himself has told us what to look for:

> "Double mirror waver" is a structure point. Mutually reflected mirrors. Like, you see yourself many times reflected in a barber's shop. You look and you see yourself going that way and you see yourself going that way. It's a key image in *Avatamsaka* philosophy, Buddhist interdependence philosophy. Multiple reflections in multiple mirrors, that's what the universe is like. (Faas 135)

Interdependent reflections begin with the barbershop's "double mirrors" in the first line of the poem and continue in the fixity of time and space found in the "splendid alpine scene" of the wall calendar, itself a reflection of the coming trip to the High Sierra as well as of past trips. The barber is a "scab" barber, thus acting as a substitute (nonunion) for the "real" thing (union member). The structural reflection in the poem is apparent in the way it opens inside the barbershop and closes on the same double-mirrored barbershop scene:

> the lotion and the spittoon glitter rises
> chair turns and in the double mirror waver
> the old man cranks me down and cracks a chuckle
>
> "Your Bubbs Creek haircut, boy."
> (*MRWE* 38)

Time obviously oscillates between past and future during the actual time of the haircut. Indeed, any notion of fixity in time or space begins to seem slippery. As Edward Conze tells us: "The basis of all our illusions consists in that we regard the objectifications of our own mind as a world independent of that mind, which is really mind and substance" (167). The mirrors in the barbershop represent the mind itself and, like a mirror, reflect a vast parade of images that flow and change. In order to empty the mirror of images and get back to the void state of "mind only" or "mirror empty," one must dissolve the apparent solidity of these illusions by noting their place in a vast scheme of interminable interrelated cause and effect. "Bubbs Creek Haircut" embodies enlightenment insofar as it dramatizes the speaker's recognition of emptiness, the illusion at the core of things.

Interrelationships are everywhere. The "sag-asst rocker" turns up again as "somebody's rocking chair." It is significant that this chair, mentioned several times in the poem and which Snyder's persona refers to as a "boulder in my mind's eye," is a rocker. The detail emphasizes the wavering movement of the entire poem. A line in all earlier published versions of the section symbolically assimilated the chair to a planetary "rocking lotus throne," one which, like Māyā's womb, contained "a universe of junk, all left alone." The green hat connects several experiences spread out over a period of years; Snyder's persona serves as a link when he carries insulting messages between two trail crewmen. Moorehead's message to McCool, "go to hell," is an echo of McCool's three-syllable return message, "*kiss my ass.*" Consider also these briefer moments of repetition and mirroring: the stained white barber gown and the birdblood-stained Filson jacket; the triplication of Goodwill, St. Vincent de Paul, and the Salvation Army; the imagistic interaction of various trips to the mountains with different hiking partners; the clean yodeling echo off Mount Whitney's peak; the insistent presence of rock; the double mirror waver in the barbershop and the reflections that wobble in the alpine lake, including its "boulder bank" and the "boulder" in Snyder's mind's eye. Ultimately, the visions "of fire-thrust, or of tilted, twisted, faulted / cast-out from this lava belly globe" that Snyder's speaker sees from his high vantage point—a "view that few men see"—become revelations of the essential "interdependent co-creation" of voidness with suchness, of the "bare" sunlight and the "empty" sky molding itself to fit the shape of the substantial mountains. What once appeared to be solid now begins to flow. One is reminded here of the silk void in the upper reaches of a Chinese landscape scroll as it intermingles with the upthrusted mountain peaks. Whiteness becomes tangible cloud and fog, which in turn slips among and into the rocks.

The poem itself becomes, like the green hat or Snyder's hiking message-carrier, a thread that binds readers to the "jeweled net of interconnectedness" as we attempt to unravel its strands. The metaphysical question of the poem concerns the nature of Goodness and Will. In a universe of junk, of loneliness, or of *things* being cast off and crippled, what exactly is "good"? The drag-legged manager of all the junk found in the "Goodwill" store is at first called a "Master of the limbo," yet his disability later marks him as the "King" of either "Hell" or perhaps a "paradise of sorts." For Snyder the three spaces managed by this Goodwill God are merged into one, a locus much wider than the Christian frame of reference that it seems to allude to. The meaning is relatively clear: the "junk" of the world becomes evil or good in accordance with how we manage it, how we apply our will to it. The value we put on the things of the world is an illusion of our minds; things in themselves exist in an indifferent limbo; attachment to things will lead us astray. This idea crops up again in the last section of *Mountains and Rivers:* there on a rock in the desert we may read a "carved stone inscription" that tells us "[t]he best things in life are not things" (150).

The "[s]inister ritual histories" that Snyder associates with this drag-legged figure belong to the mythology of world cultures, not merely that of modern Western civilization. The "Mountain God" who is possibly a "gimp" is easily linked by Western readers to swollen-footed Oedipus Rex or even to the Christian Jesus (his feet nailed to the cross) or any one of several other limping heroes and/or godlike figures, but for Snyder there are other connections. The manager of this cosmic "junk shop" is more likely the consort of the goddess Māyā, Shiva-Natarāja, Shiva the Dancer, whose uplifted left foot is symbolic of "release and is the refuge and salvation of the devotee" (Zimmer 153).

> As . . . King of Dancers, his gestures, wild and full of grace, precipitate the cosmic illusion; his flying arms and legs and the swaying of his torso produce—indeed they are—the continuous creation-destruction of the universe, death exactly balancing birth, annihilation the end of every coming-forth. (Zimmer 155)

The ambiguity of the dancing Shiva—god of both creation and destruction—fits the questioning mood of Snyder's persona as he tries to come to terms with the "halting metrics" and "ritual limp" associated with these symbols. On several occasions Snyder has said that Shiva corresponds mythologically to "the devil," a suggestion that takes into account the etymological derivation of the modern word "sinister" from "the left" and associates all these "sinister" rituals and histories. Whether good or evil, right or left, these "things" are produced by the dance of Shiva and Māyā. However "halting," the same creative-destructive dance is also the measure for the flow of the poetic imagination.

The myths and legends associated with the Dancing Shiva are indicative of "immensely old" traditions (Zimmer 169–70 passim). As a student of the Paleolithic, Snyder would certainly agree. The paintings found in the caves of southern France, sites that Snyder knows well, depict bulls, cows, hand prints, and what Joseph Campbell calls "buffalo dancers"—half-human, half-animal figures, perhaps representative of Paleolithic hunting magic, whose destinies are interlinked forever with the animals they hunt (Campbell, *Primitive* 286). As in the later section, "The Bear Mother," these pictured "animals are great shamans and great teachers. . . . They fill the world of the hunter, inside and out" (*Primitive* 295). A line from earlier printings of "Bubbs Creek Haircut"—"*Le Roi Boeuf*"—apparently confirms that the section is connected in Snyder's mind with these caves, and the dropped reference calls up the haunting image of one such "buffalo dancer," often called "The Animal Master." Snyder refers to him in his essay on "Poetry and the Primitive": "The antlered and pelted figure painted on the cave wall of Trois Frères, a shaman-dancer-poet, is a prototype of both Shiva and the Devil" (*EHH* 122). The Paleolithic era, for Snyder, always raises issues of community and wholeness:

> What [primitive cultures] . . . have is this knowledge of connection and responsibility which amounts to a spiritual ascesis for the whole community. Monks of Christianity or Buddhism, "leaving the world" (which means the games of society) are trying, in a decadent way, to achieve what whole primitive communities—men, women, and children—live by daily; and with more wholeness. The Shaman-poet is simply the man whose mind reaches easily out into all manners of shapes and other lives, and gives song to dreams. (*EHH* 121–22)

As far as Snyder is concerned, the present *yuga,* or world age (which is itself merely a part of an immensely larger world cycle), begins with "Nature and Man—the great Paleolithic Goddess and the antler'd dancer—magic paintings in caves; red hands; red dots" (*EHH* 131). The dance of The Goddess and the poet—a dyad that is neither one nor the other but a web of pure energy produced by an eternal dynamic coupling—is at the heart of things. A return to the primitive is not a "backward" journey but a recognition of our whole being. The truly "objective eye of science" would go beyond both "subject" and "object" finally to look into "the very Eye that looks" (*EHH* 131). How can there be a fixed good or a free will when it is clear that actions are willed into being by what has already been seen or by what one hopes to see. To recognize that "any given cultural outlook is arbitrary" is to "discover that all of us carry within us caves; with animals and gods on the walls; a place of ritual and magic" (*EHH* 131–32). Like a journeying *waki* in a Nō play, Snyder's narrator has encountered a "drag-legged" figure in the Goodwill store who will not leave his consciousness. Haunted by what that mythological figure represents, the poet-narrator in "Bubbs Creek Haircut" must decide if he will "leave the world" as "[m]onks of Christianity or Buddhism" have done or if he will, like the "mat-haired mountain sitter" Shiva, don the fur, antlers, and role of the "Shaman-poet" to "give song to dreams." In ritualistic terms, will he undergo the rite of tonsure or let his hair grow? The long-haired path is the path of "halting metrics," a poet's attempt to provide a "knowledge of connection and responsibility" for the whole community.

The metaphysical question is posed in quite mundane terms by the barber: "Now why you want your hair cut back like that." Heinrich Zimmer elucidates the significance of the shaving of the head as found in the story of the "great departure" of the Buddha: "Anyone renouncing the generative forces of the vegetable-animal realm, revolting against the procreative principle of life, sex, earth, and nature, to enter upon the spiritual path of absolute asceticism has first to be shaved" (157). "Bubbs Creek Haircut" commemorates the ritual setting-out of an initiate on the traditional Buddhist path of detachment. Like the Buddha, Snyder's speaker encounters old age, disease, and death. The barber is an old man. He "built the cabin / up at Cedar Grove. In nineteen five." The "[o]ld haircut smell" that the speaker remarks on is his recognition that this "scab barber" may know something of the road that the speaker must yet encounter. In fact, in the legendary story of the Buddha's life, we find just such a figure:

> Vissakama . . . came on the instant, by his superhuman power, into the presence of the Future Buddha [Gautama Buddha]. And assuming the guise of a barber, he took from the real barber the turban-cloth, and began to wind it round the Future Buddha's head; but as soon as the Future Buddha felt the touch of his hand, he knew that it was no man, but a god. (Stryk 27)

The next encounter is with disease—the man from the Goodwill store who is deformed by his "drag-legged" condition. The Buddha's confrontation with death is represented here by the heaped-up piles of "unfixed junk" in the Goodwill store, the dead and dying things of civilization. Making the long climb up to Mount Whitney, Snyder's hiker reflects on the ascetic condition of Shiva, who is entranced away from his solitude by the "slippery dance" of "[s]ome flowing girl." In metaphorical terms, the poet reenacts the ongoing dance of the hydrological cycle. The thunder and phallic lightning associated with the male god on the peak is produced by a fusion with the female spirits of the valleys who invite the fertilizing rain to fall on the slopes until the rivers flow; mountains and rivers are dynamically interlinked without end. In sexual-spiritual terms, the conjoining with the "dark and female gate" is to become aware of the presence of love and wisdom. Although intrigued by the role of the ascetic, Snyder's lonely mountain wanderer is lured into becoming a devotee of The Goddess. Ultimately, "Bubbs Creek Haircut" is Snyder's poetic rendering of his decision to take the Tantric rather than the monastic path. Having married Joanne Kyger just three months before the completion of the poem, it seems obvious that the personal dance Snyder had in mind at the time was with Joanne Kyger, his Pārvāti.

Encountering visions of vast dimensions, mythological deities, and metaphysical realities, Snyder's hiker moves past the middle of his poem to make the connections on the other, or double, side of it. The green hat brings together several events separated by years and several realities. It has links with another fictive reality for those readers who remember Jack Kerouac's description of Japhy's typical attire in *The Dharma Bums:* "In fact in his little knapsack he also had a funny green alpine cap that he wore when he got to the foot of a mountain, usually with a yodel, before starting to tromp up a few thousand feet" (11). Three years before the present "Bubbs Creek" hike, Ginsberg and Snyder hitchhiked home from a trip they took north to "B.C." (British Columbia). The "green hat got a ride" for them in Oregon because the driver of the truck who picked them up remembered Gary's hat from "two years before / a whole state north." Now on the "Bubbs Creek" hike, nine days after starting out on the trail, Snyder the hiker finally delivers Moorhead's message to McCool. With fifty mosquitoes sitting on the brim of his green hat, Snyder then suggests that humans must come to terms with the insect world as well as that of rock and water. We hear his yodel in "Bubbs Creek Haircut" too. With the "tingling static" of lightning standing his "hair on end," more than likely symbolic of Shiva's piled tresses, Snyder's hiker holds himself steady on the peak of Mount Whitney as he is assailed by the brute forces of nature. His "yodel," a voice from deep within, sails forth over the river valleys as if the sounds were the entrancing dance of Sarasvatī, echoing cleanly off the highest peak, acknowledging the path through poetry and love that he will take.

> [T]he muse remains a woman. Poetry is voice, and according to Indian tradition, voice, vāk (vox)—is a Goddess. Vāk is also called Sarasvati, she is the lover of Brahma and his actual creative energy. . . . The name Sarasvati means "the flowing one." . . .
>
> As Vāk is wife to Brahma . . . so the voice, in everyone, is a mirror of his own deepest self. (*EHH* 124–25)

The poetic voice, the flowing rivers, the dance of Tantric loving: all merge into one dynamic burst of energy. This is the dance of the dyads: of poet and goddess, of mountains with rivers, of Fudō with Kannon, of Shiva with Pārvāti, "daughter of mountains." It is the dance of Ame-no-uzume as she entices the sun goddess, Amaterasu, out of her cave ("The Dance"); it is the eternal spiraling energy expressed by the wanderings of Yamamba across the world's landscapes ("The Mountain Spirit"). It is the quiet interpenetration of mind, body, and heart—literal and sacred—in "Cross Legg'd." An awareness of such moments of interpenetrating conjunction with this goddess, this Other, is a recognition of the void behind Māyā's mirror of illusion. It is at the core of "Bubbs Creek Haircut," Snyder's earliest full expression of these universal and eternal movements of pure energy.

Once again Snyder destroys any sense of logical time progression we might develop as he asserts that "all this comes after." Returning us to the barbershop, he reminds us that the actual trip with Locke McCorkle to the mountains, preceded by a stop in the Goodwill store, and accompanied by a meditation on the nature of good will, has not yet taken place. Moreover, some of the concluding events appear to float in no particular time frame. The "diamond drill" he speaks of is a reference to the *Diamond Sūtra,* so called because, like a sharp diamond, it cuts away the unnecessary, showing "that all phenomenal appearances are not ultimate reality but rather illusions, projections of one's own mind" ("Diamond Sūtra" *Shambhala Dictionary*). The image is also geological: "racing icemelt waters" act as a drill on mountain rock, cutting paths and tunnels through the seemingly impenetrable stone. The speaker may well have watched buildings being razed and garbage acres burning in the San Francisco Bay Area, yet the events seem more metaphorically true to the poem than factual occurrences. In these last lines, the speaker's attitude becomes detached; he appears as an observer more than a participant. Equanimity of mind may be seen in the perfectly ambiguous phrase "buildings raze." Such buildings may either be raised/lifted or razed/destroyed. As if it were yet another image of Shiva, creator and destroyer, this con-/de-struction also refers to images raised or razed in the mind of the young man as he sits in the barber's chair looking into the mirror. The "skid-row / cripple's daughter" who may have been, in actuality, a cashier in the Goodwill store is transformed into the valley spirit, the flowing girl with the "slippery dance," Pārvāti-Anahita-Sarasvatī, "the dark and female gate of all the world" that lures the other half of the dyad into full participation. Now her image drops down, fades away again. Snyder the poet speaks of the truth found by Snyder the young hiker among the events of this section. He alludes to the Buddha's architectural metaphor spoken at the moment he at last attained the knowledge of interdependent co-creation, thus freeing himself from desire:

> O builder! I've discovered thee!
> This fabric thou shalt ne'er rebuild!
> Thy rafters all are broken now,
> And pointed roof demolished lies!
> This mind has demolition reached,
> And seen the last of all desire!
> (Stryk 43)

With a final twist of reality, everything just described to the readers appears to have arisen "out of the memory of smoking pine," an image conjuring up the Nō drama's phantasms as evoked against a painted pine tree backdrop on a stage constructed of pine wood. Out of this haze slowly we return to the "present reality" as the mind/mirror images clear, bringing us back to the "lotion and the spittoon glitter" of the barbershop.

As with the events in "The Elwha River" we have been confronted with a time beyond time, a reality beyond any single reality; everything flows when there is no fixity. The barber cranks down the chair on Snyder's young hiker. Like the poet, we too face the multiple illusions of the double mirror waver, the smell of the lotion, the glitter of Māyā's net. If we perceive a universe of objects, with identity, solidity, and a fixed nature, we only continue to delude ourselves; our consciousness remains willful and ego-centered. If, however, we see the ever-changing, interconnecting, fleeting character of things, we will at least recognize the universe for what it really is: a mirage, or, as Zimmer puts it, "*Māyā-māyā*, 'of the stuff of *Māyā*'" (24). Given

Snyder's view of time, there is always another setting forth on another trip to the mountains where we will meet the flowing female dancer and spin the web of energy again.

BOAT OF A MILLION YEARS

The *Sappa Creek*, the old T–2 tanker on which Snyder worked as a fireman from August 1957 to April 1958, floats at the center of the numerous symbols encountered in this short section. It turns up in "Things to Do Around a Ship at Sea," a subsection of the earlier "Three Worlds, Three Realms, "Six Roads." Selected dates and locations of the boat's actual progress were noted in *Earth House Hold:*

> At Sea   Arabian Sea   6:XI
> Suez canal   eleven eleven
> At Sea   29: XI
> At Sea   Arabian Sea   8: XII
> Iskenderun, Turkey   20: XII: 57
> Istanbul   25: XII
> Back through Suez   4: I: 58
> At Sea
> 18: II: 58   heading back into the Persian Gulf
> Ras Tanura   20: II: 58
> At Sea   20: III: 58.
>
> ("Tanker Notes" 58–68)[12]

In Snyder's diary jottings, we imaginatively sail with him on the seas of the Middle East, our lilliputian ship voyaging along the coastlines of both the modern and ancient worlds. More than once, as if propelled by the unwinding and rewinding of scenes on a horizontal scroll, the ship travels from the oil depots of the Persian Gulf, up the narrow Red Sea, and through the Suez Canal into the Mediterranean. The port city Ras Tanura, a terminus for Arabian pipelines, marks the boat's role as a transporter of the black-gold liquid from Middle Eastern oil fields to the cities of modern civilization. Always mindful of global ecology, Snyder is well aware of his compromised position on the *Sappa Creek;* in "T–2 Tanker Blues" he points out his "hatred of machinery and money & whoring my hands and back to move this military oil—" (*Riprap, & Cold Mountain Poems* 27). Yet Snyder's writing captures the world as it is, a dynamic interaction of workaday humans in the context of their technologies. *Myths & Texts* describes the logging environment in its totality; the voyage on the *Sappa Creek* records the world of seamanship and oil. Like Walt Whitman (whose poetry he was reading on this particular journey), Snyder is no stranger to contradiction; nor is he troubled by it. Zen Buddhism thrives on it.

With service to the Oil God (or Goddess) at its literal core, "Boat of a Million

Years" nevertheless transforms the journey of the *Sappa Creek* into several other realms of significance. On November 10, while sailing the Red Sea "in the narrow place just south of Suez heading Northwest," Snyder writes to Will Petersen:

> *all the long way southwest the southern coast of Arabia never out of sight of what is really an enormous thousand-mile scarp with stratification clear to view, a straight cliff well over a thousand feet high, not a sign of life not even one spit of a seed* (Halper 84)

Geological observations like these provide some insight into the title phrase "Million Years." To voyage on the veritable Red Sea is to float on waters that fill an immense rift in the planetary crust. A knowledgeable traveler on the *Sappa Creek* gets an authentic look at the ancient landscape of Gaia as it has evolved, and continues to evolve, in time. Gaia's "face" on these escarpments reveals a "million year" journey that extends well back into the period of Pleistocene glaciation.

The beings inhabiting these waters are both mythical and factual. Although Snyder plants himself as a tangible referent—"sun already fries my shoulder blades, I / kneel on ragged steel decks chipping paint"—the images ultimately lead away from the literal events he records. In his correspondence with Petersen, Snyder's enchantment with "the classical world" he was encountering—Crete, Sicily, Pompeii, Byzantium, Turkestan—is manifest:

> *This is the sea where heroes sailed.*
> *& goddesses came to shepherds on mountaintops, & the dawn is* REALLY *rosy-fingered, the sea wine-dark, & I intoxicate myself with Classical memories & look about for pagan deities & long prowed galleys.* (Halper 86)

Immensely impressed by the palpability of myth in this landscape, he told Petersen that Byzantium (Istanbul) "hit me like bricks," and he made special mention of "the terrible silence of Hagia Sophia that has been Christian & Moslem & is now void." With its primary locus in the Red Sea, "Boat of a Million Years" makes no direct mention of Hagia Sophia's empty dome, yet Byzantium is demonstrably not far from Snyder's poetic thinking in this section. Allusions to William Butler Yeats, another poet fascinated by Byzantium, are found in Snyder's letter to Petersen and in the emphatic references to dolphins in the poem. In two major poems—"Byzantium" and "News for the Delphic Oracle"—Yeats drew on the traditional symbol of dolphins as "bearer[s] of the souls of the departed to the island of the blessed" (Jobes 1: 459). In both poems, spirits straddle the backs of dolphins who swim in Yeats's metaphoric seas. In Snyder's poem the boat itself appears to ride the backs of the dolphins as they "streak in, swirl and tangle / under the forward-arching wave roll / of the cleaving bow." Similarly, passengers on this million-yeared planet endlessly fare forward, riding the back of the dolphinlike earth-boat as it arches and spirals its cyclical way through the cosmos. There is no terminus, no mythical "island of the blessed" to reach. With no human beings, as Teilhard said, "to seize the tiller of the planet,"[13] and steer it purposefully into the waters of its future, we are "led by the dolphins." The journey "toward morning" becomes its own satisfaction. Snyder openly mocks the philosophical position espoused by the Jesuit paleontologist Pierre Teilhard de Chardin. Although Teilhard de Chardin is viewed as one of the early enthusiasts for a Gaia hypothesis, his mystical vision of human evolution toward an "Omega-point," a realm of higher consciousness that "leaves animal and material life virtually behind" (*Phenomenon* 278), is far too detached from the veritable earth for Snyder to accept it. For Gary Snyder, humans must attend to the "forward-arching wave roll" of the planet and note the natural rhythms of other beings as all move together toward morning, again and then again. There is no other life.

Although the word *dolphin* is linguistically related to "Delphi," the name of the sanctuary dedicated to the Greek sun god Apollo, the locus for "Boat of a Million Years" is the Red Sea, far closer to Egyptian culture than Grecian traditions. The gods that concern us prefigure Apollo. Indeed, it is sun imagery, clearly stressed in Snyder's poem as it "fries" his "shoulder blades" on this "boat of the sun," that links us to yet another myth. On one level, the sun is the energy supply for the planet, the ultimate source of the oil welling up from within. On another the sun is transfigured into one of the boats of the Egyptian God Rā (Re), a sun god who sails through the skies on a never-ending cycle as the planet turns.

> Rā sailed over the sky in two boats; his morning boat was called "Mäntchet," or "Mätet," or "Ätet," and his evening boat "Semktet." His course was guided by Maāt, the personification of law, order, unfailing regularity, etc. After he set in the west in the evening he entered the Tuat under a different form, . . . and appeared in the sky of this world the next morning in his usual form. . . . Two fishes swam before the boat of Rā, and acted as pilots and warned him of coming danger; these were called "Abtu" and "Ant," respectively. (Budge, *Book of the Dead* 166)

Here, clearly, is Snyder's "boat of morning" and the two fish that "play in the waves" before it, albeit under slightly different names.[14] In yet another book on Egyptian mythology, in the course of explaining the sacred nature of certain trees, E. A. Wallis Budge mentions that "the god Rā appeared each morning from between two sycamore trees of turquoise" (*Osiris* II: 259). Like Rā's "Mäntchet" boat, Snyder's "boat of morning" sails between the "sycamores of turquoise" as the earth turns under it and the sun rises in the sky until it becomes the "boat of the sun." The sycamore is the "Egyptian tree of life. In the east of heaven, gods sat in it, and it provided them with fruit. After death humans went to the tree" (Jobes II: 1521). Finally, Snyder's actual title for the section is derived from Budge's translation of the Egyptian hieroglyphics representing the "sky boat" as the "Boat of Millions of Years" (*Osiris* I: 95–96).

"Turquoise" has further echoes. According to the *Dictionary of Mythology, Folklore, and Symbols*, Rā has "hair of lapis lazuli" (Jobes II: 1315), the Egyptian goddess Isis is designated as "Lady of Turquoise," and her brother/husband/lover Osiris is referred to as the "God of Turquoise and Lapis Lazuli" (Jobes II: 1609). Indeed, both the turquoise and the locale of this Red Sea poem strongly suggest the interlinked stories of Isis and Osiris. Isis, whose hallmarks are faith, loyalty, and maternal care, eventually became the supreme goddess of Egypt. Osiris, once honored as a nature deity, a dying and resurrected god symbolizing the mystery of eternally recurring vegetation, ultimately became the mythical ruler of the souls of the dead. When Set, their jealous brother, murders and dismembers Osiris—his penis is swallowed by a fish—it is Isis who restores and reanimates him, even to the point of conceiving a child, Horus, with him. Few of these mythical elements are openly manifested in the lines of "Boat of a Million Years," yet tokens of Egyptian mythology clearly hover in the background as harbingers of the poet's developing relationship with a wise and compassionate goddess, lover as well as mother. Isis, both river goddess and type of the Great Goddess, the Magna Mater, is often pictured with her son Horus on her lap, much as the Virgin Mary holds the infant Jesus, or the Bear Mother holds her infant. Osiris's role as a dying and resurrected god, revivified by Isis's animating power, underscores the dyadic nature of their common story. Snyder may even have the nurturing aspect of The Goddess in mind as he envisions the *Sappa Creek* sucking oil from a pipeline nipple at Ras Tanura, drawing sustenance from the maternal earth.

Because the dwindling resource of precious Persian Gulf oil openly drives this section even as it energizes the mechanized world, a melancholy mood hangs over the poem, one that ultimately explains the presence of the Dutch freighter. Snyder may be recording an actual encounter with a Dutch ship with a red stack—a Shell tanker would match this description—yet its color and nationality may have additional significance. This "[d]awn white" boat with a "red stack" may be a prefiguration of Rā's midday "boat of the sun," but its "Dutchness" extends the pipeline spatially into the Netherlands, thereby establishing an energy link between Europe and the Middle East. However, Snyder's letter to Will Petersen reveals still another myth rising out of this text. Snyder remarks, on "22 December 1957," that the *Sappa Creek* has had a change of orders and will return to the Red Sea, then proceed through the Suez into the Mediterranean for a port in Turkey. His frustration is evident:

> This damned ship
>
> *just goes on & on like the flying Dutchman, I sort of begin to believe it will never go home or stay anywhere more than a day, until the last drop of deep-down Arabian oil is drawn &*

> *the last gearbox oiled & the ultimate airplane wrecked & all the paint gone & the Sappa Creek just floating around in its own rust & ruin with its hoary white-bearded crew re-reading the ten thousandth time the same magazine & wondering when we'll ever get home.* (Halper 86)[15]

The "[d]awn white Dutch freighter" with a rhythmic "red stack" in a "Red Sea" is a token for the *Flying Dutchman,* a ghostly presence whose eternal passing and re-passing mirrors the seemingly endless voyage of the *Sappa Creek,* apparently doomed to never find the peace of home again. This tortured cycling equally reflects the ceaseless walking of Yamamba, Snyder's "Mountain Spirit," condemned to wander the earth's pathways endlessly in a cosmic Nō play called *Mountains and Rivers Without End.*

THE BLUE SKY

Aboard our "Boat of a Million Years" we sail through the "sycamores of turquoise" and into "The Blue Sky." Slipping away from the Red Sea where "sun . . . fries . . . shoulder blades," we voyage into a cool blue ocean of air. Inspired by the *jo* rhythms of the Nō, in this section Snyder ascends to a moment of poetic intensity and then pauses, tableau-like, long enough to focus on blue colors and mantric sounds that he believes will promote wholeness and, therefore, healing for the "sickness" of our oil-dependent "civilized world." Before continuing on to successive sections, Snyder uses "The Blue Sky" as an all-encompassing poem, one that will bring East and West together as "comrades" under the same "arched cover" of the curving sky. "[H]ere in the twentieth century," as Snyder said years ago, "we find occidentals and orientals studying each other's Wisdom and a few people on both sides studying what came before both—before they forked off" ("Re-inhabitation" 61–62). The message is clear: there was a time of wholeness before that "fork" in the path of human development. Paradoxically, to approach that wholeness, to see ourselves more completely, we must first understand our limits. Snyder points first to a planetary consciousness:

> Stewart Brand said that the photograph of the earth (taken from outer space by a satellite) that shows the whole blue orb with spirals and whorls of cloud, was a great landmark for human consciousness. We see that it has a shape, and it has limits. We are back again, now, in the position of our Mesolithic forebears—working off the coasts of southern Britain, or the shores of Lake Chad or the swamps of southeast China, learning how to live by the sun and the green at that spot. We once more know that we live in a system that is enclosed in a certain way; that has its own kinds of limits, and that we are interdependent with it. ("Re-inhabitation" 62–63)

At the center of such interdependent nonduality is the image of a spiraling blue orb, a space we must learn to reinhabit. "The Blue Sky," as Snyder himself has said on more than one occasion, *is* a poem of healing. As recorded by Katherine McNeil, he remarked:

> That poem is based on the sūtra of the Buddha of healing, Bhaishajyaguru, otherwise known as Yakushi. To get a sense of lapis lazuli . . . read Ed Schafer's *The Golden Peaches of Samarkand,* where he talks about lapis lazuli in Chinese culture. It's just a beautiful stone, a really magical stone. It's the jump from the healing impulse in Buddhism to a North American shamanistic healing that I'm really trying to get across. (McNeil 52)

First published in *Caterpillar* and then in a limited edition broadside,"The Blue Sky" became the seventh section of the 1970 *Six Sections from "Mountains and Rivers Without End" Plus One.* Notably, the paperback "second" edition of *Mountains and Rivers* was bound in deep blue covers. Manuscript fragments and early typed versions of the poem that exist at the Davis archive reveal that Snyder originally planned to entitle this poem "Azure," a detail that gives even greater emphasis to the intermingling of rich blue colors in the section (GSP B1:F98–99–100). The word "azure" remains within the section as a visual description of the Buddha called "Master of Healing"; his essence or suchness (*tathata*) is, in fact, defined by his "AZURE RADIANCE," his color fusing with the magic of blue beads and the enchanting stone blue allure of "lapis lazuli."

> Shades of blue through the day.
> T'u chüeh a border tribe near China
> Türc
> Turquoise . . .
> . . . .
> Tibetans say that goddesses have lapis lazuli hair.
>
> Azure Old French *azur,*
> Persian *lazhward,* "lapis lazuli"
> —blue bead charms against the evil eye—
> (*MRWE* 41–42)

Snyder's notes for the final version tell us that there is "ancient lore" about the "protective and healing powers of the color blue and of certain blue stones" (*MRWE* 160), and Bob Steuding, Charles Molesworth, and Sherman Paul all point to non-*Mountains and Rivers* poems, such as "Magpie's Song" from *Turtle Island,* that connect "healing" with "turquoise blue" (Steuding 108; Molesworth 117; Paul 277). One of Snyder's major sources for the poem provides several significant interconnections:

> It appears that the men of T'ang bought their lapis lazuli in Khotan, the city of the quintuple forts, dear to the earth goddess, whose rivers were rich in jade. . . .
>
> The real home of lapis lazuli was salubrious and well-pastured Badakhshan, its ancient and classical source. Here in the valley of the Kokcha, a branch of the Oxus River, the mineral azure, sometimes fine indigo blue, sometimes pale blue, sometimes green or gray, was chopped out of its limestone matrix. . . . The existence of these mines was known to the Chinese, who place them correctly southeast of Chāch (modern Tashkent), the home of the celebrated dancers. . . .
>
> Though the principal supplier for Central and East Asia was Chāch, and its eastern market was Khotan, the Chinese thought of lapis lazuli as the *Persian* gem par excellence. . . .
>
> The Chinese were not alone among the Far Eastern peoples in their admiration for the blue mineral. The Tibetans valued it above all others, even ahead of gold, and those highlanders saw in it the image of the azure sky, and said that the hair of their goddesses had its color. (Schafer, *Golden Peaches* 231–32)

Earth goddesses, trade routes journeyed between the Near and Far East, celebrated dancers, Tibetan goddesses with blue hair—all these figure importantly in the poem.

Similar associations appear in "The Hump-backed Flute Player." We notice the "high blue tiles" at Nalanda University, the Indian monastic center where the "Logicians of Emptiness" carried on "delicate debates" about the void. At Nalanda the legendary Chinese pilgrim Hsüan-tsang studied Yogāchāra thought as he "sought to revitalize" an older tradition of Buddhist thinking "in light of the Mahāyāna concept of emptiness (*śūnyatā*)" ("Hsüan-tsang" *Encyclopedia of Religion*). The term "Yogāchāra" refers to the philosophy of "mind only"; that is, that "things exist only as *processes* of knowing, not as objects" ("Yogāchāra" *Shambhala Dictionary*). Snyder himself tells us that the Chinese character *k'ung* is used for both "emptiness" and "sky" (*MRWE* 160). Thus the cluster of "blue-turquoise-lapis lazuli-azure" mingles with that of "emptiness-sky-void," and the enlightenment that comes with meditating on "emptiness" is akin to the healing that will come from reflecting on azure or lapis or the blue sky itself. Why? Because the planet itself is a spherical being bathed in the blueness of both sky and water even as it encompasses all of the beings who live upon it. If the flute playing of Kokop'ele may be said to be the sound of emptiness, then blue is its color.

Snyder's use of a drawing of the Kokop'ele petroglyph as a printer's device to mark off subsections of "The Blue Sky" in the *"Plus One"* edition literally connects it with "The Hump-backed Flute Player." In the Counterpoint edition, Kokop'ele has been replaced by simple centered bullets, yet several links remain between these two sections of *Mountains and Rivers.* They share parallel positions of importance within the structural framework of the entire sequence: "The Blue Sky" ends part I of the long poem; "The Hump-backed Flute Player" ends part II. "The Hump-backed Flute Player" invokes Tārā, "[s]he who saves," while "The Blue Sky" conjures up the healing powers of Bhaishajyaguru, Old Man Medicine Buddha. In both sections the concern for rehabilitation is evident, and the power of emptiness is evoked to bring about healing. Nor should we disregard Snyder's meshing of the word "medicine" with the goddess "Maya," thereby focusing on her healing role, as mother of Kama, God of Love. In this way she serves as a counterpart to Tārā, both of them being feminine presences that "save."

The celestial curve established by "The Blue Sky" forges a structural and conceptual link between parts I and II of *Mountains and Rivers Without End.* Hearing the echoes across the sections, we might say that if indeed we are made "whole" in "The Blue Sky," we may see (or hear) the "whole" world, as Black Coyote did, in the "hole" of Wovoka's empty hat. Snyder's "whole/hole" pun embodies three senses: "totality," "wellness," and "the tangible void." The "arched cover" of the sky, with its "bent curved bow" shape, finds a congruent echo in the geometry of Hsüan-tsang's "curved frame pack," the curved shape of the flute player's "hump," and in the arching pathways described by the historical and legendary journeys that loop back and forth from east to west in "The Hump-backed Flute Player." Like little beings on the unrolling landscape scroll, we see ourselves—along with earlier travelers and ideas —traversing the paths from Asia to North America, all under the same curving, arching, blue sky that encompasses the entire planet we live on. The culture and history of the "East" intersect with that of the "West"; the wisdom of equality is one thing, not two.

The basic spatial metaphor of "The Blue Sky" is set forth in its opening lines, which refer to an enchanting lapis lazuli world, somewhere to the east, presided over by the Buddha of Healing, Bhaishajyaguru. This Buddha of the eastern realm, also known as Yakushi, should be distinguished from Amitābha, who is mentioned at the end of the poem in connection with "his *western* paradise." In Mahāyāna Buddhism there are countless "pure lands" (also known as buddha-realms or buddha-paradises), each of which is ruled over by a Buddha:

> The most important is Sukhāvatī, the pure land of the west or the western paradise, ruled by Buddha Amitābha. An eastern paradise is the pure land of Bhaishajya-guru Buddha ("Medicine Guru Buddha"). . . .
>
> These pure lands are transcendent in nature. They are the hope of believers who wish to be reborn in them. . . . In folk belief these paradises are geographically localizable places of bliss; however, fundamentally they stand for aspects of the awakened state of mind, and the directions (east south, etc.) have iconographical meanings. The pure lands are not, however, the final stage on the way, but are the stage before nirvāna. ("Pure land" *Shambhala Dictionary*)

In one sense, then, the poem moves from "east to west" as we locate its beginning in Asia and "drive east" in the direction of Bhaishajyaguru's "lapis lazuli realm," a movement that would take us toward North America much as the geography of "The Hump-backed Flute Player" does. At the end of the section the poet "looks back" momentarily to meditate on Sukhāvatī, the "western paradise" of Amitābha. Although belief in Amitābha's power is so strong, especially in Japan where he is called "Amida," that merely calling on his name at the time of death will be enough to gain entrance to his realm, Snyder's poem actually focuses on the realm of Bhaishajyaguru, "the Master of Healing," whose world evokes the morning and the blue sky rather than the setting sun. It would be false, however, to reify either domain, east or west, since the poem is essentially a poem of motion. It is the turning world with its continual movement *into* the east that is stressed.

In Snyder's poem, the mythical "lapis lazuli realm" that lies "[e]ast across the sea" becomes the "yellow sand land / Coyote Old Man land / Silver, and stone blue" of the Great Basin. At first mysterious, there is a correlation. The preeminence of Asian lapis lazuli is echoed in the well-known use of turquoise and silver jewelry by southwestern Native American tribes. Similarly, mandala-like sand paintings, comparable to those created by Tibetan monks, are also found among the art of the Navajo. On Turtle Island, Snyder suggests poetically, Coyote Old Man is the name and face given to the Master of Healing.

Ultimately the geographical location does not count as much as the "pure land," the state of heightened consciousness that the geography represents. In this sense, the poem itself acts as a mandala—"a symbolic representation of cosmic forces in two- or three-dimensional form"—for meditative purposes ("Mandala" *Shambhala Dictionary*). We hear the chanted rhythms of "The Blue Sky" and visualize its physical and psychic worlds. According to Raoul Birnbaum, in Chinese Buddhist practice there is a widespread devotion to a trinity of buddhas—Shākyamuni, Amitābha, and Bhaishajyaguru—with Bhaishajyaguru (to the east or left of Shākyamuni) and Amitābha (to the west or right of Shākyamuni) representing "the Divine forces watching over the living and the dead," respectively (90–91). If Shākyamuni, as Snyder tells us in his poem, is "lord of the present world of sorrow," then we may imagine the realm of Bhaishajyaguru as the world of constant becoming as we continuously turn east into a future while leaving Amitābha's world behind as a past. Starting from wherever "here" is, we apparently get somewhere, but not to a "there," an actual place, that we can name. Once more we are made aware of the dynamic interconnectedness of what appear to be opposite worlds: in this case, east and west, or future and past, or life and death.

"The Blue Sky" draws on an English version of Hsüan-tsang's translation of the *Sūtra on the Merits of the Fundamental Vows of the Master of Healing, The Lapis Lazuli Radiance Tathāgata*. That the sūtra is associated with Hsüan-tsang only reinforces the link between "The Blue Sky" and "The Hump-backed Flute Player":

> The Buddha told Mañjuśrī: "If you go eastward beyond as many Buddha fields as there are ten times the number of grains of sand in the Ganges River, you will find a realm known as 'Pure Lapis Lazuli.' The Buddha there is known as Master of Healing, the Lapis Lazuli Radiance Tathāgata." (Birnbaum 152)

For Snyder, these lines "translate" as

"Eastward from here,

beyond Buddha-worlds ten times as
numerous as the sands of the Ganges
there is a world called
PURE AS LAPIS LAZULI
its Buddha is called Master of Healing,
AZURE RADIANCE TATHAGATA"
(*MRWE* 40)

The poet injects a bit of contemporary culture, and humor, when he adds that "it would take you twelve thousand summer vacations / driving a car due east all day every day" just to get to the "edge" of this world. With little change from the original, he also repeats—in both Sanskrit and English—the "mystic formula for dispelling disease and suffering" included in the original sūtra. This *dhāranī* is retitled in the poem as simply "*The Spell of the Master of Healing,*" because Snyder wishes to emphasize the positive aspect of wellness, rather than to focus on bodily disease and suffering (Birnbaum 160, 171 n. 11). Yet, by Buddhist definition, not to be enlightened is to be "ill," and both the sūtra and the poem are strategies for a "wholeness" comprising much more than the physical. Modern doctors and nurses, for example, should wear something different from their ordinary "authoritarian" costumes, something more on the order of shamanistic "masks and feathers," to indicate that their role in healing is as spiritual as it is technical. Snyder's example of spiritual healing is a fragment from the life of the young Japanese poet Ono-no-Komachi, a celebrated beauty from the mid-ninth century who is the subject of more than one Nō play. In Snyder's version she becomes sick while on a quest for her father. She has a dream-vision of the Master of Healing—"AZURE RADIANCE THUS-COME MEDICINE MASTER"—who tells her he will lead her to health and to her lost father. This dream of the "strange girl poet," as Sherman Paul suggests, echoes that of the "girl" in "The Elwha River," albeit with different results (296).

In an imaginative leap from "east" to "west," Snyder juxtaposes the reveries of seventeen-year-old Japanese girl poets with Texans who have visions that involve the blue sky. Leaping from Asia to North America, Snyder quotes two lines about the strange enchantment of the blue sky from the 1940s Bob Wills song "San Antonio Rose." The song's lyrics allude to a cowboy who "in dreams" still yearns for a woman he once met "beside the Alamo." Apparently he returns at night, "beneath the stars all alone" to "a moonlit pass," a specific location that holds vivid memories of their love affair. There he sings his "broken song of love" to the moon itself, for it is only the moon in all its "splendor" that can know his heart. This particular portrait of the "blue sky" refers not to the daylight sky but to the cool silvery-blue light that bathes the land on a moonlit evening. The entire scene of the cowboy's song is reminiscent of scenes depicted in *Mountains and Rivers;* both "The Hump-backed Flute Player" and "The Mountain Spirit" describe narrators on mountaintops interacting with the moon and the evening stars. The title of the short section "New Moon Tongue" literally "speaks" the moon's enchantment for the poet. The feminine spirit of the moon shines powerfully in many forms throughout *Mountains and Rivers.*

Where there are cowboys, there are also horses. Hidden among the etymological derivations for "sky" ("*sku*"—"skewed"—"skewbald"—"'Stewball'") is a famous folkloric horse.

> Skew Ball was an Irish race horse of broadside fame. The song came over to America and was turned into a work song by the slaves as some of the stanzas will testify. And now Skew Ball has become "Stewball" and his race is sung in the prisons of Louisiana, Texas, Mississippi, and Tennessee. It is the most widely known of the chain-gang songs in the states we visited, and by far the most constant as to tune and words. (Lomax and Lomax 68).

The horse described in the Lomax version is white and red, "born" in "Californy" where "all de jockeys / in de country" say that he "blew there / in a storm." When he races it seems that his feet hardly touch the ground. Although the folkloric Stewball may not be the right color for Snyder's poem, he surely is a "sky horse," which provides Snyder with a connective leap from African American folksong into the realm of Native American myth where the horse is found as part of a Navajo "medicine chant."

> [A] mythical story or inside song that has given rise to a poem may be cited from the Navajo "Song of the Horse." The inside song connected with the poem concerns the Sun-God, who has five horses: one of turquoise; one of white shell; one of pearl shell; one of red shell; and one of coal. As the Sun-God rides across the skies each day from the East to the West, he carries the shining, golden disk of the sun. In fair weather, the Sun-God, Johano-ai, rides either his turquoise steed, his white shell charger, or his pearl charger; but on dark stormy days he rides his pony of red shell or of coal. . . .
>
> The Sun-God feeds his coursers on flower blossoms. . . .
>
> The Navajos believe that the mist on the horizon is the pollen offered to the gods. Therefore, standing amidst his herds, a Navajo will sing of the Sun-God's

> horses so that he too can have steeds like those of Johano-ai. He will scatter the holy pollen in order to call down the blessing and protection of the Sun-God on his ponies. (Howard 24–25; also see Day 78–79)

Snyder's "turquoise horse," a "horse with lightning feet" and "a mane like distant rain" is a composite of Johano-ai's sky horses. Moreover, "Stewball," the "dappled cloud zone" horse, merges with a "[p]ony that feeds on the pollen of flowers"; together, as one being, they are entreated by the poet to bring the "blue fire" of the sky to heal the listener: "may he / make thee whole." Sky horses, like the blue planet ball rolling in space, are reminders of a certain "boat of a million years" that sails through the "sycamores of turquoise."

This new consciousness attached to turquoise shades of sky is further associated with visions of a feminine presence. As the moonstruck western cowboy is enchanted by his "San Antonio Rose" so Tibetans are charmed by—protected "against the evil eye" by—"goddesses" with "lapis lazuli hair." Taking different forms for different cultures, The Goddess appears globally as a captivating vision radiating the protective power of love. Nor is it insignificant that these are "cow" boys; both Gary Snyder and Krishna have an attachment to cows. In interviews Snyder is fond of stating that he was raised on a dairy farm in Washington State. Milk, in one form or another, is an image that repeats in *Mountains and Rivers.* The reader may remember Sokei-an's Zen-like reference in "Night Highway 99" to the story of Sujata who offered "buttermilk" to the Buddha. In *Earth House Hold,* Snyder uses "yogurt" in his sketch of "The Buddha as Son and Lover of the Goddess": "and [the Buddha] underwent *austerities;* when near death brought *yogurt* by a *girl,* which restored him; near a *river*" (132). Snyder's use of the dairy image is almost always a touchstone for renewal and healing. The Hindu god Krishna, Snyder's cowboy "comrade" (as in "Kama God of Love"), is known for his legendary adventures as a young man among the milkmaids, stories that are not without echoes in the early life of Gary Snyder:

> When Krishna was five, Nanda and Yashoda went to live in the forest of Vrindavana (Radha's forest), and there Krishna insisted upon becoming a cowherd. He grew up in the forest, ever playing his flute, with which he charmed the cowherds, the milkmaids, and the cows alike. Once he came upon a party of milkmaids while they were bathing and he stole their clothes and took them to the top of a tree, making them beg for their return. . . . The love of Krishna and the milkmaids (gopis) and especially his love of Radha are celebrated in lyrics, paintings, sculpture, and there is a whole body of erotic literature and even of erotic cult practice connected with this aspect of the Krishna myth. He dances with the gopis; he swings with them, above all with Radha; he is shown with the god of love Kama in company with them. (Kramer 300)

Krishna is literally charming as a "cow-boy"; often depicted with blue skin, he brings about ecstatic visions with his magic flute. One wonders if, like Snyder and Kokop'ele, he too carries a pack on his back. Additionally, Krishna's act of stealing the clothes of the maidens has echoes with the Swan Maiden motif that continually fascinates Snyder. Kama, linked by virtue of love deeds with Krishna, embodies a curving arch in the blue sky, the "*kam*" or "[a]rched cover" or "bent . . . bow," an image cluster conveyed also by the bow and arrow of the Western love god, Cupid. The implication seems evident; Snyder's imagery encourages a common bond of love and friendship among and toward all beings on the planet, including the planet itself. We are all "sharing the same tent or sky." As if to ground his sky imagery, "Cross Legg'd," one of the final poems in the sequence, returns to a literal act of love under such "a low tent roof."

Buttermilk is mentioned in connection with the dream vision Snyder associates with Ramana Maharshi. In actual fact, as well as dream, Snyder visited the ashram of Sri Ramana Maharshi in Tiruvannamalai on his trip through India. Snyder defines an ashram as a uniquely Indian "institution, . . . a religious community based around some teacher and branch of Hinduism; the person of the teacher being very important" (*Passage* 19). His account of his stay there includes a description of the yogin, who passed away in the early '50s.

> Ramana Maharshi was a genuine Jnana-yogin (adept of wisdom-yoga, as compared with devotional-yoga) who became totally enlightened without any great effort while still a young man. He went up on Arunachala mountain and lived in a cave by a spring for many years, then a few of his followers built an ashram for him at the foot of the hill. He was apparently a very sweet person, talking very little and having almost no teaching method or even interest in teaching. He had a pet cow named Lakshmi. . . .
>
> . . . Many old pictures of Ramana Maharshi on the walls, including one giant portrait of him standing by his cow Lakshmi. Since Maharshi is no longer there, it is the aura of his previous presence which brings people here, or as the Ashram pamphlet described it—"Saturated with the Benign Presence of Sri Maharshi the Ashram confers the unequalled blessing of peace, bliss, and happiness to the devotee, whatsoever the religion he may profess." (*Passage* 24–25)

While "enchanted" may be too strong a word, Snyder was moved by the simple sanctity he witnessed at the ashram. Quoting from an ashram pamphlet he had been given, he took special note of the cows: "The resonant chant of the Vedas by the pupils and the gentle looks of the cows of several breeds enchant the visitor, Indian and other." In his own words Snyder says: "Cows begin to creep up on you here." He concluded in admiration: "Maharshi's place . . . had the nicest feeling of any ashram in South India, and was one of our pleasantest stops" (26–27). It was, in other words, a healing place. While there, he and Kyger actually walked barefoot on a seven-mile *pradakshina* around the sacred mountain of Arunachala, a walk that has obvious associations with "The Circumambulation of Mt. Tamalpais."

In the dream that Snyder's alter ego associates with his stay at the ashram, the "old man" with the "grizzled face—neither eastern or western" is most likely a fanciful depiction of Ramana Maharshi himself, but may also be an emanation of Bhaishajyaguru, the Master of Healing. The old man's sudden appearance again reminds us of encounters in Nō plays where the traveler meets a ghost-spirit in the form of an ordinary human. This old man has a "glass of buttermilk" in his hand that comes from a dairy outside of town. Buttermilk appears as an elixir of wholeness; to find its source, to become "O K" again, one must "leave town," where one can reconnect with the natural world. The dream also includes "Ko-san" (in actuality Morinaga Soko, one of Snyder's teachers at Daitoku-ji), the same monk from "Journeys" who presumably enlightens Snyder in that section by grabbing his collar and pulling him over the edge of a cliff.

Snyder's background as a linguist is much in evidence in this section as he demonstrates one of his favorite ways of getting back to "roots." Throughout the poem an underlying rhythmic cadence is evoked by an etymological litany of interconnecting root words: blue-belo-flamen-brahman-beltane; sky-*sku*-skewed-skewbald-skybald; *heal*-hale-whole; T'u chüeh-Türc-Turquoise; azure-*azur-lazhward*-lapis lazuli; medicine-measure-"Maya"; cover-*kam*-comrade-Kama. Although such words carry meaning, their dronelike recitation reverberates in the background as melodic images and thematic ideas course through the reader's mind. Thus, the poet uses the very sounds of the words and the rhythms of the lines to open up the reader's mind to the healing wholeness or "pure land" consciousness where presumably one will have all ghosts exorcised. If words and their sounds aren't enough, a more literal connection with visions emerges when one realizes that "[g]lory of morning" is both a paean to the rising blue dawn sky and a reference to using the seeds of the morning glory flower for hallucinogenic purposes. Among the many species associated with the morning glory (genus *Ipomoea*) is *violacea,* whose seeds known as *tlitliltzin,* were sacred to the Mayans. These black seeds—especially from strains such as "Heavenly Blue," "Pearly Gates," and "Wedding Bells," among others—are the source of the well-known drug LSD, which of course explains Snyder's references to "pearly gates" and "heavenly blue" in the poem. Several variations exist between the original publication of the poem and its Counterpoint edition version: some, like the mention of *tlitliltzin* are additions; others, like a reference to "hemp" (*Cannabis sativa,* or marijuana), are omissions. Nevertheless, it is perfectly clear that this section is about visions, whether they are induced by meditation, words, sounds, or seeds. The poet obviously feels that "opening the mind" in some manner is the root-beginning for new health. Even the structure of the section—its manner of leaping from vision to vision, at times in a disjointed manner—may represent more than the typical design of much modernist experimental poetry, if Snyder intends to emulate the process of hallucinogenic revelations.

In this unrolling landscape, walking the trails side by side or perhaps drifting along in our tiny boats, we have come with the poet to a significant point in time and space, a place for awareness among the winding paths of *Mountains and Rivers Without End.* Attentive readers of "The Blue Sky" are now encouraged to meet the Old Man himself, the Master of Healing, in whatever guise is most comfortable for their culture: Bhaishajyaguru (Sanskrit), Yao-Shih Fo (Chinese), Yakushi Nyorai (Japanese), or Old Man Medicine Buddha (Snyder's merging of the Native American Coyote Old Man with the Buddha). In the modernity of our space-age culture, there, in the distance, even as we imagine, or actually hear, the vibrating hum of chanted sounds, is a vision that looms larger and larger as it rises into our consciousness, coming closer, ever closer, filling the small window of our sight, as if our vision took place through an astronaut's portal:

> The blue sky
>
> the blue sky.
>
> The Blue Sky
>
> is the land of
>
> OLD MAN MEDICINE BUDDHA
>
> (*MRWE* 44)

The sūtras revered by Mahāyāna Buddhists are gathered collectively under the name *Prajñāpāramitā-sūtra,* which literally translates as "wisdom that goes beyond to the other shore." Analogously, the "eagle that flies out of sight" is in the process of "going beyond." Since paradise is not a fixed location, the eagle's flight is never concluded; instead, the eagle continuously "flies." Reaching for the healing "pure land" produces visions out of the depths of one's inner consciousness: the revelation, pure and simple, of the interminable interdependence of the "self" with all other beings, and a magical image of this factual, ever-turning, liquid, sky-blue planet that bequeaths wholeness to its inhabitants. The eagle in "The Blue Sky" points the way to the "Space in the Heart."

Part II

THE MARKET

"The Market," as its opening lines indicate, inserts the countryside into the very heart of the city. There, in the "down" part of town, the well-oiled commercial machine is spinning its wheels, buying and selling or, in earlier times, bartering ingredients. Snyder implies that this ongoing process has led to, and continues to sustain, modern civilization. As such, "The Market" may be seen, in part, as an ironic diatribe against the capitalistic market economies that pervade modern life. Behind wry statements of what gets exchanged for what, Snyder urges us to negate human greed and possessiveness in order to find the space in the "heart" that is called for in the last section of *Mountains and Rivers Without End.* Completely different in tone from the ecstatic visions experienced in "The Blue Sky," "The Market" opens part II in a declarative mode. It is a *jo* poem, the concise statement of a major theme that pervades *Mountains and Rivers.*

The opening subsection (as established by printer's bullets in the text) establishes certain dominant notes in the entire section as it sets John Muir alongside the adolescent Gary Snyder. We might say that John Muir's dawn trips "on the morning milk-run train" in order to sell pears at San Francisco's Crystal Palace Market EQUAL the young boy-poet's literal milk run on his bike in Seattle. Regardless of their respective success or failure as entrepreneurs (Snyder manages to break nine bottles of milk), both are involved in the competitive economy of a capitalistic market scheme. The "Seattle" lines also emphasize the importance of the food chain: to drink high-quality creamy milk one must begin with animals, manure, confusion, and darkness. Each of these thematic motifs is heard in other subsections of "The Market," and throughout *Mountains and Rivers.*

Having begun with markets closer to his "native" region in the western United States, the poet adds examples from the markets of Saigon (Vietnam), Kathmandu (Nepal), and Varanasi (formerly Benares, a city on the Ganges in India). Snyder visited each of these eastern locales during a six-month trip to India (December 1961 to May 1962) with his second wife, Joanne Kyger. They were in Saigon in mid-December and again on May 1 on their return trip to Kyoto. February 6–9 was spent in Kathmandu. Coming out of the mountains of Nepal, they reached Benares on the evening of the 10th of February and stayed until the morning of the 17th, in the interim taking a two-day side trip to Sarnath.

> Coasting South Vietnam—come into muddy waters, the smell from ashore—go in a bay and up the river. . . . One P.M. land in Saigon—surrounded by shaggy ricefield delta plains, a few thatched houses in clumps of palm. Long bridge and double-spire church visible . . . Saigon is really French. They sell French bread everywhere, right along with funny-looking broiled animal innards, fruits and kinds of fish and vegetables which knowing the name wouldn't help you. The women are all beautiful and wear silk pajamas with a silk tunic and long loose hair, and apparently brassieres that make them all come to sharp points in front. Walked a bit in the afternoon, and then out in the night street stalls—fruit juices, caged birds, crushed sugarcane with ice and lime.. . . [Next

> day . . .] [s]ail back down the river at 1:30 in the afternoon. You'd never guess there was any kind of war going on around here, but for a very rare truck going through with soldiers in jungle outfits, but no weapons visible. . . . Yet we read in the newspapers of ambushes and kidnappings just 15 miles out of town. Government of South Vietnam is bunch of Catholic elite westernized prudes anyhow, completely out of touch with "the people." (*Passage* 5–6)[16]

The exact words of the journal entry are not used, yet details from the journal are immediately seen in the poem, artistically reconfigured for alliterative effect and phrasal parallelism:

> Papayas banana sliced fish grated ginger
> fruit for fish, meat for flowers
>   french bread for ladle
>
> (*MRWE* 48)

Along with abundant fruit, fish, and french bread, the poem's "strong women" and "valley thatch houses / palmgroves for hedges" are indicated by the journal entry. To make a point Snyder adds the "glimmering" eye of the "bound pullets" that watch us. Dead though they may appear when we eat them, we will not eat these chickens unknowingly; we sustain our lives with the flesh of these beings. Out of the hard work of the peasants, particularly the women marked with "[d]irt from the hills" (The Goddess in her everyday attire . . .), the white rice undergoes several stages of change from the ricefield and thrasher as it makes its way to the market where it is ultimately exchanged for money. Somehow the people become disconnected from their labors; the product is emphasized and then only in terms of its monetary value. A significant moment in both the poem and the journal comes with Snyder's mention of the war in South Vietnam and the presence, or absence, of observable change among the people. The "Saigon" section of "The Market" ends with "changes, how much / is our change:" and we know the poet is talking about more than the coins left over in his hand after a purchase. A tiny observation made in his journal on his return to Saigon the following spring emphasizes the point: "1 May: Saigon—quieter than before; the Viet Cong were getting more serious" (*Passage* 99). Social upheaval, the poet seems to suggest, is another force in the marketplace.

The Kathmandu subsection of "The Market" is a meditation on the concept of value—"was it worth it? / How can I tell," but the subsection seems unrelated to Snyder's journal entry. The description of their short trip to Nepal is three pages long in the journal, but the reference to Kathmandu's market is brief:

> The market, early morning, in the open on the stoneflagged square: young men bring in enormous loads of firewood on their backs to sell; they are barelegged and barefoot, though the hills around town and right down to our level almost

> are covered with snow (one morning). I bought curds, and an orange that was so bright and juicy looking, but turned out to be bitter and all seed. Cracked barefeet, calloused thick stubby toes. (*Passage* 44)

It may be that the lines from the poem—"I gave a man seventy paise / in return for a clay pot / of curds"—are based on the simple journal description, "I bought curds," but the link hardly seems significant. Still, almost any quotation from this subsection reveals the content to be an ironic comment on market value. Snyder's tone can be heard in lines like "equals one gross inflatable / plastic pillows" where the word "gross" does double duty to indicate both the number of pillows and his sarcastic attitude toward the very idea of plastic pillows. It is just as important, however, to hear the rhythm of the words:

> Seventy-five feet hoed rows equals
> one hour explaining power steering
> equals two big crayfish =
>   all the buttermilk you can drink
> = twelve pounds cauliflower
> = five cartons greek olives = hitchhiking
>   from Ogden Utah to Burns Oregon
> = aspirin, iodine and bandages
> = a lay in Naples = beef
>
> (*MRWE* 49)

Both rhythm and content are based on the repetition of the word "equals." Snyder cleverly "equals" the verbal expression to its corresponding mathematical symbol "=" thus establishing that it is the process of equation itself and the evaluation of that action that he wishes to deal with and not its superficial representation. It may even be that in repeating the sound of "equals / =" he intends to set up the sound as a rhythmic drone to offset and emphasize the content of the lines. This use of rhythm is basic to much of classical Indian music and is well known to the poet. For a brief moment in the 1960s and early '70s, the sound was popularized in the American market through the work of Ravi Shankar. At the time of experiencing the events that eventually became "The Market," Snyder also recorded a meeting with the internationally known tabla player Chattur Lal (who accompanied Shankar on an American concert tour). Snyder commented on the powerful effect of Indian music:

> This was the second time I'd heard Chattur Lal play, the first time was when we were in Delhi previously, and had attended a special concert given by Chattur Lal and a woman sarod player (sarod a stringed instrument with many strings played with a plectrum and held like a guitar). . . . Complex rhythms and a fantastic structure, building up from the simply stated theme ("raga") at the be-

> ginning, and developing to a powerful climax, taking a good hour of solid playing, the sarod-player and the tabla player constantly watching and checking each other, . . . because after the statement raga, most of the whole performance is improvisation. (*Passage* 74)

In the poem, the droning sound set up by constant references to "equals" is reinforced by the heard assonance of groups of words ("hour," "power," "cauliflower"; "aspirin," "iodine") and the visual parallelism of Ogden with Oregon. It takes a moment to realize that these rhythms have distracted us from the just-mentioned locations in "Utah" and "Oregon" as well as market items that are "greek." Items that are "equalized" in this subsection are not always to be found in Nepal or even in the Orient. Particularly in this "Kathmandu" subsection Snyder is interested in the global market, the exchanges that take place among beings wherever they may be found on the globe. A "lay in Naples," especially as juxtaposed with "beef," has far less to do with Italy than with the action taking place. What exactly *is* the value of a night of whoring in Italy? Is the woman merely a piece of meat to be exchanged on the market? If so, how can one equate the value of her body with twelve pounds of cauliflower? Surely to a lonely sailor, say one on the *Sappa Creek* who has spent endless days and nights at sea, the value of the exchange would differ from that perceived by the woman providing the "service." Each one has his or her own needs. How does one judge the true value of money spent or actions performed? Are not such actions equal in value to "all the buttermilk you can drink," especially if one is fixed on buttermilk as an object of immense desire. In these statements of only apparently absurd equivalency the nature of the grasping individual is exposed. With greed, need, and desire at the root of our very being, the "market" becomes the symbolic locus of our fundamental nature. In fact, Snyder spends as much time in this subsection on the dirtiness of our "market" and the "equal" need for "cleanup" as he does on setting forth the equations of exchange.

> & wash down   hose off aisles
> reach under fruit stands
>   green gross rack
>   meat scum on chop blocks
>   bloody butcher concrete floor
>   old knives sharpened down to scalpels
>   brown wrap paper rolls, stiff
>   push-broom back
> wet spilled food
>   when the market is closed
>   the cleanup comes
>   equals

a billygoat pushing through people
stinking and grabbing a cabbage
(*MRWE* 50)

These lines function as if they were an inventory of market technology: hoses, racks, chop blocks, knives sharpened like scalpels, paper rolls, push brooms, and even billygoats who function as part of the "cleanup." The yin and yang of the market is present; the implements for cleaning up are set beside those that have processed the food. The gross scum and wet spilled food are washed away or brushed away or eaten by animals. And tomorrow is another day in the endless revolution of the market cycle, the food chain, the exchange of beings.

The final subsection of "The Market" is dark, even forbidding. Snyder's time in India, especially as caught in this section of *Mountains and Rivers,* was an ambiguous revelation for him. Although he energetically sought out places of spirituality and praised the Indians for what he called their "rude" kind of straightforwardness, there was much that he was not comfortable with during his travels there, particularly in matters of food and health:

> Now we are about to leave India, and feeling very lucky to have come through it all intact, with nothing worse than diarrhea a few times, quite elated really. And glad to be leaving, then, because India is not comfortable, nor is the food really good enough to stay healthy on forever. If you were settled in one spot and could do your own cooking and fix up your own quarters to suit yourself it would be different, of course.
>
> But India in any case is not a comfortable country, the way Japan is. (*Passage* 95)

He reveals the same discomfort when he refers to the particular problem of beggars or those who are deformed or disabled, a topic that comes up more than once in his journal notes.

> Something of the same feeling about beggars—I did not give to all the beggars who approached me by any means; never to able-bodied adults, and never to children. They are growing up in a society which is gradually eliminating beggars and the need for beggars; and it is doing them no favor to help set them in a pattern of professional begging when the whole thing will be made illegal and eliminated (supposedly) in about ten more years. Deformed and crippled people are a different thing—God knows there are enough of them. Deformed people and deformed animals, India. Lepers without fingers are a common sight; they stand along train platforms or at bus stops, whining under the windows. In the south, people with elephantiasis are frequent, a great stumpy leg, or two, drip-

> ping lymph. Blind people. People with genetic deformities, or sores, or awful ailments of unidentifiable sorts. Gypsy girls of nine or ten carrying babies, hanging around trains and buses. It is a real moral dilemma. (*Passage* 57–58)

Thus it is no surprise to find the concluding lines on the "Varanasi" market commenting in a similar fashion:

> They eat feces
> in the dark
> on stone floors
> one-legged monkeys, hopping cows
> limping dogs blind cats
> crunching garbage in the market
> broken fingers
> cabbage
> head on the ground.
>
> (*MRWE* 51)

The "they" of these lines is deliberately ambiguous; Snyder soon adds to these crippled, feces-eating animals a picture of a naked beggar, a young blind man with "open pit eyes" whose "dark scrotum" is "spilled on the street" as his penis extends over his thigh. He also deliberately juxtaposes the vegetable world of cabbage heads with the head of the young beggar. The man obviously made a deep impression on Snyder; he describes him in his journal entry for February 15: "blind man about 35 sitting on the pavement, . . . his crotch uncovered, a black penis and balls, a rather handsome face" (*Passage* 50). Although it is a somber jumble of beings who inhabit this market, the blind man's torso is last seen turning—as a flower might—with the sun. Nor is one allowed to forget that these events have taken place beside the holy Ganges River. With an almost flippant gesture of ironic intent, Snyder further undercuts the significance of the entire section. He casually suggests to the reader that these scenes took place at the same time that he was offhandedly buying "a few bananas by the Ganges / while waiting for my wife." The very insignificance of this action "equals" its significance.

JOURNEYS

In "Mythic and Fantastic: Gary Snyder's *Mountains and Rivers Without End,*" Patrick Murphy draws on Tzetvan Todorov to discuss the "fantastic hesitation" of readers who encounter poems that are openly dreamlike, mythical, or visionary.

> [P]oetry can also present an event which requires the reader to choose between a logical explanation and a supernatural one, and fantastic hesitation may appear in the process of that choosing, as it does in Snyder's *Mountains and Rivers Without End.* (292)

Any reader of the nine subsections that make up "Journeys" must indeed hesitate, wondering exactly who is doing what to whom, where, and when these events are happening, and, most of all, how these tiny poems interconnect. In a later essay, Murphy describes "Journeys" as an "interpenetration of dream imagery and historical memory" (*Place for Wayfaring* 194), and surely he is correct. Although certain subsections of "Journeys" have the appearance of historical actuality—a story told by an old-timer about a girl in a red skirt or a bus ride with Lew Welch along the coast of Washington State—all of these short lyrics are finally reminiscent of the unearthly intermingling of realities found in the earlier "Elwha River" section. It seems as if Snyder planned a section entitled: "Things to Do Around Some Dreamworlds." Simply put, dreams, in Snyder's world, *are* to be confused with reality. For Snyder "seeing a bear in a dream" is "like seeing a bear" (Snyder, "Interview" [Flaherty] 66). In this light, the dream-poems of "Journeys" are real; it makes no difference whether the activities described actually happened or were dreamed. We are reminded, perhaps, of Dōgen's comments on the multiple realities involved with the "Painting of a Rice Cake," especially when combinations of these tiny poems appear to produce still another level of "reality." Murphy, using "Bubbs Creek Haircut" as his primary example, makes the point that the hesitant reader has three choices when faced with such scenarios: (1) "the realm of figurative poetic discourse" where one might interpret the images as metaphors for actual events; (2) "the realm of the uncanny" where one interprets the "spiritual visions and feelings of purification as neurotic guilt displacement"; or (3) "the realm of the marvelous" in which one may interpret the "spiritual vision" encountered in the poem as "relating a new set of universal laws by which the world operates" ("Mythic and Fantastic" 295). Verbally the correspondences among figurative/literal, uncanny/psychological, and marvelous/spiritual arrange themselves logically, but, in the final analysis, as Murphy admits, there is no easy categorizing of the subsections of "Journeys."

The first subsection is "evidently a dream, but whether a figurative one or a real one experienced by an autobiographical narrator remains unclear as the literary and symbolic mix with the narrative representation because of the heavy presence of archetypal material" ("Mythic and Fantastic" 295–96). The next two journeys are described as narratives where "archetypes and myths appear"; Murphy labels these poems as "figurative" stories. The following two, concerning the girl in a red skirt and a return to an old house, are labeled as "experiences in the familiar world [whose] quotidian reality calls into question the extraordinary reality of the previous parts" (296). As Murphy turns to the sixth small lyric in the sequence, he writes: "The reader of the poem is probably confused at this point" (296). Indeed, "Journeys" is a complicated mix of narratives. In his later commentary on this poem, Murphy concludes that "all are journeys, with the physical and psychic interpenetrating" (*Place for Wayfaring* 195).

What becomes perfectly evident, regardless of which categories one might impose, is that the poems of "Journeys" are only vaguely systematic in arrangement. Like dreams they float in a world of amorphous structure. Referring to the eighth segment, Murphy admits as much: "the distinction between dream narratives and travel narratives has blurred—both are journeys" ("Mythic and Fantastic" 297). True enough, as one attempts to impose a logical framework on the irrational, the scheme, any scheme, will break down. Distinctions will, and do, blur. Despite the confusion, however, an insistent pull toward consistency and purpose remains; readers will continue to predict and confirm (or disavow) as they read line after line, short poem after short poem, in an attempt to discover coherence. One will always wonder why nine poems and not six or twelve or twenty? Why does the first poem come first and the last poem come last? In fact, Eric Todd Smith's reading of "Journeys" shows the importance of both the first and last "journeys" (29–33), but omits a discussion of the middle seven.

The first poem is easily described as an archetypal call to adventure. It starts with a realistic detail—"Genji" was the name Snyder gave to his tomcat in Berkeley—but soon moves beyond the expected. The speaker hits a wounded bird with a shovel, intending to put it out of its misery; instead, the bird metamorphoses into a larger being, eventually becoming a woman. The speaker embraces this magical creature, and through her agency he wanders in a maze of underground passageways. Then, at the point of becoming utterly lost, the speaker receives a piece of archetypal apple taken from her mouth and instantly awakens. Both Murphy and Smith relate the woman, and her apple, to Eve in the Garden of Eden while recognizing that Snyder's version is a reversal of the Christian story of the Fall (Murphy, *Place for Wayfaring* 194). The speaker is "awakened" by his taste of apple. Whether or not, as Smith suggests, this woman is the savioress Tārā, she is surely, as he says, a feminine presence whose meeting with the speaker here prefigures the one that will take place in "The Mountain Spirit" (*Reading* 29–31).

> The second and third parts, with no apparent indication of being dreams, depict the narrator and others as traveling in a strange land. As primitive hunters they reach a plateau where they flee the sun in awe of its power while shooting arrows at it.
>
> The next two parts seem to be individual recollections of real events but their relationship to the primitive hunter story remains unclear. (Murphy, *Place for Wayfaring* 194)

With no preparation given or observable association, the reader swings, as Murphy suggests, from the pseudo-mythical time of the first tiny poem into the roughly datable world of primitive hunters. At first we find ourselves in an eerie, and seemingly lonely, world of multiple perspectives: looking out "through deep forests to the coast," standing on "a white sandspit looking in," or wandering in lowland places "where no one had ever been" with a "view of the Olympic Mountains in a chill clear wind." It is difficult to know who is seeing or even speaking these lines; no "I" can be heard or seen. Suddenly, with the third lyric, "we" become part of the dream story; we are Paleolithic hunters staring at the "flaming pulsing sun." Frightened, we escape, stumbling on "the bright lit plain."

The speaker's voice in the fourth subsection, that of an old-timer reminiscing, tells us that we have become listeners, not doers, in a world of storytelling: now "Where were we—" and "—Lemme tell you something kid—." The story we hear—a memory recollected in bits as if it were a dream—involves yet another woman, a sexual encounter with a high-heeled "girl in a red skirt." There may be poverty in this place where the whitewash is peeling, but there is no denigration; the couple lives together in a "loft" on "cool bare boards." Is this another relationship with The Goddess? What starts out as sexual energy is transformed into a life lived together, and then a life lived alone, in memory and dream. Perhaps hearing the voice of an elder brings Snyder to the point of remembering his own home. The fifth poem appears to be the poet's own voice as he relates his return—in a dream—to his boyhood homestead. Here we find a "big red cedar," perhaps the one that the poet has spoken of as his youthful "counselor." Yet things are not as they used to be: the speaker thinks his father is in jail and that he ought to bring his sister back to this place. Curiously he wonders why his mother has never died, a line that has echoes on several levels: a link with the Mother Goddess who appears to be eternal; a simple factual description of what was actually dreamed; or perhaps a remark that points to the speaker's divided sensibilities concerning his parents.

The sixth poem describes what is seen below as one descends lower and lower into a damp world from the dry heights. The inclusion of "rice fields" seems to indicate a tropical setting for this dream journey. Nevertheless, the stress is on the "LOWLANDS," a phrase Snyder uses to describe the actual world we live in, whether equatorial or otherwise. Perhaps this view incorporates Buddhist thought insofar as the quotidian world *is* the world of enlightenment; beyond duality, nirvana is immanent—in and of this humid, clouded level world—as well as transcendent.

Yet Snyder's seventh journey takes us lower than the lowlands. Once more the "I" disappears as "we"—"we all head in here somewhere"—emerge into a literally surrealistic vision of a hellish life on earth: "underground building chambers . . . refuse . . . old nails . . . rotting plaster . . . the movie always running . . . toilets full of shit . . . and a vast hat rack." To be able to take the mask off the world's appearance and see it for what it is, to know the reality of its underbelly—for it is this horrific vision too—is a stage of wisdom.

The eighth journey can be traced, almost word for word, to a 1960 notebook entry. Once more Snyder's voice speaks to us as we travel with him into his personal world. Immensely significant in his dream world, the journey taken in the eighth poem reminds him of an earlier visionary experience in the Olympics:

> Last night another version of the "magic Olympics" dream—Riding in a bus over mountainous rutted roads and along the coast of Washington—no real coast—through groves of Redwood—with Lew Welch. . . . Lew and I sitting in the back of the almost empty bus, talking and riding through. Yellow aspen-like leaves fluttering down. Passing occasionally through tiny towns—damp cabins under dark groves of trees. Then beaches with estuaries and sandbars, and views of the mountains. I brought [name given in Japanese characters] here once, in another dream. The feeling again, the same—of passing through too quick, of missing something precious. (14 Dec. 1960. GSP B30:F13)

Snyder's notebook entry also includes a sketchy map of the northwest corner of Washington State's Olympic Peninsula; the Olympic Range is clearly marked as "magic mountains." The magic continues when we notice the redwood trees, a dream-fact in conflict with his statement in "The Elwha River" that "[t]here are no redwoods north of southern / Curry County, Oregon." The contradiction serves to underscore the fact that this is "no real coast." Similarly, there is "a woman" associated with the landscape: Snyder's journal entry cloaks her in mystery by identifying her name only in Japanese characters; the poem completely conceals her by generalizing her.

For readers who believe these nine short poems are stages in some grand linear journey, the terminus becomes the ninth poem, which coyly eventuates in an absurd leap into the back country. What had promised to be an end is no end. Not even death is an end. Ko-san, whom we met in an earlier dream in "The Blue Sky," pulls Snyder over a cliff so that they may experience the realm of death. As Snyder describes it, death looks just like the land he has been traveling in. The jump into the void becomes a return to reality. The land of enlightenment turns out to be no different from the land in which we now live; there is no other land. The encounter with death is the final human encounter, but to know that death is nothing special—and, in fact, may be an enlightening trip into the wild—is obviously to have complete wisdom: the wisdom of compassion begins with emptiness.

What do we finally know about "Journeys"? There is demonstrable proof given here that Snyder at times writes with freedom and spontaneity. As controlled and disciplined a writer as he is, he obviously scribbles selected—"selected" remains a key word—dreams into notebooks and later transcribes them literally into published poems. Although the notebooks themselves are not always available, Snyder's penciled-in dates for various subsections of the UC-Davis manuscript copy of "Journeys" indicate that other subsections of "Journeys" were also taken from recorded notebook dreams: the third part ("We moved across dark stony ground . . .") is dated "30.VIII.1962"; the sixth part ("High up in a yellow-gold . . .") is dated "6:II:1963"; the eighth part ("With Lew rode in a bus . . .") is dated "14.XII 1960"; and the ninth part ("We were following a long river . . .") is dated "29:x:1962." We know that the persona in "Journeys" changes from subsection to subsection, as in a dream. Scenes shift and figures are metamorphosed. Particularized events take place in ambiguous settings, or ambiguous events take place in realistic settings. Lumped together the nine subsections of "Journeys" represent an interwoven multidimensional journey—partly personal, partly historical, partly cultural, partly mythical, partly spiritual. A poem in its own right with its own narrative crescendo, "Journeys" is a mirror for the larger *Mountains and Rivers Without End,* itself a journey with stages and a culminating point that implies newfound wisdom.

MĀ

The straightforward content, misspelled words, and nonstandard grammar of "Mā" conjure up an unlettered, working-class world of logging and subsistence farming. Both poverty and alcoholism inhabit this environment; it is a migrant worker's world, with men constantly on the move toward the next opportunity for work. The father's absence is as noticeable as is the quiet, enduring power of matriarchy shining forth in Ma herself. Her relationship with her son, strong as it is, is not the only focus of the letter we read; her narrative tells us that she functions as the head of an extended social group. As personal as the letter is, it is equally a depiction of a community of survivors.

Snyder has said that "Mā" is an actual letter he discovered in an abandoned shack in the mountains not far from his home on the western slopes of the Sierra Nevada (Steuding 104). Indeed, it is most important, from Snyder's viewpoint, to have readers believe that the words of this section represent a veritable letter from an actual woman. On the other hand, Snyder recognizes the symbolic value of this letter-poem in the simple twist he has given to its title: it is not "Ma" but "Mā." As one commentator on the poem wrote:

> He [Snyder] edited it, changed all the names and gave it the title Mā—the macron over the "a" changing the word's meaning from its usual one of "mother" to the Sanskrit word for Earth Mother, or "goddess." ("In Print" 22)

As we know from "The Elwha River" and "Journeys," several levels of reality may be present simultaneously in *Mountains and Rivers.* If on one level we meet an ordinary mother alternately chiding and encouraging her departed son, on another we see in these plaintive words an embodiment of the nurturing goddess, one who knows reality in all its suchness. A flesh-and-blood portrait of Compassion itself, Mā might as well be Tārā, "She who saves."

As a type of the found poem, Ma's letter is generic, a cautionary statement from mother to son that indicates a nurturing and worried mother. She subscribes to her boy's need for independence even as she shows her obvious concern for his welfare. She is not merely "glad," but "very glad" to hear from him. She knows him well enough, as all mothers should know their sons, to tell from the way he writes that he is "ok." These small touches tell the reader immediately that Ma carries a deeper worry: perhaps things might not have been all right or perhaps, as his mother, she just misses him. We quickly discover that her boy is "up there" working "in the timber" and that his $15 per day is the result of long working hours. Rather than agree with him about how little he is being paid, Ma takes the typical older person's stance ("well, in my day . . .") as she lectures him about how little money she earned for her day's work ($5). Neither of them—then or now—have earned a sufficient wage. Thus this section, like others in the poem, comments indirectly on the economics of poverty. Labor itself has value, but the monetary reward for work seems pitiful. As we make our way through "Mā" we will find yet others working at a subsistence level. These too are the "little people" we see time and again walking the paths on an unrolling scroll-poem journey.

Is there a personal connection in this relation of mother to son? Is this woman a token for Lois Snyder Hennessy writing to her son, Gary Snyder, on one of those summer occasions when he was, in fact, engaged as a logger? Certainly the journals of Snyder, like those of Henry David Thoreau before him, show him to be thrifty, a life lesson perhaps learned from his "Ma." Nor are hard work, drinking, and technology strangers to Snyder. Ma even reveals that she has been involved in dairy farming, another detail in accord with the factual life of the Snyders. Tempting parallels perhaps, but there is not much to be gained by working out exact correspondences. It is doubtful that Ruby is a version of Snyder's sister, Thea. Still, like some of the details in "Journeys," there are just enough coincident features to make one wonder if Snyder has manipulated the original letter to reflect some of his own childhood.

Although Snyder wishes readers to accept the verisimilitude of his found letter, it is easy to argue the case for his poetic manipulation of certain facts by examining changes that took place in the poem as it developed from its original version, published in *Coyote's Journal* (1974), to the final version that appears in *Mountains and Rivers.* In a set of crucial lines from the earlier version, Ma underscores her boy's problem with alcohol and, in the process, identifies the entire community as Native American:

> Nothing here same old thing
> Indians are allways drinking then dieing.
> Dont seem to mind tho.
> (*Coyote's Journal* 10 [1974]: 31)

In the book version, "Indians" is generalized to "People" ("People allways drinking then dieing"). The later version targets a segment of society with a disadvantaged economic status, but it doesn't allow readers to target a specific ethnic group. Others might have substituted "Native Americans" for "Indians," but the phrase is not sonorous. "People" avoids offense, keeps the rhythm, and broadens the base of that "same old thing" to a wider community. That the poet has clearly tinkered with the text of the original letter, if indeed it was factual to begin with, is the issue here.

One could write at great length about the details of this poem, shaping a firm picture of the seasonal and daily activities of this extended family. They are involved in logging, subsistence farming, and ranching. They drink and they die; they are sensitive to the vicissitudes of nature, its fires, its drought, its wild berries. Ma knows, and comments on, all of it, exhibiting her own wisdom and compassion as she speaks. The important point, however, is *not* to discuss these particulars in and for themselves, but to note how that profusion of detail gives a hard cold edge to reality. The more details and the more specific they are, the more "real" it all seems. How absolutely realistic these particulars seem when compared to the dream realm of "Journeys"!

Paradoxically, it is exactly because Ma is "one of the people" and not a spirit descended from some higher plane of divinity that she is to be seen as an aspect of The Goddess. In her down-to-earth quality and her stress on the quotidian necessities, she emphasizes the role of all mothers. In the essay "On the Path, Off the Trail," Snyder emphasizes the wisdom derived from the practice of such everyday, repetitive tasks. These are part of the "suchness," or *tathata,* of life.

> [O]ur models for practice, training, and dedication need not be limited to monasteries or vocational training. . . . [T]here are all the ecological-economical connections of humans with other living beings, which cannot be ignored for long, pushing us toward a profound consideration of planting and harvesting, breeding and slaughtering. All of us are apprenticed to the same teacher that the religious institutions originally worked with: reality.
>
> . . . It is as hard to get the children herded into the car pool and down the road to the bus as it is to chant sutras in the Buddha-hall on a cold morning. One move is not better than the other, each can be quite boring, and they both have the virtuous quality of repetition. Repetition and ritual and their good results come in many forms. Changing the filter, wiping noses, going to meetings, picking up around the house, washing dishes, checking the dipstick—don't let yourself think these are distracting you from your more serious pursuits. Such a round of chores is not a set of difficulties we hope to escape from so that we may do our "practice" which will put us on a "path"—it *is* our path. (*Practice* 152–53)

Not surprisingly, considering that Snyder's life as a Zen Buddhist has more than once focused intensely on a relationship to a *rōshi* (old master), the transmission of wisdom from teacher to apprentice is a major theme in his writing, especially when he speaks of daily routines and rituals. In "Axe Handles," for example, Snyder depicts himself as a link in a long chain of teacher-learners (Lu Ji, Ezra Pound, Shih-hsiang Chen, Snyder, Kai) engaged in passing on guidelines for existence.

More than likely, the portrait of mother and son given in "Mā" is an echo of the archetypal mother-son relationship found in several other poems. Snyder has spoken, for example, of Yamamba's relationship with her son, Kintaro (sometimes called Kintochi or Kintoki). She, the mountain woman, nurtures him, and Japanese folklore has many tales of the heroic deeds he accomplishes in later life. In *North Pacific Lands & Waters,* Snyder included "Greasy Boy" among the "further six sections." In its original journal publication, under the title of "Two Poems," "Greasy Boy" is linked with a poem devoted to seeing "the Mother." The Goddess, then, is sometimes an ecstatic dancing partner; at other times she is the nurturing mother. In order to "save" her children she offers her wisdom to them. Mā is The Goddess, in all her suchness, in her aspect as matriarch. Mā is Mother; Ma is Mom.

INSTRUCTIONS

The clipped poetic rhythms of "Instructions" are distinctly different from the prosaic cadence of "Mā." The taciturn drawl of Ma's voice and the rambling nature of her letter are in clear contrast to the succinct beat in the lines of this short poem. Yet thematically the two poems are both concerned with directions. If Ma delivers a sermonette to her son about how to survive in the modern world; the speaker of "Instructions" presents readers with an environmental impact statement on the nature of fossil fuel that originates from and returns to the same source: "Just / two places. Forever, // or, not even one." Plainly, it's a lesson in nonduality.

The images function with an obvious symbolic intent. The opening stanza seems elliptical at first, yet anyone who has twisted off an actual "[f]uel filler cap" in preparation for putting gasoline into the tank knows the feel of the cap's metallic (frequently "dull silver" in color) "knurled rim." The "[o]il filler cap" is equally familiar. Often bright yellow or orange to make it easy to spot, it typically has "horns," a double-arched piece of metal welded onto the top of its flat cap to facilitate the twisting motion of the fingers needed to open or close the cap. Undoubtedly the models for these images are as actual as they are generic; perhaps the caps belong to Snyder's 1958 Willys pickup, a wondrous piece of modern technology celebrated in other poems, but they might just as easily "fit" similar gasoline-driven engines. The "[o]il drain plug" is not described specifically; there is only the instruction that it is best to let oil drain when it is hot. Similarly, the "[e]ngine switch" has been abstracted to its single "off, on" function.

What are these "Instructions"? What wisdom is being passed on here? Evidently Snyder is speaking of energy cycles related to the "engine" known as "Planet Earth." It is "sunlight" that drives the fuel-transforming process that takes place "under the eaves" of the earth's skin. There, in the "mottled / shadow" of the centuries it gathers into the liquid that lubricates and propels the machine of modern human civilization. Less directly, the curving rim of "dull silver metal" may hint at the moon's subtle presence in this work of transformation. The "snail" of the second stanza seems representative not just of the "horns" on the cap and the sluggish flow of the viscous amber fluid we call "oil," but also of the snail-like pace of transforming matter into oil. Moreover, this liquid that we draw forth from its deep pit in the earth is made from decomposed matter buried under pressure and over time: old trees, old beings of all kinds. The snail, slimy to the touch, denizen of the dark and the wet, literally becomes the oil over the millennia.

"Fuel filler cap / —haven't I seen this before?" asks the speaker. "Yes, indeed" we answer to such rhetorical questions. Related images were encountered in "Boat of a Million Years," where the "oil filler cap" plugs one end of the Arabian pipeline at "Ras Tanura." Turn the valve on and the oil flows into use; turn it off and its ooze into the cities via the tanker ships ceases, but these valves and switches are short-term devices. Snyder comments on the discrepancy between the time it takes for the planet to regenerate the oil and how quickly humans use it: "so short, from in to out." On a more positive note, no matter what humans do, Snyder seems to say, the fuel and oil that are produced from deep within the womb of Mā-Gaia-Earth will rise from the depths and ultimately return again to the pit, eternally. Seen from the perspective of geological time, the continual switching of this world engine—

off, on. Off, on. Just
two places. Forever,

or, not even one.

is really not two things. What we remove from the earth's womb will eventually "[fall] back to its pit" once more. The planet's business is actually beyond the comprehension of the discriminating mind. Snyder's "instructions" caution us—because the mention of a "one" implies at least an "other"—that the entire process is "not even one."

Awareness of the Buddhist concept of nonduality runs throughout *Mountains and Rivers.* It is encountered explicitly in many places: for example, among others, in "Afloat" when a merging of "two souls in one body" takes place within the skin boat kayak; in the merge of the two lovers facing one another in "Cross-Legg'd"; or in the Koyukon riddle at the end of "Arctic Midnight Twilight": "It really snowed hard / in opposite directions / on my head // who am I?" It figures even more importantly in the basic premise of the entire poem, that all beings—humans, animals, plants, rocks, dirt, air, and water—are interlinked in an eternal ongoing process of the planet and thus there can only be "emptiness" at the heart of "suchness" or "suchness" at the heart of "emptiness." Nothing is the heart of everything, yet one cannot know "nothing" without knowing "something"; the best that words can do is to say, as Zen practitioners say on a daily basis, "neither one nor the other, not even one."

NIGHT SONG OF THE LOS ANGELES BASIN

Like an archaeologist, Snyder carefully uncovers the layered depositions of what went before to reveal how the past gives shape to the present on this whirling blue globe we inhabit, this network of energies we call "Earth." Immense geological stratifications underlie the domain of the modern era; interlocking tiers of species development provide a context for the human race. As a poem of discovery *Mountains and Rivers Without End* again and again reveals what is *there:* the forms, the emptiness; the spaces, the shapes.

Reading "Night Song of the Los Angeles Basin" is to experience, yet again, the interconnectedness of such layers. Beneath the bustle of the cityscape, other settings are uncovered, landscapes that give structure to the flow and shape of Los Angeles's present-day energy patterns. Significantly, as a "city" poem, where we least expect to encounter it, we discover the wilderness. The wilderness of nature in a country setting, the so-called natural setting of forests and trees, important as it is in its own right, is only one instance of what Snyder calls "the wild." Wild in the city might be defined as "freedom," meaning "unregulated," an apparently desirable goal given the legal and social restrictions of city life lived. A life of total freedom might lead to "wild" abandonment, a Dionysian condition that the "urbane" citizen views as diametrically opposed to civilized living. For a Buddhist, however, "freedom" is yet another way to connote "emptiness"; to be "free" or "wild" is to go "beyond," into the realm of that which is simultaneously both "all" and "nothing." To discover "wilderness" in the city is not to discover the opposite of the city; it is, rather, to reveal the web of illusion, the void of all possibility within the very network of the city. It is to look behind the present infrastructure of roads, wires, pipes, and the flow of city living, into the ground of all networked "beings," even rivers.

There are many encounters with cities in *Mountains and Rivers.* In "Night Highway 99" one plies the roads that link the cities of the West Coast. "Three Worlds, Three Realms, Six Roads" explores, with great detail, the poet's identification with Seattle, Portland, San Francisco, and Kyoto. "The Market" takes us beyond San Francisco and Seattle to cities of another sort, the Asian markets of Saigon, Kathmandu, and Varanasi. A subsection of "Journeys" transmits us to a nightmarish vision of the modern city:

> Underground building chambers clogged with refuse
> discarded furniture, slag, old nails
> rotting plaster, faint wisps, antique newspapers
> rattle in the winds that come forever down the hall
> passing, climbing, and on from door to door.
>
> (*MRWE* 54)

"Night Song of the Los Angeles Basin," however, seems part of a city diptych that marks the east-west boundaries of Turtle Island. Much like its eastern counterpart,

"Walking the New York Bedrock," the western "Night Song" encourages us to see the old ways that existed before the city of Los Angeles came into being, ways that have had a hand in the shaping of its modern setting. To reinforce the parallelism, Snyder has placed the two sections in similar positions within their respective units: the Los Angeles poem is the fifth poem of the second part of *Mountains and Rivers,* and the New York poem is the fifth poem of the third part. To read either poem one must adopt the poet's vision of the city before one can see the encompassing wholeness (healing) that substitutes for earlier fragmentation. The torpor induced by the mechanized habits of modern life has not changed much since the first decades of the century when T. S. Eliot described a wasteland of city-people constantly sighing their way to work and back. Among the present day's "calligraphy of cars," we have merely exchanged toll booths and long lines of automobiles for feet that plod over bridges. We are "drivers all heading somewhere," more driven than driving, more riders of the light's lines than controllers of its pathways.

"Night Song" begins and ends with "[o]wl calls." What exactly are these ghostly sounds in the night? Should readers register these calls as merely a sound of nature on hilly slopes or backyards of the city, or are such "calls" a lure, a predator's call to death (and perhaps the wisdom sometimes associated with owls). When the owl calls, do small furry beings—like the voles and mice and marmots mentioned in the poem—shiver? Such calls always cause a vague premonition of danger. Should larger beings like ourselves also feel the shudder in our blood? As in so many other section-poems of this long sequence, otherworldly presences lurk behind the ordinary. There is the "ghost of the dry chaparral" that haunts the "[h]ouses with green watered gardens," a reminder that someday the water will dry up and the gardens wither. In the "[g]host / shrine to the L. A. River," there is a glimpse of The Goddess herself; she appears—like the *shité* in the second part of a two-part Nō play—in the guise of a sweeping rainstorm that suddenly floods the "pools of the channelized [Los Angeles] river." Her image as rain maiden appears again in "Earrings Dangling and Miles of Desert."

Truly a "basin" poem, "Night Song" is about water and the watershed. Snyder's description of the "calligraphy of cars" enforces a long-distance, wide-angled view that looks down on the city in the valley, encircled by its surrounding mountain slopes. Anyone who has flown into Los Angeles on a relatively clear night will see the patterns created by the "calligraphy of cars." Street lamps run for miles in a straight line, crisscrossing each other at regular intervals to display a "checkered" pattern that ultimately twists back on itself. The gnarled "knot-tying light paths" call out for some resolution. Seen from the air the concrete on-off ramps of the expressways conjure up plantlike "[f]loral loops." Groups of cars on the move become enormous unearthly beings—a "[s]wirl of light strokes writhing." They proceed along the street-ways marking their path with long white lines of headlamps in one direction and tail-lighted red ones in the opposite direction:

Dragons of light in the dark
sweep going both ways
in the night city belly

Looking down into this basin, we are provided with an awesome, dazzling description of the movement of light patterns, but this visible energy system radiates with more than human lines. Never far from Chinese painting, the poem shows us artistically traced calligraphic lines on the surface of the planet, made not only by the engineered streets and the lights of cars that move on them, but by the animals who made the pathways long before the machines took them over, and by Snyder the painter in words who memorializes all these lines on the unwinding scroll of *Mountains and Rivers Without End.* Here are the "[v]ole paths" and the "[m]ouse trails"; here, just like tubular holes designed and drilled by civil engineers for the passage of highways through the mountainside, are "[w]inding pocket-gopher tunnels." High above, from roadside vista-points where Snyder has placed us, we may look down into the basin and see the roads we have taken (or not taken), much as "marmots" use their own "lookout rocks" to see where the danger is and where and when it is safe to travel on. Besides these paths created by animate beings, we see other lines etched into the landscape. Here are the routes taken by rivers that have enlivened the basin in their own time. Here is a watershed:

> It has been raining for four days now. One can wonder: why does it rain one year, not rain so much another? But eventually the rains (or the dry days) return. This process of rain falling, streams flowing, and oceans evaporating gives us the water cycle: every molecule of water on earth makes the complete trip once every two million years. And so the earth is carved into watersheds—a kind of familial branching, a chart of relationship, and a definition of place. The watershed is the first and last nation, whose boundaries, though subtly shifting, are unarguable. Races of birds, subspecies of trees, and types of hats or raingear go by the watershed. The watershed gives us a home, and a place to go upstream, downstream, or across in. The watershed is beyond the dichotomies of orderly/disorderly, for its forms are free, but somehow inevitable. And the life that comes to flourish within it constitutes the first kind of community.
>
> For the watershed, cities and dams are ephemeral, and of no more account [than] a boulder that falls in the river, or a landslide that temporarily alters the channel. The water will always be there, and it will always find its way down. The Los Angeles river is alive and well under the city streets, running in giant culverts. It is amused by such diversions. (Snyder, "Watershed Perspectives" 3)

We inhabit this calligraphed network together: voles, mice, marmots, owls, hawks, humans, and rivers. Deep underground the Los Angeles River flows; on the surface there is little evidence of its existence. Only pools of water settle in the channelized riverbed, sitting there like a "*jinja*" (a dwelling place for a deity) that seems not to be present. Lizards wait with reverence at the place of the river's mouth, waiting gracefully in the dry spaces for the water to fall, for health and long life to ensue. In the meantime, the hawk hovers, the owl calls. The marmot watches.

If, as Snyder has said, the watershed "is beyond the dichotomies of orderly/disorderly" and "its forms are free, but somehow inevitable," then the playfulness of wilderness truly exists in the city just as surely as in the wild places of nature. In its own time, over time, the water will move—or not move—as it sees fit. Dams and concrete channels will not hold it back if it does flow, and if it dries up completely, then so be it. Rivers are "amused by such diversions" (as we may be amused by Snyder's pun). We may see any river's calligraphy etched into the places it has already been on the landscape. We may also see the calligraphy of human activity, especially that drawn by our cars, and we can clearly see where our animal neighbors have been if we only watch with care. The routes of the rivers or the animal trails become our highways as we build beside or on them. Owls, hawks, and goddesses linger in the space above all of us. The calligraphy of the planet speaks of the dynamic flow of things; all is change, inevitable change.

Snyder's rain goddess tosses a handful of meal—the water itself—into that dry chaparral "basin" known as "Los Angeles." Like a sudden downpour she provides a liquid surfeit for desperate fish in a shrinking puddle. The water flows "freely," and there is a wild and violent response. In the surreal watery scene that follows we witness a "frenzy of feeding"; human-fish desperately grab for something to sustain themselves, to satisfy their hunger. With "mouth-bubbles" and "[g]old bellies" churning up the water, Snyder says it makes little difference whether we are rare or common creatures; we are together in this "tangle and tumble." Yet the poet cannot resist an ironic lunge at the shallow society, especially apt in a setting that contains the glitz of Hollywood where the rich and famous

> . . . ride by in Rolls Royce
> wide-eyed in brokers' halls
> lifted in hotels
> being presented to, platters
> of tidbit and wine
> snatch of fame

Los Angeles, of course, is the setting for some famous water barons, men who made their fortunes on the water piped in from the Sierra Nevada to the dry city.

> In 1904, casting about for new sources of water to sustain the city's relentless growth, William Mulholland, water-bureau superintendent, explored the Owens Valley some 250 miles northeast of Los Angeles and returned with a bold plan for a long aqueduct to carry melted snow from the southern slopes of

> the Sierra Nevada to Los Angeles faucets. The plan outraged Owens Valley ranchers, enriched two syndicates of Los Angeles speculators, and gave rise to rumours of wrongdoing that historians have never quite managed to silence. ("Los Angeles," *Encyclopaedia Britannica,* 108).

Poetic references to channelized rivers alongside words like "gold," "Rolls Royce," and "brokers" undoubtedly give "rise to rumours of wrongdoing" about the city's water sources, yet Snyder surely intends a wider application to "godlings" of many kinds, such as moneyed brokers and their clients who ride in expensive cars on the freeways of Los Angeles and whose bellies suggest their love of gold. Lifted in elevators to penthouse parties in the city hotels, they wait egotistically to be presented to someone. With cocktails in hand they engage in the trivial rituals of "tidbit and wine, / snatch of fame"; their mouths constantly bubble, filled with small talk and food, as if they were fish engaged in a "frenzy of feeding." They have placed their lives in service to the Great God of Fame or Money in the hope of attaining some small crumb, some bit of meal, dropped from his table.

Chaos has its own structures. Calligraphic patterns exist beyond those we see in the present moment. The landscape of the Los Angeles Basin is sure to be drastically redesigned by the wild as its watershed patterns change—as they have in the past and will in the future. Moreover, answers proposed by city engineers are no match for the energy of the watershed. In the long run, "cities," as Snyder reminds us, "are ephemeral." Floods are not a matter of "if" but of "when," since a water cycle is, by nature, a rhythm that promises return. Drought may appear to take longer, but it is an equally effective agent of change. In any moment, the recognizable calligraphy of the Los Angeles landscape may be rearranged by the churning and roiling of nature's flow: earthquakes, mud slides, or floods. In planetary time even mouse trails will come and go, vole pathways will change, and the freeways of Los Angeles will certainly be remembered as a thing of the past. The energy itself remains, rearranging itself in new calligraphic patterns.

Following the example of lizards who respect the place "[w]here the river debouches," who "clap hands there" in reverent and "trembling" expectation, humans need a little more awe and much less arrogance toward the forces of the wild. The hawk waits; the owl calls. Snyder's poem tells us we should listen. Above the basin, the horned moon of The Goddess rises above the setting. She may toss us some "meal"—or not—all in her own time

COVERS THE GROUND

With references to California's past and a further look at the "calligraphy" of its freeway system, the "Covers the Ground" section continues some of the motifs found in "Night Song of the Los Angeles Basin." Rather than the specters of The Goddess and the water barons, here the figural presence of John Muir, a strong influence on the life and thinking of Gary Snyder, asserts itself. Muir is mentioned in the opening verses of "The Market"; he is subliminally present in "Bubbs Creek Haircut" since it is his path, the John Muir Trail, that Snyder's persona travels to the top of Mount Whitney.

Snyder once suggested that each poem in *Mountains and Rivers Without End* would have a *ku*, a "focal image" or "key phrase," around which the section would develop (Faas 135). Written between 1988 and 1993, "Covers the Ground" was first published in David Burks's *Place of the Wild: A Wildlands Anthology*. The title of that book, in conjunction with the word "wild" in the epigraph attributed to John Muir, indicates that "wild" is the *ku* for this poem. Like the previous Los Angeles Basin section, "Covers the Ground" contrasts the "wildness" evident in the landscape of an earlier era with the "stuff" of modern society that has since been deposited on the scene.

In the late 1860s, John Muir personally walked the 400-mile-long "sweet bee-garden" of California's "Great Central Plain." At the time of his journey it was a landscape of flowers, "one sheet of plant gold"; "all the ground was covered" with hundreds of different species of blooming color and fragrance. Yet by 1894, when "The Bee Pastures" was published as a chapter in *The Mountains of California*, Muir was already lamenting the loss of the wild flowers. The nostalgic opening line of his essay—"When California was wild, it was one sweet bee-garden . . ."—serves as the epigraph for Snyder's poem. Muir knows that the wildness of the Central Valley has begun to slip into the past, to be replaced either by destruction or inappropriate cultivation:

> But of late years plows and sheep have made sad havoc in these glorious pastures, destroying tens of thousands of the flowery acres like a fire, and banishing many species of the best honey-plants to rocky cliffs and fence-corners, while, on the other hand, cultivation thus far has given no adequate compensation, at least in kind; only acres of alfalfa for miles of the richest wild pasture, ornamental roses and honeysuckles around cottage doors for cascades of wild roses in the dells, and small, square orchards and orange-groves for broad mountain belts of chaparral. ("Bee Pastures" 338–39)

If Muir were alive today he would find the wild bees and flowers that enchanted him to be fully domesticated in commercialized "beehives" that "sit tight between fruit tree ranks." The landscape of the present day, as described in Snyder's "Covers the Ground," has been thoroughly arranged and systematized for the purposes of capital enterprise. No feminine spirit exists here; masculinized trucks named "Ken" and "Peter" and "Mack" now speed up and down the valley once paced off by the deliberate steps of the aesthetically sensitive John Muir.

According to a note on a copy of the poem Snyder sent me in December of 1993, the actual setting for the poem is "Down highway 99 toward Merced." One pre sumes that somewhere along that stretch of highway are the commercial enterprises of both "Blue Diamond Almonds" and Ralston Purina Cat Food ("& the tower that holds cat food / with a red/white checkered sign"). The journey described in this section continues one made earlier by the poet—at least as early as 1961—in "Night Highway 99," where the narrator proclaimed a similar aversion to a world of trucks—"trucks [that] roll by / kicking up dust dead flowers" (*MRWE* 23) Yet, as in "The Elwha River" section, the actuality of such realities does not matter as much as the psychic scenery—especially the shock of perceiving contrasting landscapes over time. Instead of conjuring up the sweet taste of honey manufactured by busy bees among the blossoming present-day almond trees, Snyder overwhelms our imagination with the "stuff" of modern agricultural life in the Central Valley. Here, among other items, we find "cement culverts," "mobile homes," "johnny-on the spots," "tractors," "fork trucks," and "wornout car tires." The culverts, of course, remind us of the "channelized river" in the Los Angeles Basin poem: the water is no longer wild when its flow has been committed to cement cylinders in the service of commercial interests. The "house-high" six-foot wide culverts belittle the human habitations, "mobile homes, pint-size portable housing," which Snyder further demeans by linking them with typical portable outhouses used by construction workers. The flowers of John Muir's day have been reduced to the "exit floreals, entrance curtsies" of the concrete freeways. There is little evidence of nature's graceful beauty. In contrast, Muir's description of multiple flowering species is exquisite:

> *The Great Central Plain of California,* during the months of March, April, and May, *was one smooth,* continuous *bed of honey-bloom,* so marvelously rich that, in walking from one end of it to the other, a distance of more than *400 miles, your foot would press* about *a hundred flowers at every step.* Mints, gilias, nemophilas, castilleias, and innumerable compositae were so crowded together that, had ninety-nine per cent of them been taken away, the plain would still have seemed to any but Californians extravagantly flowery. The radiant, honeyful corollas, touching and overlapping, and rising above one another, glowed in the living light like a sunset sky—one sheet of purple and gold, with the bright Sacramento pouring through the midst of it from the north, the San Joaquin from the south, and their many tributaries sweeping in at right angles from the mountains, dividing the plain into sections fringed with trees. ("Bee Pastures" 339; phrases quoted in "Covers the Ground" are emphasized)

In contrast, Snyder gives us an unenthralling landscape consisting of "long straight miles of divider oleanders; / scrappy ratty grass and thistle." The normally colorful oleanders are mentioned only for their use as freeway dividers. The flowers of Muir's day are all but gone, and it seems that the "stuff" of machines has sprouted in their place. There is, ironically, some color in the landscape: "new bright-painted" agricultural combine units, "yellow fork trucks," "rows of red-roofed houses" and "a pale blue hip-roof / house" all stand in the fields as the trucks speed by. Trees and the work of builders compete for space in the sky. The tall cylindrical "spires" of "cypress trees," conjoined with a singular "frizzy lonely palm tree" are apparently losing the battle to the "steep and gleaming / fertilizer tank towers" with their "fine-line catwalk in the sky." Perhaps Snyder intends to comment wryly on changes in spiritual attitudes by introducing a lonely Middle Eastern palm and the churchlike spires of the cypress.

A measured and artificial arrangement, rather than wildness, is evident from the opening stanza of the poem with its "lines of tree trunks," all in "rows." The list of orderly "stuff," reminiscent of the recyclable junk in the "Bubbs Creek Haircut" Goodwill store, is extensive. There are "yards of tractors," and the agricultural "combines" are "lined up." The walnut orchard has been "irrigated, pruned and trimmed." "Cement bricks" are waiting for the fork trucks in "palleted stacks." There are "quarter-acre stacks of wornout car tires," and the vineyards are "taut-strung" and "trimmed out even on the top." Not the fresh fruit itself, but the "loading boxes" that will contain it are in "cubic blocks," and not the chickens, but the "long aluminum . . . chicken-feeder houses" are depicted. Ironically, the chicken houses are "automated." Measured and stacked as everything is, there is little that is "wild" about the things of this landscape. Perhaps, in the corners, one notices the "spring fur of green weed" or the "eucalyptus boughs" (an introduced species) that "shimmer in the wind," but in general it is a desolate scene with an unmistakable potential for disaster. The "new bright-painted units down at one end" of the field will inevitably become "old stuff broke and smashed down at the other." One spots the "tumbled barn" from "another age" and knows the message we should be hearing about cycles of human civilization. There are already "dust clouds blowing off the new plowed fields" and ominous "crows" that "whuff over almond blossoms."

As a final gesture, Snyder prompts us once again to listen to the ancient earth-rhythm he hears behind the tempo of modern life. The rumbling of the diesel trucks, rolling like boulders along the course of today's freeway-rivers, is a reminder of the energy that comes from deep within the planet to drive our modern civilization. Both diesel trucks and primeval boulders change the landscape, and both are literally propelled along their respective rivers by planetary energy sources larger than themselves. The great pity, Snyder seems to say in this section, is the speed with which we have moved away from the "wildness"—that might have been preserved—toward the "sad havoc" John Muir noted even in his own time. Muir's "not-so-ancient text" celebrates a landscape that existed less than a hundred and fifty years ago, when

> *[a]ll the ground was covered,* not with grass and green leaves, but *with radiant corollas,* about *ankle-deep* next the foot-hills, knee-deep or more. . . . Here were *bahia, madia, madaria, burrielia, chrysopsis,* corethrogyne, *grindelia,*

> etc., growing in close social congregations of various shades of yellow, blending finely with the purples of clarkia, orthocarpus, and oenothera, whose delicate petals were drinking the vital sunbeams without giving back any sparkling glow. ("Bee Pastures" 340, 342; phrases quoted in "Covers the Ground" are emphasized)

"Covers the Ground" demonstrates Snyder's artistry as evidenced by his careful selection from Muir's words, especially in the names of the flowers:

> *bahia, madia, madaria, burielia,*
> *chrysopsis, grindelia,*
> *wherever a bee might fly—*

Here we see the craft of the poet as he prunes the words of the passage to represent the vocabulary of a knowledgeable botanist and then trims them once more to preserve the rhythm of his poem. It is clear that "burielia" and "grindelia" are emphasized as rhyming words; it is just as clear that Muir's word "corethrogyne" has been omitted because of the discordant rhythmical note it would introduce. Poets, of course, are free to use structure whenever they choose.

In the vastness of geological time, it may seem little has been gained or lost between Muir's day and our own. Yet if the identity of beings arises in part from the places they inhabit, readers will experience sadness in the knowledge that they shall not see such flowery abundance again. The human psyche intuitively suffers when it loses touch with wildness, and both wild bees and human beings thrive on the honeyed sight, taste, smell, and touch of wild flowers. In "Covers the Ground" Snyder appeals to that essential part of the human spirit willing to reject the strictures of artificially imposed structures in favor of the freedom to fly "wherever a bee might fly," a freedom of the wild.

THE FLOWING

As it originally appeared in the journal *Kyoi-Kuksu* in 1974, "The Flowing" was divided into four parts: "Watershed," "Riverbed," "Floods," and "Mouth." "Floods" mentions the Eel and Feather Rivers of California, the waters of [Babylon], and the dry bed of the ancient Great Basin Lake Lahontan, later used as the setting of "Finding the Space in the Heart." Thematically, "Floods" focuses on what is left behind after a landscape is flooded: silt, water-polished stones, the powdered alkali of a playa, bodies in trees, the delta's mud. The delta image led Snyder to write several lines critical of U.S. military involvement in Vietnam, specifically about battles in the Mekong Delta: "The USA will never take the delta." By 1981 when the poem was republished in the journal *Conjunctions,* Snyder replaced the "Floods" subsection with another poem known as "Falls." This revised four-part section was designated for the first time as part of *Mountains and Rivers Without End.*

As late as the summer of 1988, when I interviewed him at his home, Snyder was thinking about using only selected parts of "The Flowing" in *Mountains and Rivers;* "Watershed" and "Rivermouth" were both mentioned to me as possible sections, and "Falls" had just appeared in the journal *Sierra* as a separate poem with an identifying tag line, "from *Mountains and Rivers Without End.*" Although Snyder never specifies the falls, his model was Yosemite Falls, a fact revealed by David Robertson: "In the late 1970s Snyder took his family and Japanese parents-in-law to Yosemite. It was his first trip to the valley proper since 1955." Robertson relates that "one morning before dawn," Snyder "went to the bottom of Yosemite Falls." He then quotes Snyder as saying:

> I meditated by the falls from different angles. I had just finished writing a poem about the water cycle in the Sierra Nevada, so I was full of thinking in those metaphors. And so the [following] poem just came. I was moved very deeply to actually pray somehow by being there. (*West of Eden* 160–61)

Robertson then reprints "Falls" in its entirety. In the same essay Robertson quotes a remark made by Snyder about encountering the "Other," a comment with far broader application:

> The experience from which these Yosemite poems comes is the experience of interacting with the Other—of constantly trying to be aware of the Universe as all one body, of trying not to be separate from it but recognize every part of it as part of yourself. There is nothing alien in it at all. Sometimes interacting with the Other remains theoretical. Even then it is interesting. Sometimes it is an experience. When it is, I can make a poem out of it. It takes on the force of poetry. (160)

Interpenetration of the Self and the Other is at the heart of "The Flowing," not just its subsection "Falls." Significantly, when "The Flowing" was published in *Head/Waters* in 1994, the title of the first subsection was changed from its original "Watershed" to "Headwaters," and the four principal subsections took their final shape as: "Headwaters," "Riverbed," "Falls," and "Rivermouth" (65–68). Exterior landscapes mesh with interiors. The river's headwaters are energy flows in the brain. As we shall see, the mouth of the river, like other mouths, offers up vomit from the interior, and the climax of the poem is a literal interpenetration between the river and the poet. Snyder shows his awareness "of the Universe as all one body."

The publication history of "The Flowing" demonstrates Snyder's approach to craft in *Mountains and Rivers Without End.* Although parts of the complete section have been separated and treated as independent units on several occasions, in terms of its subject matter and formal arrangement, "The Flowing" has the consistent feel of any river's journey from the heights of its headwaters to its rivermouth where it merges with the universal ocean to begin the cycle once more. It is a journey emulated in the recurrent exchange and flow of energy within the human body and between it and the Other: the inflow and outflow of orifices, the coursing movements along its channels.

The poem starts high above Kyoto where the headwaters of the Kamo River gush forth through the "dragon-mouth jet" of a bronze pipe sticking out of the wall of the cliff. An artisan has turned the pipe's end into a literal figure of a dragon, yet the image also hints at the presence of the Kundalini dragon, whose spiraling coils connect head to bowels along the spine or ridge of the body. Nearby is a statue of Fudō. Snyder repeats his name for emphasis as well as rhythm—"Blue-faced growling Fudō"—and proceeds to tell us that he is "Lord of the Headwaters." As readers of *Mountains and Rivers* surely recognize by now, if Fudō is present, Kannon (Kwannon, Avalokiteshvara, Kuan-yin, Tārā) cannot be far away; as a dyad they dance together.

> Mountains also have mythic associations of verticality, spirit, height, transcendence, hardness, resistance, and masculinity. For the Chinese they are exemplars of the "yang": dry, hard, male, and bright. Waters are feminine: wet, soft, dark "yin" with associations of fluid-but-strong, seeking (and carving) the lowest, soulful, life-giving, shapeshifting. Folk (and Vajrayana) Buddhist iconography personifies "mountains and waters" in the *rupas*—"images" of Fudō Myō-ō (Immovable Wisdom King) and Kannon Bosatsu (The Bodhisattva Who Watches the Waves). Fudō is almost comically ferocious-looking with a blind eye and a fang, seated or standing on a slab of rock enveloped in flames. He is known as an ally of mountain ascetics. Kannon (Kuan-yin, Avalokitesvara) gracefully leans forward with her lotus and vase of water, a figure of compassion. The two are seen as buddha-work partners: ascetic discipline and relentless spirituality balanced by compassionate tolerance and detached forgiveness. Mountains and Waters are a dyad that together make wholeness possible: wisdom and compassion are the two components of realization. (*Practice* 101)

So it is that a poem about feminine waters, "fluid-but-strong, seeking (and carving) the lowest," begins its trip to the valley from Fudō's masculine heights at the headwaters of the "Kamo / River back of Kyoto." Coincidentally, Dōgen is also associated with this landscape: "at the age of twelve" he was climbing the trails of Mount Hiei, a "three-thousand-foot range at the northeast corner of the Kamo River basin, the broad valley now occupied by the huge city of Kyoto" (*Practice* 97–98). As we know, to walk such mountain peaks and ridges is more than aimless wandering. Snyder's concern, and Dōgen's, is with "sacred mountains and pilgrimages to them," a feature of Buddhist devotion that readers of *Mountains and Rivers* recognize easily in "The Circumambulation of Mt. Tamalpais." In "The Flowing," however, we meet a type of sacred pilgrimage that at first seems to be linear rather than circular. Indeed, the flow of a river seems to be straightforward before one takes the water cycle into account.

In 1956, when Snyder first lived in Kyoto, he set out to know the mountains and rivers of the area. "Eventually," as he says, he "was inducted as a novice Yamabushi (*sentachi*) and introduced to the deity of the range, Zaō Gogen, and to Fudō Myō-ō" ("Walking the Great Ridge" 71). His reference is to extended walking over sacred areas—"perhaps many dozens of square miles" where the landscape itself may be seen as a "mandala," a holy text to be walked upon for spiritual purposes.

> Some friends and I once walked the ancient pilgrimage route of the Ōmine Yamabushi (mountain ascetics) in Nara prefecture from Yoshino to Kumano. In doing so we crossed the traditional center of the "Diamond-Realm Mandala" at the summit of Mt. Ōmine (close to six thousand feet) and four hiking days later descended to the center of the "Womb-Realm Mandala" at the Kumano ("Bear Field") Shrine, deep in a valley. . . . This projection of complex teaching diagrams onto the landscape comes from the Japanese variety of Vajrayana Buddhism, the Shingon sect, in its interaction with the shamanistic tradition of the mountain brotherhood. (*Practice* 99–100)

Although the Yoshino-to-Kumano route is not the route marked by the Kamo River, nevertheless the forward-flowing descent of this pilgrimage from the masculine "Diamond-Realm" peaks—the peaks of Fudō—to the feminine "Womb-Realm" in the valley at Kumano four days later is a clear echo of the river's flow from headwaters to rivermouth. At first this dropping down from the heights into the world of ordinary events, the Buddhist "dusty world," may seem linear, but there is no divorce between the peaks and the valleys. Like similar symbols of interaction such as the jewel in the lotus or the *lingam* (male genital organ) in the *yoni* (female genital organ), they represent interpenetrating realities. These highland-lowland interconnections, as we know, are numerous in *Mountains and Rivers,* resonating with the fundamental dyad of peaks and valleys depicted in "Bubbs Creek Haircut" or the interlacing of misty cloud-void and mountain peaks in "Endless Streams and Mountains." "The Flowing" highlights the course of an archetypal feminine river, but the Vajrayana images constantly remind us of the larger interpenetrating whole. On another level, the movement behind this ideal journey of a river to the sea depicts another kind of "*walking on walking*": Gary Snyder walking in the footsteps of Dōgen and walking the diamond-womb mandala.

"Riverbed" focuses on those who live by—both in close proximity to and by the agency of—the river. The people who live on the banks of the river are at home there. Snyder draws a picture of a hiker's or hobo's camp, a romanticized spot by a stream where some carefree dharma bum, "singing a little tune," might support a cooking utensil with a forked stick over a campfire. The riverbed depicted here is a place for the unfettered life traditionally associated with gypsies, those whose dancing wives and clownish children happily accept impermanence, those whose "rags and tatters" signify that the commodities of the material world are of lesser importance than their attitude toward living. When associated with Japan, Snyder's emphasis on communal performance ("actors," "dancers," "clowns") easily alludes to the origins of the present-day stylized Nō drama in early informal song-dance-mime entertainments and harvest celebrations known respectively as *sarugaku* and *dengaku* (Keene 47–48). Indeed, Snyder provides a specific example of such a riverbank performance in the outrageous and laughable dance of Ame-no-uzume that readers encounter in part IV of *Mountains and Rivers.* Then, too, audiences brought together by these performances are the same kinds of communal people who inhabit the open desert void—the "foolish loving spaces"—of "Finding the Space in the Heart": "old friends, old trucks, drawn around; / great arcs of kids on bikes" (*MRWE* 151). The freedom, foolishness, and wild play reverberate with the same kind of carefree love that Mother Nature dishes out in "Haida Gwai North Coast, Naikoon Beach": "Love hard, playing, fighting, / rough and rowdy love-rassling / she can take it, she gives it // kissing, pounding, laughing—" (*MRWE* 104). At one with the natural world, people who live "by"—or like—the river personify the "flowing" as they "come skipping down / hop on boulders, clever—free—."

Snyder also gives us examples of those who make their living by the river. In the "[g]ravel scoop bed of the Kamo" there is a digger rig busily winnowing the stones and other material out of the water. The river's flow carves the highlands, moving its material to the lowlands where it becomes a gift of the river to be used for building the habitats of humans. In the screens of these sifters is proof that there are indeed "rocks of water." Moving to the other side of the Pacific, Snyder describes the work of several Native American tribes—the Yakima, Wasco, Wishram, Warmspring—who live by the Columbia River, sifting its waters with their traditional fishing technology. Like the gypsies, they seem at home in this locale, "talking / napping scattered through the rocks." As they work the men stand on wooden planks that extend out over and into the spray of the Columbia's rushing flow; they dip their nets into the water on long poles, sweeping them against the current—much like the screens of the gravel sievers—catching the salmon as they leap upstream. Equivalent to Su Tung-p'o's observation noted in "The Canyon Wren" that the water moves with "unspeakable slowness," here we see the "standing spray" of the water. Whether fish or men or technological instruments, the dynamic captured in this subsection is a lifting and curling motion, a "straining" that takes place against the current. Yet the "against-ness" is only apparent. Snyder portrays the same dyadic interpenetration of energies seen throughout the poem. In the present images of the salmon arching in the spray and the "one wet plank" entering the water, the implications are clearly sexual, yet each image seems to capture tension in absolute balance.

"Falls," as noted earlier, is a poem inspired by the leap of the Yosemite River. One might glean this fact by associating the lines "fault block uplift / thrust of westward slipping crust" with the formation of the Sierra Nevada, yet there are many waterfalls in the Sierra and ultimately the specific location of these falls is not of primary importance. What does matter in this subsection is another variation on paired movements, that of rising and falling. We also note the continued analogy with the body: this river that commences in snowfields that lie among the "ribs" of granite, leaps out over the "lip" of the cliff as if issuing forth from a mouth. Diversity emanates from a single source as the creek that "leaps out as one" quickly "divides in spray and streamers." The natural freedom of the wild is caught in the river's total abandon; it "lets it all go." We see a variation on this image in other sections: in "Night Highway 99" when the "network womb" is "stretched loose all / things slip through" and perhaps in the nourishing milk that comes from the "[l]oose vulva, droopy udder" of Mother *Bos* ("With This Flesh") who transforms the sun's energy into liquid sustenance for all. As with the compassion of Kuan-yin, Gaia freely dispenses herself in an ongoing gift.

If the flow of the Kamo begins with water that springs out of rock, the river in "Falls" precipitates out of the sky as snow rocked into being by the mountain. It then meanders downward through muck as well as flower roots and "seeps through swampy meadows" and "sandy shiny flats" before it "soars" once more into the air. Throughout the river's journey, we are reminded of its carefree movements, its playfulness. The shape-shifting river water finally thunders on boulders below before regathering itself into droplets on its interminable trip downward into "gravelly beds," a clear echo of the granite-to-gravel journey mentioned in "Riverbed."

The water cycle, generous to all beings and of no practical use to itself, proceeds relentlessly. As rivers descend they become watery air or seep into planetary rock only to be lifted again in an eternal round of recommencement. Spiraling and cyclical, the water's movement is part of a dyadic dynamic; no flowing would take place unless great mountain ranges, like the Sierra Nevada or the Himalayas, were lifted to attract the clouds to their peaks. These same heights engender the flow of water even as they are given shape by its steady descent on their slopes. It is Shiva and Sarasvatī, cross-legg'd, wholly enmeshed in one another; it is the "Mountain Spirit" on her perpetual earth-turning rounds "*walking on walking.*" Intermingling the body of the Self with the Other, Snyder uses a fundamental metaphor of meditation—the act of breathing—to join the pairs. The rocky heights and flowing waters literally provide an inspirational dance of "soft breath, world-wide," in and out, "night and day, / rising, falling." These interpenetrating motions that go "each way" are the "fine-honed thoughts" of "The Great Mind" that moves in both directions. The dance provides moisture and minerals for leaf cells and roots, allowing trees to utilize the sun as they "leapfrog" higher and higher up the sides of mountains. The water must flow down for the trees to rise. As Snyder's "grizzled black-eyed jackrabbit" shows us in "The Black-tailed Hare," the flow is a utilitarian gift for "the people to use it"; they "do it for us // said the rabbit" (*MRWE* 74). Even a cedar log born and nurtured by these dyadic forces "hopes / to get to sea at last and be / a great canoe." Wanting us to hear the music of the "magic song" of this river-mountain dyad, Snyder even provides us with some rare poetic rhyme—"song"/"along"; "sea"/"be"; "spill"/"still"—to hear it.

In the last lines of the "Falls," Snyder momentarily steps back from the entire dynamic as his song becomes a prayer. With the "steady" yet "slightly wavering" rainbow of pure light energy hanging over—like a misty arch that enmeshes land, water, and air—as a backdrop, the lines "between the rising and the falling / stands still" hint at a moment similar to Su Tung-p'o's enlightenment when he perceived nature move with "unspeakable slowness" (*MRWE* 90) during a long night of listening to the valley streams (Cook, *Sounds of Valley Streams* 101–2).

In "Rivermouth," the final subsection of "The Flowing," the water reaches the end of its linear journey. Like detritus vomited from the inner body, so the river disgorges all that it has gathered on its downward trip in a muddy yet cleansing outburst into the ocean. Issuing forth "end over end," the projectile movement echoes the implacable motion of the flowing river that we have already experienced in "Falls." However, Snyder's main focus in this subsection is a sexual metaphor that enables the linear to become cyclical in an act of copulation that will engender a rebirth. Once again, The Goddess steps forth: transformed much like the shapeshifting *shité* in a Nō play, the river reveals herself as Sarasvatī ("the flowing one") whose liquid song (vāk, vox, voice) sexually presses against the poet—his fingers, thigh, eye, testicles, and fishlike "lazy swimming cock"—as he stands in the watery current (*EHH* 124). Imagistically we return to the salmon leaping against the river's rush or the fisherman with his one wet plank extended into the water.

Interpenetration becomes literal as Snyder makes love to the River Goddess. Her flow—the current of the world beginning in the high headwaters and coursing downward until it "NOW" becomes a "vast loosing / of all that was found, sucked, held, / born, drowned"—is the total abandonment of Māyā's womb, which gives us the gift of our world of things and activities. In a final, obviously climactic, interaction of the Self with the Other, the "root" penis of the poet "hardens and lifts" as it penetrates the "thick flowing river" swirling around it. The jewel is in the lotus; the realms of the diamond peak and valley womb merge in the mandala of NOW. With a shiver of the skin, an act of ejaculation takes place. The Goddess and The Poet have met body to body, "cross legg'd." In this moment of enlightenment a rainbow hangs steadily between the rising and the falling.

Their intercourse over, Snyder quits making this particular section, but *Mountains and Rivers Without End* flows on and on. There will be other opportunities to merge with The Goddess; she will come again, and again.

THE BLACK-TAILED HARE

Attention to the flowing, the water cycle, continues in the short poem "The Black-tailed Hare." On the other hand, Snyder is not going to remain with a picture of this jackrabbit as a listener, like the large-eared hare in "Jackrabbit" in part I. Instead, he draws attention to gender issues by using "grizzled" as a word to describe the jackrabbit of the present section. This black-tailed hare feels "male," while the earlier jackrabbit may be seen as an emanation of the female Bodhisattva Kuan-yin (Avalokiteshvara). Any confusion disappears, however, when one discovers that Kuan-yin has been represented under both forms, male and female:

> Kuan-yin manifests himself in any conceivable form wherever a being needs his help, especially when someone is menaced by water, demons, fire, or sword. . . .
>
> In China Kuan-yin was depicted up until the time of the early Sung Dynasty as a man, and in the grotto paintings of Tun-huang is even shown with a mustache. From approximately the 10th century on, the figure of Kuan-yin in a white robe (Pai-i Kuan-yin) with feminine facial traits is predominant. This development is probably due, on the one hand, to the admixture of Taoistic folk religious ideas. . . . On the other hand, it can also be connected with the incursion of Tantric elements. ("Kuan-yin" *Shambhala Dictionary*)

With the hare's link to East Asian mythology, it makes little difference whether it is male or female. More telling is the hare's link with the moon. Western folklore speaks of a Man in the Moon, but several Asian cultures perceive the face of a hare among the configurations and shadows of the moon's surface. The Jataka tales of India relate a story of a Hare in the Moon that seems especially fitting.

> One day the Bodhisattva came to life as a hare. The hare lived in a wood with three friends. . . . [T]hey chose the hare as their leader because he was the most intelligent among them. He taught his friends the need for charity, contentment and self-sacrifice. One day Shakra (Indra) came down from heaven to test the hare's charity. Disguised as a beggar he asked the hare for food. (Knappert 115)

The hare, embarrassed by having nothing to offer this poor man, ultimately threw itself on the fire in an attempt to offer itself as food. The gods prevented the fire from burning the hare, and Indra was "so impressed by this extreme hospitality" that, reassuming his divine form, he

> picked up a mountain, squeezed it out like a fruit in his gigantic hand and with the juice painted the figure of a hare on the face of the moon. The picture of the hare still adorns the moon, or so say the Indians. (115)

The story emphasizes the compassionate role of the hare, a role always attributed to Kuan-yin/Avalokiteshvara and one that the rabbit aligns himself with in the final lines of "The Black-tailed Hare": "the / mountains and juniper / do it for us / said the rabbit." Nor should we overlook Indra's analogous action of squeezing juice from a mountain. The entire section is a celebration of the way mountains gather liquid from the sky and send it down their flanks and folds for the use of all the beings.

Further light is shed on the poem by remembering its publishing history. As one of "Eight Songs of Clouds and Water" published in *Poetry* (March 1968), the poem did not reappear with the other "Songs" when they were later republished.

> When these "Songs" were published in 1969 and again in 1970 in *Regarding Wave,* "The Rabbit" was not included. It is intended for a place in the final version of *Mountains and Rivers Without End.* This poem marks the beginning of the second phase (1968-mid–1976) in the development of *Mountains and Rivers Without End.* (Steuding 94)

Steuding feels that those sections written after 1968 demonstrate that Snyder shifted his "emphasis back to the topography of the American West," and he therefore discusses several of them in terms of Native American myth and history. Although his comments on "The Rabbit" are minimal, Steuding adds another dimension to an understanding of the section: "This 'grizzled black-eyed,' trickster-like figure, drawn from Amerindian mythology, tells the poet the source of the water which nourishes those roots: 'the / mountains and juniper / Do it for men'" (104). Steuding implies that the "roots" are, metaphorically, Snyder's return to his own grounding in the American West. Given a setting with "pines," "junipers," and "arroyos," the jackrabbit in "The Black-tailed Hare" seems far less Asian and more in league with mythological trickster figures, especially as found among the Native American peoples of North America.

Still, a comparison of several versions of this short poem shows us Snyder carefully working to broaden his base. Whereas the mountains and junipers of the earlier version "do it for men," an interim unpublished version became "Do it for People" (GSP B7:F12). The final version changes to "do it for us / said the rabbit." The "us" does not just reflect a greater sensitivity to gender roles; it is far more literal. The mountains and junipers do it for all beings, and the rabbit includes himself/herself/itself among those beings. Snyder's Buddhism is based on the figure of the Bodhisattva, the one who will not enter the world of final enlightenment until all beings "have been saved." As readers contemplate these lines, a great poetic truth dawns: for Snyder the real bodhisattvas, both in these lines and elsewhere in *Mountains and Rivers,* are the mountains, trees, and rivers that form the endless water cycle and "do it for us." The jackrabbit merely points us in the direction of the truth. Is this "grizzled black-eyed jackrabbit" the poet himself?

Joseph Campbell, a renowned authority on myth, brings the theoretical trickster a little closer to the "grizzled, black-eyed jackrabbit" who seems to be "showing" Gary Snyder a great teaching about the water cycle:

> This ambiguous, curiously fascinating figure of the trickster appears to have been the chief mythological character of the Paleolithic world of story. A fool, and a cruel, lecherous cheat, an epitome of the principle of disorder, he is nevertheless the culture-bringer also. And he appeared in many guises, both animal and human. Among the North American Plains Indians his usual form was Coyote. Among the woodland tribes of the north and east, he was The Great Hare, the Master Rabbit, some of whose deeds were assimilated by the Negroes of America to an African rabbit-trickster whom we know in the folktales of Br'er Rabbit. The tribes of the Northwest Coast knew him as Raven. Blue Jay is another of his forms. . . .
>
> In the Paleolithic sphere from which this figure [the trickster] derives, he was the archetype of the hero, the giver of all great boons—the fire-bringer and the teacher of mankind. (*Primitive* 273–74)

Snyder is not drawing particular attention to "The Great Hare, the Master Rabbit" in this section, although, as a student of anthropology, he is certainly aware of Paul Radin's well-known book on trickster figures, which includes a full account of the Winnebago Hare as a Trickster-Transformer. However, Snyder's writing—in both prose and poetry—shows a demonstrable fondness for Coyote and the lessons he passes on to us. The poet has also used Magpie to deliver a teaching about the "turquoise blue" of the mind ("Magpie's Song," *Turtle Island*). In a later section of *Mountains and Rivers,* Raven functions openly as a "teacher of mankind." In this section, then, the "grizzled black-eyed jackrabbit" is yet another animal "giver of all great boons" and "teacher of mankind." In short, in Snyder's poetry animal tricksters spend far less time "tricking" us, the two-legged beings, than they do teaching us.

On the pathways of *Mountains and Rivers,* the meeting with the animals, jackrabbit included, always seems to be a locus for visions of an earlier time, a time "in the distant past in which the world was different and people could not be distinguished from animals." Snyder speaks to animals and listens to what they teach. For him and for Native Americans the "animals have souls or spirits that give them supernatural power." In poems like these, the animals "come . . . in visions, and in . . . stories they help the hero out of trouble" ("Arts of American Indian Peoples," *Encyclopaedia Britannica* 659). One of the primary purposes of *Mountains and Rivers Without End* is to reestablish that contact with the animal world for the wisdom that it contains.

"The Black-tailed Hare" seems to divide into two connected parts: what the rabbit shows the poet and, consequently, what the rabbit says to him. Through the poet's eyes, we see what the jackrabbit is pointing to: irrigation ditches by the side of the paved highway stretching far away, leading off, like a white line disappearing into emptiness, over great distances to the farms and cities where the water will be used. Looking in the other direction, our eyes take in the peaks of the mountains against a stark blue sky with white clouds flying like banners around them. Looking more closely, readers see the juniper trees on the sides of the mountains even down to the small buds on the tips of their branches and the scale of their bark. We can see, almost feel, the tough skin, the surface of the planet with its "rock scrabble, picklers, boulders."

Then, as in the earlier "Jackrabbit" poem with the hare's "great ears shining," Snyder asks readers to focus on listening. We hear the song of mountains and trees. As if in a chorus, perhaps a chant, they sing to the blue sky—the "bell chill blue jewel sky"—for water. The mist gathers, the snow falls; from the snow and mist the water accrues, flowing down the sides of the mountains by means of arroyos and ditches, finally leading off to the cities for the people to use. The form of the sky—the "bell" is as much shape as sound—may remind us of the curving arc of "The Blue Sky," an earlier section dedicated to "making things whole." Like Indra's Hare, the planet gives itself to us, says Gary Snyder; a little grateful behavior on our part would not be out of place. Jackrabbits, especially the grizzled black-eyed trickster species, know this a little; perhaps these rabbits know a lot more than we give them credit for.

WITH THIS FLESH

In contrast with "The Black-tailed Hare" and "The Flowing," which entreat water to come down from the mountain peaks and the clouds above them, "With This Flesh," originally entitled "Reeds," concentrates on "roots" at the base of things and draws up the waters, or other "inspiring spirits," that are down in the wells, deep under the dusty earth. The section opens with an epigraph from the *Avatamsaka Sūtra:*

> *Why should we cherish all sentient beings?*
> *Because sentient beings*
> *are the roots of the tree-of-awakening.*
> *The Bodhisattvas and the Buddhas are the flowers and fruits.*
> *Compassion is the water for the roots.*

Reminiscent of William Butler Yeats's famous question about a tree's essence—"O chestnut-tree, great-rooted blossomer / Are you the leaf, the blossom or the bole?" ("Among School Children")—the basic meaning of the sūtra's lines is easily paraphrased: the roots, flowers, and fruits are interconnected; watering the "bottom" will bring about profusion at the "top." Compassion leads to the flowering or fruitfulness of becoming an enlightened being. There is, however, a necessary recycling, a return to the roots; the essence of being enlightened is to know that one must be compassionate toward all sentient beings. This theme, incarnated in "With This Flesh," is central to an understanding of *Mountains and Rivers Without End.*

The *Avatamsaka Sūtra,* according to Snyder, points toward a way of seeing a "vast interrelated network in which all objects and creatures are necessary and illuminated" (*EHH* 92). In a different context, the fundamental idea of the sūtra arises when Snyder muses on the "dreamtime" of Australian aboriginals:

> "Dreaming" or "dreamtime" refers to a time of fluidity, shapeshifting, interspecies conversation and intersexuality, radically creative moves, whole landscapes being altered. It is often taken to be a "mythical past," but it is not really in *any* time. We might as well say it is *right now.* It is the mode of the eternal moment of creating, of being, as contrasted with the mode of cause and effect in time. Time is the realm where people mainly live and within which history, evolution, and progress are imagined to take place. ("Good, Wild, Sacred" 84–85)

This shape-shifting, out-of-time dreamtime that might as well be "right now" is rooted in the flowing experiences that emanate from living in an actual place, albeit a sacred place. The "dreaming place" is much more than a special location for the people who visit it; it is composed of all the beings and events that have inhabited it, become attached to it, or flowed out of it over time ("Good, Wild, Sacred" 85). Dreamtime is, in other words, an all-encompassing experience much like the "vast interrelated network" of the *Avatamsaka Sūtra.*

In "With This Flesh" Snyder visits a "dreamtime" site of his own choosing: one of the few places in the dry landscape of Baja California where water flows, an "arroyo" not far from San Ignacio. Snyder's "sacred" spot is first and foremost a place for cows: "Mother *Bos* / in her green-grass body at / Arroyo de Camanjue—arroyo of reeds—." Here we will find associated archetypes and bridges among humanity, cows, and the locale. In the lines of this poem one can trace the "tracks of ancestors" of all sorts that have moved, and continue to move, in and through the landscape. Reeds are not just grass for cows to eat; they are hollow stalks with which one might extract essential liquids. If musical, one might fashion a crude wind instrument, such as a flute, to play upon. At the very least, breathing in the atmosphere of this section through its metaphorical reeds, readers will find themselves spiraling outward and across the face of the planet in a web of interconnections.

The region surrounding San Ignacio, which includes Santa Gertrudis, San Ignacio, La Purísima, and San Javier, is known as the "Comondú." Here the pre-Hispanic inhabitants spoke a language known as Cochimí. Originally there were three native languages spoken in Baja California—Pericú, Guaycura, and Cochimí—but only Cochimí survived into the twentieth century and then "only by a few monolinguistic individuals who still exist in the northern part of the peninsula" (Martinez 48). The name "Comondú" is derived from the native words *caamanc ca-*

deú, which mean "reed creek." "Kadekaman," formed by the same words, *cadeú caamanc*, is the name given by natives to the place the Spanish renamed as "San Ignacio." Snyder, ethnolinguist that he is, makes the connections clear in the title he gives to part II: "San Ignacio, *Cadacaaman*, 'Reed Creek.'" His use of native words throughout "With This Flesh" honors inhabitory roots, and the linguistic traces of the native population are clearly seen in the landscape of his poem (Martinez 54–55). The section's original title, "Reeds," not only pays homage to the names hidden beneath the names, but marks the landscape for what it is. As any standard travel book on Baja California points out, present-day San Ignacio is a surprisingly verdant agricultural center in the midst of Baja California's inhospitable desert. In addition to the water that runs deep under its surface, there are prehistoric cave paintings and wintering grounds for gray whales nearby. Readers of Snyder's work see the immediate attraction of such a place for this poet. Yet "With this Flesh" ("Reeds") is one of the few poems in *Mountains and Rivers* that is difficult to locate in terms of Snyder's chronology. The poem was published in 1994, but the trip to Baja California described by the poet more than likely took place years before then. The point is intriguing because the poem draws on an act of rejuvenation; it appears to celebrate "a trip to the well" in the midst of an arid spell. Hearkening back to the watering imagery of the poem's epigraph, perhaps it was here, drawing deeply through these reeds, that the poet felt inspiration rising again from "deep wells." Perhaps it was here that Snyder first recognized his long poem would encompass desert spaces alongside its mountains and rivers. The practice of the wild takes place both on the path and off the trail; it occurs in cities as well as in "wilderness areas"; it connects deserts to high mountain peaks and water to aridity. Ultimately it goes beyond any such simplistic dyads, but one must move through them, even as one holds on to them, in order to experience the simultaneity of what is beyond either and of both.

The unexpected prosaic lines that begin "With This Flesh" open readers to seemingly new tracks crisscrossing in this multidimensional long poem. Snyder ventures forth on "a beach in Baja" with the Spanish conquistadors. His feelings about the Spanish invasion of Turtle Island, first expressed in 1957, have not changed much in forty years:

> Rape of the world: destructiveness of Western civilization. Those insane Spaniards in Central America—answering to abstractions of gold and religion. The nature, wildlife, Indian life, Mississippi, Grand Canyon, didn't move them. The whole Western hemisphere a gift to Spain from the Pope. ("Tanker Notes," *EHH* 54)

The opening lines of "With This Flesh" are composed wholly of a quotation from an affidavit written, as it says, in 1539, by a member of a Spanish expedition exploring the coasts of Baja California. Impelled by repeated stories of the so-called Seven Cities of Gold, Hernán Cortés, the conqueror of Mexico City, had authorized three ships under the direction of Francisco de Ulloa to discover the truth about those "mythical cities and lands" and, if possible, to "possess" them. Ulloa left Acapulco in July but was soon forced to abandon one of the ships; continuing his travels up the Pacific coast with the two remaining boats, he entered the Gulf of California, exploring for the first time both "interior coasts of that gulf." By September 28 he reached the mouth of the Colorado "to which he gave the name of 'Ancón de San Andrés.'" Here, the Spaniard "took possession" of the bay and its surrounding lands "in the name of the Emperor our king of Castille." Snyder reproduces the event as he found it in a translation of the original testament written down by Pedro de Palenzia:

> on the twenty-eighth day of the month of September, 1539, the very excellent señor Francisco de Ulloa, lieutenant of the Governor and Captain of this armada by grace of the most illustrious señor Marqués del Valle de Oaxaca, took possession of the bay of San Andrés [the mouth of the Colorado River] and the Bermeja sea [the reddish-colored waters of the northern Gulf of California], that is on the coast of this New Spain toward the north, at thirty-three and a half degrees, for the said Marqués del Valle in the name of the Emperor our king of Castille, at the present time and in reality, *placing a hand on the sword, saying that if anyone contradicts this, he is ready to defend it, cutting trees with his sword, uprooting grass, removing rocks from one place to another, and taking water from the sea;* all as a sign of possession. . . . I, Pedro de Palenzia, notary public of this armada, write what happened before me. (Martinez 82–83, my emphasis and brackets)

Notably, although Snyder drops out a line or two of nonessential names from the original, the only real change that he makes is to rearrange a block of prose lines (emphasized above) for greater poetic effect, a technique that not only enhances the poetic rhythms latent in the prose but follows the distribution of rhythms that might be found here if this were a segment from a Nō play. One suspects that Snyder chanted these lines in his head as he wrote them down. In terms of meaning, the poeticized lines speak directly to what has ultimately taken place under the "sign of possession" in the New World: trees have been cut down to provide lumber for cities, grass has been uprooted, and rocks have been moved to make way for plowed fields or, later, shopping malls. As in so many other sections of *Mountains and Rivers,* there is an anti-imperialist, anti-capitalistic edge to these lines. As a Buddhist, the thought of taking possession of anything is anathema to Snyder. As an intellectual anarchist whose grandfather "had soapboxed for the Wobblies" (*Practice* 124), Snyder has little love for capitalistic ownership. For Snyder, "[c]apitalism plus big government often looks like welfare for the rich" (*Practice* 143). A look backward at "The Market" will confirm that this stance persists in *Mountains and Rivers.*

Ulloa and his ships next sailed south from the mouth of the Colorado. Rounding the Cape of San Lucas at the tip of the Baja peninsula, the Spaniard explored northward along the Pacific coast, was wounded in a fight with some Indians, and then vanished, seemingly without a trace:

> On April 5, 1540, he [Ulloa] directed to Cortéz from the Isle of Cedars a detailed account of the events of the explorations, sending it by one of the ships; in the other he continued navigating, but no one knows what ultimately happened. So it was that the waves of the western California coast swallowed up the first European who dared to plow through them. (Martinez 83, my brackets)

Momentous events come and go; apparently only a name here and there remains. Yet, as readers discover in part III of this section, one significant trace left by the Spaniards are the cows they introduced to the Southwest.

With the feel of an interlude, part II of the section opens on a vine-covered cottage in San Ignacio. The ninety-eight-year-old "Señora" who rules in this house—the "Casa Leree"—is almost as old as the century-old grapevine that covers her home. Resting in her "dark cool room at full noon," she is distinctly at home, at one with her habitation. As in "Mā," we find ourselves in a matriarchy; this elderly woman has no husband at her side, and even at her advanced age she still tells people what to do. Perhaps it is not by accident that Snyder, the "poeta," will find "inspiration" in this place. In the voice of the narrator we are introduced to Rebecca, Señora Maria Leree's daughter, who must be over seventy years of age herself. As she says, she has "six kids in Guaymas" that she only sees "three days a month"; moreover she "lived fifty-five years in Los Angeles" before returning to Baja. Her husband, Dagobert, drives a beer truck "all day every day / and some nights . . . to ranches / all through central Baja." Not unexpectedly in a poem that begins with the Spaniard threatening to "[remove] rocks from one place to another," as a "sign of possession," we find Snyder putting wry words in Dagobert's mouth about the salt works at Guerrero Negro that "sell most of their salt to Japan."

For the most part, however, one wonders what purpose these mundane details serve. As in all *Mountains and Rivers* poems, landscape is important. San Ignacio is "Reed Creek," a place where the water flows in the midst of aridity. Even Dagobert's beer provides refreshing liquid for the dry rancherias throughout the surrounding area. Two of Rebecca's sons are painters, and she plays a mandolin because she "needs some music down here." One begins to imagine the Casa Leree at Reed Creek, imbued with water, music, and art, as a "sacred" spot, a place to enhance inspiration. A mandolin? Ancient stringed instrument that it is, in Rebecca's hands it may stimulate readers to think of her as a Muse, one of the nine mythical figures "known as Pierides inasmuch as they supposedly first saw the light of day at Pieria, a Thracian district famous for its rivulets which produced sweet soothing songs" (Jobes II: 1138). Thus "[r]ising early" gives a "poeta" a chance to meet the muse and hear sweet songs. And the name, "Rebecca"? In another guise she is Isaac's wife, found by Abraham's servant at a well where she "let down her pitcher upon her hand, and gave him drink," a sign that she was marked by the Lord (Genesis 24:17–21). This must be the place for inspiration. Here are "[d]eep wells"; here is "[w]here we breathe" in deeply through the reeds. Here Snyder bows in gratitude for the creative flowing that must have started here, perhaps after a dry spell.

If the narrative of the second part of the section has the feel of an interlude, it nevertheless remains firmly linked to the other parts of the section. Among talk of the Señora, her daughter Rebecca, and their extended family, there is a brief set of lines of a more general nature—the lines are indented and made rhythmically repetitive to set them off. In these lines we find an emphasis on the food chain at work, a theme that predominates in the last part of "With This Flesh." The hummingbird's four-egg nest is juxtaposed with four watchful Mexican black hawks; one egg for each hawk, we presume. The carrion-eating, falconlike "caracara" waits vigilantly on top of a "cardón" cactus; the bobcat stalks. It may be that this "wadi full of cheeping evening birds" is about to be decimated. Even supposedly domesticated cats are watching from above as they "walk the fan-palm roof." In almost the same breath with "deep wells," the poet mentions "[d]ry leather," which looks forward to the "[d]ried meat" and "[l]eathery twisted ropy Christ / figure racked to dry" of the next part. However dry they may be, both are "flesh" intended to be eaten, which brings us to the bulls and cows of Baja California, the subject of the third part, "The Arroyo."

In part III Snyder establishes a circumplanetary line for the genus *Bos,* one that can be traced back and forth from India to Crete to Spain and finally on to the New World on the ships of the Spaniards. For those who know the circumpolar implications of the story of "The Bear Mother," Snyder's latitudinal cow track seems analogous to that of the bear cult. Like the paths followed across the face of the landscape scroll, the long-distance travel of beings via a network of interconnections is often celebrated in Snyder's long poem, most notably in "The Hump-backed Flute Player," significantly the next section of *Mountains and Rivers.*

Scholars of myth connect Europa's story—a young woman so charmed by Zeus, disguised as a bull, that she climbed onto his back and disappeared across the Mediterranean Sea—to tribal migrations involving Crete. In earlier essays Snyder has used the word "Europa" to represent the geopolitical unit known as Europe. Indeed, in the immediately following lines of this poem, he calls our attention to the Vouet painting *The Rape of Europa,* now located in Madrid. In clearly negative tones, he concludes that this patriarchal rape of the ancient goddess figure has left us with "modern Europe and its states and wars." Europe has become plainly masculinized, yet as Snyder has written the passage one sees The Goddess as one who has allowed these events to happen, knowing that in some future era she will have her day, or night. For now, starting from the Madrid gallery and Snyder's mention of "the bulls of Iberia," readers are asked to leap imaginatively across the Atlantic with the Spanish colonizers who brought the "cow" with them to, among other places, Baja California. That leap is the basic connection between parts I and III.

Snyder juxtaposes Europa's love for the Father with India's love for the "big-eyed Mother Cow." Joseph Campbell, speaking of an archaeological "galaxy of female figurines" belonging to the "Near East c. 4500," makes some important connections for us. He spots a "prominent motif" among these neolithic images and symbols:

> the head of a bull . . . with long, curving horns—suggesting that the widely known myth must already have been developed, of the earth-goddess fertilized by the moon-bull who dies and is resurrected. Familiar derivatives of this myth are the Late Classical legends of Europa and the Bull of Zeus, Pasiphaë and the Bull of Poseidon, Io turned into a cow, and the killing of the Minotaur. Moreover the earliest temple compounds of the Near East—indeed, the earliest temple compounds in the history of the world—reinforce the evidence for the bull-god and goddess-cow as leading fertility symbols of the period. (*Oriental* 36–37)

Following the trace of Mesopotamian temple compounds in which these apparently sacred figures were found, Campbell links this Near Eastern complex of images to goddess-mother rituals to be found later in India. Citing a Sumerian seal from 3500 B.C. ("just before the invention of the art of letters"), he implies that all such rituals belong to a cycle of "life-in-being-through-mutual-killing," which, he says, represents "the mythological theme . . . of the self-consuming, ever-dying, ever-living generative energy that is the life and death in all things" (*Oriental* 39–40). Before another millennium has elapsed, according to Campbell, the archaeological evidence of a cosmic goddess Cow increases:

> a cult of the tilled earth fertilized by that noblest and most powerful beast of the recently developed holy barnyard, the bull—who not only sired the milk-yielding cows, but also drew the plow, which in that early period simultaneously broke and seeded the earth. Moreover, by analogy, the horned moon, lord of the rhythm of the womb and of the rains and dews, was equated with the bull; so that the animal became a cosmological symbol, uniting the fields and laws of sky and earth. And the whole mystery of being could thus be poetically illustrated through the metaphor of the cow, the bull, and their calf, liturgically rendered within the precincts of the early temple compounds—which were symbolic of the womb of the cosmic goddess Cow herself. (*Oriental* 41)

Snyder himself has commented on these temples. In *Earth House Hold* he mentions seeing (in the work of G. R. Levy) "illustrations of a 'temple dairy farm' at the neolithic temple site of Al 'Ubaid: 'the Goddess of the pastures was herself the Cow'" (132–33). Surely these ideas belong to "With This Flesh," a poem that ultimately celebrates a food chain based on the sacrifice of a (cow) being for the betterment of (human) beings. Starting with the "green grass body" of "Mother *Bos,*" a clear indication that this skinny cow has consumed the grassy reeds in the arroyo at San Ignacio, the chain is evident: from sun to grass to flesh to jerky to shoes, saddles, sheaths, buttons, buckets of lard, glue, milk, and buttermilk. Even though the "horny forehead" in this poem belongs to "a skinny cow," the horns, like the horns of other beings in *Mountains and Rivers,* reinforce the spiral image. This cow has "sweet breath spiraling outward." In fact, this complex of linked images—dying and resurrected gods, flute players, crescent moons, spiraling horns—has echoes throughout *Mountains and Rivers.*

"With this flesh" is a linguistic echo of "with this ring," a phrase used at wedding ceremonies around the world: "With this ring, I thee wed." Snyder adapts the phrase in the last line of the section: "with this flesh I thee wed." Marking a sacred communal event, the expression is similar to another well-known ceremonial phrase: "This is my body." Both phrases have a distinctly Christian tone to them, even while they resonate with the sound of rituals from a far more ancient period. It is not wholly surprising that Christ's "[l]eathery twisted ropy" body, like that of the "bony cows of Baja," is turned into "jerky," dried meat to keep for good years and bad. Sacramental jerky becomes the sanctified host to be consumed. A true wedding is a complete communion: "with this meat I thee feed / with this flesh I thee wed." The intermingling of these sacred acts is echoed in the natural landscape. Snyder suggests that the physical hoof of the cow has been formed by ("is a trace of") the grasslands she walks on. In other words, Mother *Bos*'s shape is determined by Gaia. The converse is equally true: the form of the earth is altered by the presence of the cow's hooves.

We may imagine the change in Snyder's poetic tone of voice as he chants, Nō-like, an inventory of water in its native rhythms. In the earlier version of the section, published in the journal *Sulfur,* Snyder used a different litany of native words. As translated phrases, the four words in the journal version were "creek of the large ranges," "running water," "high mountain," "plateau of the mountains." In the Counterpoint edition there are six terms that, when translated, depict a common motif:

Aggvacaamanc — creek of the hawks
Camané caamanc — creek of the cardón cactus
Cahelulevit — running water
Vaba cahel — water of the camp
Cunitca cahel — water of the large rocks
Cahelmet — water and earth

Obviously the poet has dropped the earlier images of range, mountain, and plateau in favor of water, water, water. The change helps to depict the landscape as it must have been seen in the imagination of its earliest inhabitants. One way or another, this arroyo has always been a veritable oasis in the midst of an arid region, a source of magical flowing, a well of inspiration.

"A su servicio!" says the white bearded vaquero; "Adios!" "Go with God!" Here then is a section dedicated to flowing, not just that of the poet's creativity, but in terms of an eternally revolving food chain, a compassionate and sacred sacrifice of beings for the preservation of other beings, a *puja,* that we will experience again in "An Offering for Tārā."

THE HUMP-BACKED FLUTE PLAYER

The Buddhist concept of emptiness permeates *Mountains and Rivers Without End.* Some sections of the poem imply it; others actually invoke it. It may shine with the fullness of the moon; it may be represented by metaphors of unending spirals or boundless jeweled nets. It dwells in the curl of the horns of sheep and goats and cows. It inhabits the vast spaces of the Brooks Range and the Black Rock Desert. In "The Hump-backed Flute Player" we are witness to the poet's meditation on emptiness (Hunt "Hump-backed"). Here Snyder connects the void with an extensive list of motifs and images: the music of Kokop'ele's soundless flute; the conveyors of emptiness—Hsüan-tsang's "curved frame pack," or Kokop'ele's hump, or Snyder's backpack; the "whispers" that Snyder shares with the "pecked-out pictures of some mountain sheep with curling horns"; the "delicate debates" of Tārā's devotees; the Nalanda monks whom Snyder refers to as "Logicians of Emptiness"; the rhythmic movement of the resurrected ghost animals and the swirling bodies of the Native Americans who danced the Ghost Dance in the 1890s; the "conch spiral corridors" or the spiraling twists of the Kundalini "dragon in the spine"; the "bottomless sky" seen in Wovoka's empty hat; the mystic message whispered to the poet by the ancient "Bristlecone Pine." It is, nevertheless, the icon of Kokop'ele (or Kokopilau or Kokopelli—Snyder has used them all) that integrates this diverse collection.

It is not an accident that "The Hump-backed Flute Player" is found in a climactic location at the exact middle of *Mountains and Rivers Without End* and the end of part II. Readers now have their first sustained contact with the heart of emptiness. Attuned to the rhythms of the Nō drama, we have journeyed to a place of higher intensity from our setting forth; yet here we stand on a preliminary peak from which we may perceive further valleys and even loftier pinnacles before us. The highest point in the distance is the meeting with "The Mountain Spirit" of part IV, the evident narrative summit of the poem and a mirror image of this one. It takes place, as much of "The Hump-backed Flute Player" does, among the bristlecone pines in the White Mountains of California on the edge of the Great Basin. These two counterpointed sections may even be evidence of Snyder's structural imitation of the two-scene Nō play: In "The Hump-backed Flute Player" we encounter the pines in their "normal" guise; in "The Mountain Spirit" the pines are transformed into Yamamba herself. Meetings like these—whether in the Nō or in *Mountains and Rivers With-*

out End or in actuality—are transformative, and transformation is at the heart of enlightenment.

Additionally, "The Hump-backed Flute Player" has a significant structural relationship to "The Blue Sky." The former poem ends part II, as the latter ends part I. These poems have always been linked in Snyder's mind. As published in the second edition of *Mountains and Rivers Without End* (1970), "The Blue Sky" used tiny Kokop'ele figures as printer's devices to mark off internal subsections of the poem. Moreover, the mythical "lapis lazuli realm" of "The Blue Sky" that lies "east across the sea" is identified with the "yellow sand land / Coyote old man land / Silver, and stone blue" of the American Great Basin. Asia becomes America; the emptiness of the Great Basin is suddenly filled with turquoise and lapis lazuli jewels of consciousness.

The geographical arc between Asia and the "New World," a counterpart of the "healing" curve mentioned in "The Blue Sky," follows a path across the Pacific Snyder once described in the small book *North Sea Road.* Like Paleolithic hunters tracking game, we traverse the path of the named rivers in "The Hump-backed Flute Player" from the Asian Amur to the North American Tanana and Mackenzie by way of Beringia, the ancient land bridge between Asia and Turtle Island.

> Sweetwater, Quileute, Hoh
> Amur, Tanana, Mackenzie, Old Man,
> Bighorn, Platte, the San Juan

Once on the North American continent, migration groups during the Ice Age followed one of two open main pathways: one route south follows the Tanana, a tributary of the Yukon, as it flows just east of the great Alaskan and Canadian Pacific coastal ranges. This route eventually leads migrating peoples into the Pacific Northwest culture area tagged by the names of the Quileute and Hoh Rivers of the Olympic Peninsula in Washington. The other route follows the Mackenzie River, the primary path south into the heart of a glacier-locked North America. The remaining rivers on this list are found progressively further south until one reaches the San Juan River, which begins on the Colorado Plateau and meanders through the Four Corners area of Arizona/New Mexico/Colorado/Utah, about fifty miles north of Canyon de Chelly where the poet's persona converses in whispers with Kokop'ele and "the pecked-out pictures of some mountain sheep with curling horns."

In the opposite direction we trace the path of the legendary journey of the missionary Hsüan-tsang, traveling west and south from China across mountain ranges and deserts to the holy rivers of India:

> the Pamir   the Tarim   Turfan
> the Punjab   the doab
> of Ganga and Yamuna

These ranges and rivers mark the transmission path for the emptiness school of Buddhism as it was transplanted from India to China in Hsüan-tsang's "curved frame pack." Reaching India after such immense journeys, Hsüan-tsang remained for an extended period at Nalanda University studying the Vijñaptimātra school of Yogāchāra thought. Eventually he returned to China with the knowledge he had gained. His translations of several key sūtras, including the *Heart Sūtra* referred to in "Finding the Space in the Heart," helped in the spread of Buddhism, especially the concept of emptiness. Tracing both paths—Hsüan-tsang's round-trip between China and India and the migration routes from Asia to North America—is Snyder's way of describing an overarching trajectory for the Buddhist emptiness that he suggests has one foot planted in Buddhist Nalanda and the other set down amid the cultures of Native American peoples. The emptiness contained in Hsüan-tsang's pack is also carried in Kokop'ele's hump. In Native American folklore the curved back of the petroglyph is said to be a "pack" containing the seeds of plants and flowers with which to start a new world. We see the beginning of such a new world in the visions of Wovoka, the Paiute Indian prophet of the 1890s, whose shamanistic insights led to ritualistic Ghost Dances designed to regenerate the world and rid it of the White Man. Wovoka's hat, like the pack of Hsüan-tsang and the hump of the flute player, becomes a magical source of pure possibility for the future growth of the universe. Snyder points out several of these connections in his notes to the poem, including the idea that Kokop'ele's emblem continues into the present day as a reminder of the need for genetic diversity of beings and cultures (*MRWE* 160–61). The trip along these pathways is not restricted to human travel, as Bert Almon has pointed out.

> The Buddhist, like the North American Indian, gives a kind of equality to ". . . the other people—what the Sioux Indians called the creeping people, and the standing people, and the swimming people . . ." [*Turtle Island,* "The Wilderness"]. Many of Snyder's "people" are birds, coyotes, whales, insects, or even plants. It is easy to dismiss this sympathy as sentimental pantheism but Snyder knows that the ecological crisis grows out of such attitudes. (121, brackets original)

Snyder feels the weight of this significance. As his poetic persona says: "Ah, what am I carrying? What's this load?" Emptiness is a heavy burden; "taming and teaching" oneself and then passing it on is an arduous assignment. Those who carry forward a tradition—be they teachers, poets, literary critics, philosophers, scientists, or engineers—are charged with the difficult task of clarifying, and at times changing, perceptions. One does not do these things merely for the self; one must do them equally for the "earth house hold" we all live in. A world of ego and fragmentation calls into being its opposite, a coming to wholeness; yet one must continue to respect the diversity of parts. Each of us must listen to the music of the biosphere as it is whispered to us by the trees.

Much of the poem's energy relies on aural, visual, and dynamic devices similar to those found in Vajrayana (i.e., Tantric) Buddhist rituals. It is possible to see the entire poem as Snyder's informal version of a ritual known as "meditating on a deity."

> The Tantra worked out a system of meditation on deities which is marked by a sequence of four steps:
>
> *First of all,* there is the understanding of emptiness and the sinking of one's separate individuality into that emptiness.
>
> *Secondly,* one must repeat and visualize *germ-syllables* (*bija*).
>
> *Thirdly,* one forms a conception of the external representation of a deity, as shown in statues, paintings, etc.
>
> *Fourthly,* through identification one becomes the deity.
>
> (Conze 185)

Though I do not envision an exact correspondence between this four-stage ritual and what I see as the "strategy" behind this section, there are certain general similarities. "The Hump-backed Flute Player" both describes and offers some "understanding of emptiness" by depicting its transmission in mythical and actual time across geographical space from Asia to North America, across the space that stretches from the earth to the stars, and across the void that exists between our inner and outer being. The speaker is attempting to "sink" his individual self into the felt reality of emptiness as he transports himself from whispering among the petroglyphs of Canyon de Chelly to the whispering of the "Oldest of Beings" and the song of "a young throng // of Pinyon Pine" that he hears on the peaks of the White Mountains. Listening to birds is one thing; listening to rocks and trees is quite another.

What should we listen for in this poem? It seems highly probable to me that Snyder is deliberately repeating "*germ-syllables*" (*bija*) for an effect. This repetitive rhythm of syllables, words, and phrases creates a chantlike quality in the poem that seems decidedly mantric and brings out the magical power inherent in the very sound of words. "According to the Tantra, different syllables not only correspond to different spiritual forces or deities, but a syllable or letter can be used to conjure up a deity" (Conze 186). Snyder has said that "we proceed to learn from the sense of sound better than from any other sense, in the very specific terms of Zen enlightenment. . . . [S]ound is essentially your path in" (Snyder, "Coyote-Mind" 165). As we have already seen, in Vajrayana mythology Kuan-yin's name means "observe the sounds," and the very title of "The Hump-backed Flute Player" indicates that this poem must be listened to: the chantlike quality in some of its lines: "Ghost bison, ghost bears, ghost bighorns, ghost lynx, ghost pronghorns, ghost panthers, ghost marmots, ghost owls"; the repetitive phrasing in lines like "[t]he hump-backed flute player" and "[h]is hump is a pack" and parallel phrasing in "he carried / 'emptiness'" and "he carried / 'mind only'" or "the oldest of trees . . . the Oldest of Beings / the Oldest of Trees"; obviously related assonantal and consonantal phrases seen in "scattered—books burned—banners tattered—statues shattered—by the Türks." The places associated with Hsüan-tsang's journey are arranged according to their sound value: both counterpoint and echoing are heard in "Pa*mir*" and "Ta*rim*," "Pun*jab*" and "do*ab*," "Ga*n*ga" and "Yamu*na*." The rivers that trace the migration patterns of the Native Americans are actually arranged more in accordance with their sound value than with the importance of their geographical locations. Thus, in addition to marking dispersions in space, the words "A*m*ur, Ta*n*a*n*a, Macke*n*zie, Old *M*a*n*, / Big Hor*n*, Platte, the Sa*n* Jua*n*" share a preponderance of *m* and *n* sounds, sounds that reinforce the sound of the word "*em*pti*n*ess."

A form of mantric "vibration" takes place within this section. Generally, mantras are classified into two broad types: "*kanthika*, 'throated' or mantras given expression to by the voice"; and "*ajapa*, or 'non-uttered'" mantras which are not spoken but repeated internally" (Walker 2: 26). Among the throated mantras are several subtypes:

> (a) *vāchika*, "spoken" or uttered aloud . . . ; (b) *bhramara*, "humming," the method generally used for japa or repetition; (c) *janāṇtikā*, (lit. "people nearby"), whispered or spoken in a low voice, so as not to be overheard; (d) *karnika*, whispered into the "ear"; a special class of initiatory mantra, conveyed to the pupil by this means directly. (Walker 2: 26)

Snyder has filled this section, consciously or not, with repetitive, resonant, humming, nasalized, whispering sounds, starting with the "hum" in "hump-backed," continuing through the sibilant whisperings among the flute player, the mountain sheep, and the poet's persona in Canyon de Chelly, and ending with the enlightening "it" that was "whispered" directly into the ear of the poet "by the Oldest of Trees" on the summit of the White Mountains. The sound becomes the form; the form becomes the sound. All this mantric "ringing" in our ears is, finally, a healing vibration; it is the sound of the "cricket in the stars" as it interpenetrates with the world we live in. When one is enlightened, visions of a new world join with the sonorous sounds of all beings; perhaps even the sound of butterfly wings may be heard "on slopes of grass and aspen."

Snyder uses visualization as a significant technique in "The Hump-backed Flute Player." The poem records many dreamlike images from different times and places, but it is the underlying stick-figure icon of Kokop'ele, with his curved pack full of "nothing" and the music of his soundless flute playing in the poet's ears, that becomes Snyder's "external representation" of the "deity" of "emptiness." According to Frank Waters, Kokop'ele plays a prominent part in the Native American creation/migration stories of the Hopis, especially those that point to the settling of a new world (3–48 passim). Helping the Hopis in their four migrations (west, south, east, north), were insect people, or *máhus*. The locust *máhu*, the hump-backed flute player, also known as Kokop'ele, carried seeds of plants and flowers in his hump and created warmth with the music of his phallic flute. In their migrations the people carved pictures of him on rocks from the tip of South America to Canada. Incidentally, the locust *máhu* could just as well be the "cricket" that we hear and see "in the stars."

The directional turnings of the Hopi migrations—from a common center outward to four extremities and back again—are often represented in rock art by a drawing of a swastika, originally a sacred design. Others see the design as a spiraling pattern that easily relates to the formal patterns seen in the poem's "conch spiral corridors" or to the "curly horns" of the desert sheep or the spiraling energetic movements of "the dragon in the spine" of Kundalini Yogic practice. In terms of Tantric practice, some of these patterns may be seen as yantras, sacred designs to be meditated on that embody the energy of a deity. Presumably, the ideas, images, and sounds of "The Hump-backed Flute Player" become the seeds of the reader's meditation, thereby transmitting the tradition of emptiness from "teacher" to "disciple" once more.

In the third section of the poem, using spatial relationships and linguistic derivations, Snyder takes us still further back in time as he carefully connects Nalanda with the teaching of the historical Gautama Buddha.

> In the plains of Bihar, near Rajgir, are the ruins of Nalanda. The name Bihar comes from "vihara"—Buddhist temple—the Diamond Seat is in Bihar, and Vulture Peak—Tibetan pilgrims come down to these plains. The six-foot-thick walls of Nalanda, the monks all scattered—books burned—banners tattered—statues shattered—by the Türks.

The Diamond Seat, Vulture Peak, and the ruins of Nalanda are all located in Bihar, associated linguistically with "vihara." Since "vihara" is defined as a "dwelling place" or a "condition of heart" (Humphreys 211), it represents both the human body-spirit and a geographical location. Similarly, the English word "temple" also doubles as a term for the frontal lobe of the brain and a place of worship. Snyder's sacred places often equate states of mind with geographical locations, and he fills the reader's mental temple with the flowing interconnections of emptiness. Vulture Peak, one of the named "mountains" in this section, is the location for some of the Buddha's most famous sermons ("Buddhist Literature: Exegesis and Hermeneutics," *Encyclopedia of Religion* 537). The Diamond Seat refers to the spot where Gautama Buddha found enlightenment as he sat under the Bodhi tree. The word "diamond" translates as *vajra*, the root syllable in "Vajrayana," the third great "vehicle" or "way" (*yana*) in Buddhism. Not only did the Vajrayana flourish in the sacred region of Bihar, it was transmitted to Tibet, no doubt by the very "Tibetan pilgrims" that Snyder locates at Nalanda, where it flourishes today, especially in its devotion to Tārā, "[s]he who saves." Its system of meditational aids—that is, mantras, yantras, and mandalas—forms the structural backbone of "The Hump-backed Flute Player."

Referring to the Ghost Dance ritual practiced among Native Americans in the 1890s, Snyder again combines images of emptiness and wholeness as he tells us that "*Black Coyote saw the whole world / In Wovoka's empty hat.*" Wovoka, also known as Jack Wilson, was a Paiute prophet from the Great Basin area who had shamanistic visions about regenerating the world as it was before the white man came along. His visions became the basis for the formal circling movements and songs of the Ghost Dance. Snyder provides us with his version of Wovoka's vision and dance:

> Ghost bison, ghost bears, ghost bighorns, ghost lynx, ghost pronghorns, ghost panthers, ghost marmots, ghost owls: swirling and gathering, sweeping down,
> Then the white man will be gone.

When asked for proof of his supernatural power, Wovoka passed his hand into his hat and pulled out "something black"—"Tall Bull saw only an empty hat" but "Black Coyote saw the whole spirit world" (Mooney 17–18). Before the Ghost Dancing had ended, Wovoka's new world visions led to the tragic massacre of the Sioux at Wounded Knee. In *Mountains and Rivers,* Snyder's dance with emptiness, a ghost dance of another kind, continues Wovoka's visionary quest for rehabilitation by perceiving wholeness through emptiness.

For Snyder, a sacred spot for meditating on such sounds, patterns, and meanings is near a petroglyph of Kokop'ele on a rock situated on the north wall in Canyon de Chelly. The place is marked by dualities that must be overcome: a north wall and south wall; it is warm but there is ice; it is in sun as well as in shadow. The sound of the flute may be heard. Another profound dreamtime location would be on the peaks of the White Mountains, just east of Bishop, California, where there is a grove of bristlecone pine trees, the "oldest of trees," the "oldest of Beings" on the surface of the planet. There, in silent meditation, sitting, like the Buddha on a diamond seat, under the very Oldest Tree, one could listen "all night long" for the sound of emptiness.

Kokop'ele's mythical function, like that of Old Man Medicine Buddha in "The Blue Sky," is that of a healer, and we are invited to listen to the music of his flute, the music of wholeness. There is "nothing" in the curve of his humped back, or in Snyder's backpack, yet a new world arises out of such emptiness. "The Hump-backed Flute Player" is, ultimately, an ecstatic apocalyptic poem. As ghostly animal beings dance in "swirling and gathering" motions all around, the human world of egotism and divisive desire is swept away. The "shining rain" of regeneration, the beginning of an apocalyptic flood that will overwhelm our consciousness, starts to fall from "thunderheads the deep blue of Krishna." Drops of "tiny" rain-people-buddhas glide down from the sky world to join once more with earth's rooted "grass-seed-buddhas." Because "all manner of beings" swim in Krishna's sea, plant, animal, and human realms combine in a spiraling, harmonic, ecological vision: body and mind, earth, sea, and sky, all are entwined and mirrored in one another's being. This revelation is the lesson of the Tantric "dragon" coiling along "the spine." The diamond (*vajra*) "jewel" of emptiness conjoins the "pearl" of the sea with the "crystal" of the stars. Along with Snyder, we are invited to meditate on the "spiral," the "wheel," the "breath of mind" in the "bottomless sky," Tārā's "night of starlight." As we breathe quietly in the silence, we hear the music of the hump-backed flute player Kokop'ele, the "echoing" sounds of Krishna's "conch" shell, the whispers of the petroglyphic sheep and those of the "Oldest of Beings"—the "Bristlecone Pine." Sound is the way in.

In one sense, "The Hump-backed Flute Player" captures the moment of an actual meditation on emptiness—or several meditations collapsed into one—by the poet. Readers observe Snyder as he listens to himself, finding a way to work through his own illusions. As Snyder has heard the wisdom of emptiness whispered to him by the "Oldest of Beings, / Oldest of Trees," as he has heard it also from the sheep while lying on his back, his shirt off, warming to the sun under the image of Kokop'ele, listening to the silent playing of a flute in Canyon de Chelly, so he whispers on the tradition to us. This section is not only *about* meditation; reading it *is* a meditation exercise. If we hear the sounds of the poem, see the interconnections among its images, and become attentive to its dynamic flow of energies, we too are meditating on the deity of emptiness in the depths of our consciousness.

Part III

THE CIRCUMAMBULATION OF MT. TAMALPAIS

"The Circumambulation of Mt. Tamalpais" was not always considered part of *Mountains and Rivers Without End.* First published in 1966 in two different journals, one version was tagged as a section while the other made no mention of a connection to the longer poem. The section was not included in a first draft of the completed book that Snyder sent to me in June of 1995. Perhaps its overtly ritualistic nature caused Snyder to hesitate; certainly, no other section is as openly and totally ceremonial as this one. Others—like "The Blue Sky" and "An Offering for Tārā"—contain mantric verses, and "Raven's Beak River / At the End" is so unremittingly rhythmical that it has the feel of a religious litany, but "The Circumambulation of Mt. Tamalpais" is a complete ritual in and for itself.

With this section we begin part III, ten sections constituting a second *ha,* or "agitated development," phase of *Mountains and Rivers.* As we journey across this new poetic landscape we should expect to catch echoes of what we have already encountered; further interconnections should accumulate and unfold. Theoretically the level of complexity and intensity of these sections should be greater than that which we experience in part II, a first *ha* stage. Yet this comparison can only be made in retrospect and then only with some imaginative appreciation for the poem as performance. Certainly, given that the concluding sections of part II—"With This Flesh" and "The Hump-backed Flute Player"—are intricately written in both style and theme, it would be difficult to maintain the level of intensity established in them. As an opening section, therefore, "The Circumambulation of Mt. Tamalpais" is written in an introductory, or *jo,* mode; it begins a new aesthetic cycle in a lower register. Like each of the other three leadoff section poems—"Endless Streams and Mountains," "The Market," and "Old Woodrat's Stinky House"—it has a prefatory quality to it. Emulating the practice of circumambulation, the section goes nowhere thematically. Its form is its message. Snyder may also intend it to stand in juxtaposition with "The Market." If the latter poem is a catalog of ruinous commercialism, perhaps the chanted spells, songs, and sūtras of "The Circumambulation of Mt. Tamalpais" will serve as an antidote. As Snyder explains in his note for the section,

> Walking meditation, circumambulation, *pradakshina,* is one of the most ancient human spiritual exercises. On such walks one stops at notable spots to sing a song, or to chant invocations and praises, such as mantras, songs, or little sūtras. (*MRWE* 161)

In other words, this section asks the reader not merely to think or feel but to practice. Structured as a religious ritual, it mirrors the performance mode of the larger poem. In his detailed analysis of the importance of Mount Tamalpais for Gary Snyder, David Robertson has pointed out that

> [h]iking for Snyder is a way of furthering a political, social, and spiritual revolution. The ground of all right living (one of the meanings of *dharma*) is, literally, the ground we walk on. Hiking at one and the same time frees us from a dependency on nonessential things (the products of *dharma* in another of its senses). The essential nature of things is not an Aristotelian plot nor a Hegelian dialectic, and does not lead to a goal. Therefore, it cannot be the object of a quest, as for the grail. Instead, it goes round and round and on and on, rather like the hike that Kerouac and Snyder took [on Mount Tamalpais] and even more like the poem that Snyder projected writing and told Kerouac about as they walked. ("Real Matter" 220, my brackets)

Following Robertson's suggestion, I would add that hiking the trails of Mount Tamalpais is an equivalent for still other ongoing journeys. Not only is *Mountains and Rivers* a compositional journey that took forty years of going round and round, it is a colophon to be affixed to a planetary landscape scroll or a commentary on Mahāyāna doctrines, and it provides a model for devotional practice in the service of The Goddess Gaia. Like Hsüan-tsang before him, Gary Snyder is committed to the transmission of Buddhism. Both ideas and techniques learned in Asia have come to North America in Snyder's backpack.

Sound and motion are at the heart of this section. We listen as Snyder, Whalen, and Ginsberg ascend, circle (clockwise), and descend the San Francisco Bay Area's most prominent mountain ("Mt. Tamalpais" = "Bay Mountain"), stopping at selected spots along the way to chant mantras, *dhāranīs* (magic spells), vows, sūtras, and other short verses. Although the spiraling trip was completed in a single day, it must have been a satisfying consequence for Snyder's promise, made to himself in Japan in 1957, that when he got back to America he would do a "100-day walking practice around Hieizan = Tamalpais" (Journal entry—12 Jan. [1957]. GSP B30:F6). A few years after his promise, as an initiate of the Yamabushi, he reiterated to Whalen that he wanted to "do magic on mountaintops" and that he would "sacredize Tamalpais" when he returned (17 June 1961. Reed–PWP). It was October 22, 1965, before the *pradakshina* recorded in "The Circumambulation of Mt. Tamalpais" fulfilled his wish. The Yamabushi connection is preserved in a note to the *Agenda* publication of the poem: "Gary Snyder, *Shugendo sentachi,* in company with Philip Whalen and Allen Ginsberg, 22.X.1965" (35). The label in apposition to Snyder's name rather proudly announces his status as an initiate (*sentachi*) in the Shugendo sect.

> The Yamabushi ("those who stay in the mountains") are back country Shaman-Buddhists with strong Shinto connections, who make walking and climbing in deep mountain ranges a large part of their practice. . . . The tradition is also known as Shugendo, "the way of hard practice." The Yamabushi do not constitute a sect, but rather a society with special initiations and rites whose members may be lay or priesthood of any Buddhist sect, or also of Shinto affiliation. The main Buddhist affinity is with the Shingon sect, which is the Sino-Japanese version of Vajrayana, esoteric Buddhism, the Buddhism we often call "Tibetan." (Snyder, "Walking" 71)

Snyder's Yamabushi connection unites this meditative walking practice to shamanism, which has its roots in the primitive. As Snyder told Robertson, the lore of circumambulation "is a part of ancient Indo-European lore, Indo-Aryan lore, that probably goes back to central Asia, and which includes the Celts" (Robertson, "Circumambulation" 5). Robertson reports Whalen's general agreement:

> I probably thought of it as some ancient magical tradition that preceded the Buddhist or Tantric traditions. . . . I thought of it as more in the shamanic tradition. I think that Gary is right that the ancient magical tradition became, at least in Buddhism, a walking meditation. (11–12)

The Yamabushi costume, which includes straw sandals and a deer pelt, reinforces their shamanistic appearance. They carry a "conch shell in a net bag across the shoulder" and "the shakujo staff with its loose hanging bronze rings on top." Not surprisingly, Fudō, whom we meet in other sections of *Mountains and Rivers,* is the protector of the Shingon Yamabushi brotherhood, whose teachings intermingle the Vajra [Diamond] Realm peaks with the valleys of the Garbha [Womb] realm. Their practice is to combine these landscape mandalas by walking them (Snyder, "Walking" 72). Readers of "The Circumambulation of Mt. Tamalpais" hear the blowing of the conch and the rattling of the rings as the staffs are shaken ceremonially. Given Snyder's status as a Yamabushi initiate, this ritual trip around Mount Tamalpais—from the shadowy redwood valley in Muir Woods to the bright lookout summit and back—is a one-day walking of the diamond-womb mandala. Moreover, as a Vajrayana practice, this ritualistic section prepares us for our meeting with the Tibetan bodhisattva Tārā in the climactic moments of part III of *Mountains and Rivers.*

Robertson has traced Snyder's ongoing relationship to Mount Tamalpais from a first visit to Muir Woods at the age of nine all the way to the present day ("Real Matter" and "Circumambulation"). In his interviews with Snyder and Whalen, both poets reveal important points about their pilgrimage around the mountain on October 22, 1965. For one thing, their circumambulation that day was the first time that either poet walked the trails in an "intentionally ceremonial" way. On the other hand, there was nothing special about the choice of the day. As Snyder told Robertson:

> It just happened to be the day we could all get together. But we did make a decision. Let's all go do a formal circumambulation of Tamalpais and establish sacred spots on it and pay our respects and do some chanting. Allen was doing a lot of chanting at that time. So was I. (Robertson, "Circumambulation" 4)

Four types of chants were selected: the *Heart Sūtra* as a "statement of 'the total truth of the universe' as the three of them understood it"; a magic spell, or *dhāranī,* for the protection of all beings; various mantras addressing "rocks, animals, plants, human beings, watersheds, upthrusts, all spiritual beings"; and the "Four Vows" of Buddhism (Robertson, "Circumambulation" 6–7). The continuing importance of the *Heart Sūtra* cannot be overemphasized: besides Hsüan-tsang's role in its transmission, Snyder notes that it is a "one-page condensation of the whole philosophy of transcendent wisdom" (*MRWE* 160–61); and it is the heart of "Finding the Space in the Heart."

Ritualistically, Buddhism is rife with items of thought or practice being divided into five phases or ten steps or fifteen conditions. Snyder's division of the section into ten stages may or may not relate to a preexisting Buddhist ritual. Whalen's poetic version of the hike marks off only eight spots of formal significance, which he calls "shrines" instead of "stages." Robertson explains:

> I was under the impression that the stations had been chosen in advance on the basis of hikes Snyder had taken on Mt. Tamalpais in the decade or so before 1965. Both he and Whalen assured me that I was mistaken. "We just felt the

> magic vibrations," he said, as Whalen chuckled. "We decided on them the day that we walked it, by being finely tuned," a sentence punctuated by Whalen's "Right, right!" ("Circumambulation" 7)

Perhaps, then, when Snyder climbed Glacier Peak with Allen Ginsberg just a month before, it was in the same vein that he divided his ascent into nine stages (*EHH* 98–101). What seems to be significant is the ability to stop at regular intervals, to pay attention, to feel the "vibrations."

Whalen and Snyder gave Robertson several reasons for making the ritual journey around the mountain. They both told him they wanted to give "tribute" to Mount Tamalpais. An extended explanation from Snyder touches on the mountain's physical, almost magical, prominence in the Bay Area landscape and its power as a storehouse of special memories for the poet. It was, and is, a wild place within easy reach of the cities of San Francisco and Berkeley, serving equally as a site for extended communal hiking or for personal solitude. Snyder therefore wished to pay "respect and gratitude" to the mountain. Both poets acknowledged their desire "to make an opening for Buddhism in American culture." Their ritual of "opening the mountain" was an overt action, a way that could be followed by others. Snyder told Robertson that he wanted to "consecrate Tamalpais" as a "sacred mountain for future generations to do the same kind of pilgrimage on." Finally, Snyder added that their circumambulation had been a simple act of religious "devotion" ("Circumambulation" 14–15).

For the most part, a reading of the poem is straightforward. Though it may be mantric, it is not overly metaphorical. Readers should substitute the full texts or chants—if familiar with them—for the indicated titles (i.e., "Four Vows," "Dhāranī for Removing Disasters," etc.), and the majority of the lines in the section should be actively chanted. Overall, these are not lines from a book to be reflected on quietly. Nevertheless, there are instances of wordplay and an example or two of significant ambiguity or irony. Robertson mentions most of them in his essay. The "book called Harmony" found in a shack near Rifle Camp resonates, as does the cynical tone that attaches itself to "Peacock Gap Country Club." Ginsberg's mix-up of the smell of California laurel leaves with that of fried chicken is humorous while being emblematic of modern civilization's confusion about nature. There is a mini-jeremiad over the Bay Area's "smog and sense of heat. May the whole planet not get like this." Snyder never lets us forget that the world of humans is close, perhaps too close, at hand: "Parking lot of Mountain Home. Cars whiz by, sun glare from the west." The poem, in fact, ends with the circumambulators "blowing the conch, shaking the staff rings, right in the parking lot." Here, perhaps, is where the "Dhāranī for Removing Disasters" most needs to be chanted.

One can spot interconnections with other sections of *Mountains and Rivers.* Perhaps the cows should remind us of other cows and their "cowboys," or of their inherent status as symbols for Mother *Bos,* nurturing goddesses all, but it seems more to the point that this cow with the big eyes stands out because she is in the midst of a "huge pissing." At Rock Springs the trickle that issues forth is of a different kind, yet it is still enough to call forth a chant for Sarasvatī, the flowing river goddess we have seen in other sections. There are sumptuous food offerings that, in the context of the Tārā mantra, seem to prefigure "An Offering for Tārā." And, in a small but telling echo, the "chinquapin" found on Mount Tamalpais has its parallel as a named tree in the East Asian scroll "Endless Streams and Mountains."

Among the birds, trees, and animals encountered, what stands out, especially with the addition of new lines in the Counterpoint edition, is Snyder's consistent attention to water and rock. These are the places where he naturally stops to pay obeisance. For water there is: "mountains make springs"; "[s]plash across the creek"; "Rock *springs.* A trickle even now—"; "[l]unch by the stream, too tiny a trickle, we drink water from our bota"; "Collier Spring . . . water trickling out a pipe"; "[t]he gleam of water storage in the brushy hills." For rock we find: "ancient interior live oak splitting a rock outcrop"; "a tiny chörten" (a small group of memorial stones); "[a] ring of outcropped rocks. A natural little dolmen-circle"; "*Rock* springs"; "[a] notable serpentine outcropping"; "[r]ocky brush climb up"; "[a] ring of rock pinnacles around the lookout."

If one focuses on the Hindu/Buddhist aspects of Snyder's poem, it appears to be exotic. Most non-Buddhists will be distanced by his use of Sanskrit phrases like "*Prajñāpāramitā-hridaya-sūtra*" (*The Heart of Understanding Sūtra*) or the mention of magical *dhāranīs* or mantras. Having led several circumambulations of Mount Tamalpais himself, Robertson specifically mentions the problem of choosing texts for chanting by non-Buddhists during these *pradakshinas.* Snyder's answer to the problem is equally instructive for readers of the section.

> It is too burdensome to say that it must be a Buddhist ritual. I would rather think that it is open for anyone to be as creative as they like. They can stop at those points we stopped at, or they can stop at other points. The main thing is to pay your regards, to play, to engage, to stop and pay attention. It's just a way of stopping and looking—at yourself too. In a way that is what ceremony is for. (Robertson, "Circumambulation" 20)

As disciplined as Snyder is, he is rarely if ever programmatic. The final message of "The Circumambulation of Mt. Tamalpais" is to be creative and attentive. The same could be said of the larger *Mountains and Rivers Without End.* Snyder's long poem recognizes, with respect and gratitude, the myriad interconnections of the sacred planet we inhabit. Stopping places—in the sections of this long poem or in the world—are everywhere; we have only to choose them and to adopt a ceremonious attitude toward what we find there. Stop we should, says Snyder.

THE CANYON WREN

In "The Canyon Wren" Snyder quotes Dōgen as saying that "mountains flow / water is the palace of the dragon / it does not flow away." Snyder's essay "Blue Mountains Constantly Walking" also cites Dōgen's words, albeit in a broader context:

> Now when dragons and fish see water as a palace, it is just like human beings seeing a palace. They do not think it flows. If an outsider tells them, "What you see as a palace is running water," the dragons and fish will be astonished, just as we are when we hear the words, "Mountains flow." (*Practice* 108–9)

Juxtaposing apparent absurdity with exquisite truth, Zen master Dōgen informs us that fish and dragons view water, their dwelling place, as a fixed and stationary "palace." For all we humans know, their perception of water as a solid entity is true. It may even be that we would bring some enlightenment to the fish and dragons if we could share with them our human understanding of their abode as a place of flowing water. The real issue for Dōgen is that human beings, like fish and dragons, may not be quick to recognize the nature of their own abode as they live in it.[17] At first human perception endorses the concept that mountains are solid; surely, the eye says, these huge earth forms are fixed in place. Further reflection, however, reveals that mountains have indeed shifted, settled, and uplifted in time. It is, after all, only in the last half of the twentieth century that the formerly astonishing geological theories of continental drift and plate tectonics have been accepted as scientific truth.

"The Canyon Wren," however, is not about the flowing of mountains or continents; it focuses instead on the other half of the dyad, the equally astonishing perception that rivers, though apparently moving, may stand still.

> Shooting the Hundred-Pace Rapids
> Su Tung P'o saw, for a moment,
> it all stand still.
> "I stare at the water:
> it moves with unspeakable slowness."

Who is this "Su Tung P'o" who, just for a moment, sees the movement of these hurried rapids become unspeakably slow? What is his significance for Snyder? Also known as Su Shih, Su Tung-p'o (1036–1101) was a Chinese poet, essayist, painter, calligrapher, and politician. An optimistic and forgiving man, he held no grudges against his superiors although he was banished on two occasions for opposing their reforms. As a poet he tried to loosen some of the restrictions on form and content imposed by the existing conventions of poetry in China ("Su Tung-p'o" *Encyclopaedia Britannica*). Even in this simple sketch it is evident that Su Tung-p'o's biography has interesting parallels with Snyder's. As one of the early Beat poets, Snyder plainly had a hand in liberating poetry from its academic conventions. Although never "banished," Snyder's years of residence in Japan, his months on the *Sappa Creek*, and his home in the Sierra Nevada foothills far from the city have all contributed to his profound understanding of seclusion, an intentional isolation from which Snyder unquestionably gathers wisdom. On the other hand, as onetime head of former governor Jerry Brown's California Arts Council, the poet has also had a taste of the political life, to which one should add his ongoing involvement in the politics of ecology at local, regional, national, and international levels. Still, for all their aptness, these comparisons do not reveal the heart of the comparison. As a Buddhist, Su Tung-p'o spoke of becoming enlightened on Mount Lu

> when he heard the sound of valley streams flowing in the night. He composed a verse and presented it to Ch'an [Zen] master Ch'ang-tsung . . .
>
> The sounds of the valley streams are His long, broad tongue
> The forms of the mountains are his pure Body.
> At night I heard the myriad sutra-verses uttered
> How can I relate to others what they say?
> (Cook, *Sounds of Valley Streams* 101–2)

Like his eleventh-century counterpart, Snyder attaches enormous significance to the sound of water flowing (or not flowing). Curiously, one could just as easily reverse the phrase and lose none of its importance: the flow of sound (or silence, its nonflow). Snyder drew attention to the links between enlightenment and sound in his 1967 essay "Poetry and the Primitive":

> THE VOICE AS A GIRL
>
> "Everything was alive—the trees, grasses, and winds were dancing with me, talking with me; I could understand the songs of the birds." This ancient experience is not so much—in spite of later commentators—"religious" as it is a pure perception of beauty. The phenomenal world experienced at certain pitches is totally living, exciting, mysterious, filling one with a trembling awe, leaving one grateful and humble. The wonder of the mystery returns direct to one's own senses and consciousness: inside and outside; the voice breathes, "Ah!" (*EHH* 123)

Snyder's visionary experience, as quoted above, easily associates with Su Tung-p'o's enlightenment as he listened in the dark to the sound of valley streams. Sound, for Snyder too, is an awesome and beautiful wave pattern. Experiencing the "pitch" of the phenomenal world causes one to tremble. Sound is associated with the feminine—"the voice as a girl." The breath—the same breath focused on during the practice of meditation—is at the core of one's life experience. "Breath is the outer world coming into one's body"; "breath is spirit, 'inspiration.'" Expelling the breath is to give "voice" to it; it is the basis for community since it "makes the signals by which the species connects." When "certain emotions and states occasionally seize the body, one becomes a whole tube of air vibrating; all voice" (123). Breath is at the heart of poetry, the flow of its phonemes. Moreover, as we know from "Bubbs Creek Haircut," Snyder equates the voice of poetry with the Goddess Vāk (Sarasvatī), whose name means "the flowing one." Snyder puts these ideas into poetic practice in his 1970 collection of poems, *Regarding Wave.* We see the same ideas in his evocation of figures like Kuan-yin (Avalokiteshvara), whose name, according to the *Shambhala Dictionary of Buddhism and Zen,* literally means "Who Contemplates the [Supplicating] Sound of the World." Thus a cluster of interconnecting images and ideas becomes evident: sound, flowing, breath, meditation, feminine, goddess, muse, voice, poetry, rivers, waves, rhythms, energy, and so on. To focus on any one aspect is to bring forth the others. Sound, as Snyder has said more than once, is the "way in" to awareness.

Like Su Tung-p'o, Snyder has recorded occasions when he sensed the forces of enlightenment at work on him; yet, unlike his predecessor, there seems to be no single poem that expresses the intensity of those moments. Perhaps Snyder has earmarked *Mountains and Rivers Without End* to be, retrospectively, his enlightenment poem, not a tiny lyric that responds to a single moment but a work of epic intent that compresses a lifetime of attentiveness into a large poetic event. It has been presented not to a Zen master but to the world of its readers. In our recapturing of this dyadic landscape of mountains and rivers (and much more) as presented by Snyder's rhythms, images, and ideas, we may feel the spirit of Su Tung-p'o reincarnate itself in Snyder's long poem. The song of the Buddha's long broad tongue may be heard in the sounds of the rivers; the body of the Buddha may be visualized among the forms of the verbalized mountains.

We hear echoes of Su Tung-p'o's verse in other sections of *Mountains and Rivers* such as "An Offering for Tārā" and "We Wash Our Bowls in This Water," but in "The Canyon Wren" sound, water, and motion become the primary focus. The section commences with frenzied activity and multidirectional energy. The rafts containing the speaker and his party are "swept on by downriver"; their motion is not of their own making. On this river between the "rock walls" of the canyon, the "shimmer[ing]" boulders also lie just under the water until one cannot tell the rock from the water, nor the water from the rock. All is "wobble" and "roils" and "arching" and "spinning" and "churning" as they paddle "forward, backstroke, turn" in an attempt to harmonize their energies with that of the river. "Above the roar," like moments taken and held in balance, one hears the melodic breath of the canyon wren steadily expressed in song: "ti ti ti ti tee tee tee." Suddenly there is a "smooth stretch" to the river, and the frantic motions become mere "drifting and resting." The "delicate downward song" of the bird merges with the "song" of the river and the motion of the raft as all drop down through the canyon, descending "through ancient beds." It is the awareness of the bird's song that makes "it all stand still."

"The Canyon Wren" sets out to capture more than the sound of a single wren at home within its habitat. This section depicts the "sound of a valley stream" in its entirety, the sound of the habitat itself, including all of its significant components. Sounds exist beyond the audible sounds heard in this canyon. With a touch of poignancy and irony, this section eulogizes a harmony heard along a river that would soon be gone. As Snyder tells us in his notes, the poem commemorates the Stanislaus River, which flows westward out of the central Sierra Nevada.

> The twists and turns of the river, the layering, swirling stone cliffs of the gorges, are cut in nine-million-year-old latites. We ran the river to see its face once more before it went under the rising water of the New Mellones Dam. The song of the canyon wren stayed with us the whole time. (*MRWE* 161)

History, the "nine-million-year-old" record of the river's flow evidenced in geological waves left behind on canyon walls, is a major concern in this poem. All this history—of rock, river, vegetation, and animal—was about to be submerged. Indeed, the river's rapids were soon to become "unspeakably slow" as much of the river was transformed into a lake. In an interview, Snyder distinguished several kinds of history. Acknowledging his respect for the "2,000–3,000-year-old habits of mind and philosophical positions" that make up "European and Occidental history at large," Snyder also spoke of a "history of place":

> From another standpoint, my identity . . . is as much California as it is Europe. . . . I enjoy thinking of what has happened in the last 12,000 years since the ice caps melted . . . and the saber-toothed tigers and wooley mammoths ceased to be here, and we came into our moment. . . . This is our moment. . . . That's another history. It's what we smell when we smell the breeze in the morning that has a little manzanita bloom in it. That's 12,000 years of history. That smell hasn't changed. Or the bird songs that are going on in the early morning behind you. That's the same set of bird songs that have been going on for 12,000 years. ("Voice in the Wilderness" 10)

The song of "The Canyon Wren" has a similar history. This section, like "Arctic Midnight Twilight," which follows, explores the harmony of beings in place, yet with a difference: an abiding plaintive tone accompanies the knowledge that these twelve-thousand-year-old songs and nine-million-year-old latites will soon be gone from view. This sobering thought leads to a moment for enlightened awareness. Perhaps, like the "channelized" Los Angeles River or the hidden streams coursing under the bedrock of Manhattan, the Stanislaus will reappear as a river in some other time, some other place. In the meantime, even though the rush of the Stanislaus is about to be stemmed, the river "does not flow away." Snyder reinforces his idea with small historical particulars inserted toward the end of the poem. Tying past human events to the history of the river, Snyder reports that the rafting party beaches at "China Camp" where "black-haired miners" once stacked up "piles of stone." Thus the stones tell the history of Asian labor imported into California to work the gold mines. And this too is part of the "song" one hears by this river. Like Su Tung-p'o and Dōgen, Snyder spends the night by the stream listening in the dark to the flow.

Here and gone, but not forgotten, these intermingled melodies of birds, river, rocks, and humans remain to "purify our ears."

ARCTIC MIDNIGHT TWILIGHT
COOL NORTH BREEZE WITH LOW CLOUDS
GREEN MOUNTAIN SLOPES, WHITE MOUNTAIN SHEEP

We move on from birds to sheep. "Arctic Midnight Twilight" continues the theme of enlightenment through sound as we hear yet another song of being-in-place, at homeness on the planet. This "*Dibée* Song" refers to the perceptible harmony of Alaskan Dall mountain sheep in their age-old habitat. Not identified as a *Mountains and Rivers* poem at the time of its first journal publication, the section was, however, located and dated as "Headwaters of the Koyukuk, Brooks Range, Alaska, VIII 40085 [1985]." Its slightly different title—"Daylight All Day / Cool North Breeze with Low Clouds / Midnight Twilight / Steep Rock Slope Mountain Sheep / Green Summer Slopes Song"—focuses on the medley of landscape elements rather than on the song of the sheep. Yet, in either form, the haiku-like title implies a blending of beings and forms. The "white dots on far slopes" may be perceived as cloud tatters or as sheep; either way they appear to be "constellations, / slowly changing." Living half in the sky, all is orderly and interwoven. Beings are held in a "web of clan / and kin." The floating white spaces should remind us of the misty cloud-void seen in Chinese landscape scrolls. The "music" to be heard in this section is a rhythmical amalgam of cloud, air, water, sheep, slopes, greenness, and light—the wild harmony produced by the natural composure of a landscape and its inhabitants.

Snyder uses the same images in "Blue Mountains Constantly Walking," his essay on Dōgen's *Mountains and Waters Sūtra.* In that commentary the poet explains the circumstances behind "Arctic Midnight Twilight":

> One July walking down from the headwaters of the Koyukuk River in the Brooks Range of Alaska I found myself able to look into the realm of Dall (mountain) Sheep. The green cloudy tundra summer alps—in which I was a frail visitor—were the most hospitable they would ever be to a hairless primate. The long dark winters do not daunt the Dall Sheep, though—they do not even migrate down. . . . Dall Sheep (in Athapaskan called *dibee*) see mountains—Dōgen might say—"as a palace or pavilion." But that provisional phrase "palace

> or pavilion" is too high-class, urban, and human to really show how totally and uniquely *at home* each life-form must be in its own unique "buddha-field." (*Practice* 107–8)

Snyder's essay contains the opening lines of "Arctic Midnight Twilight" as an example of the unique "at-homeness," or "buddha-field," of the sheep. The poet disagrees with Dōgen's aristocratic and anthropomorphic images, but his point, and Dōgen's, remains clear: one must make the attempt to experience life with the perceptions of other beings. Dall sheep see their green slope mountains differently from humans. Both compassion and wisdom demand that humans should attempt to see such mountains from the homely perspective of Dall sheep. Reflecting on the harmony of their being-in-place, we may then see the need for coming to terms with our own sense of at-homeness. Snyder's point is that green summer slopes "call forth" the Dall sheep just as "[h]uckleberries and salmon call for bear." What then, as he asks in his essay, "sucks *our* [human] lineage into form?" His answer is "mountains and rivers without end," this very planet we live upon and with (*Practice* 109). Here, then, is a not-so-distant parallel between "Arctic Midnight Twilight" and Snyder's earlier section on being-at-home, "Three Worlds, Three Realms, Six Roads." Whether sheep or human, whatever life form one happens to be, we are the places we live in, especially when we live in harmony with those places. Dōgen's "midnight" appearance in "The Canyon Wren" provides a superficial link to the "midnight" twilight of the *dibée* poem, but the two sections—one a river and the other a mountain landscape—are connected far more profoundly by their emphasis on the harmonics of living in place.

Snyder is not alone in his observation of the Dall sheep's rapport with their setting. Dale Brown pointed out long ago that these sheep are so "at home" in their landscape that if a sheep crosses "valleys on its way from mountain to mountain, it chooses to walk on gravelly stream beds rather than on the grassy banks." He says the sheep "spring about on hoofs that are soft and concave at the center to provide traction on rocks" (Brown 126). This interaction of animal and landscape makes a striking parallel with Snyder's observation about "Mother *Bos*" in "With This Flesh," where he says "the hoof of the cow is a trace of the grasslands / —the print in the grass is the hoof of a cow." Following these sheep tracks along with Snyder, we are asked to perceive the floating world that the sheep experience—its green summer slopes, its "cliff-edge of life and death," and its dynamic cycling cloud processes—even as *the sheep themselves* experience it. Brown, who has followed such sheep trails, describes their world in identical terms:

> Where it is possible to walk on them at all, this is rather like traversing a steep roof, with talus slopes falling dizzily away on one side and rising precipitously on the other; but the reward is a sheeps'-eye view of the tundra. It is the kind of landscape that requires a deep breath to absorb. Valleys and mountains roll

> everywhere toward infinity. The carpet of vegetation washes up the slopes, stopping at the point where rockslides have fallen or where the brown, tan, red and ocher soil receives the full brunt of the wind. (126)

Alternating between a sheeps'-eye view and a human perspective, we also envision this Arctic realm in the entirety of both its vast magnitude and its smaller details. We find ourselves simultaneously in and out of the landscape, observer and participant once more. Here, "at the roof of the planet" where the globe's longitudinal lines gather to a common planetary point and the eerie midnight twilight of summertime glows with a light that is both day and night, both shadow and sun, we are in a landscape of magical possibilities. Like their pictorial representation in Chinese scrolls, the clouds that float among these peaks and valleys embody both substance and intangibility. In such places we discover yet again the significance of emptiness.

This land is, after all, the abode of the "*vajra*," or "diamond" sheep. (The journal publication of the poem calls them "diamond sheep.") In Buddhism the adjective automatically calls forth *The Diamond-Cutter Sūtra* (*Vajrachchedikā-Prajñāpāramita-Sūtra*), a treatise that depicts how "all phenomenal appearances are not ultimate reality but rather illusions, projections of one's own mind" ("Diamond Sūtra" *Shambhala Dictionary*). "Diamond," or "*vajra*," not only implies the act of cutting through illusion but becomes a metaphor for the "spotless purity and translucency" of emptiness, which is "untainted by all the appearances that arise out of it"; it conveys the meaning of "indestructible," or "adamantine," because it is at the heart of all existence. It is a symbol of "true reality": "This emptiness . . . is not different from things, from all phenomena. It is one and identical with them. This cannot be conceptually 'understood' but can be experienced in enlightenment" ("Vajra" *Shambhala Dictionary*). For Snyder, then, these "Vajra Sheep" are a vehicle for contemplating emptiness in a pure and direct manner. Meditating on the harmonious at-homeness of the sheep, the poet suggests that we may also merge with the actual experience of the sheep. Following their trails provides a discovery of their "hidden / sheltered beds." Smelling the "[s]weet rank smell" of these "sheep dreaming place[s]" is enough to make "the heart beat." Would that humans too should be so at-home. In this way one vividly comprehends the cyclic planetary rhythms of another being. Moving outward from human time to the experience of "[s]heep time" is a means to interacting with all beings "[a]ll over the world."

As if reenacting Hamlet's meditation on Yorick's skull, the narrator invites us to contemplate a "sheepskull forehead with its horn prongs / sitting on a boulder." Concentrating on its "emptiness of intelligence," we find nothingness in this singular skull, yet the bony skeleton, like a cow's hoof formed by the grasslands on which it has walked, is the product of untold numbers of sheep lives that, on these slopes, have nibbled "forbs." Metaphorically this skull is a blossoming "flower" that commemorates the ongoing process of sheep having lived in this place. We hold the skull in our hand, feel the sharpness of its prongs, feel the solidity of the boulder it rests on. Putting our experiences together we realize that "emptiness" cannot be perceived outside of "things." Recognition of "sheep impermanence, sheep practice, / sheep shapeshifting" is a step along the path toward enlightenment. A process, as tangible as it may be, is, by definition, dynamic and impermanent. To observe these sheep "hanging out" on their ledges, chasing each other, "napping" or "scratching"; to examine the detritus of their "[p]ellet piles in moss"; to contemplate a "spiral horn in the grass" is to experience the endlessly flowing, rock-hard stability of persistent life cycles. These activities, Snyder suggests, compose the at-homeness of the sheep. They are in their place; it is their history.

Like "The Canyon Wren" before it, "Arctic Midnight Twilight" acknowledges a "history of place" that exhibits sameness—like bird song or flower smell—in the midst of thousands of years of change (Snyder, "Voice" 10). Although we follow the sheep of "Arctic Midnight Twilight" in great detail and can even count their specific numbers as we watch from a distance—here are three, there are six, or sometimes thirty-one—we also know that these individual beings are repeating ancient processes, tracing Paleolithic pathways, fulfilling prototypical patterns, so much so that their lives are perceived as forms: dots, constellations, spirals, slopes, circles, tangents, slants, and peaks. We find their new, age-old "hidden / sheltered beds," and experience the "[s]weet rank smell" so deeply that it "makes the heart beat," yet another reference that goes beyond the rhythms of the heart muscle to the enlightening mystery of the *Heart Sūtra:* form is emptiness; emptiness is form. A sacred place, this is a "sheep dreaming place" both in and out of time. As Snyder says: "12,000 years of history. That smell hasn't changed" ("Voice" 10). If sheep time is "in time," it should be reckoned with the time of the glaciers as part of planetary time "[a]ll over the world." Both sheep and glaciers leave a trace on the surface of the globe. The cosmic network has many pathways besides the human track that may be followed.

In this place we will hear—as the wild sheep do—"[t]he beat of her unseen feet." "Her"? By now most readers of *Mountains and Rivers* should be attuned to the entrance of a goddess. The encounters reverberate among the differing landscapes, becoming more frequent the further we move into the poem. In part III, we find her lying "Under the Hills Near the Morava River" among the bones of the mammoth, reindeer, and wolf. Tārā awaits us on the high Tibetan Plateau. "The Bear Mother" approaches amid the "gullies and folds" of Alaskan mountains with her gift of blueberries. In the tropical jungles of southern Taiwan, a mother macaque will leap from branch to branch crossing the sky realm before us as if she were the Milky Way, the "mother of the heavens." Yet the "her" of "Arctic Midnight Twilight," while clearly associated with a landscape, is not revealed as clearly as other emanations of the shape-shifting Goddess. Connecting "[t]he beat of her unseen feet" with the earlier line "by the midnight breezes strewn" will lead readers to Percy Bysshe Shelley's "The Cloud," an eighty-four-line poem in six stanzas. There we find the context for the two quoted lines, and discover a clear identification for "her":

> That orbèd maiden with white fire laden,
> Whom mortals call the Moon
> Glides glimmering o'er my fleece-like floor,
> *By the midnight breezes strewn*
> And wherever *the beat of her unseen feet,*
> Which only the angels hear,
> May have broken the woof of my tent's thin roof,
> The stars peep behind her and peer
> And I laugh to see them whirl and flee,
> Like a swarm of golden bees,
> When I widen the rent in my wind-built tent,
> Till the calm rivers, lakes, and seas,
> Like strips of the sky fallen through me on high,
> Are each paved with the moon and these.
> (my emphasis)

The personified "I" of Shelley's poem is a fleecy cloud bank spread out across a shining midnight sky. The "her" whose "unseen feet" glide rhythmically across the midnight sky is "that orbèd maiden" called the "Moon" whose white fiery light breaks though the clouds wherever the breezes have parted them. Snyder uses other bits of Shelley's poem. His "roof" of the planet echoes Shelley's "my tent's thin roof," and his "rips in the wind-built tent" is clearly parallel with "rent in my wind-built tent." This moon goddess appears in many sections of *Mountains and Rivers.* "Arctic Midnight Twilight" may reveal how phases and cycles of the moon influence cycles of growth on earth, but it also depicts another moment of Buddhist enlightenment. Here, on these cloud-driven, shining, midnight peaks of the Brooks Range, among these ethereal, yet absolutely commonplace, sheep, the poet hears the sound of the The Goddess's feet. As in the lyrics from "San Antonio Rose," alluded to in "The Blue Sky," here indeed is strange enchantment found in another moonlit mountain pass, a love song sung to the moon in all its "splendor."

It is misleading, however, to suggest that Snyder's focus is on the moon in this section. Shelley's poem is, after all, entitled "The Cloud," and Snyder's emphasis is much more clearly on breezes and clouds, on "gulfs of air," and "floods of rising, falling, / warmer, cooler, air-mass swirls / like the curls / of Dall sheep horns." One may follow the trail of the sheep or the recognizable trace of liquid vapor and water cycles. Both Snyder and the sheep utilize the water; the poet's tea comes from the icepack; the sheep's grass is watered by the dew created when the clouds blow south through the passes. Similarly, one hears the Bear Mother, her mouth full of blueberries, nodding her head: "we share."

We approach the end of the poem amid contrarieties: "the trail crosses over and heads down a glacier, / tracks fade in the snow." The lines present a visual analogue to the sound of a Nō flute subsiding into silence. Having built his vision out of the blowing cloud whiteness, Snyder will unbuild it again, reminding us of Milarepa who built and unbuilt stone houses on his path to enlightenment. Snyder has followed the sheep to a point where, at the base of a "knife ridge," on a "cliff-edge of life and death / over endless mountains," he arrives at a cutting point, a *vajra* moment. From here "the trail crosses over and heads down." Ahead the "tracks" of the sheep "fade in the snow" . . . beyond. Snyder rests among the rocks; he will then "arise to descend."

Readers are left with a Koyukon riddle, a "song" proposed by a Dall sheep (*dibée*). Like a Zen kōan, the riddle clearly challenges the validity of the ego ("who am I?") and wrestles with the mystery of oneness beyond duality, the enlightenment that comes with the interpenetration of *shūnyatā* and *tathata*. The riddle, originally composed by Ten'a people of Alaska, reflects Snyder's physical position and mental condition on the edge. As translated by Julius Jetté, the full riddle is explained in the following manner:

> Riddle me: on the top of my head the snow has fallen in two mounds; or, the hair is parted in two. —The mountain-sheep; the head of the mountain-sheep.
>
> On the mountain-sheep's head the hair is naturally parted in the middle, hanging on both sides, and leaving a strip of bare skin between the two bunches. Being white, the hair is naturally compared to snow. (Jetté 193–94)

One head with two mounds of woolly white hair on either side of the strip of bare skin? Or two kinds of whiteness: one woolly fur and the other snow? Or two beings: Snyder the human and *dibée* the Dall sheep? Or the at-homeness of the sheep on its green summer slopes juxtaposed with the discord of human habitation among their mountains and rivers? The riddle also conveys a statement of impending ecological anguish for the sheep. Father Jetté continues:

> This riddle is now current among the people of the Koyukuk river, in whose hunting grounds the big-horn is not to be found. As the riddles are generally not imported from one tribe into another, even when their object is equally familiar to both, it would seem probable that the habitat of the big-horn formerly extended to the westward as far as the Koyukuk river, and that this riddle antedates their disappearance from the tract of country lying between the Koyukuk and Chandlar rivers. (194)

The riddle, we find, speaks of a species whose "tracks" have indeed faded in the snow of the Koyukon region. Their range, which once included this area, no longer does.

These are truly visionary sheep, veritable "ghost sheep" who body forth a new world order. Similar sheep have already whispered to the poet in "The Hump-backed Flute Player."

Like kōans, riddles are often proposed for the purpose of contemplating the nature of reality. Since, for a Zen adept "the tea-room [is] an oasis in the dreary waste of existence where weary travelers . . . meet to drink from the common spring of art-appreciation" (Kakuzo 43–44), perhaps we should accept the poet's offer, given at the beginning of the section, and have a cup of tea while we ponder our response to this blossoming sheep skull.

UNDER THE HILLS NEAR THE MORAVA RIVER

Reminiscent of "Old Bones" from part I, the small section titled "Under the Hills Near the Morava River" takes its inspiration from an archaeological discovery of a unique Upper Paleolithic burial site in Dolni Vestonice, a site where several well-known Upper Paleolithic "goddess" figurines were once uncovered. Snyder tells us the figures described in his poem are based on "excavations by Bohuslav Klima at the Dolni Vestonice site in the Pavlovske Kopce hills of southern Moravia (Czech Republic)" (*MRWE* 161). Although others had already reported on the discovery, in 1988 it was described in English by Paul G. Bahn:

> On 13 August 1986 . . . a remarkable triple burial was found. . . . The skeletons were in a shallow pit, in an extended position, side by side, with their heads towards the south. All three were young, between 16 and 23 years of age. The youngest, lying supine in the centre (DV XV), was very gracile; this fact, together with pelvic shape, points to a female. On her left was a big robust skeleton (DV XIV, a male) lying on its stomach, with its head turned away to the west; its left arm covered the female's hand, as if holding her. On her right was a smaller robust specimen (DV XIII) lying on its left side and facing the female; both of its arms touched her pelvis. . . . [T]he red crust around their frontals contained the remains of "diadems" of wolf and fox teeth and small ivory beads. . . . There was also a considerable concentration of ochre under the female's pelvis and between her thighs. The pit contained a few small fragments of animal bone (reindeer and wolf), some flint flakes, an engraved pebble and a cluster of unperforated shells. (302)

The find was dated from carbonized wood fragments that produced a radiocarbon date of "26,640 ± 110 years BP (before the present)" (302). Deformation in the bones of the female suggest to the archaeologists that she may have had "rickets or encephalitis at a very early age"; the "fragment of burnt reindeer pelvis" found in her mouth may have been a "clamp to bite on during times of great pain as it has traces of scratches and pressure" (302). Considering the near exact verbal parallels between the poem and the article, it is abundantly clear that Snyder's section is a found poem based on Bahn's report of the burials.

There is some significance in the eastern European setting of the section; it is, after all, one of only a handful of sections that mention a European location. The headwaters of the Morava River are in the mountains that separate the Polish plain from the Czech highlands. On the northern slopes of these mountains the Odra River flows to the North Sea, while the Morava issues forth from the southern slopes to merge, just east of Vienna, with the Danube, which in turn ultimately joins the Black Sea. Geographically the Morava functions as part of an ancient route called the "Moravian corridor" that passed between northern and southern Europe, a pathway that conceivably extended into both Mediterranean and Middle Eastern lands. In this fashion one may see a resemblance between this river and the ice-free Mackenzie River corridor that Snyder alludes to in the "The Hump-backed Flute Player."

It is far more likely that the section's significance is linked in Snyder's mind to its location in time, rather than to its geography. During a reading of selected sections from *Mountains and Rivers* given at the Library of Congress in October of 1996, Snyder referred to the "she" in this section as a "Paleolithic Kali." Yet, old as she may be, her bones are still with us in the same way that the sheep skulls of "Arctic Midnight Twilight" are with us, both instant reminders of the ongoing passage of history from the time of the glaciers. Although the poet, following the carbon date recorded in Bahn's essay, gives her age as some "26,640 plus or minus 110 years before 'now,'" this goddess figure is as real to Snyder "now" as she might have been "then." She belongs to dreamtime, a time beyond historical time, a fact made obvious by Snyder's ironic use of quotation marks around the word "now." Following Dōgen's thought in "Painting of a Rice Cake," these bony shapes provide us with a tangible reality that exists beyond any limiting specific time frame. Similarly, a rice cake is both real and painted, and an unrolling landscape scroll bodies forth an actuality that both is and is not the veritable reality of misty peaks and falling watercourses.

Even before the language of cave painting, adornment of the body signified the power of human expression. Although this nearly 27,000-year-old female is considerably younger than the earliest cave paintings, her decorative fox teeth, ocher, and reindeer pelvis bone bits invite the reader to consider the nature of prehistoric nonverbal artistic and ritual impulses. The spell cast by this female form appears ominous. By focusing on the centrality of the female in the entire picture, Snyder diminishes the role of the two males. Six of the seven lines of the section are devoted to her; the males are merely the "[b]ones of two men lying by her, / one each side." Snyder does not point out that "the remains of 'diadems' of wolf and fox teeth and small ivory beads" were found in the red-crusted frontals of all three figures. Without reference to Bahn's article we imagine only a crowned female—her forehead ringed with a "[d]iadem of fox teeth"—who, by the "[o]cher under her hips," is enigmatically connected with the allure of sexual passion and the mystery of giving birth. Snyder does not overtly connect her with destructive capabilities, nor does he mention Bahn's hypothesis that perhaps "these two apparently healthy and powerful men met violent deaths, perhaps sacrificed to accompany the dead female" (303). Overall, the images of the section remain ambiguous. Is she a central figure, or should they be considered as a triplet? Have these two men been sacrificed to or for her, or should they be seen as her protectors? Hindu Shaktism, the worship of Kali in her many aspects, allows both answers, among others:

> Shyama-Kali (the Black One) . . . is the Dispenser of boons and the Dispeller of fear. People worship Raksha-Kali, the Protectress. . . . Shmashana-Kali [Kali of the Burning Ground] is the embodiment of the power of destruction. (Campbell, *Oriental* 165)

However, given Snyder's emphasis on her singular foxtooth crown and her encirclement by mammoth, reindeer, and wolf bones, this woman is less a Kali figure than an emblem of the Goddess of Wild Animals, a figure the Greeks associated with Artemis. In addition to being seen as a protector of wild animals, Artemis is linked with the hunt itself, wild vegetation, chastity and childbirth, dancing nymphs, and a tree cult. She was worshipped in Crete, and "many scholars have held that Artemis was originally a mother goddess, descended from a Cretan Mother of the Mountains similar to the Asian Magna Mater" ("Artemis" *Encyclopaedia Britannica*). Mircea Eliade points out that her names in other languages include "Cybele" in Thrace and "Ma" in Cappadocia (Eliade I: 279). While the orgiastic personality of Artemis seems distant from the maternal figure who speaks in Snyder's "Mā," it is worth pointing out that the mother in that poem insists that she "can shoot. / I killed several rabbits in my garden." No stranger to Snyder, Artemis is addressed directly by him in "Earrings Dangling and Miles of Desert." She is "the least civilized of all the Greek goddesses" and her lineage is the oldest, reflecting

> backwards into the ancient time before the cultivation of land and the construction of cities. To a twentieth century sensibility, she embodies a wisdom that has been largely lost, both of outer nature and of that untamed animal region of human nature, and of the necessary relation between them. (Baring and Cashford 323)

Comparable to the portrayal of a multivalent Kali, Artemis is paradoxically both goddess of the hunt and protector of the animals, both "hunted and huntress." The ambiguity is explained by Baring and Cashford:

> [I]f both hunted animal and the person who hunts it are under the protection of the goddess—or, at a deeper level, are two aspects of the goddess herself as two necessary dimensions of life—then the sacred order cannot be truly violated. It is ultimately she who gives and she who takes away. (324)

Similarly, just as the powdery ocher under the skeleton's hips may indicate both her sexuality and fertility, so Artemis was extolled both as a goddess of unmarried girls and of mothers in childbirth. The fact that "young girls danced to Artemis as bears, wearing masks of bears on their faces and costumes of bears on their bodies," links her with Snyder's nurturing "Bear Mother," yet she was equally well known as a figure who required blood to be sacrificed to her (326–27). As a virgin, Artemis personified the new moon, reminding us of "New Moon Tongue." Her dark aspect—"the underworldly being she might become if she were offended and withdrew her light"—is identified with Hecate, the dark moon. Notably, we witness just such a withdrawal of light in Snyder's section "The Dance" when Amaterasu, the mythological Japanese sun goddess, withdraws into her cave after her brother insults her. Coming full circle, we learn from Baring and Cashford that some depictions of Hecate are reminiscent of the Hindu goddess Kali (328). Snyder's own fascination with Artemis can be seen in early letters and poems. Writing to Whalen in 1957 from the *Sappa Creek*, he mentions her, under her Roman name of Diana, as part of his general enchantment with the ancient Middle East:

> All Xmas Eve & Day prowling Byzantium—Hagia Sophia the uttermost & beyond which O of religious interior building. Got drunk in Pera & caught a bus in Chalcedon; touched a marble pillar taken from the temple of Diana at Ephesus; now at port in Sea of Marmara at Izmit, anciently Nicomedia. I can't bear it! Snow on the hills about; white spire minarets of isolated mountain mosques. . . . G. (26 Dec. [1957]. Reed–PWP).

The Temple of Artemis at Ephesus, one of the "Seven Wonders of the World," was "destroyed by invading Goths in A.D. 262 and was never rebuilt"; yet there are extant copies of a prominent statue of Artemis, depicted with what appear to be multiple breasts, that once stood there. Originally made of "gold, ebony, silver, and black stone, the legs and hips [were] covered by a garment decorated with reliefs of animals and bees and the top of the body festooned with breasts or eggs; her head was adorned with a high-pillared headdresses" ("Artemis, Temple of" *Encyclopaedia Britannica*). The "many-breastedness" of the statue is striking, an imagistic detail that Snyder surely connects with the overt naked-breastedness of Hindu (Pārvāti) and Tibetan (Tārā) goddesses mentioned in *Mountains and Rivers*. In the "Kali" section of Snyder's *The Back Country* (1968), we find a short poem commemorating the sacred, yet destructive, aspect of this goddess:

Artemis,
Artemis,

so I saw you naked—
well GO and get your goddam'd
    virginity back

me, me,
I've got to feed my hounds.
("Artemis" 77)

The story of Artemis and Actaeon is taken to be another version of the encounter of The Goddess and her Son-Lover, a myth to be traced in the Isis-Osiris allusions of "Boat of a Million Years" and the implied marriage of bull-god and cow-goddess in "With This Flesh."

Like the Mountain Spirit on her peak, Artemis belongs to "remote, lonely places—the solitude of the forest, grove and mountain, the tumbling stream down the mountain side, the meadow with unpicked flowers, the rough, bare land far from the tilled husbandry of crops" (Baring and Cashford 321). She is a primary force in *Mountains and Rivers,* and "Under the Hills Near the Morava River" seems a proper locale for her. As insignificant as she appears to be, lying there, between the bones of two men, she nevertheless radiates the ambiguous and vigorous energy of mythical truth. As a literal embodiment of the "playful" practice of the wild, she is the one who gives and the one who takes away.

WALKING THE NEW YORK BEDROCK ALIVE IN THE SEA OF INFORMATION

Like "Night Song of the Los Angeles Basin," a similarly placed section in the middle of part II, "Walking the New York Bedrock" is a poem about experiencing the wild within the city. Linearly we have traversed two-thirds of a reader's pathway through *Mountains and Rivers.* Since our journey in Snyder's Nō play has brought us to the midpoint of the second *ha,* anyone familiar with the fractal rhythms of the Nō would expect a more extensive treatment of the theme as we return to its elaboration a second time, albeit in a different setting. And so it will be. We spiral around; our backward glance recognizes the similarity of these two sections, but we are about to experience a greater richness of detail, a more intense presentation of the wild-in-the-city theme, as we walk the times and spaces of Manhattan's bedrock with the narrator. Both sections catalog the plant and animal life within the urban environment, and both comment on cars, underground rivers, and the pretentious urbanity symbolized by cocktail foods such as "tidbit and wine" or "sushi" or shellfish ("ostracods"). Yet in contrast with the Los Angeles poem, a perceivable narrative thread exists in "Walking the New York Bedrock." Moreover, it appears to capture Snyder's illuminating moment of discovery that the city and the world of "nature" are not two things. One does not have to go to the mountain for enlightenment.

In a 1991 article John Whalen-Bridge points to a new "attitude of tolerance and good humor for America at its most urban" in "Walking the New York Bedrock," a stance he attributes to Snyder's reworking of "his theory of space and wildness in *Practice*" ("Spirit of Place" 123, 125). According to Whalen-Bridge, earlier poems, such as "Marin-an" from *The Back Country*, display a judgmental and dualistic attitude toward cities. Yet, "from a theoretical point of view, a Buddhist aesthetic of nonduality should not lead to a hostile approach to the concept of 'cities'" (125). If indeed "Walking the New York Bedrock" marks an acceptance of the city and a turning away from duality, it would be a celebratory poem of discovery for its composer as well as a model of instruction for attentive readers.

As published in *The Whole Earth Review*, the section was subdivided into five subsections. These internal divisions have not been maintained in the final version; yet, after the first set of introductory lines, readers can spot the subsequent divisions by Snyder's summative use of the words "Information" and "Economy" as in "Alive in the Sea of Information" or in the "Sea of Economy" or just "of Economy." With the rhythmical use of these phrases, the entire section appears to have been structured along the lines of musical harmony and cadence rather than logical division of subject matter. Many of its images overlap and repeat as if Snyder is not only providing a profusion of details about life in the city-wild but imitating the city's normal method for delivering information: a stream of jumbled bits-and-bites to be processed by the reader. Throughout the section, however, we follow the trail of the narrator who is "*walking on walking*" through this city that turns under and over him.

The first subsection might be entitled "wake up." Beginning with the speaker's literal awakening in the "[h]ot sun dapple" to a vision of trees, leaves, and green, we watch as he slides off the rock he has been napping on (or perhaps sitting in meditation on) and enters the living currents of New York City. Walking away from his motionless rock, perhaps in Riverside Park near Columbia University, and out of the "woods," he strides past a familiar squirrel and toward humanity and urbanity, a "[r]are" realm for him to explore, one that he has only "[s]een from a safe distance" before. As the humming of mantric sounds signal the opening of a ritual, so the energetic and ominous tones of the nearby city invade his mind: murmuring, howling, and vibrating. Ready to confront the city, dressed "fast and light" for anything that might happen, he leaps over the wall that has enclosed and protected him in his "natural" green park. With the first obstacle eliminated, he becomes one with "the migrating flow."

Bracketed by the lines "New York like a sea anemone / Wide and waving in the Sea of Economy" (*MRWE* 97) and "Anemone / colony / Alive, in the Sea of Information" (*MRWE* 98), the second subsection initiates a sea theme. With one stroke Snyder performs an amazing feat of metaphoric amalgamation. The entire city is bathed in liquid air as if it were underwater. The buildings become tentacles of a vast waving colony of sea anemones gripping the bedrock of the planet, interconnected by currents of energy and conduits of information. In order to see these structures as they are, Snyder empties them of their daily residents, "[c]adres of educated youth," sent out to enjoy the night life and good food after a day's work. Without humanity, the inner breath energy ("prana-subtle"), the "[h]eartbeat" of the buildings, may be discovered. The power comes from being "fired / Deep at the bottom." How deep? "[U]nder the basement" is Snyder's way of connecting the raw energy of the city buildings to the molten energy at the core of the planet. Fueled by coal and oil and constructed of earth's substances, these places of humming power, structures to be found in all modern cities, are merely a reshaping of planetary materials: "Glass, aluminum, aggregate gravel, / Iron. Stainless steel." Snyder notes the passage of time—and energy sources—by substituting heat- and power-monitoring computers for the men who formerly shoveled coal into basement boilers. Continuing the sea theme, he says these ex-fire-tenders were former merchant marine sailors who left the ships of the sea for these boatlike buildings on land. "Streams" of "keen-eyed" people with "[b]risk flesh" flow in and out and around. The women, most probably office workers, exhibit sexual energy as they are transformed into sensual primitives with "[d]elicate jiggle, rouge on the nipple, / kohl under the eyes." The vastness of this flowing space is captured in the statistic that sixty thousand people discharge their daily labors in just two buildings. Like a cosmic breath, energy pulses incessantly even as technologies and management teams come and go. As with Tibetan prayer flags flapping in the breeze, the wind ripples the banners of "Time" and "Life," a sign that Impermanence is everywhere. Flowing currents shift from being watery or airy to being lines of electricity or, even more broadly, of cultural and political power. So it is that Columbia University may be said to be the intellectual landlord of this colony in the Sea of Information. Its cerebral currents ripple throughout the city, like invisible pathways followed by bees, from its "honeycomb brain-buildings." This city, and all cities like it, is a live pulsating being awash in the sea of information that surrounds it. It thrives on the process of exchange itself.

The third subsection opens with a historical lesson in buying and selling:

> "Claus the Wild man"
> Lived mostly with Indians,
> Was there as a witness when the old lady
> "Karacapacomont"
> Sold the last bit of Washington Heights, 1701

Claus, also known as "Long Clause" (because he was tall) and "Claus the Indian Interpreter," was a member of the Reckgawawanc tribe, which was involved in several transactions between Europeans and tribal groups who lived in the area of Washington Heights. According to Reginald Bolton, who has compiled lists of native names from extensive study of deeds involving land sales in and around New York City in the seventeenth century, the "last appearance" of "*Clause de Wilt native Indian* (de

Wilt being literally 'the wild man')" on such a deed was "in . . . 1701, confirming to Van Cortlandt the last possession of the Reckgawawanc" (96). Bolton also lists under the "Squaws of the Weckquaesgeek" one "Karacapacomont" who "joined in the deed confirming the Van Cortlandt tract in the northwestern part of the Bronx in 1701" (122). It is, of course, typical of Snyder to present the history of a place; research is one way to know the spirit of any place. In this particular happening in the "sea of economy," the poet's melancholic tone is apparent; merely listing these details of sale is one more example of the European displacement of native inhabitants. In addition, Snyder indicates that Claus was, perhaps, the last "wild man" in Washington Heights. Yet, like the deep rivers mentioned in the next lines of the poem—"[d]own deep grates hear the watercourse, / [r]ivers that never give up"—these economic "deeds" only appear to have disappeared. The true history of the Native American is very much alive in the psyche of the present power structure. Snyder also intends a literal river here. As in "Night Song of the Los Angles Basin," it is an image of the persistence of the watershed:

> The watershed is the first and last nation whose boundaries, though subtly shifting, are unarguable. . . . For the watershed, cities and dams are ephemeral and of no more account than a boulder that falls in the river or a landslide that temporarily alters the channel. The water will always be there, . . . in the larger picture that river [the Los Angeles River] is alive and well under the city streets. (*Place* 229, my brackets)

Shifting quickly away from river imagery, Snyder implants yet another perception of the city. A bird seen in the cityscape gives us its eyes, and a gap between buildings becomes a mountain gorge. We see from great height and distance as, for a moment, Snyder assaults our senses with the urban scene about us. As the speaker waits on a corner for the signal light to change, sounds caught in the street canyons echo in darkness; looking up the chasm he sees light from the sky cutting across the shadowy street in "[c]risscrossing . . . threads." This natural sound and light show is mingled with the squeal of automobile tires and the gleam of headlights. The images turn fantastic and ominous: "One growl shadow / in an egg of bright lights, / Lick of black on the tongue." Is this some wild dog in a corner, or have we seen a momentary glimpse of the fearsome black-tongued Kali lingering here in the shadows? Sirens echo, the light changes, and Snyder's alter ego looks again, this time toward the sky. He sees the false gods of commercial profit and culture arrayed before him in the shape of the buildings that house their combined energies. Corporation names like Equitable, hardly plain dealing, and Celanese, hardly "noble," ring with irony. These international capitalistic giants block out stock market shares; their tall buildings literally dole out patterns of the sunlight in the streets below. They utilize far more than their share of the sun's energy as they go about the business of processing information and materials. Snyder is not much kinder to the art barons, targeting the way they have bought and packaged the world's art for easier viewing. More a reminder that this assembled art is someone else's idea of what is tasteful, and that culture is based on commerce, Snyder's diatribe does not appear to be against art museums as such. Still, the unnaturalness of "water lilies," Monet's or anyone's, being seen under glass, signals a broadening of the imagery. Culture, it seems, has become a matter of drifting through room after room, passively observing rather than partaking or performing, as guards watch all our movements. Instead of these sterile rooms, culture should take place in "a nourishing habitat" (*Practice* 15). Once again outside, the city blends with nature as a helicopter mutates into a hummingbird. The image captures both poetic truth and scientific fact. Regardless of what sweet things they may transport, the whirling blades of the helicopter surely do dissipate pollen throughout the city air. The subsection ends rhythmically "[i]n the air / of the / Sea of Economy." Economics has indeed been the prime concern of these lines.

In subsection four we once again drop under the surface with the narrator's continuing walk through the city. We enter the subway, a network of underground tunnels alive with "spiderwebs, fungus, lichen," all blown by the wind. As Snyder has said, "wildness is . . . everywhere":

> ineradicable populations of fungi, moss, mold, yeasts, and such that surround and inhabit us. Deer mice on the back porch, deer bounding across the freeway, pigeons in the park, spiders in the corners. (*Practice* 14)

The spray painting and etched-in graffiti on the subway walls reminds Snyder of another kind of art, the pictographs and petroglyphs of prehistory. In someone's artificial attempt to bring nature into this dank modern cave, there is, perhaps, a potted ginkgo tree or two for ornament. The trees stand as a mute reminder of how plants travel the planet through space and time. Gondwanaland was the hypothetical continent of the Mesozoic era linking the southern continents of South America, Africa, India, and Australia. Either these trees are a long way from home or they have managed to make the entire planet their home. Once again on the surface, the speaker meditates on buildings now undergoing construction—without windows they cannot have souls—that will become "new, Big / city Gods." As in the second subsection, the network of water and wire conduits will ultimately activate them. Once energized they will become the minds of their workers as, some say, gods truly are. Playing off a reversal of Juliana of Norwich's mystical "cloud of unknowing," Snyder's building-gods exist in a "cloud of . . . knowing," that is, the exchange of information that takes place within their confines on a daily basis. The word "cloud" imputes a certain muddled manner of thinking to these processes. Still, like most higher beings, these godlike structures exist in the sky or in the air. In Snyder's special sense of air/sea currents, they also may be found in the "Sea / Of Information." The encounter with construction brings about its opposite. Cutting across several alleys and ducking under some trucks, the narrator confronts a sign that ironically says "Under Destruction." Newspaper headlines are written in roman letters, a fact of literacy that ensures both a historical and a partial view of the world, one that hearkens back to Rome and not, say, to Asia. The periodicals speak of "Economy." Is this merely a pun on reading about money in the *Wall Street Journal,* or has the narrator begun to think of "economy" as the true business of minding one's house without waste?

The opening lines of the final subsection remind one of the dreamlike visions recorded in "Journeys." In an "[e]mpty room" with "no walls," a "cellar" with "clear air," one is reminded of Buddhist emptiness and the meditative process of "going down" to "contentless ground." We hear the sound of a "Skilsaw" cutting bricks with its carbide blade. Is this construction for the new building gods? Or is our thought "under destruction." Is this Skilsaw the city's version of the Diamond Cutter? The bricks are shown in all their impermanence. Each brick is, in itself, a "rusty house bod[y]" containing the earth's materials, "cooked clay." In the millions, red or "rusty" bricks make a building, a house body, just bigger, now containing people and the processes of information and economy. In the heart of this city, "form is no other than emptiness, emptiness no other than form" (*Heart Sūtra*). The fixity of such buildings, and their practices and systems, wavers in the mind. They are real; they are illusion. While contemplating these sounds, and ideas, a "[b]lue-chested" female runs skillfully, like the Skilsaw's cutting edge, like a ray of illuminating light, between the lines of blocked city traffic. She, perhaps a glimpse of the turquoise Goddess in jogging outfit, flows beyond. The mind follows. One could escape this city for the wild—toward woods and rivers nearby—but there is no need. There is illumination in the city as well as the country. They are not two things. Wherever one is, one must inhabit the place, know it deeply, flow with it. Like the ginkgo tree in the subway, the wild peregrine hawk is "at home" on a ledge "at the thirty-fifth floor."

The narrator now has a final vision of the interpenetrating network of the city's "at homeness." Returning to the mountain imagery of previous lines, he speaks of street people with shopping-cart homes who look at rows of condominium apartment buildings as if they were sharp-edged ridges or ledges and buttresses to be attained. Those urban professionals who live at the higher-up levels are a picture of clean crisp whiteness, including their white skin. As we imagine a cocktail party we hear cascading laughter while shellfish and sushi appetizers are passed around. Finding "ostracods" on these "layered stratigraphy cliffs" reverses our perception. Land that was once under water rises as a range of hills or mountains; among the depositions of its layered cliffs, now bathed in the air, one will find traces of the ocean life that once teemed there. Recalling "Claus the Wild man," we remember that vast shell middens have been found in the soil of Manhattan, left behind by the Native Americans who inhabited the island before the Europeans. The current shifting relationship between the "street-bottom feeders" and those who "occupy sunnier niches / Higher up" seems to be a matter of the food chain at work among human beings. In this pecking order, those at home in the lower status "check out the air for the fall of excess, / . . . From the higher-up folks in the sky." The peregrine hawk, now at home on its city ledge, has "snapped up" the information it needs to survive; it feeds off the lower-down pigeons. Snyder's play with the word "condominium" indicates that these relationships are constantly shifting. As a matter of economics, or "household management," in this Sea of Economy, being "at home," in one's "domus," does not have to be a matter of dominion over others or even of becoming inured to the other's fate; the condition of "con domus," to live in harmony with others and with the place one calls home, is still a possibility. As John Whalen-Bridge puts it:

> The gap between the rich and the poor, between the bottom feeders on the street and the species in the high-rise condominium is not *accepted* in this poem, but the gap is understandable. A younger Snyder would have left out the humorous touches, the sushi, the photosynthesis and the cascading laughs.
>
> This sense of humor, this sense of gratitude for even the most oppressive elements of city life, has an important political effect. The voice of "Walking the New York Bedrock" is not intimidated by the dangers of the city, and so the satire is not the reflexive/defensive sort. . . . Thus, the city loses its "epic distance" and is cut down to size, to a habitable size. ("Spirit of Place" 130–31)

Acceptance, in the sense of an enlightened understanding of how things interconnect and interpenetrate, how they flow, is the basis for full living. Compassion and Emptiness go hand in hand. As the sun sets on the narrator's long ambulation through the city, even the glass faces of New York's buildings turn to "[s]oft liquid silver." Life among these storied buildings becomes stories to be told endlessly. Like fish swimming among anemones, humans float and feed in, drift in and out of, these foam and steel habitats. The very buildings waver like tentacles in the liquid that surrounds them. The bedrock is molten; the air is the sea. Bathed in the bits and bites of information, "Walking the New York Bedrock" reveals the wild diffused throughout the city.

> The lessons we learn from the wild become the etiquette of freedom. We can enjoy our humanity with its flashy brains and sexual buzz, its social cravings and stubborn tantrums, and take ourselves as no more and no less than another being in the Big Watershed. . . . No expectations,. alert and sufficient, grateful and careful, generous and direct. . . . The wild requires that we learn the terrain, nod to all the plants and animals and birds, ford the streams and cross the ridges, and tell a good story when we get back home. (*Practice* 24)

These are lessons to be learned, stories to be told, anywhere, even in New York City.

HAIDA GWAI NORTH COAST, NAIKOON BEACH, HIELLEN RIVER RAVEN CROAKS

> Earlier generations of Haida called their archipelago *Xhaaidlagha Gwaayaai or Xhaaidla Gwaayaai,* The Islands at the Boundary of the World. The shorter form, *Haida Gwaii,* which means The Islands of the People, is recent coinage, though the connection it names between the people and the place is ancient fact. This shortened form of the name has also been officially adopted by the Council of the Haida Nation and now is widely used. (Bringhurst 7)

In overt contrast, from the east coast of Turtle Island to its western outreaches, from Manhattan Island floating in its Sea of Information to the "Islands of the People" surrounded by the Pacific Ocean, from wild-in-the-city to wild-in-the-wild, the "Haida Gwai North Coast" section brings us to the region of one of Snyder's earliest influences. Jon Halper, writing of their visit to the Queen Charlotte Islands, gives the flavor of the site and something of its special meaning for Snyder:

> We were poking around Haida Gwaii, South Moresby, Lyell Island, in the Queen Charlottes, following the curve of islands, and had come to Skedans, a long-deserted Haida village. Skedans was, once, a place where longhouses and totem poles expressed *home* for human beings surrounded by the wealth of many other Beings. The wealth remains, but the people are gone. . . . We were visitors, come there to imagine and explore lightly. Gary and I were alone then, and at one point we kneeled in the wet beach grass, looking at a fallen cedar, Bear and Eagle discernible still [on the fallen totem pole], if one looked carefully, but their once bright edges blurred, slowly returning to soil and wind. There wasn't anything to say and we didn't. I realized how special this moment was for him, the *now* of a life lived strongly, following dreams and imaginings, journeys begun in a childhood far south of here in Puget Sound and pursued in studies of this actual place and its people when he attended Reed College. (Halper ix, my brackets)

As a young student at Reed College, his mind brimming with scholarship about the Haida, Snyder produced his imaginative and disciplined senior thesis, published years later as *He Who Hunted Birds in His Father's Village: The Dimensions of a Haida Myth.* It was a definitive step on the poetic and intellectual path he would follow for the rest of his life. In "Haida Gwai North Coast," albeit for different purposes, the poet revisits the physical landscape that went with that first stride.

Typically, Snyder has chosen the specific setting of his poem with great care. With dark rain forest standing behind it, this is Naikoon Beach where the Hiellen River meets the ocean at "Rose Point" or "Rose Spit." "Naikoon," the Haida name for Rose Point, means "Long Nose." Under the present circumstances of geography, this region is part of Naikoon Provincial Park, 179,000 acres of coastal wilderness along the northeast corner of Graham Island, the largest and most populous of the Queen Charlotte Islands, sometimes called the "Galapagos of the North" for their unique and plentiful wildlife. According to guidebooks the surf pounds the north coast incessantly; it is a place of sunshine and mist and storm clouds; tidal change and sand dunes and driftwood; seals, golden eagles, sea birds, and, of course, ravens. Inland is a "wildland of stunted pines, muskeg, meandering oxbow streams, meadows, and low flat-topped hills" (Landi 702). Watery junctures often function as significant poetic locales for Snyder: the holy doab of the Ganga and Yamuna mentioned in "The Hump-backed Flute Player"; in "Raven's Beak River," where the Tatshenshini River meets Alsek Lake; in "The Flowing," where the mouth of the universalized river spews forth into the ocean what it has collected in its descent.

Similarly, the Hiellen River discharges its "wash of inland / hard-won forest natural trash" into the ocean at this site on the north coast of Haida Gwai. However, Naikoon Beach is more than a mere dumping ground, it is a "sacred place." As Snyder himself has said:

> Certain places are perceived to be of high spiritual density because of plant or animal habitat intensities, or associations with legend, or connections with human totemic ancestry, or because of geomorphological anomaly, or some combination of qualities. These places are gates through which one can—it would be said—more easily be touched by a larger-than-human, larger-than-personal, view. (*Practice* 93)

In mythological time, on this same wild beach, Raven digs up a clamshell. Finding people inside its confines, he opens it and releases them. Thus Naikoon is a place of first emergence, a gateway for the Haida Nation as well as for one who would be "touched by a larger-than-human, larger-than-personal, view." Standing with the poet on the long nose, rose spit, with the surf crashing about us, we too may hear Raven croaking. Like those of other trickster figures, Raven's deeds are usually motivated by sheer mischievousness or by his selfish pursuit of pleasure or food. Nevertheless, his actions transform both himself and the world around him, bringing it closer to its present state. At times he seems human (male or female); at times he is all raven. He causes laughter as well as sorrow; he is capable of killing and resurrecting himself or other beings. A Pacific Northwest version of Coyote, this particular Trickster-Transformer has a reputation that extends well beyond the Haida; his stories are "shared by other societies along the north Pacific, from Siberia to Vancouver Island" (Boelscher 178). The raven (*Corvus corax*) "is both common and prominent along the Pacific Northwest Coast. Its heavy bill, black colour, and prominent wedge-shaped tail are its distinguishing features, along with its repertoire of calls, ranging from aggressive caws and mocking chuckles to eerie clucks. It is a carrion eater and omnivore" (Boelscher 178). "Haida Gwaii North Coast" certainly has its share of ravens; twelve of them sound off in the opening line of the section: "squawk, squork, crork." At the end of the section we will find two more, the carrion-eating "twa corbies" who "rork and flutter." Mythological or actual, the orderly disorder of the world of these raucous and disruptive ravens is an emblem of our present world. The entire section is a tangible example of chaos theory in action; everywhere we look or listen in this jumbled world there is unrelenting noise and kinesthetic conflict, yet everything is ultimately part of the routine of "Mother / Earth" who "loves to love."

In addition to the cacophony of the ravens, there are "[t]wo eagles squabbling" who "twitter" in their "meeting / bumping flying overhead." Where the Hiellen River meets the ocean, we find dark, murky, acidic water rolling toward a wall of "drumming" tidal surf. Punning on "eagerness," Snyder uses the unorthodox word "eagre" (from Old English *ēagor*, flood tide) in consort with the later "twa corbies," to build an atmosphere of a more primitive time. Above the sound of the surf, the assembled "wheeling birds"—the seagulls, ravens, and eagles—"make comment" about the sky, sea, seasons, and especially the "humpy salmon." The repetition of the word "comment" calls attention to itself. As a verb it means to "talk" or "gossip" or "remark" on something; as a noun referring to conversation it involves "personal reaction" or "personal attitude." In either case the phrase humanizes the conversational communication of the birds and fish; we overhear them speaking personally to one another. In Haida mythology animals regularly take on human form and humans take animal forms. Essentially the birds, with their minds on dinner, are remarking on the conditions necessary for the salmon to make their spawning run. The salmon, in the meantime, comment about the debris they will confront as they leave the "flot and jet of sea crud" to swim upstream against the "natural trash" flowing downriver. The same process that drives the salmon to overcome all obstacles by an urge to procreate will provide the birds with fish for dinner. Moreover, the obstacles perceived by the salmon are the detritus of a natural and ancient ongoing flushing process of materials from the "older wildness" and "climax lowland" fostered by the river's downstream flow.

Snyder's metaphor for these natural processes is bound up in the concepts of "climax" and "virgin system," phrases that explain why this section of *Mountains and Rivers* celebrates diversity, the necessity of the food chain, and an accepting attitude toward the preservation of wild systems. As Snyder explained in an important early interview:

> Every given natural region has a potential top situation where all of the plants that will grow there have grown up now and all of those that will push out something else have pushed out something else, and it reaches a point of stability. If you cut all the forests and you wait many hundreds of years, it'll come to something again. . . . This condition, called "climax," is an optimum condition of diversity—optimum stability. When a system reaches climax, it levels out for centuries or millennia. By virtue of its diversity it has the capacity to absorb

> all sorts of impacts. Insects, fungi, weather conditions come and go. . . . [A]lmost half the energy that flows in the system does not come from annual growth, it comes from the recycling of dead growth. . . . [T]here is a rich population of fungi, and beetles, and birds that feed on bugs, and predators that feed on birds that feed on bugs that eat the rotten wood; you've then achieved the maximum optimal biomass (actual quantity of living beings) in one place. This is also what is called "maturity." By some oddity in the language it's also what we call a virgin forest, although it's actually very experienced, wise and mature. Margalef, a Spanish ecologist, theoretician, genius, has suggested that the evolution of species flows in line with the tendency of systems to reach climax. ("*East West* Interview," *Real Work* 115–16)

In the offhand juxtaposition of words like "virgin" and "climax," there are poetic echoes of Artemis, the wise virginal Lady of the Forest. More to the point is the concept that optimum stability for the planet depends heavily on diversity and the recycling of dead material. All of which explains Snyder's reference at the end of the poem to the "twa corbies" who are apparently croaking over "the old food / the new food." A well-known Scottish border ballad, "The Twa Corbies" serves as a counterpart to an equally well-known version of the same events entitled "The Three Ravens." The latter poem tells the story of a dead knight's faithful hounds, hawks, and sweetheart who protect his dead body from being eaten by the three ravens for breakfast. The former poem, Snyder's reference, reverses the situation; the knight's hound, hawks, and lady fair are all busy elsewhere, allowing the "twa corbies" to "mak our dinner sweet."

> Ye'll sit on his white hause-bane,
> And I'll pike out his bonny blue een
> Wi ae lock o his gowden hair
> We'll theek our es when it grows bare.
> (Sargent and Kittredge 45)

Acknowledging our place in the food chain, that every being is intended to be utilized, if not directly eaten, by some other being, is to accept the existence of apparent chaos—the "flot and jet of sea crud," the "tangled" nature of seasonal "fall flood streams"—as the pattern of our present world. It is a situation mythologized in the stories of changes brought about by the Trickster-Transformer's selfishness, curiosity, and desire. Raven's croaking is the voice of a natural wildness; it calls forth the free and natural side of living on this planet:

> Love hard, playing, fighting,
> rough and rowdy love-rassling
> she can take it, she gives it,
>
> kissing, pounding, laughing—

These lines are not a call to abuse the earth or, for that matter, to be abused by her; rather, they sing a song of acceptance and confidence in the diversity of forces that exist beyond the arrogance of human intent and assumed superiority. It is a song of freedom:

> To be truly free one must take on the basic conditions as they are—painful, impermanent, open, imperfect—and then be grateful for impermanence and the freedom it grants us. For in a fixed universe there would be no freedom. . . . The world is nature, and in the long run inevitably wild, because the wild, as the process and essence of nature, is also an ordering of impermanence. (*Practice* 5)

For all our lamenting over the fate of the world and our attempts to regulate its direction, the planet will survive long after the human species has passed on. Snyder continually encourages dedicated personal involvement in matters of the environment, but his allegiance to the Buddhist teaching of impermanence leads him to accept imperfection and confusion as part of our existence. Accordingly, he says "we can be long-run optimists even if we are short-run pessimists. The universe can take care of itself. We can't save the universe, and we can't do it much damage either" (Snyder, "When Life Starts" 71). Readers should recall Snyder's jovial cynicism toward Teilhard de Chardin's notion that we humans should "seize the tiller of the planet" ("Boat of a Million Years"). In Snyder's view, we may be passengers on the boat and we might even have an occasional turn at the wheel as pilot, but we are certainly not its captain. More to the point would be for us to learn to love the sometimes smooth, sometimes wild, ride as we "wobble and slide over roils of water" ("The Canyon Wren").

NEW MOON TONGUE

As if singing his way up and down the scale of some mountain peak, Snyder climbs from the brief understated "Under the Hills Near the Morava River" to walk on an elevated plateau in "Walking the New York Bedrock." Written in an entirely different mode, the midlength "Haida Gwai North Coast" maintains a lyrical intensity until it reaches closure in its final lines. We then return, in the seven-line section "New Moon Tongue," to a quieter mode. With the lengthy and complex "An Offering for Tārā" still to come, the momentary change in rhythm and duration of "New Moon Tongue" gives it the feel of a brief interlude, as if it were between phases of the moon itself. To be short, however, does not mean to be flat or insignificant. This tiny section picks up echoes of earlier sections and distills several important ideas found in *Mountains and Rivers Without End.*

We may, for example, recall the lovelorn Texas cowboy from "The Blue Sky" literally mooning over his lost Rose of San Antone. Standing in a mountain pass of our imagination, he looks into the moonlit night sky, one similar to the "[b]lue eve" in "New Moon Tongue," and is struck by the "enchantment" he feels "as strange as /

the Blue up above." Then again we may hear the "[o]wl / calls" associated with the "late-rising moon" that hangs over the setting of "Night Song of the Los Angeles Basin." The resulting overlay of owl and moon implies a horned, or crescent, moon such as the one that we infer in "New Moon Tongue." Whether we focus on the owl or the moon, the image remains that of watchful waiting, primitive and prehuman. In the magical landscape of "Arctic Midnight Twilight," where sheep are at home on their green summer slopes, the only sound heard is that of the "unseen feet" of the moon, a vigilant goddess ambling among the clouds of the midnight sky. In each of these cases, whether in the city or in nature, the moon provides a pervading ethereal atmosphere that hints at a wild world beyond the one humans ordinarily inhabit.

Snyder's moon is a "new moon," a detail that instantly implies the dynamic change of the moon's phases and the symbolism associated with it: growth and the waxing moon; the completeness and totality of the full moon; loss and the waning moon; the darkness of the moon's invisible phase; and the sense of a "resurgence of new life" with the "reappearance of the crescent moon" (Baring and Cashford 19). The horned crescent moon brings forth a wealth of associations. In this "[f]aint new moon arc, curl" we will see the shape of Artemis, Lady of the Animals, who, in her virginal aspect, personifies the new moon. Given that the poem takes place in a "deer-moving dusk," her presence in this setting is assured. Yet knowing Snyder's predilection for the Paleolithic, we may remember a host of goddess figures linked with the moon: "As the great light shining in the darkness of the night, the moon, in all mythologies up to the Iron Age (c. 1250 B.C.), was regarded as one of the supreme images of The Goddess, the unifying power of the Mother of All" (Baring and Cashford 21). Few figures were more appropriately tied to the new moon than the 20,000-year-old "Venus of Laussel":

> Over a rock shelter in Laussel in the Dordogne, only a few miles from the great cave at Lascaux . . . , the figure of a woman 17 inches (43 cm) tall once gazed out over the valley. . . . Palaeolithic sculptors chiselled her out of limestone with tools of flint, and gave her to hold in her right hand a bison's horn, crescent-shaped like the moon, notched with the thirteen days of the waxing moon and the thirteen months of the lunar year. With her left hand she points to her swelling womb. Her head is tilted toward the crescent moon, drawing a curve of relationship from her fingers on the womb up though the incline of her head to the crescent horn in her hand, so creating a connection between the waxing phase of the moon and the fecundity of the human womb. In this way the pattern of relationship between the earthly and the heavenly orders is acknowledged. (Baring and Cashford 6)

Woman, animal, crescent moon, and fecundity are all linked in a single stone sculpture, a haunting cluster of relationships that calls forth the mystery of human imagining. To this day the moon's ancient magic invades our minds in the form of folkloric fantasies: we continue to associate the moon with lovers, whose passionate obsession may change them into lunatics or, more sweetly, honeymooners; some men are believed to become half-human werewolves when the moon is full. "New Moon Tongue," however, does not manifest human forms to be seen or heard. The deer move quietly in the "[b]lue eve"; the "plant-realm" thrives in the "[p]urple shade." The "million years" of "sniffs, / licks, lip and / reaching tongue" seem far more suitable to the prehuman plant and animal world. In that sense, the section is a celebration of fecundity itself, wherever it may have been found. As if it were an act of planetary *yab-yum,* this omnipresent licking phallic tongue reaches into the lip of a yonic new moon eternally. It was so in the beginning; it is so in the present.

As is often the case, Gary Snyder is best at elucidating his own poetry. In a foreword he wrote for *Mirror for the Moon,* William LaFleur's translations of Saigyō's poems, he commented extensively on the meaning of moonlight, both for Buddhists and for all beings who live under the moon's influence:

> Moonlight has been pouring down on this planet for billions of years, and for all us beings tuned to—nay, fed by—the energy of the sun, the light of the moon has long been an odd and unsettling force. We have it inside us, like sea-water and calcium, a cool light that is always in motion, but stable and recurrent in its changes. The full moon has long been a Buddhist symbol of the Tathagata—of perfect and complete enlightenment. Even enlightenment may be understood as just a fine high phase in a cycle—who does not also love the sight of the new crescent moon in a lavender sunset sky? ("Energy from the Moon," *Place* 118)

Clearly Snyder's "lavender sunset sky" in this essay connects with the "[p]urple shade in a plant-realm" that he writes of in "New Moon Tongue." Indeed, among other comments about Saigyō's poems and LaFleur's translations, Snyder says that "the flowers of flowering plants coevolved with insects and are beautiful and sweet-scented for them, not for human beings" (*Place* 118). Similarly, "New Moon Tongue" does not describe a world for humans or even one to be seen from a human vantage point. This short poem is written for plants and animals in their own realms and on equal footing with the human realm. Since all beings may be "heard," all beings "speak" in some fashion. All have tongues; all are embraced by the moon.

AN OFFERING FOR TĀRĀ

"An Offering for Tārā" brings us to a point of utmost importance in *Mountains and Rivers Without End.* Structurally it is at the apex of a crescendo of sections that make up part III. Remembering the *jo-ha-kyū* principle, the nine sections of part I, taken together, make up the *jo,* or introductory unit, of the complete *Mountains and Rivers Without End.* The sections of parts II and III contribute to the developing, or *ha,* rhythms, and the complexity and intensity of the sections in part III are noticeably more elaborate than those of part II. With part IV we will begin the *kyū*, or "fast close," segment for the entire poem. Within part III we move forward from its ritualistic introductory *jo* section, "The Circumambulation of Mt. Tamalpais," through increasingly more intricate pulses of energetic poetry—"The Canyon Wren," "Arctic Midnight Twilight," "Walking the New York Bedrock"—until we reach a point of climax in "An Offering for Tārā." After "An Offering for Tārā," part III closes quickly with two intense, if shorter, sections: "The Bear Mother" and "Macaques in the Sky." The "Tārā" poem is parallel with, and prefigures, "The Mountain Spirit," the climactic section of both part IV and the entire long poem; each is the eighth poem within its unit. In fact, both the Tibetan Tārā and the Japanese Yamamba are "mountain spirits"; together they are two of the most important feminine figures in *Mountains and Rivers.* Yet any named goddess of Snyder's meditations is an incarnation of a greater nongendered mystery, a shimmering veil that will never be lifted entirely. The best one can do, he suggests, is to be attentive and to show respect. Hence, at this meaningful moment in the long poem, we have a *puja,* an offering, for Tārā.

To experience the full impact of *Mountains and Rivers,* readers must comprehend Tārā's role. In his notes for the long poem, Snyder tells us that "Tārā, 'She Who Brings Across,' is a female Buddha of both Compassion and Wisdom. She is one of the most revered figures in Buddhism, especially in Tibet, Mongolia, and Nepal" (*MRWE* 162). Her centrality to Snyder's long poem becomes evident if one links her to other goddess figures. In the shimmering mirrors of "Bubbs Creek Haircut," the world's fixity and permanence is discovered to be an illusion, most often experienced in the form of dualities. The goddess Māyā is not only the mother or fountainhead of illusion in the world, she also embodies its dynamic nature, its impermanence, the interconnectedness or web of all things. Similarly Pārvāti's flowing dance eternally entrances Shiva, the mat-haired mountain god, luring him from his sitting position. In gendered and sexual terms, this duality of spiraling and rootedness is a feminine river that coils about a masculine mountain peak in an eternal Tantric entwining, an ecstatic sexual embrace that goes on "without end," in an act designed to dissolve or go beyond duality even while acknowledging the reality of its dyadic nature. In whatever guise she appears, even when the "dance" becomes a horrific encounter with Kali, The Goddess brings about change and incarnates movement itself; she is, in other words, "the flowing." A crucial first step on the road to becoming an enlightened being, that is, one who has "reached the other shore" beyond dualities, is a realization that we live in and are part of a flowing, dynamic, illusory world. This is true wisdom, the knowledge represented by yet another goddess, Prajñāpāramitā ("Wisdom That Reaches the Other Shore"), herself a symbol of the collected Mahāyāna wisdom sūtras. When Snyder says that Tārā "brings [us] across" he points to her aspect as a "savior," a goddess of wisdom. Tārā proffers the ability to recognize the impermanence (illusion) of all things, a recognition of the very heart of the *Heart Sū-*

tra: "form is emptiness, emptiness is form." These words are spoken by the gender-shifting god/goddess Avalokiteshvara, out of whose tears of compassion Tārā is said to have arisen. This chain of reasoning results in the understanding that, as Snyder told his graduate class, "the Goddess who is nature and illusion is ALSO the Goddess who liberates us from herself, and in doing so both she and we are transformed—into the presence of an enlightened universe" (Snyder "onward"). As lover the Goddess engenders the spark of worldly creation, as mother she nurtures the created world, as savior she works to enable all beings to accept the wisdom that transforms the world. Tārā is the authentic heart of *Mountains and Rivers.*

"An Offering for Tārā" focuses on the concept of a *puja,* an exchange of gifts, or "potluck," as Snyder calls it in the third part of the section. At a potluck supper everyone brings a dish for everyone else; everyone eats from someone else's dish. Expanding the metaphor reminds us that we bring ourselves to the table as part of the repast, that all beings eat and are eaten at this banquet. In fact, Snyder's metaphoric *puja* becomes a token for his thinking about the food chain, which, in turn, is a specific illustration of his fundamental reasoning about the interdependent exchange of energy on the planet.

> A key transaction in natural systems is energy-exchange, which means the food-chains and the food-webs, which means that many living beings live by eating other beings. Our bodies—or the energy they represent—are thus continually being passed around. We are all guests at the feast, and we are also the meal! All of biological nature can be seen as an enormous puja (ceremonial food offering). (Snyder, "Village Council" 10, 12)

"An Offering for Tārā," ultimately, honors the universal interconnectedness of all beings as tiny moments of energy transfer flowing in time, another way of understanding the principle that all things are truly interdependent, a realization of emptiness, the beginning of wisdom, the starting place for true compassion.

The poem is divided into three subsections. Snyder begins the first part by singing: "Have you seen my companion / With her moon-like forehead / Has she passed this way?" The song is a variation on a traditional Ladakhi folk song, in this case a love song in a question-answer format:

> Have you seen my companion,
> The companion Tsering Skit?
> I know not your companion,
> The companion Tsering Skit,
> Who has the moon like forehead,
> And just passed by this way.
> (Shakspo 13)

Snyder's deletions from the original leave us with the suggestion of moons and therefore moon-goddesses: Artemis, certainly; the Paleolithic "Venus of Laussel" with her uplifted horned moon; and Tārā herself whose moonlike face can be seen as an illustration accompanying the section (*MRWE* 112). Knowing that the original is a "love song" helps to set the tone; the question-answer format establishes an archetypal plot line with echoes throughout *Mountains and Rivers:* a lover in quest for a beloved. Unlike the original, Snyder's question goes unanswered, implying that his companion may indeed have wandered the pathways of the Tibetan Plateau. For readers of Nō plays, the question has a certain resonance with the kind posed by a journeying *waki* when he encounters an unassuming yet mysterious person on the path: "Who is this person standing before me?" The answer presented in the Nō play usually calls up the significance of the locale along with the ghostly presence of the spirit who abides in that place. When the spirit appears, the encounter, culminating in a dance, transforms all. So Tārā, Tibetan goddess, appears with her love magic in this section.

Snyder traveled with his son Gen to Tārā's abode in September of 1992. He was invited to present a talk at the Rethinking Progress conference sponsored by the Ladakh Ecological Development Group. There, in the remote region of India known as Ladakh, in the upper Indus River watershed on the Western Tibetan Plateau, he came to "the town of Leh":

> Leh is built on the gravelly slope coming down from the ridges to the north, and alluvial outflow, fed by water from snowfields and glaciers far above and behind. It is built on what we call—here in the west—a *bajada.* Looking up and down the Indus Valley, I could see that there were other villages, each of them built on a *bajada,* and in some cases such fans coming out of gulches with no villages and farms. . . . [W]here there is glacial meltwater there is a village and fields—gentle terraces rising back with stone walls, houses raised of stone and mud brick, and the village or town somewhere in there. (Snyder, "High Dry Place" 11)

What is obvious about both Snyder's travel notes and "An Offering for Tārā" is his emphasis on structures. Whether speaking of the Tibetan Plateau, the town of Leh, the "rock-edged channels" that bring the water to the fields, Milarepa's chores, or "tabletop mandalas," the focus is on "building" and "making." Starting with the geomorphological features of the landscape, Snyder mentions "Gondwana," making a subtle link with the same term in "Walking the New York Bedrock," another section about the making and unmaking of edifices. Furthermore, the image of the "New York" buildings, said to be submerged like anemones in a Sea of Information, resonates when juxtaposed with the picture of a Tibetan plateau that once existed wholly underwater. Echoes of Dōgen from "The Canyon Wren"—"mountains flow / water . . . does not flow away"—may also be heard in the seemingly unmovable rivers that "sat their seats" while "million-yeared" mountains were rising around them. Geologically, these facts belong to scientific theories of drifting continental plates. Millions of years ago, the subcontinent of India moved north, crossing the ancient Tethys Sea. It rammed up against the underbelly of Eurasia, forcing the upward thrust of the Himalayan Mountains. As the Tibetan Plateau lifted, the body of waters that preexisted there became the major rivers that today flow out of these mountains: the Indus, the Sutlej, and others not named in the section.

In this same ancient place, the town of Leh is "now" built on a *bajada,* a fanlike deposition of mountain materials—"glacial-flour and outwash gravel"—that has descended over thousands of years from the same forces. Leh's very buildings are made of these substances. The food grown in this place is dependent on the flow of rock and water. The barley grows on terraces that have been "built up" from the rocks; it is irrigated by crisscrossing "rock-edged channels." Wherever one looks there is rock. Whether New York City or Leh, the buildings are fixed in more than one manner on their respective bedrock.

And then there is the "flowing." Following the rhythmic model of the Nō, Snyder switches to prose, posing three kōanlike questions for the enlightenment of those readers who would ponder them. In more poetically structured lines, answers, derived from the simple mysteries of life, are then suggested for each question. (1) "Glaciers, and how high must they be to catch the snow and make year-round streams in a land of no rain?" The "[w]ater from the icefields" is the "long wide tongue of the Buddha," answers Snyder. As we will discover in "We Wash Our Bowls in This Water," if we did not already know it, the glacier-tongue metaphor derives from the enlightenment poem of Su Tung-p'o: "The stream with its sounds is a long broad tongue." In "An Offering for Tārā" the stream is a glacier, another way of capturing Dōgen's meaning in saying "water does not flow" even while admitting that it does. For now, in this "land of no rain" the Buddha-glacier-tongue speaks of life for the villagers below. (2) "Where was the hearth of high altitude barley and when did it spread?" As with questions about the origins of glaciers, there is no way to know where barley first grew, yet the spread of its fields is clearly consequent upon the "[w]ater from the icefields" that is economically managed by the "rock-edged channels" and the human hands that create the "terraces" where it "passes through barley plots." It will not spread without such care. (3) "Did these people move here to escape some tyrant, or because they were crazy and bold?" The people came here as "hunters . . . for sheep before farmers or lamas, / but now they move rocks." The sheep, wild like those we have seen in "Arctic Midnight Twilight," were here long before the people who followed them. Following the sheep, the Paleolithic hunters had their lives changed by the place they had come to. Thousands of years later, perhaps merely as a ritual unconnected to its ancient reality, the people of the place now worship the sheep as part of a "woven rooftop shrine." In each case—glacier water, the harvest of barley, the establishment of towns—what is, at first, "wild" eventually flows into, or interpenetrates with, the structured "now" of present-day life.

Turning again to prose, Snyder tells us a well-known story about Milarepa, Tibet's most famous saintly figure. Among the purifying and enlightening trials imposed on him by Marpa, his teacher, were orders to build, and rebuild, houses of stone. Marpa's objective was obviously a lesson about impermanence, one particularly apt in a landscape such as Ladakh where the people even today continue to "raise gravel outwash into walls and houses." With this example Snyder turns to yet another aspect of culture built on rock: the temples, or *gompas,* "built on some peak or cliff" out of the mountain's materials. An act of "confidence, patience, good humor," temple building is "the work of hands with the stone and grit of the world." In the same way the magical practices of Tibetan Buddhism—symbolized by the "[t]abletop mandalas"—are derived from "fine-ground minerals" and "pulverized rocks" taken from the surrounding landscape. As abstractions, mandalas are "vision palaces" or "maps of stages of the soul and all its pathways," but they are made out of "mountain dust." One may remember the equally apt example of East Asian painting in which the very materials—the colored inks—used to create vast artistic landscapes are prepared from the substance of the land itself. As artists, the Tibetan monks labor meticulously—grain by tangible grain—over their visionary soul maps. Similarly, the painters of landscape scrolls work painstakingly to etch in the details of their tiny created universes. Yet both know that the "entire phenomenal universe and the empty sky are nothing but a painting." The implications are obvious: all constructions, even those religious temples of Leh-Ladakh-Tibet-Vajrayana Buddhism, are founded on a "rock" that for all its corporeality is finally impermanent. No wonder then that Milarepa's enlightenment came from building stone houses again, and then again, many times. The emptiness of edifices is a way in. Constantly shifting and changing, the turning world—the entire phenomenal universe—and all of its regional or universal ecosystems, make up a Promethean mandala. Yet even as we construe it, we are constructed and reconstructed by our changing location within it.

The second and third parts of "An Offering for Tārā" continue to be based on Snyder's activities during his stay in Leh, especially his encounters with Tibetan rituals and customs. Although the parts remain separately labeled as "II" and "III," they are bracketed, and thus enfolded into a singular entity, by subsequent verses from a Ladakhi song. Part II begins with:

In the lofty sky
Is the nest of a vulture
May it remain unchanged.
The unchanged bird,
May you remain unchanged.

And part III ends with:

> *On the lofty mountain*
> *Is the nest of a hawk*
> *On the lofty rock,*
> *The nest of a white hawk*
>
> *The unchanged bird,*
> *May you remain unchanged.*[18]

Although the presence of a specific vulture and hawk remains perplexing, at least to a non-Tibetan mind, the original thirty-two-line Ladakhi song that Snyder draws on is said to be a "marriage song" that is intended to "express the community's good wishes for the future happiness and prosperity of the young couple in their new life" (Shakspo 16). Snyder's eleven-line selection, in its repetitive phrasing, emphasizes the ritualistic tone of his own poem. Its source in a marriage song reveals Snyder's primary intent in this section and in the poem as a whole: "An Offering for Tārā" is the poet's song in honor of "Tārā's love magic," especially as her compassion may affect the youth of future generations. *Mountains and Rivers* is, after all, dedicated to his children—Gen, Kai, Mika, and Kyung-jin—and Snyder states in his "Notes" that he thinks of his long poem as "a sort of sūtra—an extended poetic, philosophic, and mythic narrative of the female Buddha Tārā—" for the "young people" that showed him "how" to end his poem (158). Finally, his selection from the original focuses on lines that respectfully request "the unchanged bird" to "remain unchanged," a plea for constancy in the midst of illusion. Tārā is that constancy; it is she who saves. Amid the vicissitudes of daily life that are perhaps symbolized here as "vulture" or "hawk," Tārā is the sky goddess, the goddess of the lofty mountain whose compassion is unchanging.

Ironically, in part II of the section we find that Tārā's stability is rooted in her ability to shift gender. Immediately after the opening five-line song of the unchanging vulture, Snyder sets the stage for a literal offering to The Goddess. Stepping into the "half-built house" of "Angdu's parents," the poet and his companion (his son, Gen) are served "butter tea and black tea." They notice the "little Tārā shrine in a corner" in its humble surroundings, the point surely being that wherever one might travel in this country one will find The Goddess among the people.

> Gen and I stayed on in Leh, to wander the streets a bit more, to take the many paths back into the upper parts of the village, to listen to the songs of the harvesters, watch the little donkeys loaded with piles of straw and alfalfa come down the paths, to see the men and women squatting in the fields with short sickles harvesting barley—harvest going full bore—and to do some trekking.
>
> . . . [W]e came up with a three day itinerary that would take us into a traditional village in the Stok range. We set out one morning on foot. . . . At the end

> of a long day it [a narrow rock walled canyon] opened out in a kind of old cirque, leveled out, broadened, with barley fields in it and up one arm of that a sizable old village, which is Rumbak. Our guide, Angdu, grew up here. ("High Dry Place" 15, my brackets)

Here, in the house of Angdu, in this far-flung, hidden-away corner of the world, among people whose lives flow with that of the earth itself, they "do the Tārā mantra for the shrine." Best known for her "salvific powers," Tārā is supposed to materialize "in the instant her devotee recites her mantra, *Om tāre tuttāre ture swāhā*" (Lopez 549), and her appearance may well be what Snyder intends his readers to perceive in the lines that follow the chanting of the mantra. As the mantra concludes, a printer's bullet is inserted, and with the next line readers find themselves in the presence of Tārā. In her own voice, she tells us that she has adopted the "body of a woman" to "serve the needs of beings." The lines return us to her mythic origins, as recounted by Stephan Beyer:

> A beginningless time ago, we are told, there was a worldly realm named Various Lights, in which there appeared a Tathāgata named Sound of Drums, and to him the princess Moon of Wisdom showed great faith and devotion. For a thousand billion years she did reverence to the Buddha and the measureless host of his retinue, the Bodhisattvas and Worthy Ones, and finally she awakened the supreme thought of enlightenment. "The proper thing to do," the monks then said to the princess, "is to make an earnest wish that your body (with which you attend to the teachings) may become that of a man, for surely this desire will be granted." She replied: "Since there is no such thing as a 'man' or a 'woman' (and no such thing as a 'self' or a 'person' or 'awareness') this bondage to male and female is hollow: Oh how worldly fools delude themselves!" And this is the earnest wish she made: "Those who wish to attain supreme enlightenment in a man's body are many, but those who wish to serve the aims of beings in a woman's body are few indeed; therefore may I, until this world is emptied out, serve the aim of beings with nothing but the body of a woman." (Beyer 64–65)

This "Princess Moon of Wisdom," Snyder's "companion / With her moonlike forehead," is Tārā, the Savioress. Obviously her desire to remain in the "body of a woman" both focuses attention on the sexist thought of the male monks and provides a rationale for her appearance as a gendered half of a sexual mystery that exists beyond duality. Tārā knows, as Snyder knows, that humans "delude themselves" when they speak in sexist terms, yet it is only through illusion that illusion may be overcome. In some accounts Tārā is said to have arisen from the tears of the Bodhisattva Avalokiteshvara in order to help him spread compassion, yet Avalokiteshvara is portrayed by the Chinese and Japanese as a female ("Avalokiteshvara" *Shambhala Dictionary*). In the Tibetan depiction of *yab-yum*, as captured in "Cross Legg'd," the apparently dualistic embrace of the genders enables one woman and one man to go beyond gender.

Another twist to Tārā's appearance arises in this second part of "An Offering for Tārā." The seven stanzas following "Tārā's Vow" are all indented, indicating that these lines are a unit that proceeds from the vow just taken. Remembering that water and valleys are the abode of the feminine, it seems significant that Snyder begins this subsection by telling us that the "steep eroding mountains" of the Himalayas seem to have "no place for lakes or meadows." Earlier in the poem Snyder made a point of telling us that this high glaciated landscape is a "land of no rain." Symbolically speaking, the high backbone of the Himalayan range—no longer just the local mountainscape enclosing Ladakh—appears to be a place of rocky peaks, wholly masculine, and unfriendly to the feminine archetype. Previously, Snyder has characterized the flowing feminine dance of rivers as a coiling of the feminine around the masculine in a sexual embrace in order to indicate the "going beyond." His metaphoric strategy here is to transform the landscape into an image of mother and child. Thus, in serving the needs of beings "with my body of a woman," the spirit of Tārā is seen here as a maternal figure hovering about a landscape that is metamorphosed into "Baby Krishna Himalaya." Indeed, the nurturing presence that Tārā represents is a thread that becomes the focal point of the two short poems that follow "An Offering for Tārā." Both "The Bear Mother" and "Macaques in the Sky" focus on maternal images.

Krishna's presence abounds in *Mountains and Rivers,* and his image often intersects with Snyder's own life. Snyder was raised on a dairy farm; Krishna was taken as an infant to be nurtured by Yashoda and Nanda among the cows. Snyder's journeying persona is yet another embodiment of Kokop'ele, a wandering flute player who brings about cultural change; Krishna too is known to be a flute player. Krishna's love of butter is echoed in Snyder's mention of "buttermilk" in several sections. There are abundant women in the lives of both figures; Krishna is known as a lover of numerous butter-churning milkmaids, or *gopis,* and many poems and tales circulate about his special love for Radha (Knappert 144). The repeated mention of "blue" in this part of "An Offering for Tārā" is a reminder that Krishna was born with blue skin—as indeed Samantabhadra is often depicted iconographically as "naked" and "blue"—and that Snyder returns again and again to the color of azure radiance, turquoise, lapis lazuli, or just plain "blue" as his token for a healing wholeness. We find echoes of Krishna's love of "dirt" in both "The Hump-backed Flute Player" and in the climactic poem of *Mountains and Rivers,* "The Mountain Spirit." In the former section, rising from the "dust" where he was "sleeping on the ground" Wovoka shows "the whole world" to Black Coyote. In the latter, there are "[g]hosts of lost landscapes / herds and flocks, / towns and clans, / great teachers from all lands / tucked in Wovoka's empty hat, / stored in Baby Krishna's mouth" (*MRWE* 146). As Snyder explains: "Lord Krishna, when a baby, sometimes ate dirt. Once when his

Mother tried to take a lump of dirt off his tongue, he playfully let her see the whole universe with its stars and planets, all in his mouth" (*MRWE* 163). Apparently, for Snyder, to love dirt is to embrace this tangible world. If, as Su Tung-p'o puts it in his enlightenment poem, the "looming mountain is a wide awake body" of the Buddha (*MRWE* 138), and the body of Lord Krishna contains "the whole universe," then Snyder's intermingling of Himalaya and Baby Krishna is to tell us that these dynamic mountains, which lift and fold even now as the northward-moving Indo-Australian Plate continues to collide with the Eurasian Plate, *are* the palpable bodies of the buddhas. To look deeply into the mountains, as Dōgen has in his *Mountains and Waters Sūtra* (*Sansuikyo*), is truly to see "the whole universe" in all its "thusness" as Snyder makes clear in his commentary on the sūtra:

> Dōgen is not concerned with "sacred mountains"—or pilgrimages, or spirit allies, or wilderness as some special quality. His mountains and streams are the processes of this earth, all of existence, process, essence, action, absence; they roll being and nonbeing together. They are what we are, we are what they are. For those who would see directly into essential nature, the idea of the sacred is a delusion and an obstruction: it diverts us from seeing what is before our eyes: plain thusness. . . .
>
> This, *thusness*, is the nature of the nature of nature. The wild in wild. (*Practice* 103)

Snyder too does not wish to deify these Himalayan mountains, yet they nevertheless serve as an auspicious place to "see directly into essential nature." One picks a place to begin. Why, then, does he choose the Himalayas? The word *himalaya* literally translates as a "storehouse of snow" (*him* = "snow," *alaya* = "storehouse"). Here, at the Himalayan rooftop of the world, the planet's highest point, we find a "storehouse," a "snowbasket," a Krishna-like mouth out of which all flowing may be seen to begin. It is here that the glaciers are high enough to "catch snow and make year-round streams in a land of no rain." In this symbolic locale, on this earth we inhabit, the cycles begin; here is the process of the process.

The mention of "naked Blue Samantabhadra," alongside "Kalachakra" and "Yamantaka," reinforces essential ideas related to Buddhist thought. Snyder intends each of these three figures to be conceptualized as an embodiment of a mountain range within the Himalayas. Even though the Himalayan mountains are young, geologically speaking, and therefore "baby mountains," the various ranges are "ancient" if seen as incarnations of timeless Buddha figures. The three icons are prominent images in Tibetan Buddhism. Samantabhadra is "regarded as an embodiment of the wisdom of essential sameness, i.e., insight into the unity of sameness and difference." In the Vajrayana "his naked deep blue body symbolizes nothingness (*shūnyatā*)" ("Samantabhadra" *Shambhala Dictionary*). Symbolizing an existence with total equality and no hierarchy, Samantabhadra exists outside of time. Kalachakra, on the other hand, literally translates as the "Wheel of Time," a reference needing no other explanation if one thinks of the "ceaseless wheel of lives" spoken of in "The Mountain Spirit" or the "*[w]alking on walking, / under foot earth turns*" that opens and closes this endlessly unfolding verbal painting of "the entire phenomenal universe" ("Kālachakra" *Shambhala Dictionary*). Yamantaka, whose name translates as "Subduer of the Lord of Death" ("Mañjushrī" *Shambhala Dictionary*), is iconographically represented as a terrifying bull-headed deity. He is a "wrathful form" of Mañjushrī, the Bodhisattva of wisdom. In Tibetan Buddhism a "wrathful form" serves as a counterpart to a peaceful form of a deity, and "the energies symbolized by the wrathful deities are as helpful and necessary to the realization of enlightenment as the peaceful ones." Although a wrathful icon may seem repugnant to outsiders, its purpose is to destroy "the illusions that hinder spiritual development," especially the "illusionary ego of the practitioner" ("Forms of manifestation" *Shambhala Dictionary*). Thus these three bodies of the Buddha, these ceaselessly lifting and folding mountains, incarnate the mysteries of time, death, and the wisdom of emptiness.

The Himalayan sheep, reminiscent of the "at-home" sheep in the Brooks Range in "Arctic Midnight Twilight," are intimate with the wisdom of "Baby Krishna Himalaya." Dancing on these slopes long before the coming of humans, each one of these "blue sheep" is said to "love the Himalayas" and "thinks the Himalaya / is hers alone." The stated femininity of the sheep immediately suggests a reference to the flute-playing charm of the youthful Krishna:

> Whenever the god played his flute at night the women would leave their husbands to go and join him in the forest. There they would dance the famous dance called *lilarasa*, in which each woman had the illusion that she was the one whom the god had chosen to dance with. This scene is often depicted in art, showing a circle of women dancing, each with Krishna. The god had divided himself into as many men as there were women wanting to dance. (Knappert 144)

On the peaks of the Himalayas, no rain appears. It is a locale that is so high and cold that one is easily tricked into thinking of adjectives like "frozen," "unmoving," and "fixed." This impression calls up the image of Shiva, lord of the Himalayas, the ascetic "mat-haired mountain sitter" of "Bubbs Creek Haircut" in whose hair is entrapped the waters of the universe (the Ganges). No creation can take place, no flowing of the waters, until Shiva, unmoved and unmoving, is charmed into motion by the energies of Pārvāti, the high goddess of the Himalayas, the daughter of the mountains. This kinesthetic moment of awakening, the mingling of essence and energy in an act of creation, is plainly reflected in "An Offering for Tārā," for among this hard "[r]ock stuff" that one conceives of as "permanent," the dance continues. Sheep dance round the slopes, each completely in love with, at home with, the landscape, as if it were their own. The rock itself folds and refolds, in geological time "wrapping, twisting in and out like dough." The sinuous weaving granite dance calls up an image of Tārā, whose braided plaits correspond to the twisted, wrapped shape of the folding rock. "Black as bees are the plaits of your hair"—a reference to a poem written by the fifth Dalai Lama in honor of Tārā (Beyer 59–60)—is also an unmistakable echo of the form of Shiva's hair. A glance at the picture of Tārā in the margin of the poem (*MRWE* 112) reveals that strands of her hair flow downward about her shoulders, as a river might wander down the slopes of a mountain, while other tresses sweep upward, like the dark triangular peaks of the Himalayas ascending through the clouded heights. For good measure, the Dalai Lama's simile adds the mantric humming sound of bees to the hivelike shape of her gathered hair. In sum, aspects of Tārā's womanly body conform to the "masculine" body of the mountains; in these mountains one may find the bodies of all the Buddhas at work, unrestricted by their gender, serving the needs of all beings.

The third and final part of "An Offering for Tārā" begins with lines that echo those of the first part. Snyder returns us to the immense geological reality of the "great Indus," which, after all, would not be flowing, "running / just there by the wall," unless that "wall" had been lifted eons ago by colliding continental plates. Mentioning the Indus in tandem with the "far shore" of the Yuba (in California) imposes a planetary image on the reader. In a constant state of redistribution, the movement of rock and water is never-ending and causative: what happens on one side of the globe ultimately links up with events or reactions on the other. As a continental plate dives toward the earth's core under another plate, the heat and pressure generated by the subduction process melts the rock, a common cause of volcanic eruptions on the surface above. When plates drift and collide, mountains lift and fold. Similarly, all river systems ultimately intermingle in the unbounded oceans that encompass the planet; the waters of the Indus will meet those of the Yuba.

Unlike the previous two parts, this part does not linger over visions of the larger forces of geology as much as it accentuates human interaction with the landscape. Invited to speak at the Rethinking Progress conference in Leh, Snyder discussed the effect of progress on ecology, spirituality, and place ("Village Council" 10). In this part of "An Offering for Tārā," the impact of progress on other beings is immediately apparent in Snyder's depiction of the "wild salmon" reclaiming, or at least adapting to, a habitat tainted by an earlier misuse of technology. Swimming up river the salmon spawn in "old mine-tailing gravels" that have washed downstream. The flowing river provides a transportation medium for both fish and gravel, as well as a "bed" for the creative act of spawning.

In its simplicity, Leh's agricultural existence is portrayed as essential and meaningful. Water is "[l]ed" to the beds of "kohlrabi, peas and potatoes" to irrigate the crops. Where the water flows, channeled by the rocks, so the food grows. The "gold-dry barley" then lures the songbirds; the village rises by the fields; on the roofs of the village houses the prayer flags flutter in the breeze. What begins with water leads to the spirit. The flowing wind speaks the message on the prayer flag by causing it to undulate; the prayer is always the same—"*Om Mani Padme Hum*"—or, as Snyder states it here: "*Om, Mind, in Phenomena, Hum.*" This Sanskrit formula, an "expression of the basic attitude of compassion," is the "most important and oldest mantra of Tibetan Buddhism." Associated with Avalokiteshvara, its seed syllables literally mean "jewel in the lotus"; the linked image represents the way the enlightened mind (jewel) "arises in the lotus of human consciousness" ("OM MANI PADME HUM" *Shambhala Dictionary*). Often overtly sexual in nature, the interpenetrating jewel and lotus embody the action of "going beyond" duality. For Snyder, especially at this moment in the poem, the phrase has yet another twist as he utters his own message of compassion: "Space of joy / in the life of the moment." What follows is a tiny dramatic tableau that captures the spirit of the mantra: "sheaves . . . packed on their backs / husband and wife walk singing"—in other words, human joy seen as a result of being totally enmeshed in work, the phenomena of the harvest. It is not only the alfalfa that winds up in the "storehouse and stables" to be apportioned to humans and animals; the song of the heart is dispensed to the readers: "*and give some away.*" The nature of a *puja* is to provide. To make sure that readers understand the exchange of energies that constitute this potluck, Snyder pulls back from his tableau to describe the entire landscape, linking the endeavors of humanity with the wild. Looking up, his sweeping vision takes in the "wide-ranging cloud chaos" above; looking down he sees the "silvery Senge Chhu" (the Indus) "curving below" him. Human activity is seen in the constructed "stone towers and walkways, / apartments and chambers" as well as in the "fields by the river, white dot houses / barley laid drying." The "white dot" image echoes the sheep seen in "Arctic Midnight Twilight" and merges sheep and human habitations. Sheep were among the earliest of domesticated animals, and barley was one of the first crops to be harvested by humans. Both are gifts of the planet.

While attending the Rethinking Progress conference, Snyder and his son attended an actual *puja* at Spitok Gompa, an early fifteenth-century monastery near the river. The ceremony was so inspiring that when "An Offering for Tārā" was first published, in the *Yale Review*, Snyder marked the poem's place of composition as "Spitok Gompa, upper Indus River watershed, Western Tibetan Plateau, town of Leh, nation of Ladakh, province of Jammu & Kashmir, state of India." His first impressions of the ritual, as sketched in his travel notes, are the source for the stanzas:

> It was a Tara Puja, an offering of chanting, meditation, food-energy and spirit-energy to the Bodhisattva Tara, force of compassion, in which the food offerings are reflected back to the participants and so we all had salty butter tea, apples, and barley dough in short order. It was a powerful and moving experience to be up in this airy place, where one stepped out onto a roof and looked at the long Indus River valley. The monks are rough, funny, a trifle greasy, re-

> laxed, and clearly learned. Another room in the Gompa had a huge Buddha image, the whole Tripitaka stored in shelves on both walls, and wall paintings of all the heavy-duty Tantric guys and gals snarling at each other or fucking. ("High Dry Place" 14)

In sight and sound and spirit, readers are invited to recreate the scene. Standing in or near this "temple built above the Indus," one hears "[c]onch blows from the rooftop" and the chanting of "monks in maroon." One imagines a procession with colorful images of Tārā everywhere: Snyder speaks of her "red body, gold body, green" (*MRWE* 111). Although White Tārā and Green Tārā are most commonly seen, she appears in many colors, and she has a significant presence as Red Tārā, which we will meet a few lines later in the poem. Prayer flags flutter in Tārā's honor, some with her image on them; perhaps her icons are seen on surrounding walls, perhaps her golden statue is carried above the heads of the participants. A boy leader "makes all the bows." All seems accustomed, all is ceremonious, as Yeats once wished for his world ("A Prayer for My Daughter").

Yet Snyder's vision always includes room for diversion. The monks "grin and glance" while the boy "plays" at being leader. We have seen the word "play" before. "Mother / Earth" in "Haida Gwai North Coast" is said to "[l]ove hard, playing, fighting, / rough and rowdy love-rassling / she can take it, she gives it" (*MRWE* 103–4). In this wild world, one must embrace the unexpected, the sudden and surprising, at times the awful, alongside the rational path of planned activity. It is not surprising, therefore, that these lines call attention to "demons" that "trample" or "intestines tangling, men and women dancing screwing / head of a horse, a bull." This too is the world of all beings, all activities. Yet the word "play" is more directly assigned to this boy who is playing at a role—"leader"—that is not properly his. Snyder's phrase may serve as an allusion to the extreme youth of the historical Dalai Lama at the moment when he was first informed that he had been called to lead his people. It may also be a reminder of the significant relationship between mother and son that Snyder has planted in *Mountains and Rivers.* As Tārā is watching over these proceedings and this particular "boy," so Mā worries about her son, so Yamamba has a son, Kintaro, who will one day perform great deeds, so Krishna as the child of Yashoda has magnificent adventures in front of him. In another realm we remember the Bear Mother and her child, and the mother rhesus macaque and her baby. Although Snyder does not specifically point to them, these same images have echoes in the Christian doctrines associated with the Virgin Mother and her baby Jesus. In this "Buddha hall in the sky," under the watchful eye of the universal mother, all beings are invited to share. Each of the participants at the Tārā *puja* has a "pinch" of "barley dough," and some "salt tea and sliced apple." Each has a taste of the playful ingredient, that "drop of chang on the tongue," the intoxicating barley beer with the distinctive tang. Tārā's hands, positioned in the *mudrā* of "the giving," express her benevolence; she *is* the body of the planet. Not only does she welcome us to the table, we partake of her. This particular "potluck" may begin in Spitok Gompa, but it quickly spreads to "the whole Himalayan plateau" and beyond. We realize that we are all "guests at the feast and we are also the meal! All of biological nature can be seen as an enormous *puja*" ("Village Council" 12).

Much as a printer's bullet placed immediately after the chanting of Tārā's mantra signified a shift in the second part, so one here marks a complete change in pace and poetry. Suddenly readers are presented with a formula in prose for "Tārā's love magic," a rite associated with Red Tārā. The preceding lines referring to demonic and orgiastic forces seem to have called her form into being. Also known as Kurukullā, Tārā's frightful aspect is four-armed and equipped with a bow and arrow, a hook, and a lasso, weapons with which she may subjugate the human or demonic forces that oppose her. With a necklace of human heads and a diadem of skulls, Kurukullā is often associated with Kali's wrathful aspect. Unlike rituals of protection, Kurukullā's work of subjugation goes "beyond defense into the darker realms of offense"; the practitioner calls upon her "to crush and overwhelm the malignant forces that threaten one" (Beyer 301–2). Her aggressive activities are viewed as acts of compassion, one more way to liberate persons from illusion. In these few grotesque lines, Snyder once more reminds readers that the work of the wrathful deities is as important as that of the benevolent figures. In the final analysis the goddess is larger than all her forms; she exists beyond any particular emanation of herself.

"Tārā's love magic" is used ostensibly to bring about the union of a boy with his beloved. It is not so much an act of subjugation as the establishment of reciprocity in the union. After a great many preliminaries that involve ritualistic chanting, offerings, and visualization, the practitioner of Kurukullā's ritual—in this case the "boy"—becomes one with The Goddess and her blazing energy. The boy's heart sends out "a red beam of light . . . [that] enters . . . his arrow, . . . and [through it] shines straight to his loved one's vagina." The light that plants itself in the body of the beloved is like Kurukullā's iron hook or arrowheads. Beyer notes: "If the person to be subjugated is female, the practitioner thinks that the light strikes into the middle of her vagina, that her menstrual blood trickles down, and that she becomes full of lust" (306–7). By changing Beyer's "full of lust" to "full of desire," Snyder softens the relationship the couple shares. The beloved's passion returns to the practitioner until, after several more exchanges of sound, light, and energy, they become indissolubly one. The mention of "menstrual" blood brings up images of the cycles of the moon, an allusion that has many echoes, both direct and indirect, in *Mountains and Rivers,* not the least of which is Tārā's own "moon-like forehead." Although this "boy" might have some literal connection to Snyder's actual experience in Leh, it is far more likely that he functions symbolically. If Snyder himself is the symbolic "boy," then he is using the Red Tārā ritual to entice Tārā herself into union with him. Similarly, the passionate desire aroused in the milkmaids by the boy Krishna certainly stands out, leading readers to consider that the boy and his beloved are tokens for these young mountains, the Baby Krishna Himalaya, that have become one with the blue sheep—"each one thinks the Himalaya / is hers alone"—who live indissolubly among them. No matter which path the reader follows, it leads to a union.

The narrative thread of "taking puja" returns with the next stanza. The phrase "[c]ross-legged" underscores that fusion of mind, spirit, and body, and perhaps of sexual partners, that Tārā's love magic has just led to. Nor should we forget that parts II and III are framed by verses from a Ladakhi "marriage song." The cross-legged position—as readers will find out in the poem of the same name in part IV of *Mountains and Rivers*—equally describes a pose of meditation and of sexual embrace. The later poem also has echoes of Milarepa, tea drinking, and a love mixed with "rocks and streams," all of which may be seen here in "An Offering for Tārā."

The only beings who appear to be out of place on this "lofty mountain" slope are the members of the "Indo-Tibetan army unit" whose "jeeps clatter up the hill toward Leh." As "malignant forces" of modern chaos in this ecologically balanced locale, perhaps Kurukullā's wrath will "crush and overwhelm" them, deliver them from their nationalistic purposes and bring them to an enlightening "space of joy / in the heart of the moment." The reader does not hear the flutter of Tārā's prayer flags at this moment, nor the exotic resonance of Tārā's mantra. Instead, deep in the engines of the modern phenomenal world, in its planetary crankcase so to speak, lies a recognition that civilization's dependence on irreplaceable fossil fuels will be its own undoing. Earlier poems in *Mountains and Rivers*—for example, "Boat of a Million Years" or "Instructions"—have already hinted at society's upcoming liberation from that dependency. It is just a question of time; one only has to listen to the sound of the "prayer" that "spins in the crankcase."

In the meantime, high up on this ancient plateau, in these "baby" mountains where there is only rock and water, butter and dirt, barley and birds, sheep and humans, Snyder presents readers with his vision of a biological community, with all its units interlinked as if they were part of an ongoing ceremonial sharing, a *puja*. "The village," he says, "can be defined as the distant communal pastures . . . and the total linkage of the larger area that is usually called a watershed, as well as the cultivated fields and households." In political terms, this village should be governed by what he calls an "ecological village council," a body that includes several of the same animals that turn up in the final lines of the poem: "a Council, that is, that includes the trees and birds, the sheep, goats, cows, and yaks and also the wild animals of the high pastures (ibex, argali, antelope, wild yak) as part of the village's local community" ("Village Council" 12). In "An Offering for Tārā" Snyder describes a viable village community based on "the old ways," run by and for all beings. Tārā's presence may be heard humming everywhere in the air. It is not an easy existence on this "lofty mountain" habitat, yet insofar as the day-to-day life has evolved from and is firmly grounded in the landscape, life in Ladakh becomes a model for emulation.

Emphasizing the dyads once more, the section closes with references to Krishna and Tārā. Lord Krishna, "Baby Himalaya," is the god who "loves the herdgirls" and the curl in the horns of the ibex. Like the phenomenal emptiness in Wovoka's hat, the "taste of dirt" in his mouth is a reminder that "when his Mother tried to take a lump of dirt off his tongue, he playfully let her see the whole universe with its stars and planets, all in his mouth" (*MRWE* 163). Like Yamamba who will soon follow, Tārā, "lady of the stars," is associated with the never-ending "*walking on walking,*" the hard work of keeping the planet going, a dynamic flow caught in the ancient, and essential, tradition of work—"grimy handed cutting barley, / leading water, / moving stones." We commemorate their eternal relationship, the planetary dance of dirt and stars, with a prayer of constancy: "The unchanged bird, / May you remain unchanged."

THE BEAR MOTHER

Although hidden from view, the bear is present almost from the outset of Snyder's long poem. "Old Bones," the second section of *Mountains and Rivers Without End,* is dedicated to Paul Shepard, the coauthor of *The Sacred Paw,* an intriguing compendium of facts and myths about the bear. The bear is one of Snyder's favorite animals, and factual encounters with the "old man in a fur coat" in and around Kitkitdizze or while walking mountain trails are only part of the story. In 1954 he was reading Irving Hallowell's "Bear Ceremonialism in the Northern Hemisphere" (9 Dec. 1954. Reed–PWP). Even before then, as he researched the folklore of the Pacific Northwest for his Reed thesis, it is likely that Snyder had read Marius Barbeau's article on "Bear Mother." Barbeau cites Hallowell's monograph in pointing out that "customs and rituals relating to the killing of the Bear" are widely distributed throughout the northern perimeter of Eurasia and North America, and he suggests that "there is a hidden or symbolic meaning behind the mass of related observances and rituals, all of which are somehow interrelated historically" (1–2). The "symbolic meaning" of the "Bear Mother and her Cubs" for Barbeau—and more than likely for Gary Snyder—is global. Her story entails the following "basic motifs":

1. The mystic union between a spirit or a divinity and a human being for the procreation of offspring, which offspring shares in both the supernatural and natural attributes of his parents, and becomes an intermediary or intercessor between two worlds
2. The self-sacrifice and the immolation of a supernatural being for the benefit or salvation of a clan, a tribe, or mankind
3. The communion or sacrament of partaking reverently, after self-purification, of the sacred flesh of the immolated supernatural being
4. Atonement, rituals, offerings and prayers addressed by representatives of human society below to the powers above. (Barbeau 10)

Mystic union, self-sacrifice, communion, and atonement are all interwoven threads in the thought and writing of Gary Snyder; they recur as major themes in *Mountains and Rivers.* Not only is the reader invited to participate in lucid meetings with the supernatural, the poem constantly reminds us of the mystical sharing undertaken by the planet on behalf of all of its beings, its living landscape. Self-sacrifice for the benefit of "mankind" is a direct theme in several sections; not only do bears show us "the way," even the mountains and juniper do it for the humans, according to the black-tailed hare. The act of communion is explicit in "With This Flesh," where we are wedded to the meat we eat. The emphasis on "at-one-ment" is everywhere in *Mountains and Rivers,* as Snyder urges his readers to experience the nondual, the "not even one," to realize the compassion that ensues from an understanding of emptiness. "The Bear Mother," a tiny phrase and a tiny poem, contains all these threads.

Any encounter with Snyder's work reveals his poetic fondness for bears and, in particular, for the story behind "The Bear Mother." The poem he chose to read at the Six Gallery in 1955, the inaugural moment of the Beat movement, was "The Berry Feast." Within the lines of that early poem is an obvious reference to the Bear Mother:

> Bear has been eating the berries.
>   high meadow, late summer, snow gone
> Blackbear
>   eating berries, married
> To a woman whose breasts bleed
> From nursing the half-human cubs.
>
> (*Back Country* 13)

Another variation on the tale may be glimpsed in "this poem is for bear," a section of Snyder's first long poem, *Myths & Texts:*

> The others had all gone down
> from the blackberry brambles, but one girl
> Spilled her basket, and was picking up her
> Berries in the dark.
> A tall man stood in the shadow, took her arm,
> Led her to his home. He was a bear.
> In a house under the mountain
> She gave birth to slick dark children
> With sharp teeth, and lived in the hollow
> Mountain many years.
>
> (24)

The complete tale has been summarized by Catharine McClellan, who tells us that it is "one of the most popular stories of the southern Yukon Indians—the Inland Tlingit, Tagish, and Southern Tutchone." The story involves

> a girl who was taken away by a bear after she had insulted it. He first appears in human form, and she marries him and has children by him. Later her brothers kill the bear, who is their brother-in-law, and the girl returns home. However, when her brothers urge her to don a bearskin against her wishes, she turns into a bear forever and kills her brothers. (ix)

Snyder's prose version of the story appears in *The Practice of the Wild,* where he makes it clear that there are multiple versions of the tale by referring directly to McClellan's compendium of eleven variations on the basic theme (155–74). Snyder's "Bear Mother" in *Mountains and Rivers* both is and is not an obvious reference to the story. Few readers would spot the tale in the title unless they were already familiar with the lore of the bear. There is little else in the nine-line *Mountains and Rivers* section that connects obviously with the story of this woman who married a bear, except, perhaps, for the tantalizing lines: "Her mouth full of blueberries, / We share." The surreal image of a large she-bear looming closer and closer to the reader's lips to share a kiss with a mouth stained purple by blueberry juice is plainly compelling and provides its own pure poetic inspiration.

Snyder's appraisal of the myth behind the text in *The Practice of the Wild* reveals the full impact of this tale within Snyder's long poem. Perhaps, indeed, the connection involves berries. Snyder's commentary on the story begins with

> Salmonberries, Crowberries, Nagoonberries, Cloudberries, High Bush Cranberries, Low Bush Cranberries, Thimbleberries, Raspberries, Soapberries, Blackberries, Serviceberries, Manzanita Berries, Red Huckleberries, Blueberries . . .
>
> . . . The berries' sheen, aroma, little spike of flavor, sweetness, all handed down from long ago. Who is it for? The berries call the birds and bears to eat. It's a gift, but there's also a return, for now the seed will be moved away. The little seeds buried in the sweet globules will go traveling in birds' craws, in raccoon bowels, across the rocks, over the river, through the air, to be left on other forest soils to sprout anew.
>
> Picking berries takes patience. The bears draw over the shoots and delicately rake through the clusters with their claws. People make wooden rakes that look like bear-claws. . . . Maybe this story starts with berries. (*Practice* 161–62)

The berries not only conjoin humans with other animals in the food chain; there is a subtler relationship, even a transfer of technology. Human rakes, as Snyder points out, resemble the claws of the bear. Thus it is that knowledge of the animal world teaches us who we are, where we came from, and what we must do to regain our harmony with "the wild." The salmon eaten by the bear, for example, help to define the Pacific Rim itself: "the salmon come into rivers from as far south as the Sacramento and go all the way around the North Pacific to Korea. At every river on the rim there are bears" (162).

In his commentary, the poet tells us that "for a long time only the bears and birds were at the berry thickets and the rivers. The humans arrived later. At first they all got along." Although "the human beings in the original time weren't so bad," eventually they "seemed to drift away." They "got more and more stingy. They learned a lot of little stuff, and forgot where they came from." With his love for bears, Snyder says other animals started "avoiding human beings," but "bears sort of cared." Bears, Snyder says, are

> the closest of all animals to humans. . . . They have no enemies, no fears, they can be silly, and they are big-hearted. They are completely at home in the world. They like human beings, and they decided long ago to let the humans join them at the salmon-running rivers and the berryfields. (*Practice* 162–64)

As he so often does, the poet reverses our conventional perceptions. Instead of seeing animals through human eyes, he presents the animal's observations of the human world. The reversal is tantamount to returning to the Paleolithic world when human lives were intimately shared with the animals.

> In North America many mythologies . . . deal with a period in the distant past in which the world was different and people could not be distinguished from animals. These mythologies are related to the concept that all animals have souls or spirits that give them supernatural power. Because man has subsequently been differentiated from the animals, they come to him in visions, and in the stories they help the hero out of trouble. ("Arts of American Indian Peoples," *Encyclopaedia Britannica* 659)

Bears have particular significance if, as some anthropologists think, the bear cult is one of the oldest religions in the world. Baring and Cashford tell us that the bear is

> the oldest animal hunted for food in the northern hemisphere, and also the oldest animal whose remains have been given a ritual significance. . . . Bear skulls have been found high up in the Swiss Alps in caves over 7,000 feet (2,100 m) above sea-level, which means that they must have been put there before the beginning of the last ice age—that is, before 75,000 B.C.—when the mountains became inaccessible because of the glaciers that covered them. (28–29)

The caves are regarded by some as religious sanctuaries. Cave paintings in Europe attest to the antiquity of the bear cult, and cave paintings, as Cashford and Baring argue, may at times represent sacred ritualized acts. The "Wounded Bear" on the walls of Les Trois Frères (16,000–12,000 B.C.) is seen by them as an "ethical act" that "honours the bond between human and animal, and the bond of both with the whole." In a world where "all life is interrelated," the killing of the bear is tantamount to "taking the life of a 'brother,'" which must be "atoned for by careful ritual" since in killing the animal, "the 'One' is wounded" (29).

"The Bear Mother," then, is Snyder's way of shifting our perspective toward what he regards as a more enlightened—and sacred—view of animal-human interaction. The rituals of Pacific Rim bear ceremonialism enact the bear's willingness to give itself up for the people even as they respectfully express their gratitude for its self-sacrificing act.

> The attitude of the Indians of the Northwest Coast toward animals is expressed in rituals such as the first salmon ceremony and the ceremonial attitude toward the bear. . . . The bear is never killed wantonly. When seen, it is addressed in terms of kinship, expressing an attitude that is known sporadically from the Ainu of northern Japan to many places in northwestern America. ("Arts of American Indian Peoples," *Encyclopaedia Britannica* 660)

Snyder's commentary on "The Woman Who Married a Bear" is in the same mold. He tells us that the bears "still wanted to be seen by people, to surprise them sometimes, even to be caught or killed by them, so they might go inside the houses and hear their music. Maybe that's why bears leave droppings in the trails" (*Practice* 163). The full story of the woman who married the bear begins with the young girl's indelicate step into the middle of bear feces, unquestionably the other side of the spirit world, but not separate from it. They are "not two." At every level "The Bear Mother" is a story of continual transformation—from bear to human, from sky to earth, from phenomenal world to spiritual world, from text to myth, from berries to excrement—and back again.

Snyder's "The Bear Mother" extends the Native American "Bear Mother" story into another meeting with The Goddess. In Snyder's mind these two—Bear and Goddess—are "not two," but partakers at the same polysemic feast. There may be no direct references to bears in the previous "An Offering for Tārā" or the subsequent "Macaques in the Sky," but there are connections in those sections to "The Bear Mother." As one of Tārā's epithets is "Joy of Starlight" (from "The Hump-backed Flute Player"), it is not unrealistic to identify the macaque as a different emanation of the starlight goddess, leaping from branch to branch, the night sky behind her, with her monkey-child clasped to her belly. Similarly, the epigraph for "Arktos," a non-*Mountains and Rivers* poem, quotes Pythagoras for an epigraph: "She-bears are the hands of Rhea" (*Left Out in the Rain* 141).[19] In other words, she-bears are emanations of The Goddess. She-bears might just as well be the hands of Tārā. "Arktos" concludes with "Joy of the Mountains / 'The Great She Bear.'" Thus, joy-of-starlight and joy-of-mountains come together in this mothering bear who must be seen not only as the lumbering bear that ambles *through* the mountains, but as an image of the entire physical mountain range, perhaps lying on her side or back, a connector between the ethereal and earthly realms, the defined peaks reaching into the rarefied cloud-sky as a veil of misty water falls endlessly over her rocky ledges. The layers, gullies, folds may be seen as the slopes and valleys of the mountain range or the physical layers of fat and skin of the heavy bear's body.

As originally published, this small poem was tagged by Snyder as "Brooks Range VIII: 86," possibly deriving from an actual bear sighting, perhaps a grizzly eating blueberries or salmon late in the Alaskan summer. Yet readers are asked to hold in mind that the poem also portrays an encounter with a symbolic bear, the mountain range itself, indeed all mountains ranges on the observable landscape of Mother Gaia Earth. To meet the bear is to meet the mountains that nourish our lives. To meet the bear is to meet The Goddess, although both are veiled. The Goddess Māyā is "illusion" itself. The truth of the phenomenal world as we know it will always be veiled. The Bear Mother-Goddess is both mother and coquette, perhaps even harlot; she nurtures us as she teases us—even "kisses" us—into wonder: "What do you know of my ways." We will never completely know the ways of The Goddess or of Gaia or of any corporeal species, but we are still invited, even tempted, to try. To taste of the blueberries or to eat of the salmon is a sacred act; a communion with the mystery of The Goddess, the enigma of the planet. We share.

MACAQUES IN THE SKY

From its first publication in the journal *Wild Earth,* we know that "Macaques in the Sky" is set somewhere in "South Taiwan"; its date is given as "September 1990." The poem commences prosaically by listing who was there ("Wang Ch'ing-hua, Red Pine, Lo Ch'ing, and Carole") and which trail they were walking ("from Nanren Lake"), but it quickly moves toward a lyrical mode. As often happens with poems in *Mountains and Rivers,* the poet, following the introductory *jo* rhythms of the Nō, begins a section with relatively unrhythmical pedestrian details so as to heighten the contrast with subsequent lines of greater poetic intensity. Nonetheless, these introductory lines are not devoid of thematic significance. In this "lookout on the forest slope," the hikers discover "a clear spot in the jungle canopy," "a high point arch of heavy limbs." Here is a place where one may learn to see clearly; here, in this place of heavy limbs, is a geometrical "arch," like so many others encountered in *Mountains and Rivers,* that echoes the curvature of the sky world and the lighthearted leap we are about to take through it.

Snyder deliberately blends the beings in this section. As we read, even if we somehow were not familiar with human evolutionary genealogy, we would come to know that we humans belong to this community of macaques: "A mother . . . sits and nurses // A couple . . . side by side // A face peeks . . . pink cheeks, / shining eyes // An old male . . . furrowed face." Undoubtedly these "faces among the leaves" are meant to be seen as kindred to the human species. The inference is confirmed when

Snyder switches pronouns to describe the baby monkey dangling from its mother's belly as she leaps: "*as we hang on beneath with all we have.*" The "we" can only be read as "we humans." Unlike in "The Bear Mother" where we humans stand apart from the bears, learning to share with them and from them, Snyder here directly reconnects us to our animal heritage. Descended literally from the trees, we are still primates, and the poet firmly binds us to our life among the branches. The old silver-bellied male is "laid back in a crotch" of a tree; the faces are seen "among the leaves"; and "soft hands and haunches [are] pressed on boughs and vines." In the interim line—"being ears and eyes of trees"—the word "being" functions as a participle that goes beyond modifying the "faces" to identify them as a living part of the trees. Thus in this literal "lookout" these faces—faces like our own—become the ears and eyes of trees; we see one being. Akin to the Dall sheep in "Arctic Midnight Twilight," the macaques are completely at home in their habitat. The implication for human primates is clear; we must relearn our love for the trees. The forest is our true home.

The poem then moves into action: " . . . *wha!*" The mother monkey leaps into the sky with her baby. Like the rapids in "The Canyon Wren" that Su Tung-p'o saw stand still or a river that leaps off the lip of a cliff in "The Flowing," just for a moment "out in the air . . . // they float there," anchored in time. Before the monkey "settles in" again, Snyder's moment of inspiration has taken place. This Mother Macaque—"*mother of the heavens, / crossing realm to realm / full of stars*"—is a sky goddess. Associated with the Milky Way, her nurturing aspect connects her to that mother of all cows, "Mother *Bos,*" and takes us even further back in time, to many-breasted Artemis, or to those heavy-breasted stone goddess shapes found in the Paleolithic, figurines that may have been modeled on celestial patterns:

> The flowing breast is the essential image of trust in the universe. Even the faintest pattern of stars was once seen as iridescent drops of milk streaming from the breast of the Mother Goddess: the galaxy that came to be called the Milky Way. (Baring and Cashford 10)

The macaque's skyworld "*arching*" may remind us of the "[c]elestial. Arched cover . . . a bent curved bow" of comradely love in "The Blue Sky." She is, in one consummate image, "Tārā, 'Joy of Starlight,' naked breasted. She who saves" ("The Hump-backed Flute Player").

In the penultimate lines of the poem, as we hang on to her "*with all we have,*" we are asked to "*enjoy her flight / Drink her light.*" The milk we ultimately drink is the energy from the stars. The poet's reminder that we should "*enjoy*" this flight seems apt, for there is little else we can do except to learn to flow with nature's playful wildness; it is "*all we have.*" Typically, Snyder ends the poem by returning us to this factual earth. Moments of illumination, when we "[d]rink" the "light," remain grounded in tangible data. We are not allowed to linger in some abstract ethereal sky without acknowledging that, as scientists know, this monkey is, factually, a "Rhesus macaque."

Starting in prose and ending on an unpoetic note of scientific fact, the entire section remains highly poetic. Parallel grammatical phrasing contributes to rhythmical balance: "A mother . . . A couple . . . A face . . . An old male"; "she leaps out . . . she fetches up . . . "; "enjoy her flight / Drink her light." Alliteration is common: "mother monkey," "peeks . . . pink," "furrowed face," "cough-calls echo," "baby . . . belly." Rhyme is used throughout: "peeks/cheeks," "leaves/trees," "air/there," "limb/in," "flight/light."

Short as it is, the poem has been carefully crafted for effect, more so because of its prominent place as the concluding poem of part III. The Nō structure followed by Snyder specifies that we have come to the end of the *ha,* or "agitated development" phase, of *Mountains and Rivers Without End.* As we turn to part IV, we will enter the final *kyū,* or "fast close" stage. Yet due to the fractal nature of the principle of *jo-ha-kyū,* what we actually perceive in "Macaques in the Sky" is a fast close to part III. Intriguingly, the section can be divided into five observable parts that may also imitate the basic structure of the Nō (*jo-ha-ha-ha-kyū*): prose beginning, the description of the macaques in the trees, the realistic leap of the mother monkey, the symbolic import of that leap printed in italics, and the final scientific naming. Thus the words "Rhesus macaque" serve as the *kyū,* or "fast close," to the section itself.

Looking back over the sections that make up part III, we may conclude that, taken together, "The Bear Mother" and "Macaques in the Sky" form the *kyū* for the entire unit. The eighth poem, "An Offering for Tārā," is undeniably the significant moment, the apex of the *ha* phase among these ten poems. Having met Tārā in her Tibetan abode, Snyder closes quickly with the two short poems revealing The Goddess in animal incarnations. In a similar fashion, as we turn to part IV we may look forward to a meeting with the Mountain Spirit in her western home among the bristlecone pines of the White Mountains on the edge of the Great Basin.

Part IV

OLD WOODRAT'S STINKY HOUSE

The issues raised by *Mountains and Rivers Without End* are not truly matters for closure; the poem calls on its readers to develop both a heightened attentiveness to—and respect for—the planet and new strategies for sharing it with other beings. These are matters for continual practice. However, according to the aesthetic of the Nō, the fourth part of *Mountains and Rivers* is the *kyū,* or "fast close," of the long poem. The *kyū* of a two-part Nō play invariably ends with the *shité*'s transforming reenactment in dance of all that has come before. Thus key poems within this ten-section unit draw the long poem toward artistic resolution by spiraling around, often providing faint echoes from earlier parts albeit with a new tone or a fresh vision. And Snyder surely has the *kyū* aspect of Nō in mind as he repeats the dance motif several times in these last sections.

"Old Woodrat's Stinky House" serves a double function in that it is equally a *jo* poem, an introduction to the final gathering of sections. The section begins with an epigraph—itself in the mood of a two-line introductory *jo*—that focuses on a dance of energy exchange: waves of life and death washing endlessly over a universal ocean of dazzling light. In *How to Raise an Ox* Francis Dojun Cook translates and comments on ten essays from Dōgen Zenji's *Shōbōgenzō* in order "to help the reader to gain a better understanding of what it means to practice Zen" (xv). Cook's commentaries emphasize Dōgen's insistence on the ceaseless practice of Zen. In "Giving Life to Our Lives," Cook's chapter on the present moment, the Zen "now" moment, he too refers to the line used by Snyder as an epigraph to "Old Woodrat's Stinky House": "The whole universe is an ocean of dazzling light" (Cook 82).

> For the purposes of our practice, it is important to remember that it is the whole universe which is an ocean of dazzling light, not just half the universe or the rather meager portion we have habitually come to associate with light. This means we can find that light everywhere, in every event, in every new "now" as it unfolds and becomes an actuality. None of these "nows" is deficient in light, no matter how deficient or terrible, ordinary or dull they may appear. Eating plain rice and drinking tea are part of this ocean of dazzling light. The task of the individual who trains in Zen is to learn to see this, for Zen practice is no more and no less than this.
>
> How ordinary, plain and simple Zen is! It is a life with one's feet on the ground of one's native home, toes buried in the fragrant dirt. It is a life of appreciation for the wonderful taste of plain boiled rice and green tea. (83)

Snyder's vision of the home "[u]s critters" share does not neglect this totality of "nows," and the wholeness of the picture he sketches in this section is indeed dazzling. Beginning in myth with the floating meadowlark nest stretched and shaped by Coyote and Earthmaker into the land we live on, actuality informs the mythical as Snyder turns to a "venerable desert woodrat nest of twigs and shreds," a "family house" that scientists believe has been in use for "eight thousand years." Both nests are metaphors for the nest-planet we now inhabit; Snyder's focus is on its content over the millennia. Like Chinese boxes within boxes, Snyder's painted images of the real contain lists of the ordinary, the dull, the plain, and the simple. He conjures up the fragrance of the dirt we stand on as he reminds us of the feces—"5,086 coyote scats" and "thousands [of] paleo human droppings"—we will find under our feet; if we inhale deeply we may drink in the smell of woodrat's nest "plastered down with ambered urine." Probing the contents of the coyote feces reveals bits of previous lives and creatures ranging from "[p]ocket gopher [and] elk" to "rubber, tinfoil, shoestring, paint rag, [and] two pieces of a shirt." Ten-thousand-year-old human feces found in Lovelock Cave reveal another diversity in appetite: "cattail pollen . . . raw baby birds . . . beetles . . . and suckers." These scraps of the past, as processed by ancient digestive tracks, reinforce the notion of the food chain; more significantly, they are a subtle reminder that, as Gary Snyder likes to tell audiences, we too will be eaten. Every being ultimately winds up in the stomach of some other being; more crassly, it all comes down to feces.

The poem is unquestionably a criticism of the way humans have "fouled" their nest. Like "Woodrat" who is "[s]hitting on his grandmother's blankets— / stinking everything up—pissing on everything," reckless human greediness and consumerism have made our "whole house stink" until it is in danger of becoming uninhabitable for ourselves and for other species. Earlier poems, like "The Market," make it clear that this criticism belongs to Snyder's outlook in *Mountains and Rivers.* Yet the present poem does not insist on the awful as much as it as calls up the awe-full, that which brings forth wonder. Snyder's attribution of the two-line epigraph to "*a service for the spirits of the dead*" is clarified by Cook's statement that it is a "line in the memorial service . . . recited in the Dharma hall on the occasion of remembering and honoring our spiritual ancestors" (82). "Old Woodrat's Stinky House" is not so much a diatribe against our foolishness as it is a commemoration, in amazement, of diversity over time and space. The smallest bits of dirt are the focus of thousands of previous lives; the tiniest moments of time should be seen in the context of all previous time. The moment is not one of nostalgic melancholy or morbidity but a time for honor and respect. Snyder places the present moment, the "now" of "a breath is a breath," a timeless meditative breath such as one might take while sitting "cross-legg'd," in the context of successively larger sequences of chronological units: a four-minute song, a twenty-four-hour day, a twenty-eight-day cycle of the moon, four seasons to a year, groups of years gathered into significant patterns of eight or ten, twenty, eighty, "a couple hundred," the life span of a bristlecone pine (the "Oldest of Beings" as we know from "The Hump-backed Flute Player"), the durability of both spoken and written languages, a desert woodrat's nest containing thousands of years of collected detritus, not unlike the "flot . . . jet . . . crud . . . and natural trash" that floats in the waters of "Haida Gwai North Coast," the time of an ice age and the time between those ages, all tapering off into the realm of unimaginable numbers ending in words like "millions" and "billions." Measured in time and discovered amid the waste matter of the past, this energetic dance of the "*waves of life and death*" on the turning surface of the universe is truly dazzling.

As for resolution, "Old Woodrat's Stinky House"—even with its focus on the apparent finality of excrement—appears to be the inverse of "The Market," providing an updated commentary on this earlier *jo* poem with which it might be compared. Although "The Market" accentuates acquisition and "Old Woodrat's Stinky House" highlights elimination, both poems utilize images of feces, droppings, and waste material, and both employ the "equals" strategy: "four thousand years of using writing equals / the life of bristlecone pine" ("Old Woodrat's Stinky House") or "five cartons greek olives = hitchhiking / from Ogden Utah to Burns Oregon" ("The Market" 49). Yet the tone of "The Market" often seems caustic, and its final vision leaves readers with an image of pathetic wretchedness, while "Old Woodrat's Stinky House" admonishes gently, almost indirectly. The penultimate words expressing Cottontail boy's disgust with Woodrat are playfully modulated by a nonthreatening voice that is both rabbit and juvenile, one that uses words like "yucky." Although Cottontail boy's frustration lingers in the abiding stench of vomit, defecation, and urination emanating from Woodrat's house, rather than leaving us with hopeless pathos or despair, Snyder puts the final words of the section in the mouth of Coyote and delivers them as an instruction to humans to reinhabit the planet in a proper manner. This message is hardly new for Snyder's readers or, for that matter, for listeners of stories that were spoken long before the late twentieth century: "stay put . . . learn your place . . . do good things." While Coyote, like the Mountain Spirit (Yamamba) and the planetary Boat of a Million Years, will travel on endlessly, humans need to learn to stay put. In *The Practice of the Wild* Snyder quotes a Crow elder on just what will happen if people would learn to sit still:

> You know, I think if people stay somewhere long enough—even white people—the spirits will begin to speak to them. It's the power of the spirits coming up from the land. The spirits and the old powers aren't lost, they just need people to be around long enough and the spirits will begin to influence them. (39)

Staying put means listening to the tales of our elders, those Native Americans who inhabited these places long before modern waves of restless immigration began and, even farther back, the "old ones" whose trails may be followed in the stories told about them. In that time before human and animal were dissevered from one another, when Cottontail was still a Boy, an animal-human who mingled freely with Woodrat and Coyote, the lessons were already there for the learning. We humans are only one small species among the hundreds of thousands of "critters" who have inhabited the earth during its past three billion years. The waves of life and death—breath and excrement—extend far beyond our mere comings and goings. In every nest-home, in each tiny moment of breath, in the smallest of fecal pellets, exist universes of dazzling light.

RAVEN'S BEAK RIVER AT THE END

The scroll unrolls another turn. Between two Great Basin landscapes the trail turns temporarily north from "Old Woodrat's Stinky Nest" toward higher latitudes and the wet, crystalline chill of "Raven's Beak River / At the End." It will return to the heat of the high desert imaged in the section that follows, "Earrings Dangling and Miles of Desert." The scene before us now is the "doab of the Tatshenshini [or Raven's Beak] River and the Alsek Lake." The Tatshenshini flows out of the southwestern corner of Canada's Yukon Territories through British Columbia to meet the Alsek River before emptying into the Gulf of Alaska at Dry Bay. A typical rafting excursion, such as the one Snyder made sometime in July 1986, puts in north of Haines Junction and takes well over a week to run some 150 miles of the river, one of the wildest in North America. Fresh Tracks (Canada) describes their expedition as follows:

> We join the river at historic Dalton Post in the Yukon Territories, near the mouth of the Klukshu River. Almost immediately it enters a narrow canyon and cascades through many exciting rapids before opening into a broad U-shaped valley surrounded by the Alsek and Carmine Ranges. Further on, the river starts to meander, then to braid and eventually to create a series of gravel bars and false channels. . . . [W]e race downstream with the 10 kilometre (6 mile) per hour current. Shortly thereafter it meets the Alsek River and at Walker Glacier we will have the opportunity to walk on the ice. A short drift downstream brings us to Alsek Bay where we can watch numerous glaciers actively calving huge blocks of ice into the river in front of our rafts. Here also is Mount Fairweather rising more than 4600 metres (15,300 feet) and dominating the skyline. . . . The most visible large mammal species along the river are black and grizzly bears, moose, and mountain goats. Other wildlife species readily spotted are red fox, beaver, wolves, bald and golden eagles, peregrine falcons, and a variety of other avian life. (Fresh Tracks)

This prose description parallels the wild beauty of Snyder's poem, which begins on "a long spit of gravel, one clear day after days on the river in the rain." The poem has its own complement of bears, moose, and fox, and the poet describes the evidence of recent visits to the setting: "little fox tracks in the moose-print swales, & giant scoops of dirt took out by bears around the lupine roots." As in "Afloat," Snyder's verbal brush goes on to paint a veritable panorama of ice, water, rock, sky, and land. In the foreground on this chilly sunlit morning are boulders, gravel, flowers, and two ravens; in the distance are "ice slopes," and "mountain knuckles / Interlaced with snowfields." Everywhere one looks or listens there is a profusion of dynamic flowing and growing. The word "fall" shifts between substantive and verbal modes as we encounter "rock-fall," "ice falls," "water falling." The river is "running" and "dancing." Like the speaker, it has its "nose in the grasses." Castilleja flowers flourish among, and beyond, the gravel banks of the river; clusters of green alders actively "climb" into patterns on the distant mountain slopes. Detaching itself from the end of the glacier, a blue-tinted iceberg, now a floating goddess-queen, drifts in Alsek Lake. Like the "web of waters streaming over rocks" or the "frothy braided torrent" described in "Endless Streams and Mountains," the water in "Raven's Beak River" turns foamy as it comes down the mountain slopes. When their time comes, salmon will weave their way up braided river channels.

For all of its exquisite description of wildness in action, the central feature of this section is not its scenic beauty, and its focus is not on what is seen. Instead, in the midst of dazzling imagistic energy, the poem paradoxically insists on sitting still, on silent meditative attentiveness to one's interconnection with the flow of life, of finding the still point at the heart of this whirling circle of the senses. As visual as this section is, it remains a poem of sounds and silence. Once past the prose of its introductory *jo* lines, "Raven's Beak River," more than any other section of equal length in *Mountains and Rivers,* is metrically rhythmical. Selected words and phrases like "boulder," "gravel," "flowers," "glacier," "ice age," "rivers" are repeated often enough to act as a scenic litany of the basic locale. It has a high proportion of structurally parallel prepositional phrases ("to the . . . ," "at the . . . ," "by the . . . ," "in the . . .") and verbal phrases ("sitting on . . . ," "looking up . . . ," "resting in . . ."). The alliteration and accentual patterning of the lines call attention to the regularity of sound and rhythm, so much so that at least one contemporary musical group has composed a musical version of "Raven's Beak River" (see Zumak).

Vigorous sound patterning like this may be especially relevant in a gathering of sections belonging to the *kyū* mode, yet it is because Snyder knows that sound was a "way in" for Su Tung-p'o and Dōgen that he composes "Raven's Beak River" as an attentive meditation on sound and movement. As the chanting of the lines continues, the speaker merges with the flowing forces that at first surround him and then unite with him. He tells us directly that "two ravens" show him "the way / To a place to sit." If on the north coast of "Haida Gwai" where the Hiellen River meets the ocean, Snyder has emphasized the raucous sound of twelve ravens squawking, squorking, and crorking, in this section, at the dynamic juncture of the Tatshenshini with Alsek Lake, we encounter a different kind of raven, and the sound we hear amid the other sounds is of a different order. It is the sound of emptiness itself. An interviewer once questioned Snyder about the source of a similar image—"a gulf where a raven flaps by once"—in a non-*Mountains and Rivers* poem. Snyder responded:

> I'll tell you what that is. That was trying to deal with emptiness. If earth is a flower being offered to the Buddha, it is a flower out of emptiness, it is a flower of the void. But to say "a flower of the void" is far too abstract. So the "gulf where a raven flaps by once" is putting a little detail on the nature of emptiness. (Snyder, "Interview" [Johns] 109–10)

The poet's answer evidently applies to the ravens he encounters in "Raven's Beak River," especially when we consider the image given to us in the final lines of this section: "Flying off alone / flying off alone / flying off alone // Off alone." Stated repetitively, the chanted phrase serves as a mantra for a meditation on emptiness. Like

Dōgen, Snyder suggests the daily practice of meditation as a strategy for survival, a method for attaining a greater wholeness of being. Both philosopher and poet agree that daily "sitting" meditation is not only the path to enlightenment, it *is* enlightenment in the here and now. "Raven's Beak River / At the End," more clearly than other sections in *Mountains and Rivers,* demonstrates what takes place at such clarifying moments. Not surprisingly, Snyder turns to the animal world to explain the process, because "animals," as he told an interviewer long ago, "know all about it." They "have the capacity for sitting still and tuning in on their own inside consciousness as well as the outside consciousness for great periods of time." Moreover, as Snyder says, "they can restore themselves by doing that; you can see them doing it. The calmness of deer at rest at mid-day is the order of meditation" (Snyder, "Interview" [Flaherty] 61). This "tuning in" on inner and outer consciousness is Snyder's strategy for this section. Readers are presented with deliberate ambiguities. The "blue sky singer" is both raven and the poet who has, as we know, already written of "The Blue Sky." Sitting in his "[r]aven-sitting high spot," Snyder, now imaginatively a bird, speaks of a "[n]ose of morning" and a "[s]kin of sunlight / skin of chilly gravel." Is this a personified "nose" of the morning, or is this Snyder inhaling the morning smell? Is this his skin, now in sunlight, now in contact with the chill of the gravel, or is it the personified skin of the air and the earth? Deliberately ambiguous in nature, these references indicate Snyder's coalescence with an outer consciousness. Unsure if we are dealing with a personified earth or the nose and skin of the poet, we attribute them to both subject and object. Snyder's "mind" turns from being "in the mountains" to become a "mind of tumbling water,/ mind running rivers." With each grammatical step the mind approaches more closely to the thing that had once been outside of it. "Meditation," he has said, "is not just a rest or retreat from the turmoil of the stream or the impurity of the world. It is a way of being the stream, so that one can be at home in both the white water and the eddies" (Snyder, introduction, *Beneath* 1). A river itself, the mind sifts "flowers in the gravels," but the flower Snyder speaks of may well be a "flower out of emptiness, . . . a flower of the void." By the end of the section, presumably at the height of his meditative accomplishment, the speaker acknowledges the merger that has taken place: "we are the bears, we are the ravens, / We are the salmon." Catherine Ingram refers to Snyder's use of meditation as a way of opening his mind "to the point that it's empty enough that other things can walk into it, so that a rabbit can walk in your mind, so that trees or rocks become part of your mind" (Snyder, interview [Ingram] 228). In "Raven's Beak River," Snyder's poetic ice age—its imagistic glaciers rhythmically grinding boulders into the virtual gravel of the poem—slides directly into his mind, and presumably into that of the reader's. At the opening of the section Snyder says "I find my way"; in reading the ensuing lines one experiences the act of his finding. To read this poem is to participate in Snyder's meditation on the status of modern humans as children of the ice age, beings who must realize, once again, their oneness with the bears, the ravens, the salmon, the mountains and rivers. By the end of the section, as if it were "at the end" of the Tatshenshini River after days in the rain, a clear day dawns. The attentive mind, now attuned to the harmonious flow of sound, image, and idea in the lines, follows the raven's flight as it flies off alone, off alone . . . , into the music of the void that *is* the music we have heard. In the silence, surrounded by the flow, we comprehend the world anew.

EARRINGS DANGLING AND MILES OF DESERT

> *Hail, Artemisia,*
>
> . . . . .
>
> *I will think of you in my other poems.*
>
> (*MRWE* 127)

Snyder's adaptation of the Homeric "Second Hymn to Artemis" substitutes a botanical genus, *"Artemisia,"* for The Goddess's name. With this deft touch, sagebrush becomes a tangible, metonymical vehicle for Artemis, a predominant goddess of *Mountains and Rivers Without End,* the poet's feminine embodiment of "the wild." In either guise—botanical or mythical— *artemisia* has indeed appeared in other poems. Readers will conjure up its presence, whether actually named or not, as the North American *Artemisia tridentata,* whenever the unrolling scroll depicts a Great Basin landscape of the "arid west" ("Cross-Legg'd"). "Old Woodrat's Stinky Nest" contains it among the "[s]hreds of every bush that grew eight thousand years" in the Great Basin. In our minds the lower slopes of the White Mountains in both "The Hump-backed Flute Player" and "The Mountain Spirit" are cloaked in the "twiglets" of this omnipresent "brushy, bushy, stringybark cobwebby tangle" vegetation ("Earrings Dangling"). Carved on the face of stones found "tucked into the sagebrush" of "Finding the Space in the Heart" are sayings inscribed by a "desert sage," his sagacity giving yet another significant twist to the word. This "sagebrush" Goddess, Artemis, after all, "embodies a wisdom . . . largely lost, both of outer nature and of that untamed animal region of human nature, and of the necessary relation between them" (Baring and Cashford 323). Read as a praise song for sagebrush, "Earrings Dangling" is matched only by "Covers the Ground" as a hymn to Gaia's world of botanical beings.

In a similar manner, Snyder has certainly sung of Artemis in other poems. A Goddess of Wild Animals, decked out in her foxtooth crown, she reveals her Paleolithic heritage in "Under the Hills Near the Morava River." A "mountain-mother" in her own right, we may imagine her standing behind the matriarchal figure we meet in "Mā" or, in her animal body, as the nurturing maternal presence we encounter in "The Bear Mother." Inseparable from lunar imagery, Artemis in her virginal aspect is specifically associated with the new moon, leading us to think of her as we read "New Moon Tongue." At times Artemis's epithet is "'the sounding one,' *keladeine,* evolving out of the music of the wild, the spirit of the place, the language of animals, birds, fish, insects—the immanent presence of the whole of nature as a sacred reality" (Baring and Cashford 322). Mindful readers may sense "the beat of her unseen feet" among the floating white patterns on the green summer slopes of the Brooks Range or hear her rhythmic step again in the music of the wild "Raven's Beak River." In the present section, Snyder continues to associate her with sound by drawing attention to her ears. Her beauty, like the botanical sagebrush, may be found "worldwide"; it is presented to us in terms of her "blue-gray-green" sagebrush earrings, seen dangling from her earthly earlobes. Readers who listen with the great shining ears of the black-tailed jackrabbit, that Artemisian lunar Hare who epitomizes knowledge gained through attentive hearing, may feel the presence of The Goddess all the way "to the edge" of the desert and beyond, into its "emptiness far as the mind can see." Just as Snyder traces the journey of the Mediterranean bull to Spanish America in "With This Flesh," so he uses the global dispersal of plants to bring the dance of the Middle Eastern goddess Artemis to Turtle Island. Verbally transfigured, Artemis is transported away from the Old World forests and mountains with which she is traditionally associated and relocated in the Great Basin of the American West.

Notwithstanding its important link to sound, "Earrings Dangling," unlike "Raven's Beak River," is not presented as a straightforwardly lyrical poem. Here, as in many sections of *Mountains and Rivers,* prose paragraphs are intermingled with passages of carefully constructed verse, more than likely in accordance with Snyder's sense of the fluctuating cadences of the Nō. "Earrings Dangling" begins with a high proportion of prosaic lines, underscoring the section's distinctly informative aspect, yet it moves inexorably toward its conclusion in waves of increasingly musical rhythms, ending with a formalized poetic apostrophe to Artemis. Entering the poem, readers are confronted by a wealth of encyclopedic data. Emphasizing community, Snyder makes the point that plants get along with each other: "Sagebrush often lives with rabbitbrush . . . , saltbush . . . , and greasewood." In distinguishing "sagebrush" (*Artemisia*) from "sage," the poet identifies the genus of sage as "*Salvia*," Latin for "the healing plant." It is a subtle way of reintroducing the notion of botanical curatives, an idea we met as far back on the path as "The Blue Sky." To offset the prose, Snyder follows his first paragraph with a five-line stanza of highly alliterative verse and short dynamic images to bring the reader face to face with the living plant itself: "multi-stemmed, forking / twiglets jut sidewise, a scatter of silky tiny leaves." The next fifteen lines return to prose as Snyder expounds on the affinities of artemisia. First we learn how animals, both small and large, have traditionally used the plant for food and shelter. Always quick to point out the humor of the commonplace, Snyder tells us that "[e]lk eat it and belch a lot." He then moves on quite logically to mention human interrelationships with sagebrush. As we might expect, his examples are drawn primarily from Native American usage, especially that of the Hopi and the Cahuilla. For "tens of thousands of years," he tells us, the plant has been used to make clothing, provide firewood and incense, form the basis for a healing tea or a women's tonic. Ever the linguist, Snyder points out linguistic variations on the word from tribe to tribe as well as dialectical differences within tribes: *"wi:'kwapi," "wikwat," "sawabi," "sangwabi."* In doing so, he underscores the legitimacy of native terms alongside the nomenclature of modern science even as he composes a strangely resonant poetry based on these exotic words. The plant itself is endowed with a veneer of magical mysticism.

Turning again to a set of artfully structured and rhythmical lines, Snyder forges the actual link between the plant and The Goddess, establishing them together in their communal setting that stretches for miles across the ranges of the Great Basin: "Artemisia, / who lives across the ranges, / stretching for miles, / she's always there: / with saltbush and greasewood, with rabbitbrush / and all the little grasses." Just as the heard sound of the native words for sagebrush enchants the ear, so these seven lines induce the visual image of The Goddess to emerge, transfigured, from the "blue-gray-green" of the plant. For a brief moment we are imaginatively in the same half-natural, half-supernatural, atmosphere of the Nō play. Like the traveling *waki*, our encounter with the commonplace has suddenly left us in the presence of a spirit.

Allowing us only a glimpse of The Goddess in her "blue-gray-green," Snyder returns to prose and factual information. Moving beyond his opening description of North American sagebrush, he now establishes the plant, and therefore The Goddess, as a circumplanetary entity by linking it with both Europe and Asia. In Japan there are at least "thirty species" of artemisia, and China identifies it as "mugwort" and "moxa." In Europe, as he tells us, sagebrush plants "are known as wormwood." Literally bringing The Goddess closer to home, Snyder implies that we will find her among our kitchen seasonings: "Tarragon's a wormwood." Hidden in the technical name for tarragon—*"Artemisia dracunculus,"* or "dragon wort"—is the hint of risk; this spice belongs to the realm of the coiled serpent ("tarragon" *American Heritage*). Dismissing Pernod as harmless, he points instead to the supposed dangers of drinking absinthe tinged with the "wormwood *absinthium*"; the manufacture of absinthe was prohibited in France in 1915. Snyder connects wormwood—and the inspiration of The Goddess he associates with it—to the visionary world of French symbolist art, specifically to the poet Arthur Rimbaud:

> To Ernest Delahaye Parshit [Paris], Junish [18]72.
>
> There is a drinking place I prefer here. Long live the Academy of Absinth, in spite of the ill-temper of the waiters! It is the most delicate, the most tremulous of garments—this drunkenness induced by virtue of that *sage of the glaciers, absomphe* [absinth]! (Rimbaud 315, my emphasis and brackets)[20]

Educated by wormwood-induced drunkenness in the "Academy of Absinth," Rimbaud blends wisdom and the smack of sage in his drink. The glacier image is easily explained by the common practice of serving the drink with ice, the water and absinthe mixing to produce a cold, cloudy, greenish-white liquid. Snyder, however, deliberately translates Rimbaud's "*sauge de glaciers*" ("sage of the glaciers") as "sagebrush of the glaciers," linking the botanical images of "Earrings Dangling" with those of the ice-age glaciers presented in the previous section, "Raven's Beak River," and reinforcing Artemis's position as an ice-age goddess. These collective image clusters are reminiscent of Rimbaud, who was known for his unconventional lifestyle, his prose poems, and his unusual imagistic correlations. The French poet becomes Snyder's example of the rhapsodic artist who lives on, or beyond, the edge of common life, unafraid of visions or the substances that produce them. Even as the dangerous "[w]ormwood is sacred to Artemis," the hallucinations inspired by this wild goddess of silver moonlight may lead to derangement of one's senses or to moments of pure vision and flawless integration. In a nondual world these reveries flow together; they are not two.

Snyder's adaptation of the Homeric "Second Hymn to Artemis" is to remind us that she "loves to hunt / in the shadows of mountains / and in the wind" (Athanassakis 65; Baring and Cashford 320).[21] Incorporeal, she lurks in shadows and wind, but not just of mountains and rivers. Picking up from where his description left off earlier, Snyder tells us that "[h]er blue-gray-green" fills the "emptiness" of "sagebrush flats" that reach "to the edge" and then "bend away— / . . . far as the mind can see." In this sense, "Earrings Dangling" looks ahead to the vast desert locale of the final section in *Mountains and Rivers Without End.* Like the worldwide artemisia, The Goddess in her many guises may be found everywhere; with a "flick of danger" the allure of her dangling sagebrush earrings conveys both the adventure and the risk of listening to her song. To meet her, as Snyder surely has, is a perilous encounter, one that may end with destruction, as it did when Actaeon saw Artemis naked, or with instruction, as when Odysseus listened to the call of the sirens.

Typically, Snyder turns to etymology to enhance his imagistic associations. The poetic figure of The Goddess with the pendant sagebrush earrings is conceived of when he sees a trace of Artemis's name in the Greek word "*artem,*" glossed by the poet as "to dangle" or "earring." Indeed *artema,* a neuter noun, does mean "a hanging ornament, earring," coming from the verb *artao,* which means "to fasten to" or "hang upon" (*Intermediate Greek-English Lexicon*). Yet Snyder does not stop there. The Latin *artem,* an accusative form of *ars,* is the basis for the English word *art,* and a further chain of connections relying on the Indo-European root *ar-* (to fit together) relates these words to "articulate" (*articulatus,* or "jointed"), an especially well chosen link in that it conveys the power of speech ascribed to one who speaks clearly and distinctly ("art," "articulate," "ar-," *American Heritage* 74, 75, 1506). Inspired by artemisia and Artemis, Snyder's careful articulation of his long poem, both in its entirety and in its parts, leaves us no doubt that it is "[w]ell-connected." In Buddhist terms, of course, these verbal-visual connections continually create and recreate one another; emptiness results and compassion arises.[22]

Snyder's images, like Rimbaud's, dance surrealistically across the synapses of our brain. We imagine rain showers advancing toward us across the vast spaces of the desert. Mentally, one smells the heavy aroma of the wet sagebrush. Yet this undulation in the mind is equally a ghostly dance: Artemis / *Artemisia*'s attendant "[r]aincloud maidens," their "gray skirts sweeping and trailing" along the Great Basin playa, accompany the sagebrush Goddess as she approaches. Snyder's discovery of the Muse within himself derives from his belief that "men become creative when they touch the woman in themselves" (foreword, *Divine Woman* xii), and it is not unusual for him to couch this "male-female play in our own hearts" in terms of landscape images that are simultaneously internal and external:

> We work with the faint facts of a Neolithic past and the actual facts of a planet-wide interconnected web of living beings. The totality of this biosphere is called by some *Gaia* after the ancient Greek Earth Goddess. It should be no surprise that one singer will be inspired by the heavy breast of a slender girl and another by the wind whipping through a col plastering the cliffs with gleaming rain. (foreword, *Divine Woman* xii)

Inspired by his raincloud Muse, walking the desert with her sagebrush earrings dangling, Snyder concludes with his variation on the Second Homeric Hymn's sacred apostrophe to The Goddess of the Wild: "Hail, Artemisia, / aromatic in the rain, / I will think of you in my other poems." In this way he invokes her presence in reverence even as he acknowledges his gratitude to her. She prefigures the conclusion of his long poem. Raincloud maidens walk in the emptiness of the sagebrush flats; in the apparent void of the desert playa, Lake Lahontan will rise again.

CROSS-LEGG'D

One's relationship to The Goddess, tinged by Tantric theory and practice, is a central issue in *Mountains and Rivers Without End.* Understood as a male-female, lover-beloved dyad, this liaison expresses several ideas. As seen in "Earrings Dangling and Miles of Desert" or in "With This Flesh," a male poet maintains contact with The Goddess in order to tap the female spirit of creativity within himself even as he draws from the well of her inspiration. A far different application of the dyadic metaphor shows human beings striving for balance in their association with the abiding presence of the biosphere personified as a female (Gaia, or "Mother" Nature). In this schema, human beings are seen as "male." Moreover, it is commonplace to say that modern human societies, especially those industrial and commercial giants who consume the majority of global resources, are busily "raping" the feminine planet. Ecofeminists object to gendering the planet with such metaphors, and

Gary Snyder, undeniably a prime mover in the modern ecological movement, is obviously aware of the dangers of planetary sex-typing. Yet Snyder continues to offer gendered metaphors in *Mountains and Rivers.* In Buddhist terms, however, interpenetration is a dynamic force eternally involving both "the one" and "the other," and thus the issue becomes an "empty" matter. One goes beyond the fixity of either side of such dualities even while savoring the tangible reality of the *samsaric* world. Emptiness is always realized as a dynamic, always a matter for ongoing interconnections. In sexual terms it is an unceasing dialectic that respects both male and female, their union, and the bliss engendered by, yet literally rooted in, their here-and-now union. It is as simple as that.

When the female figures of Tantric literature "join forces with men," as Miranda Shaw informs us, "the women become spiritual allies and esteemed teachers, mystical companions, and bestowers of magical powers and enlightenment. Men are portrayed not as dominators of women but as supplicants, lovers, and spiritual sons and brothers" (Shaw 37). Reading the sections of *Mountains and Rivers,* one sees that these are modes in which Snyder approaches The Goddess: supplicant, lover, spiritual son, and brother. An early section, "The Flowing," metaphorically mates the poet with the river goddess to suggest one manner in which poems get made: "The root of me / hardens and lifts to you, / thick flowing river, // my skin shivers. I quit // making this poem" (*MRWE* 72). The image cluster, minus the river, reappears in a single line of "Cross Legg'd": "Love made, poems, makyngs." Poets are called "makers" because the word *poem* derives from the Greek *poema,* a "created thing" we might even call a "making." The antiquity of these "old touches" of verbal and sexual creation, characteristic attributes of human behavior from its beginnings, is echoed further in Snyder's use of a Middle English spelling for "makyngs," reminding the reader of other etymological links—"to construct," "to mix," "to mate" or "to match" (Indo-European root: *mag-, American Heritage* 1527)—all of which apply in this poem that not only speaks of sexual mating but returns us to the image of Milarepa who "four times built a tower of stone" on his way to enlightenment. Out of such matings and makings we construct the world again and again. Out of the merge of dualities we make the illusions we live by, yet it is only through that miragelike reality that we see the nature of the illusion we have constructed. This illusory world is real.

As the authentic "Ma" in "Mā" pins down The Goddess as a real-life mother-on-earth, so in "Cross-Legg'd" the poet appears personally as lover, and his wife, Carole Koda, to whom the section is dedicated, appears as the veritable beloved Goddess. Devotion to The Goddess in this here-and-now world means, as Snyder once said, that both lovers "must have practiced the lonely yogas and wanderings, and then seek the center of the individual-body and group-body mandala; dedicating their two loving bodies to the whole network; the man evoking the Goddess in the girl on suitable occasions and worshiping her" (*EHH* 133). "Cross-Legg'd" celebrates the sensuous tangibility of their intimate interconnected reality—their mutual carnal and mindful interpenetration—even as it reaches beyond into the abstractions of spiritual bliss.

Thus if cross-leggedness refers to the folded leg position of a devotee in meditation (i.e., the "lotus" position), in this section it refers also to the position of the partners' legs as dictated by the Vajrayana ritual of sexual union called *yab-yum*. As Joseph Campbell has pointed out,

> In the Buddhist lamaseries of Tibet, . . . the holy images and banners showed the various Buddhas and Bodhisattvas joined with their Shaktis in embrace, in the yogic posture known as Yab-Yum, "Father-Mother." And the great prayer of the old prayer wheels of Tibet, OM *maṇi padme* HUM, "The jewel (*maṇi*) in the lotus (*padme*)," signifies, on one level: the immanence of nirvana (the jewel) in samsara (the lotus); another: the arrival of the mind (the jewel) in nirvana (the lotus); but also, as in the icon of the male and female joined: the lingam in the yoni. (*Oriental* 352)

Widely represented in the Buddhist art of India, Nepal, and Tibet, this sexual embrace of the male deity with his female consort refers as well to "the mystical union" of compassion, seen as the skillful means by which a Bodhisattva guides beings toward nirvana (*upāya*, conceived of as masculine) with wisdom (*prajñā*, conceived of as feminine). It is "a fusion necessary to overcome the false duality of the world of appearances in the striving toward spiritual enlightenment" ("yab-yum" *Encyclopaedia Britannica*).

The poem has all the hallmarks of a formal rite. Since Snyder is a practitioner of Zen, the mention of "drinking tea" always signals a ritual tone, a time for thoughtful clarity, in his poems. Another measure of the poem's formality is seen in the use of two-line stanzas throughout the section and the emphasis on heavily alliterated, often monosyllabic, words. Thus, one evening in the "dim light" after "dinner" is "done" we find the poet and his beloved sitting "[c]ross-legg'd under the low tent roof." They come together in the "dry old west," its dryness reminding us of the Buddhist epithet—the "dusty world"—used to refer to the illusory surface of this veritable earth on which we live. Imbued with delicate eroticism, the lines show us the lovers, face to face, each lifting the other's shirt, revealing bare skin. Deftly, Snyder uses a single word for a double purpose: their "lean" physiques "lean" toward each other, and they "touch lips." The image tells us that the couple is face to face in the *yab-yum* position. In this loving sexual embrace, as they have—and as a multitude of others have—done many times before, they go beyond refreshing their lives to recreating them. It is always the same old "stuff / life after life," yet it is "always new," each time, like Milarepa's constructions on the way to nirvana, as if it were "the first."

This specific act of love that transpires between Koda and Snyder—"[o]ur love"—

may have taken place literally among the "rocks and streams" near their house in the Sierra Nevada; the south fork of the Yuba has an abundance of boulders along its watercourses. Yet, as a generic act that has taken place from the first moments of the planet's life until now, the metaphoric act of love has been mixed with "rocks [mountains] and streams [rivers]." Geologically, it was an intermingling of rock and water that carved the surface of the planet. The dyadic metaphor looks back to "Bubbs Creek Haircut," where Shiva, the "mat-haired mountain sitter," is entranced away from his rock-bound austerities on the peaks of the Himalayas by the "slippery dance" of Pārvāti, a "flowing girl" who coils around him. Their conjunction is enough to make the world leap forth "in fire." In "Cross-Legg'd" Snyder again calls on words to do multiple duty. "Rocks" is easily transformed into a sexual "rocking motion" of the two bodies; it may even convey the regular rhythmic beat of their hearts. The noun "streams," denoting "rivers," could just as well be a verb denoting the flow of "a heartbeat, a breath, a gaze" in the following line. Intermingled by the love act, their hearts, their breathing, their gaze become one, beyond duality. This simple clarity makes a "place" in the chaotic "dizzy eddy" of the world's flow. For a moment there is a "created space" ("Endless Streams and Mountains") into which minds and bodies may slide as if they were "two places. Forever, // or, not even one" ("Instructions"). This "old clear way" is a creative and passionate fire. Like the aftermath of volcanic upthrust, creating the land we live on, even as the flow of energy subsides, it still has "sizzle"; it still has the warm glow of "ash and embers." Phoenixlike, these energies will rise from the ashes again, and again, and again.

With a final cluster of images, Snyder accentuates the primitive. These events began "under the low tent roof," and we again hear the sound of the "[s]cratchy breeze on the tent fly." To be at home in "Cross-Legg'd" is to be among the rocks and streams, the night sky, the scratchy breeze. The final images suggest those of an earlier poem where primitive life—animal and human—is eked out in the "dust of the old bones, / old songs and tales" ("Old Bones"). The harshness of that reality has its compensations. "Primitive" peoples, according to Snyder,

> live vastly in the present. Their daily reality is a fabric of friends and family, the field of feeling and energy that one's own body is, the earth they stand on and the wind that wraps around it; and various areas of consciousness. (*EHH* 117)

Stripped of illusions and the so-called sophistications of civilization, the primitive stand—or sit—naked before one another, fully aware of the "field of feeling and energy" that comprises "one's own body . . . the earth . . . and the wind that wraps around it." By the fire over which they have cooked their dinner, as well as in the creative fire of their own making, these two—Snyder and Koda—"hunch on bones," ready for "what comes," a phrase that signifies the bliss of sexual climax as surely as it does the uncertain future. One in their coupling, they establish a communal fabric:

"one sip tea" yet "two be here." Essential, if sometimes harsh and often dangerous, the primitive, wherever Snyder finds it, is always the place to begin from, again and again.

AFLOAT

In "Afloat" we once again float on the waters of the Pacific Northwest. The poetic kayaking trip in this "inlet-basin world of cries and whistles" actually records a double-kayak voyage shared by Snyder and a companion, most likely Carole Koda, in Adams Inlet, Glacier Bay (cf. tag line to "Afloat," *North Pacific Lands & Waters*). Remarkably, in only two generations, the glaciers have retreated so extensively here that what used to be under ice is now under water: "and all this realm was under ice-fields ten miles long, / when my grandfather drove his team." What appeared solid has clearly become flowing. The second line playfully underscores such interconnecting opposites: the words "water" and "rock" are literally juxtaposed with one another.

The lines in this highly rhythmical section imply motion and sound everywhere: the paddling of the kayak, the movements of mountains and waters, the sliding of the moon, the diving of the birds, even the slow grind of the glaciers over the gravel. Snyder embodies all the motions in the rhythms of these poetic lines, leaving little that one might call prosaic in this section. Boats float and rock and ripple as the sea and sky "slip slow[ly] by." The prosody is conspicuous. There are both internal rhymes and occasional end rhymes. Using a rhythmic technique that Whitman relied on long before, Snyder repeats initial words in successive lines: like-like-like, the-the-the-the-the, in-in. Grammatical patterns abound in parallel. The progressive tense ending (*-ing*) provides a sense of insistent present movement: "[f]loating," "paddling," "crossing," "roiling," "casting." At other times insistent motion or sound appears to be caught by monosyllabic action verbs: "churn," "turn," "glint," "bob," "dip," "dive," "splash," "tweet," and "croak." Even the sizes of the stanzas give the effect of wave motion; in general the section swells and then diminishes. Beginning with a preponderance of two-line stanzas, in the middle the poem pulses with stanzas of eight and three and seven lines long. Concluding line groupings ebb in length, falling from five, to two, and finally to a single-line stanza at the end.

If these rhythms contribute to the reader's imaginative sense of actuality, that this voyage is imaginatively taking place in the here and now, the section also invites readers to join the poet on another multileveled journey. There are overtones of the magical boat that drifts in the watery foreground of "Endless Streams and Mountains" and of Rā's mythological "Boat of a Million Years" that surges forward each morning between the turquoise sycamores, sailing and sailing (*"walking on walking"*) across atmospheres above the eternally turning earth. As Snyder has reminded us in "Raven's Beak River," these are the waters of the ice age, liquid from ancient glaciers flowing out of the past and into our present (and future) time. The kayak and setting of this section may be as "real" as the *Sappa Creek* of Snyder's past, but the landscape is a primal world of water and land, current and air, one reminiscent of archetypal myths involving vast expanses of sea and sky.

> Floating in a tiny boat
> lightly on the water, rock with every ripple,
>
> another skin that slides along the water
> hung by sea and sky

Here "land meets water meets the sky." Remembering that "Afloat" was published as the leadoff poem in *North Pacific Lands & Waters* (1993), a book significantly enhanced by Bill Holm's drawings of Haida totems, we know we have returned to the world of Snyder's 1951 Reed thesis on Haida myth. The parallel with certain Native American tales is striking:

> First there was ocean . . . infinite water.
> And there was sky . . . infinite air.
> The water was strong, thick, clear . . . forever pushing upwards. The air was thin but heavy . . . forever pushing down. Invisible elements in the ashen light of precreation.
>
> And where the line was drawn between the ocean and the sky, a raft floated . . . eternal, forever bound on this unseen line of two opposing forces.
>
> (Simpson 13)

These are the opening lines of a Maidu creation myth. Snyder's tiny boat, a "husk" or "skin" in its own right, also floats on a "line drawn between the ocean and sky," a skin of another kind, a "membrane" that marks the edge of water and sky. Fragile and durable at the same time, the membrane is a portal between worlds: among others, sea and air, lower and upper, timeless spiritual and present moment. It is a sacred site where creation, or enlightenment, can occur.

> The raft came drifting from the north, moving quietly, moving quickly between those two translucent layers, carried out of voidness and in to voidness by unchallenged water currents running wildly through eternity.
>
> And the raft revolving slowly, turning first this way and then the other, was forever buffeted by fitful winds of air and made to play a whirling game of aimlessness.
>
> Thus the raft ever traveled, each movement and every direction a whim to the invisible elements of precreation. (Simpson 13)

Eventually, the Maidu tale brings Worldmaker down from an upper world of timelessness to confront Turtle and his companion, Peheipe the clown, who seem to have been drifting on the raft from the moment of their consciousness. Upon Worldmaker's insistence, Turtle dives deeply to procure a bit of slime from the bottom; with this mud the world begins. Many such tales exist among Native Americans, and considerable variation occurs from storyteller to storyteller or tribe to tribe. Even within the same tribal society variations appear over the years of telling and retelling. Another version of the myth, interesting because Snyder wrote a foreword for the book in which it appears, relates how Earthmaker floats over a world covered in water unable to find "even a tiny bit of land." Coyote appears and tells him to "imagine where in this world / some land might be" and then the two of them can "float to that place." Much as Snyder does in some sections of *Mountains and Rivers,* they attempt to sing the land into existence: "Where are you, little bit of earth?" or "Where is there land?" Earthmaker finally says: "If I could but see a little bit of land / I might do something very good with it." Then, as if by magic, "Floating along . . . / they saw something like a bird's nest." Earthmaker stretches it out to make the world (Shipley 18–20), an event already referred to in "Old Woodrat's Stinky House." The Concow Maidu also speak of a watery world at the beginning:

> This world was dark when first created, and all under water. There were no living beings and no light to be seen. The only light was Creator himself—and he rode in a boat. There was a floating Turtle down from the north, and he landed on the north end of the boat where the Creator sat. The Creator asked the Turtle, "How are you on diving?" (Chase 37)

Each of the above myths belongs to the Maidu people, a culture group that Gary Snyder has studied closely. According to Shipley, the original homeland of the Maidu was (is) at "the northern end of the Sierra Nevada, just east and south of Mount Lassen" (6). In other words, not far from Snyder's home at Kitkitdizze. Still other native groups of the North Pacific have similar tales. The Kutchin people say: "In the days when the earth was all covered with water, the animals lived on a large raft. The Crow said, 'Had I any earth, even so little, I would make it grow large enough for all the animals to live upon'" (Goodchild 34). The Bering Strait Eskimo speak of the "first days" when

> the earth was flooded except [for] a very high mountain in the middle. The water came up from the sea and covered all the land except the top of this mountain; only a few animals were saved. . . . During the flood the waves and currents cut the surface of the land into hollows and ridges, and then, as the water receded, it ran back into the sea, leaving the mountains and valleys as they are today. (Goodchild 35)

In addition to obvious echoes with the Judeo-Christian flood, many of these tales demonstrate the "Earth Diver" motif, a "popular Siberian and North American myth about an animal that created dry land (i.e., the earth as we know it) by diving down into the primordial water to bring back some mud" (Goodchild 1). Even with observable differences among the tales, the general setting for the creation myths of the North Pacific culture groups varies little. This primal world of water and air, of floating rafts, animals, and mythical beings, has few human beings in evidence; they remain to be created. In terms of our modern world, as Snyder envisions it, the human need is to be recreated, again and again and again, endlessly.

According to Robert Bringhurst, the Haida, like other Pacific Rim peoples,

> lived primarily at and on the surface of the sea: in boats and in the intertidal zone. They lived in intimate familiarity with that membrane, sometimes savage, sometimes calm, through which grebes and harbor seals and killer whales, harpoons and halibut lines and paddles vanish, refract and reappear. This membrane, called *xhaaidla* in Haida, stretches skin-tight and resonant over everything in the world of Haida myth. It is the surface of the sea, the land, the sky: the skin of the world, through which the black bears pass as they enter their dens, the killer whales as they sound, and the sharp-shin hawks and eagles as they glide behind the mountain. When they cross the boundary and enter their houses, the mythtellers say, the animals take off their feather cloaks or skins. There they appear to one another, and converse with one another, just as we do here among ourselves. They too, in other words, are people. (16–17)

Snyder's tiny skin boat also "trembles on the membrane," where "sky and water" are "stitched together." Other than the humans in the kayak and an occasional seal's head, the "animals" in "Afloat" are birds: "oystercatchers," "kittiwakes," "murres," "murrelets," "terns," "petrels," "geese," and those omnipresent birds of the Pacific Northwest, the ravens, which "tweet and croak and gurgle in the far-off / outflow alders." Like the animals of the Haida storytellers, when these birds are at home they "drop their masks and go on as they were." One can hear Snyder asking who we humans might truly be if we would "drop our masks" or forget our performances. The poet also implies, as he does with the sheep in "Arctic Midnight Twilight," that the animals and birds here are more "at home" in the world. Following the wisdom of the Native American mythtellers, we might yet discover the age-old intimate connection between the human and animal worlds. Before there were humans there were other beings. Except in the mind, the boundary line between our worlds is not impassable and divisive, but a permeable membrane through which humans could pass in an instant. Creatures of the forest, sky, and sea, in fact, can show us the way.

> Haida poets say the gods call human beings *xhaaidla xhitiit giidai*, "common surface birds,"' because we need animal escorts, nonhuman powers or guides, in order to penetrate that skin between the world we can see and the ones we dream of, sing of, paint and carve. But the usual name for us wingless, finless, gill-less, naked creatures is simply surface people, *xhaaidla xhaaidaghai*, as distinct from the people of the forest, sky and sea: *hlkkyaan isgyan sagwa isgyan taangghwan xhaaidaghai*." (Bringhurst 17)

The winglike "twin kayak paddles" work with the currents, some ethereal, some of this world: "paddling forward, paddling backward / crossing at an angle." The boat is buffeted by wind and water as the tide "sucks and coils"; the "waters churn together." And so, like the raft of the creation myth, "each movement and every direction" seems "a whim to the invisible elements of precreation." A clear connection to Pierre Teilhard de Chardin is here. Unlike the anthropocentric Teilhard who said "seize the tiller of the planet," in Gary Snyder's view "we are led by dolphins toward morning." In this vast universe, human effort—symbolized by the decisions, performances, and constructions of "judges and speechmakers, actresses and carpenters"—becomes marginal. Not negligible, but marginal. We are "small fish fry" caught in "the tide-suck dark draft sea, / floating in the weaving / of clouds, ice, tides." Where exactly are we? What is our purpose? To have a goal would indicate a direction toward a destination, but "there is no place we are / but maybe here." As always in Snyder's imagination, the other world becomes this world, endlessly returning on itself, forever creating itself anew. Emptiness is suchness. The far shore is here and now. Never a call to be indifferent or unmoved or hedonistic; there is, instead, a recognition that this, our only place, is always a beginning, a place to practice. In this grand place of motion, sound, and light, in this unceasing revolving universe, Snyder suggests we should be grateful that we are "only to be here!" "Afloat" is Gary Snyder's own creation tale, a journey toward nonduality, a fusion of sea and sky, an intermingling of the animal world and the human world. Snyder's tiny boat, a kayak, literally holds two bodies in one boat, "two souls in one body." Like a single bird with "two sets of wings," the partners paddle the air and sea together, in unison, even as the land-water-sky are also in unison. In this "tiny skin boat"—like Koda and Snyder in *yab-yum*—they are indeed only "here" in the moment.

THE DANCE

Mountains and Rivers Without End, replete with sound and the rush of energy, at times bursts forth in expressive kinesthetic imagery. "The Dance," the last section to be added to the sequence, celebrates a fundamental metaphor of movement in the long poem. Located between the rocking waves of "Afloat" and the churning waters of "We Wash Our Bowls in This Water," this section undoubtedly prefigures that visionary moment when Snyder's persona, the journeying *waki,* will come face to face with the final ecstatic dance of the *shité,* Snyder's version of Yamamba, the old woman of the mountains.

Bill Moyers, reflecting on his association with Joseph Campbell—an encounter that engendered the six-part PBS television series *The Power of Myth* and a book based on the series—retells Campbell's story of an American in Japan who didn't understand "the ideology" or the "theology" of a certain Shinto priest. Reflecting on this, the Japanese priest told the American: "I think we don't have ideology," he said. "We don't have theology. We dance" (*Power of Myth* xix). Shinto, as the *Shambhala*

Dictionary of Buddhism and Zen tells us, began as a "primitive nature religion" and is "characterized by belief in a multitude of deities. Every mountain, every river—all forms of nature are associated with a deity (*kami*)" ("Shintō"). Similarly, Snyder's *Mountains and Rivers Without End* incorporates a multitude of spirits. Behind or within every plant, every animal, every landscape there looms a presence, and, like the Shinto priest in Campbell's story, or Campbell himself, Snyder surely thinks of these presences as figures in a grand poetic dance and not as "ideology" or "theology." In this section—which focuses on Ame-no-uzume's dance to lure Amaterasu, the sun goddess, out of the darkened cave into which she had retreated—Snyder not only sketches in words the mythical beginnings of the performing arts in Japan, but underscores the essential kinesthesia of both the Nō theater and *Mountains and Rivers.*

"Dancing," as Heinrich Zimmer tells us, is "an ancient form of magic" in which "the dancer becomes amplified into a being endowed with supra-normal powers." Commenting on the "Dance of Shiva," Zimmer explains that such dancing "induces trance, ecstasy, the experience of the divine, the realization of one's own secret nature." If, on the one hand, there is ecstatic dancing, it must be complemented by "austerities of the meditation grove" based on "absolute introversion," for "[t]o work magic, to put enchantments upon others, one has first to put enchantments on oneself" (151). The dance, especially "pantomimic dance" in which the dancer is transmuted "into whatever demon, god, or earthly existence he impersonates," is "an act of creation" that is intended to bring about transformation. It "summons into the dancer a new and higher personality," but it also serves a "cosmogonic function, in that it arouses dormant energies which may then shape the world" (151–52). We have already witnessed such dancing in lines from "Bubbs Creek Haircut," where a "Daughter of mountains, stooped / moon breast Parvati" is said to entrance Shiva with her "slippery dance." Pārvāti, said to be a "flowing girl," is equated with the "valley spirit / Anahita" and the river goddess Sarasvatī. The "water . . . cuts back quartzflake sand" as it flows from peaks to valleys; the sexual "dark and female gate of all the world" invites movement from the monastic masculine Shiva, the unmoved "mat-haired mountain sitter." Ultimately he is charmed by her movements "to leap in fire" (MRWE 36). The fundamental transforming "dance" of the planet takes place as rivers carve the landscapes; in the process life forms are engendered out of the sitting earth. These movements have been noted in great detail in "The Flowing." Similarly, individuals may be transformed by the Tantric "dance" presented by the *yab-yum* ritual of "Cross-Legg'd."

The section opens with an epigraph from Otto Rössler that, in sum, suggests that when energy works against itself it produces "something productive" and when nature works against itself it produces—out of its own "self-entanglement"—something of "beauty" (Gleick 142). The connection with the story of Amaterasu is unmistakable: her self-entanglement—even against her own better judgment—leads her into darkness. Luring her from its depths necessitates the invention of Ame-no-uzume's provocative dance, the cornerstone for the Japanese performing arts.

Snyder's compressed retelling of this Shinto creation story is based on variations recorded in the *Nihongi* and *Kojiki*, the first books of Japanese mythology. He begins with Izanami's procreative energies, clearly emphasizing the feminine perspective. A poetic echo of the Hindu Pārvāti and Shiva, Izanami is the consort of Izanagi. Together they form the most significant of several original pairs of divine couples. From high above in a cloud world, Izanagi stirs the waters below him with a diamond-tipped spear until, eventually, land begins to form. Descending to this firmer ground, the couple mates and, after a false start or two, Izanami begins to produce the forms of the world. Snyder's poem starts at this point: "Izanami / gave birth to rocks, trees, rivers, mountains, grass." Tragedy soon strikes when she gives birth to fire; as Snyder says, "so burned she died." Skipping over multiple details, the poet picks up the story when the lonely Izanagi, like the Greek Orpheus, goes to the underworld (Yomi)—a "land of darkness"—in an attempt to bring Izanami back. After promising not to look at her, he then breaks his vow and is treated to a vision of her rotting corpse, "a mass of pollution." He is horrified by his encounter with decay and death; for her part, she is so mortified that she pursues him, vowing to enact retribution on him. Snyder's intent in relating this part of the myth is clear, for he has often spoken of the need to recognize the totality of life:

> Life in the wild is not just eating berries in the sunlight. I like to imagine a "depth ecology" that would go to the dark side of nature—the ball of crunched bones in a scat, the feathers in the snow, the tales of insatiable appetite. . . . [T]here is a world of nature on the decay side, a world of beings who do rot and decay in the shade. Human beings have made much of purity and are repelled by blood, pollution, putrefaction. The other side of the "sacred" is the sight of your beloved in the underworld, dripping with maggots. Coyote, Orpheus, and Izanagi cannot help but look, and they lose her. Shame, grief, embarrassment, and fear are the anaerobic fuels of the dark imagination. (*Practice* 110–11)

Ultimately, Izanagi survives by rolling a rock in front of the entrance to the underworld, sealing Izanami in Yomi forever. She vows to have thousands of people killed, and he vows to have more born than she can kill; thus the world, having encountered the mystery of death, manages to proceed.

Izanagi then commences to purify himself: "ah wash her clear stream." As he washes off the pollution, new divinities are formed. Among others Amaterasu is born from a teardrop of his left eye, and her brother, Susanowo, is born from the ooze in his nostril. Again focusing on the feminine, Snyder seems to sum up her birth, and the symbolic birth of all ensuing generations, in the lines: "—skinny little girl with *big* ears / we have passed through / passed through,   flesh out of flesh." Since there seems to be no evidence among the myths for Amaterasu to have "*big* ears," it seems likely that Snyder intends this detail to connect with the "[g]reat ears shining" of "Jackrabbit." Since Amaterasu is, after all, referred to as "Shining Heavens" and the curiosity symbolized by her big ears will ultimately bring her out of the cave, the link is obvious. Once again attentive listening is a key ingredient of *Mountains and Rivers.*

Paralleling the dyadic on-again, off-again, relationship of Izanagi and Izanami, Susanowo, jealous of his sister's position, contaminates her shining palace with "mud and shit and a half-skinned pony," which causes her, like Izanami before her, to become separated from the world: she "entered a cave [and] made the world dark." At this point in the story the literal dance of Ame-no-uzume begins, although some would say its undulations and vibrations have been present from the opening lines of the narrative. Snyder's retelling of Ame-no-uzume's dance is, as he says, taken from commentaries written by Jean Herbert and Allan Grapard. First he gives us Herbert's version of this "Outrageous Heavenly Woman." She wraps moss about her hips, bamboo grass about her wrists, and nishikigi leaves about her forehead and then stomps and stamps on the sounding board she has placed in front of Amaterasu's cave. A "goddess possessed," like Pārvāti before Shiva, Ame-no-uzume undulates erotically until all the thousands of watching gods begin to laugh, whistle, and cheer at her bawdy show. Her energetic, procreative, sensuous dance creates the sounds that titillate the curious ears of Amaterasu. Light comes out of the darkened cave; the world proceeds apace once more.

Defining the rhythms of his own lyrical dance, Snyder then breaks away from the Shinto story to describe the planetary engendering dance of the mystical Goddess, the "masked dancer" who lies behind each of the named or visible emanations of The Goddess that the reader encounters in *Mountains and Rivers.* No one will ever lift her veil completely. As in "The Flowing," Snyder eulogizes her dance as the movement of the river, "the whole river" from its beginning as a series of flowing creeklets emanating from stationary "rock-rimmed" sources high in the mountains above, winding down to the valleys and basins below. The basin appears to call forth the flow. Snyder deliberately connects this dance with that observed in the Nō theater, for he uses the technical terms associated with it: the "stamp of the foot" and the "*mai*" (dance) that forms the climactic moment of each spirit play. There may also be a secondary play on the word *mai,* in that Snyder has used it to speak of the rhythmical "pulse" or "vein" of a mountain range (*Practice* 102). If readers have any familiarity with the Nō drama, they will experience double vision in these lines, at times seeing the Nō dancer gliding and turning with consummate artistry on the stage before them, at other times envisioning the mythical goddess of the river twisting her way down the "gravelly bar" of the riverbed, coiling her way down from the "headwaters, mountains, / breathing icy bliss," bringing down the "diamond-glittered" snowmelt as water, the jeweled bits of "inorganic granite" as "grains" or "salt" or "gold dust," and the mud and dirt that forms our world and out of which we arise once more. If there are "dry riverbeds," if trees on the "[h]ills of Yugoslavia" have been "clearcut" to make boats for the imperialist Roman fleet, if springs have gone dry in some areas, it is of no consequence to the never-ending planetary dance. Among the comings and goings of a diverse world over time, its "*walking on walking*," the planet continues on its cyclical rounds; the "*earth turns*" and its "*streams and mountains never stay the same*." Surely Teilhard was joking when he said humans could control these planetary motions; we are led by goddesses dancing down the mountains.

The implication of this intense poetic interval between the two descriptions of Ame-no-uzume's dance is clear. Not only is her dance the founding dance of the Nō theater, it exemplifies the dance of the river goddess around the mountain god, the dance of Pārvāti before Shiva, the dance of the coiling Kundalini dragon about the spine, the yoking of Fudō's wisdom with Kannon's (Kuan-yin, Avalokiteshvara) compassion, the jewel in the lotus, the conjunction represented by the *yab-yum* posture, and all other dyads of motion and stillness; it is the procreative dance of energy itself, literally glimpsed "in the raw."

We return then, to Grapard's prosaic version of Ame-no-uzume's dance where she has "bound up her sleeves with a cord of heavenly *hi-kage* vine, tied around her head a head-band of the heavenly *ma-saki* vine," and "bound together bundles of sasa leaves to hold in her hands." Instead of a "sounding-board," Grapard gives her an overturned bucket to stamp on. And so she does. Once again she is "divinely possessed" and once again her dance is described erotically: she exposes her breasts and lowers her skirt as she whirls. Matching Herbert's version, the end result of Ame-no-uzume's dance is the thunderous laughter of the gods, which Amaterasu hears with her "*big* ears." Her curiosity awakened, the sun goddess is lured, in opposition to her own will, out of her cave. Although Snyder does not relate the detail, once Amaterasu steps outside she is amazed by the sight of herself reflected in a mirror hung on a tree; consequently, she is unable to return to the cave. The gods' "little faces"—and those of all planetary beings—once again shine forth in her white light (*omoshiri*).

Rather cryptically, just before the end of the section Snyder reiterates selected details of the two versions, side by side in columnar form, so that the contrast in their story elements becomes evident. The tabular layout provides a prosaic, pseudoscientific touch to the lines, yet a strange kind of rhythm—visual and verbal in nature—also emanates from the rearrangement. The columns disappear as the lines suddenly become interrogatory. As if he were asking his readers, Snyder wonders: What was Ame-no-uzume wearing as she danced? and How far down did she, in fact, push her skirt? Does her "skirt-band" go "down to her genitals" as Grapard says, or does she show herself "down below" as in Herbert's version?

Why does Snyder present differing versions of this folktale? Some clarification is found in his essays. The Rössler excerpt introducing "The Dance" is taken from a chapter entitled "Strange Attractors" in James Gleick's book *Chaos: Making a New Science.* We have already become familiar with the notion of dyadic couplings in *Mountains and Rivers,* but the story behind "The Dance" introduces some new "strange attractors": Susanowo and Amaterasu; Ame-no-uzume and Amaterasu. Moreover, Gleick's theories provide parallels between Snyder's poetics and the fractal rhythms associated with chaos theory: "visible patterns in the turbulent flow—self-entangled stream lines, spiral vortices, whorls that rise before the eye and vanish again—must reflect patterns explained by laws not yet discovered" (Gleick 138). One need go no further than the modular rhythms of the Nō play—founded on Ame-no-uzume's dance—to see the intermingling of art and science. The Nō's insistence on echoing repetitive patterns at every level of its composition establishes it as an authentic model of fractal form. Snyder's musings on the effect of raw solar energy streaming through the universe provide further examples of the dance of energy and form. Snyder quotes Lewis Thomas, who tells us that a "steady flow of energy from the inexhaustible source of the sun . . . is mathematically destined to cause the organization of matter into an increasingly ordered state." It doesn't just "flow to the earth and radiate away." Instead it is "thermodynamically inevitable" that this energy flow will "rearrange matter into symmetry, away from probability, against entropy, lifting it so to speak into a constantly changing condition of rearrangement and molecular ornamentation." Thomas concludes:

> If there were to be sounds to represent this process, they would have the arrangement of the Brandenburg concertos, but I'm open to wondering whether the same events are recalled by the rhythms of insects, the long pulsing runs of bird songs, the descants of whales, the modulated vibrations of millions of locusts in migration. (*Lives of a Cell* 27–28, as qtd. in *Place* 146)

Among these constantly changing "rearrangements" of energy, Snyder would find still others: the "rhythms and modulations of archaic music, the little chants and choruses of songs and dances" (*Place* 146). Intriguingly these ideas about energy and form are proposed in Snyder's essay on "The Politics of Ethnopoetics," an extended argument for preserving diversity in tale-telling among multiple cultures. "The study of ethnopoetics," he says, "provides would-be poets and scholars with hundreds of models of poem strategies, forms, angles of imagery, types of word play and mindplay" that will "enrich our sense of human accomplishment" (*Place* 147). In short, energy constantly interacts with matter, giving birth to new forms. Among other perceptible patterns arising from this rhythmical dance we find artistic models in the shape of myths and folktales. Just as Snyder envisions an ecosystem tending toward "climax" where maximum diversity is the key to providing for stability and maturity, so he champions multiple versions of myths and tales to "enrich our sense of human accomplishment." Monoculture in any form is anathema in Snyder's world; dynamic diversity is the rule. And so we contemplate multiple versions of the folkloric dance of Ame-no-uzume. Ultimately there is no answer to Snyder's questioning at the end of the section; there is only the ongoing dance.

Every tale of light requires a lingering darkness. If we actually knew how far down Ame-no-uzume pushed her skirt, the wildness of symbolic myth would become formulaic allegory. The veil of The Goddess, so to speak, would be lifted. The flickering patterns of the dance—at times erotic, at times horrific—provide glimpses of life-and-death-in-the-making; it is a world of ceaseless process in which one never sees the whole picture. Still, these stroboscopic revelations of energy at work are alluring; without them the world and its beings would be resigned to deep isolation, sitting unmoved in complete and total darkness.

WE WASH OUR BOWLS IN THIS WATER

Snyder tells us that this section "incorporates a Zen training-hall meal verse" (*MRWE* 162), and, indeed, the exact set of lines appears, along with two other examples, as a mealtime chant in "Survival and Sacrament," the last essay in *The Practice of the Wild.*

> We wash our bowls in this water
> It has the flavor of ambrosial dew
> We offer it to all demons and spirits
> May all be filled and satisfied
> *Om makula sai svaha*
>
> (183)[23]

Readers of *The Practice of the Wild* are given several examples of mealtime "grace" and the simple lucid thought that an enlightened attitude comes down to "conduct that is entwined with food." Since all beings are part of an immense food chain, eating should be regarded as a sacramental act, and grace becomes "part of the first and last practice of the wild."

> Everyone who ever lived took the lives of other animals, pulled plants, plucked fruit, and ate. Primary people have had their own ways of trying to understand the precept of nonharming. They knew that taking life required gratitude and care. There is no death that is not somebody's food, no life that is not somebody's death. (*Practice* 183–84)

According to Snyder, the short conventional verses spoken at mealtimes—that is, saying grace—have all the earmarks of "superstitious-sounding old ritual formulas." Their "import," he says, "is older than Buddhism or any of the world religions," and they are "at the heart of the teaching." For Snyder, to recite such prayers is to reach into that veiled time before the Neolithic, toward the truth of the primitive (183).

In "An Offering for Tārā" Snyder presents his image of life as an ongoing *puja,* a vast potluck dinner in which all guests provide themselves as a meal for another. It is not surprising, then, as we approach the final pages of *Mountains and Rivers Without End,* to find Snyder bowing in reverence, as if reciting a grace. Still, "We Wash Our Bowls in This Water" cannot be dispensed with as if it were merely a short mealtime poem, for the section also has a role to play as an interlude between "The Dance" and "The Mountain Spirit," two sections with similar kinesthetic moments of immense significance for *Mountains and Rivers.*

"We Wash Our Bowls" is *not* a poem about food, but about water. Its complete effect can be felt only when one places the epigraph's scientific description of the planetary water cycle alongside Su Tung-p'o's enlightenment verse written to capture that illuminating moment when he heard the sound of the Buddha's tongue in the valley streams. Both texts describe the awesome power of water's flow, albeit in different realms, and both are singled out for comment in Snyder's notes to the section (*MRWE* 162). A similar combination of science and reverential imagery is found in his foreword to Edward Schafer's *The Divine Woman,* where Snyder quotes the same "water cycle" lines of the epigraph alongside thoughts of inspirational "rain maiden" goddesses; he then goes on to comment that "the work of art has always been to demonstrate and celebrate the interconnectedness: not to make everything 'one' but to make the 'many' authentic, to help illuminate it all" (*Place* 89–90). Similarly, "We Wash Our Bowls" both includes and goes beyond either science or poetry to become a graceful moment of reflection celebrating Snyder's acknowledgment that water, in *all* of its many emanations, is at the energetic heart of the teaching. However one reckons truth, either with numbers or images, the endless cycling of water—the flowing rivers, the encircling oceans, the misty clouds, the approach of the rain maidens, The Goddess in all her dancing forms—sustains life on the planet and literally moves the mountains and continents of Planet Earth to assume their continually evolving shapes.

There is little doubt that "We Wash Our Bowls" is a poem about raw energy. The section opens with a litany of nature's wild playfulness-at-work on a typical "day on the ragged North Pacific coast." Among multiple "*-ing*" forms—"whipp*ing*," "tumbl*ing*," "hang*ing*," "loop*ing*," "droop*ing*"—that emphasize movement, the reader's ears and eyes are assaulted by water, water, everywhere and in every form: mist, squalls, ponds, slush, creeks, falls, snowflakes, rivers, glaciers, pools, icebergs, streams, spume, and soft rain. Soaking us in this watery energy for an entire paragraph, Snyder suddenly pulls back to a quieter moment: "sea lions lazing under the surface of the sea." Like the section itself, the energy flows madly, then languidly melds into the silence of relative nonactivity.

The middle segment takes a turn toward the specific. Readers imagine a location: a river, a sandbar, a raft beached in the shallows after a long ride through some wild water. Indeed, the lines remind us of earlier trips in the poem, down the Tatshenshini ("Raven's Beak River") or the Stanislaus ("The Canyon Wren") Rivers. Snyder deliberately scrambles human and animal when he has the unidentified speaker "shake off wetness like a bear"; with no human images to guide us we imagine this bear-human standing "on the sandbar" at "rest from the river." An effective structural space in the poem tells the reader's eye that the river too is a "being" with a life of its own, a truth that becomes evident in the turbulent whirl of the next four lines. Drawn primarily from the vocabulary of river rafting, the rush of words takes the reader along for a wild ride through the "upswellings" and "outripples" and "confluence turbulence" of the river. Someone, most likely our river guide, instructs us about a "hydraulic" and "[p]illow-rock" and a "haystack." Remembering the concluding lines of "The Flowing," readers may not be surprised to find sexual associations in the movement of the river: the rapids' "slick tongue" and the "V" to be entered. The guide talks on, images pile up, leaving readers aware of the chaos and evident danger: "some holes are 'keepers'" that "won't let you through"; "[c]urrent differential . . . can suck you down." At the end of the lecture, our naive heads filled with untested knowledge, we are encouraged to pile back into the rafts. We "head into a storm" chanting the final three lines of the mealtime grace, offering up our actions, our very selves, as a way of placating the "demons and spirits," perhaps warding off, or perhaps merely accepting, the dangers that surely lie ahead.

These fact-filled lines and realistic images are undoubtedly drawn from specific rafting experiences, but Snyder's celebration of water in this section goes well beyond a mealtime grace and the excitement, and fear, of navigating the perils of rivers. In the final segment of the section, Snyder's meditation on the power and significance of water leads him to speak of enlightenment in the context of two earlier Zen writers. Inherently ironical, profoundly attentive moments of awe and speechlessness lead to impressive attempts to communicate the fullness of what has been heard. Listening "[t]hroughout the night" to "song after song" of stream and mountain, the great Chinese poet Su Tung-p'o wondered how, when the dawn came, he would ever find the words to speak. Yet the short poem he wrote to capture his all-night-long experience was commanding enough to be approved by his master as a sign of enlightenment. "Two centuries later," Dōgen, reflecting on the same phenomena and on Su's enlightenment poem, wondered whether it was "Su who woke" or "the mountains and streams" themselves. Dogen's metaphysical musings are at the heart of his imposing treatise on mountains and rivers, the *Mountains and Waters Sūtra,* a text that Snyder read in "the late seventies." As the poet says, it "made me think more about rivers. . . . [S]o now I studied waters, spinning and dashing down many a rapids in rowdy and convivial company" (*MRWE* 157). "We Wash Our Bowls in This Water" efficiently attests that Snyder has not only meditated on "the long broad tongue" of the "stream with its sounds" and "the wide-awake body" of the "looming mountain," he has experienced directly the all-enveloping rush and spurt of flowing water, the energetic voice of The Goddess herself. Indeed, it is tempting to view this compact and rhythmical section as an "enlightenment poem," Snyder's intuitive testament to the phenomenal significance of water.

Readers also know that, like Su Tung-p'o, Snyder has heard an "all night long" song in the White Mountains, where the "cricket in the stars," the "oldest of trees," and a "young throng // of Pinyon Pine" all pour the sounds of emptiness into his ears (*MRWE* 82). It is no accident, then, that "The Mountain Spirit" immediately follows "We Wash Our Bowls." Snyder's alter ego will once more ascend the slopes of the White Mountains to interact with the planetary forces. In a recurring pattern, land and water, mountain and river, being and spirit, will interpenetrate once more; the dyads will dance again until duality drops away. Regardless of instructions from forerunners or river guides, each being must engage the spirit directly; each must listen to the sound of the stream and come to terms with the unceasing shapes of the mountains. Dōgen instructs all beings similarly: "If *you,* who are valley streams and looming / mountains, / can't throw some light on the nature of ridges and rivers, // *who can?*" (*MRWE* 139). One must begin with perception of the thing in itself, with contemplation of the literal ground of all beings, the world of streams and mountains, this here-and-now universe, a universe that is at once illuminated and illuminating in the steady gaze of our attentiveness.

THE MOUNTAIN SPIRIT

"The Mountain Spirit" has evident links with both "The Hump-backed Flute Player" and "An Offering for Tārā"; it returns us to the setting of the former while reminding us that these "western" mountains are the "far shore" of the latter poem. Snyder tells us the section is derived from the Nō play *Yamamba* (*MRWE* 163), and research reveals that a high proportion of lines allude to or actually originate from that Japanese Nō play. Still, in contrast to "An Offering for Tārā," with its esoteric symbols in exotic places, few direct references to Buddhist icons and emblems occur in "The Mountain Spirit." The focus, instead, is on this Great Basin setting as an exemplary model for planetary dynamics. Here, once again amid "the White Mountains / & the bristlecone pines," Snyder's narrator recounts his final meeting with The Goddess in a landscape he knows intimately, a place perfectly poised between rhetorical symbolism and hard-edged reality. With a "view to the Last Chance range," an actual gathering of peaks just north of Death and Saline Valleys on the California/Nevada border, Snyder allows readers a final opportunity to partake in his vision of the Dance of All Beings in Time and Space. While all of *Mountains and Rivers Without End* may be seen as a cosmic Nō play, this section serves, fractally, as a mirror of the dynamics of the larger poem.

"The Mountain Spirit" clearly accomplishes the poet's early wish to embody East Asian aesthetics and philosophy in an authentic American setting. Shortly after arriving in Kyoto in September of 1956, Snyder conceived of transplanting the Nō theater to American soil in these words: "American Nō stage: background painting a desert and distant mountains? chorus on a long low bench. Maybe one large real boulder" (EHH 37). Knowing that every Nō play has a painting of an ancient pine tree—the Yogo Pine—as a background, Snyder now adds a verbally painted bristlecone pine to the desert and distant mountains of his American Nō play. Further, it is no secret that Snyder has specifically recast the essence of the Japanese Nō play *Yamamba* in "The Mountain Spirit"; his notes tell us so (MRWE 162). Inevitably, readers want to know more about the relationship of these two works. One cannot help but be reminded of the final questions raised by Snyder about the Grapard and Herbert versions of Ame-no-uzume's dance. Which version of *Yamamba*—a play translated and adapted many times under various titles—is "authentic"? In Snyder's world, the answer might be "both" or "neither." We hear the poet intoning: "Just / two places. Forever, // or, not even one" (*MRWE* 61), and we remember that diversity enriches "our sense of human accomplishment" (*Place* 147).

When the two works are correlated, step by step, on the basis of the traditional five-scene division of a two-part Nō play, we discover that Snyder's adaptation omits some correspondences entirely and collapses others to a line or two. As always, he is flexible in his use of models. What follows is a modified summary of a far more intricate comparison worked out by David Jinsoo Lee:[24]

Yamamba (Japanese Nō Play)

PART ONE

1.1. *Artist Enters:* An entrance song (*shidai*) is sung. Hyakuma, a famous singer/dancer from the city, travels (*michi-yuki*) with her attendants on a pilgrimage to Zenkōkji Temple in the mountains. Not knowing which road to take, they ask for guidance from a villager. Suddenly the sky darkens.

1.2. *Spirit Enters:* Woman (Yamamba embodied in a young woman) offers them a place to stay.

1.3. *Spirit and Artist Converse:* Woman (Yamamba) wants to observe Hyakuma perform the song and dance (*kusemai*) that has made her famous. The Woman promises to reveal her true form after watching Hyakuma perform.

1.4. *Spirit Tells Story:* The Woman (Yamamba) narrates the story of her wanderings and promises again to show her true form as well as to dance a dance in imitation of Hyakuma's dance.

1.5. *Spirit Exits:* The Woman (Yamamba) leaves the stage.

PART TWO

2.1. *Artist Waits:* A waiting song (*shidai*) is sung as Hyakuma waits for Yamamba to return.

2.2. *Spirit Re-enters in "True" Form:* Yamamba appears in her "real" form as the "old woman of the mountains."

2.3. *Spirit and Artist Converse:* Yamamba asks Hyakuma to perform the *kusemai.*

2.4. *Spirit Dances and Sings:* The climax of the play. In fact it is Yamamba who ritualistically performs a slow dance as she, and not Hyakuma, performs the *kusemai* (a traditional song/dance) which tells the story of Yamamba's endless rounds and her agonized desire to be free from this endless attachment to the world even as she knows it is an impossible wish.

2.5. *Spirit Performs Final Dance/Exits:* The play ends with an energetic short dance (*tachimawari*) performed by Yamamba. As the chorus sings the final lines Yamamba stamps her foot and exits.

"The Mountain Spirit" (*Mountains and Rivers Without End*)

PART ONE

1.1. *Artist Enters:* An entrance song (*shidai*)—"ceaseless wheel of lives"—is heard. Snyder travels (*michi-yuki*) from Reno to Bishop. Tells the Ranger who he is (*nanori*). Asks for guidance from the Ranger. Off to White Mts. and the Bristlecone Pines (the "temple"). The sky darkens.

1.2. *Spirit Enters:* A Voice (The Mountain Spirit) says: "You had a bit of fame . . . / for poems of mountains . . . ." Surprised, Snyder wonders just what or whom he has heard . . . "What?"

1.3. *Spirit and Artist Converse:* The Spirit quotes lines from Snyder's poem, *"walking on walking."* Spirit asks what he knows about minerals . . stone . . . time. Wants to hear Snyder's poem. Snyder answers that he'll read it later (at midnight) as Perseus crosses the ridge. . . .

1.4. *Spirit Tells Story:* The Spirit implies that she knows from first hand experience the endlessly unfolding story of minerals, stone, and time.

1.5. *Spirit Exits:* The Spirit has obviously gone as Snyder says "Who am I talking to?" Snyder returns to his camp down the ridge.

PART TWO

2.1. *Artist Waits:* A "waiting song" (*shidai*) is sung: "Evening breeze up from the flats. . . . formations dip and strike my sleep."

2.2. *Spirit Re-enters in "True" Form:* "Approaching in a dream" the Mt. Spirit's "true form" is difficult to define—"Old woman? white ragged hair?"—but is connected to distant stars and meteors. She seems to sing an entrance song (*issei*): *"Bitter ghosts that kick their own skulls. . . . what's it all for?"* She "stands there" in front of Snyder's persona.

2.3. *Spirit and Artist Converse*: The Mountain Spirit says: "I came to hear—"; Snyder "can't say no" and he begins to chant his poem in her honor, entitled "The Mountain Spirit."

2.4. *Spirit Dances and Sings:* Framed by the lines *"Walking on walking, / under foot earth turns,"* Snyder's two-and-a-half-page poem "The Mountain

Spirit" (*MRWE* 143–46), within the poem "The Mountain Spirit" (*MRWE* 140–47), tells of endless planetary dynamics. Among other things, it is the climactic *kusemai* of the *Mountains and Rivers* section entitled "The Mountain Spirit."

2.5. *Spirit Performs Final Dance/Exits:* The Mountain Spirit "whispers back" wisdom about art and reality to Snyder's narrator and the two of them dance a short "pine tree" dance (*tachimawari*) and "then she's gone." There is a brief recitation of two lines that opened the poem, and then Snyder returns "to the bedroll" to "sleep till dawn."

The overall structural and narrative correspondence between the two works is striking. Moreover, given the modular construction of Japanese Nō plays, it is possible to break down several of the identifiable scenes. The most obvious example is the climactic scene (2.4) that contains the traditional *kusemai*. Following a pattern established by an earlier study of *Yamamba*, Lee's analysis of Snyder's "*kusemai*"—when the narrator reads the poem within the poem—reveals a "theme song" or *shidai* ("*Walking on walking . . . Streams and mountains never stay the same*"), an "ornate passage," or *kuri* ("into earth rock dives" to "display how it plays," 144), a "recitative" section, or *sashi* ("Buttresses fractured, looming . . ." to "limestone shines like snow / where ancient beings grow," 144–45), and a "main segment," or *kuse* ("*When the axe-strokes stop . . .*" to "*Walking on walking . . . earth turns,*" 145–46) (Bethe and Brazell 5; Lee 50–62). Because the *kuse* in a Nō play is itself often "divided into five stanzas," even further groupings may be observed within the lines of Snyder's *kuse*. However one analyzes it, to enter the world of "The Mountain Spirit" is to enter a hall of mirrors, Maya's palace, a temple of echoes, a landscape of recurring fractal patterns.

"The Mountain Spirit" is obviously not just one more poem in the entire sequence; the section is, in an unprogrammatic fashion, *Mountains and Rivers Without End* in miniature. Indeed, reading this section reveals at once one aspect of the fractal nature of Snyder's design throughout his long poem. Just as a reader familiar with the Nō can spot groups of lines in the section that are indebted to the traditional structure of the Nō, so entire sections of *Mountains and Rivers* also follow that traditional structure. In the *jo* mode, "The Mountain Spirit" begins with a six-line entrance song, while *Mountains and Rivers* begins ceremoniously with "Endless Streams and Mountains" and "Old Bones." As the traveling narrator in "The Mountain Spirit" speaks of "[d]riving all night south from Reno / through cool-porched Bridgeport, past . . . ," so "Night Highway 99" is a traveling song (or *michi-yuki*) for the entire poem. In the brief identifying lines of the narrator to the ranger in Bishop—"I'm a traveler. / I want to know the way . . ."—there is an allusion to a *nanori*, or "name-introducing" section, that has its counterpart in the larger "Three Worlds, Three Realms, Six Roads." Like the traveler (usually but not necessarily the *waki*) of the two-part Nō who first meets the *shité* in the guise of an ordinary person, unsuspecting that an enlightening second encounter with the veritable *shité* will follow in a dream vision, so readers have seen many incarnations of The Goddess throughout *Mountains and Rivers;* but only now, in this section, at midnight on this ancient peak at the boundary of land and sky, will they confront her, through the narrator, in the intense fullness of her authentic self. In "The Mountain Spirit," as in the original Nō play, Snyder's "old woman" makes her two appearances; however, unlike in *Yamamba* where the first appearance of the old mountain woman is in the body of an ordinary person, Snyder's "Mountain Spirit" appears first as a disembodied "voice." Later, closer to the form dictated by the Nō, she approaches the narrator "in a dream" vision and finally "stands there" before him at midnight. As the final meeting with The Goddess in *Mountains and Rivers Without End,* this second appearance is the climax of the "The Mountain Spirit" section, the summit of the "*kyū*" poems that make up part IV, and the apex of dramatic movement in the complete long poem. Like the *waki,* without knowing it, readers have been drawn toward her from the first pages of the book. The last lines of "Endless Streams and Mountains"—"*Walking on walking . . . Streams and mountains never stay the same*" (*MRWE* 9)—resonate unmistakably with the initial lines of "The Mountain Spirit"—"Ceaseless wheel of lives / ceaseless wheel of lives." Indeed, readers discover that the former lines, which they will hear one last time in "Finding the Space in the Heart," belong to a famous poem written by Snyder's alter ego, the narrator. It is a poem that was inspired by the Spirit's unremitting expenditure of energy in the service of all beings on the planet, one that the Bristlecone Pine-Goddess-Yamamba-Spirit insists on hearing in "person" from him. At one stroke, Snyder disrupts the stability of his readers' perception. Where, exactly, does one locate oneself in this hall of mirrors? The narrator's poem, a poem within a poem called "The Mountain Spirit," is manifestly analogous to Gary Snyder's *Mountains and Rivers Without End,* which just so happens to contain a section entitled "The Mountain Spirit." At this climax of climaxes, these endlessly interpenetrating refractions of art and life obviously call up the hard-edged reality of emptiness for Snyder.

Shortly after the narrator's encounter with the Spirit, the power of the visionary moment passes. Now, in *kyū* mode, the intensity drops away rapidly and the narrator returns "back to the bedroll" to "sleep till dawn." Corresponding to a linear journey along the unwinding paths of an unrolling scroll, readers who have read the entire long poem from "A to Z," or better yet from section "1 to 39," have only two relatively short poems before coming to the "end" of this endless poem. Both "Earth Verse" and "Finding the Space in the Heart" are *kyū* poems; the conclusion is upon us as soon as "The Mountain Spirit" ends.

Such a structural overview demonstrates only the most straightforward of connections. An in-depth look easily uncovers multiple secondary events that correspond in *Yamamba* and "The Mountain Spirit." Among the many possibilities a few examples will suffice. As the travelers in both works climb toward higher peaks, they encounter an unearthly darkness. In *Yamamba* we find this passage:

> *Villager.* How extraordinary! Night is coming on so suddenly. Had I known, I should have recommended taking lodgings at Sakaigawa. How foolish I was! *First Attendant.* It is most extraordinary. It should still be daylight, but suddenly day has given way to night. What shall we do? (NGS, *Yamamba* 165)

The "darkening" skies of "The Mountain Spirit" serve as a counterpart: "Plane after plane of desert ridges / darkening eastward into blue-black haze" (*MRWE* 141). When the Mountain Spirit approaches for the second time, her entrance song has obvious similarities in both works. First, *Yamamba:*

> Ghosts that beat their bones in wintry woods
> Bemoan the karma of their former lives;
> Celestials to their burial field bear flowers
> And bless the good deeds of their former lives.
> Nay! Good and Evil are the same;
> What is there to bless? What to lament?
> Behold, before the eye all entities!
> The rapid river flows unceasingly,
> The crags soar high and sheer.
>
> (NGS, *Yamamba* 170)

Snyder's version is obviously built on the original:

> *"Bitter ghosts that kick their own skulls like a ball*
> *happy ghosts that stick a flower*
> *into their old skull's empty eye—*
> *'good and evil'*
> *—that's another stupid dream—*
> *for streams and mountains*
> *clouds and glaciers,*
> *is there ever an escape?"*
>
> (*MRWE* 142–43)

Snyder's variation preserves the basic meaning of this tiny Buddhist sermon while managing to concretize it, wrapping it in images closer to his own poem. At the very least readers should remember the ghosts—bitter or happy—of the Native American Ghost Dance that they encountered in "The Hump-backed Flute Player"; they may also remember a "sheepskull forehead . . . on a boulder— / an offer of the flower of a / million years" from "Arctic Midnight Twilight." If things are empty, eternally interconnected, the thought of a fixed reality for good and another for evil is merely another "stupid dream," one more false illusion that humans cling to. In the never-ending processes of the turning world, good and evil intertwine just as surely as the rivers and mountains do. Finally, in the midst of the traveler's *kusemai,* sung by Yamamba in the original Nō play, and by Snyder's alter ego/poet in "The Mountain Spirit," we hear a set of lines emphasizing the silence that is woven into the sound. First, *Yamamba:*

> Blows of the woodman's axe
> Awakening distant echoes,
> Plunge the silence into deeper silence
> that closes over all again.
> (NGS, *Yamamba* 174–75)

And in "The Mountain Spirit":

> *"When the axe strokes stop*
> *the silence grows deeper—"*
> (*MRWE* 145)

Given Snyder's background as a logger and his deep commitment to environmental issues, readers may find more than one echo here. On a literal level it is easily demonstrated that the sound of silence becomes more profound in the aftermath of a heard sound. In the "silence" that "grows deeper," readers may hear a reference to the sound of emptiness. According to Royall Tyler, who translates these lines as "perhaps an axe rings out / and the mountain stillness grows," there is a reference to "a single line of a poem [unnamed] by the great Chinese poet Tu Fu" (Tyler, *Yamamba* 325). In another set of lines within the *kusemai,* Snyder's allusions become a cross-cultural bridge: his "when—bristlecone needles are green! / Scarlet penstemon / flowers are red!" (*MRWE* 146) is a reference not just to *Yamamba* but to similar lines from Su Tung-p'o's poem—"Oh! Willow leaves are green, peach-blooms pink" (NGS, *Yamamba* 175). North American green bristlecone and red penstemon reflect East Asian green willow and pink peach blossoms. Interconnections like these embody emptiness; the silence grows "deeper" as one uncovers link after link.

In such allusions Snyder is clearly following the common East Asian practice for a poet to reference lines from another poet's work. To read a poem in China or Japan is rarely to read a single poem; one is much more likely to be reading a tradition kept alive in the lines of successive poets. In this sense "The Mountain Spirit" is not just a gloss on an earlier work from the Nō; it is both a continuation and extension of that work and of the culture it has emanated from. T. S. Eliot defined a similar process of interpenetration between an "individual talent" and its "tradition," and Snyder suggests such interactive referencing again when he points out that *Mountains and*

Rivers Without End may be viewed as yet another colophon attached to a painted landscape scroll known as *Ch'i-shan wu-chin*, or *Streams and Mountains Without End*. Like Kokop'ele or Hsüan-tsang before him, Snyder's cultural backpack not only carries a tradition from Asia to North America, from the Paleolithic to the present, but intertwines that tradition with a new locale and time in a manner that will change all that has come before it and after it.

Because "The Mountain Spirit" is so indebted to the Nō, one cannot speak with assurance about its rhythms unless one has heard the poem in performance. Even then, as all modernist critics know, one performance is not "the poem." The classical Nō supplies many set patterns for the development of rhythm in its plays. Snyder, in turn, has provided some clues to his use of these models by indenting groups of lines and juxtaposing evident prosaic patterns with either loose poetic clusters or lines that are intentionally and obviously written in formal rhyming patterns or with dense imagery. Not surprisingly, readers will at times detect a countable pattern of syllables or stresses in selected lines. However, although one may begin with observable forms and patterns, hearing these rhythms is not, finally, a matter of numeric calculation. The method of delivery attached to individual lines and blocks of lines—some are to be chanted, or sung, or spoken—radically affects the perception of rhythm. Ultimately the rhythms of the Nō are based on subtle performance factors, often derived from an interplay with the chorus, the musicians, the action of the play, or the actors.

In his program notes for "The Mountain Spirit" Snyder adopts a storyteller's tone as he clearly distances himself from his own poem:

> This poem . . . retells the story of the Nō play *Yamamba*, in North American terms. . . .
>
> Throughout western North America there are tales of the Mountain Spirits—sometimes fierce and jagged as lightning, sometimes smooth and sweet as a rainbow, sometimes seen as an old ragged woman. Some years back, in San Francisco, there was a poet who made his reputation largely on the basis of a poem he had written about the Mountain Spirit, even though he had not actually visited the mountains very much himself.
>
> One year he decided to pay a visit to the unique groves of ancient bristlecone pine—the oldest living beings in the world—that are located in the remote upper elevations of the White-Inyo mountains of eastern California. After considerable travel he made his way into the White Mountains and set up camp as it was getting dark. As it happened it was the time of the annual Perseid meteor showers, which he also hoped to enjoy. While looking over the dusk landscape, a voice out of the dark challenged him, and asked that he read aloud his famous poem on the Mountain Spirit for her. He promised to do so at midnight, and then tried to put this strange encounter out of his mind. At midnight however

> he was awakened, and he saw that his visitor was indeed the legendary Mountain Spirit. As the meteors streaked through the sky, he read his poem to this mysterious personage, and then the two of them danced the dance of the bristlecone pine. The spirit suddenly slipped away, and the poet fell back to sleep. (Snyder, *Gary Snyder Reads*)

"Some years back, in San Francisco, there was a poet . . ."—"One year he decided to pay a visit . . .": Obviously Snyder has, once more, become a character in the dramatic story-poem he is about to tell. As in "Endless Streams and Mountains," where the observing eye is sometimes on the trail, sometimes in a boat drifting off the coast, and sometimes standing outside the museum in the "real" world, Snyder's personality here wavers between that of fictive participant and (fictive) narrator of the story. The nature of "reality" is always a question in *Mountains and Rivers Without End.* Most readers will be quick to substitute "Gary Snyder" for the young San Francisco poet mentioned in these notes, but the merger is difficult to sustain when they hear that this poet "had not actually visited the mountains very much himself." Can this "San Francisco poet" be the "real" Gary Snyder? In 1965, while praising his friend Drum Hadley as "the first American poet [with] a sense of the desert . . . a realm of the spirit for Americans," Snyder admitted, with a touch of humility, that he had "to a small extent captured the mountains a little for Americans" (Kherdian 13). Plainly a mountain poet in those years, one wonders if he knew then that he would also turn to the desert as a "realm of the spirit" ("Finding the Space in the Heart"). In truth, starting with the first section of *Mountains and Rivers,* there are many versions of "Gary Snyder" walking the paths of his verbalized horizontal scroll. Just as emptiness cannot and does not reside in any one place, so no single personality can achieve the wholeness of a "person." Personality is a series of endless images reflecting back and forth in the "double mirror waver" of illusion ("Bubbs Creek Haircut"), one more restatement of Dōgen's comments on the reality and unreality of "the entire phenomenal universe." Snyder's distorted portrayal of himself as a city poet "who made his reputation largely on the basis of a poem he had written about the Mountain Spirit," stems from his wish to parallel the action in *Yamamba.* Hyakuma, a city dweller, is a famous dancer whose reputation rests on her "famous song for a *kusemai* dance on the theme of Yamamba's wandering from hill to hill" (NGS, *Yamamba* 162). She performs the dance and song herself. Hyakuma's life is so intertwined with her ideal prototype that she is actually known as Hyakuma Yamamba. Following the example of Hyakuma, Snyder represents himself as a "city poet" whose art is intimately linked with the spirit of the mountains. Snyder's male artist thus corresponds to the female Hyakuma, reminding readers of the amorphous nature of gender in *Mountains and Rivers.*

Legends about Yamamba abound in Japan. In some stories she is said to be the mother of a red-skinned boy named Kintaro whose father was the god of thunder.

Kintaro, whose name means "golden boy," performs heroic deeds and is often associated with wild animals, especially bears. Distant echoes of Snyder's own predilections for wilderness, mother goddesses, and bears exist here, and it may not be far-fetched to consider the writing of a long poem intended to transform a culture as a "heroic deed." In addition to noting the obvious mother-son relationship in "Mā," some readers may see the red-skinned Kintaro in the picture of a sunburnt Snyder scraping the deck of our common "Boat of a Million Years." Not all of Yamamba's deeds are benevolent; she has been represented as a demon as well as a cannibal. Her origins appear to reach back to early shamanistic rituals, and it is likely that Snyder connects her imagistically with the Paleolithic goddesses. Not always human in form, her appearance in *Mountains and Rivers* has a certain resonance with goddess figures like "The Lady of the Animals" or the horrific Kali who encompass *all* aspects of nature, death as well as birth.

In most legends she is shown wandering among the peaks and valleys of the wild. Yamamba is always associated with mountains. Literally, the Japanese characters for *yama-uba* mean "mountain-old woman." Her name has been variously translated as "mountain crone," "mountain hag," "granny mountains," or, in Snyder's case, as "mountain spirit." Royall Tyler argues that the vigor she displays in the Nō play indicates that an "*uba*" may be a "good deal livelier than an 'old woman,' or 'crone,'" as a result "no mask could show all her faces" (Tyler, *Yamamba* 310). In calling her a "spirit" Snyder implies that she is a disembodied and ageless force. As spirit, she is pure energy, an essence measured by scientists just as surely as worshipped by the religiously inclined. In ceaseless motion, she may yet be encountered; incapable of being fixed in any one time or space, she remains clearly "there." As Snyder moves to depict her shape, to put her into words, to give form to her emptiness, his narrator is not sure that she is an old woman or that her hair is white. Both details are presented as questions to be pondered: "Old woman? white ragged hair?" If this is her blazing white hair, it is metamorphosed into meteor showers and timeworn stars. Like Tārā, also associated with starlight energy, she is that which animates the planets and rains down on all beings to nourish them. To place the Mountain Spirit in "time" as a "crone," Snyder conjures up a tangible picture of her for meditative purposes, incarnating her in a four-thousand-year-old gnarled bristlecone pine topped by a flash of starry white hair. As her hair is sky-bound, so her roots dive deeply into the earth. The bristlecone is said to derive its long age from "the taste of carbonate / dolomite." Here, thousands of feet in the air, the bristlecone's "food" is derived from age-old minerals, a calcium-rich sea that once covered the land before it lifted.

Thus, thriving "on rock and air" like the pine, the Mountain Spirit suddenly "stands there" in front of the poet, her visionary being demanding to hear his poem about "minerals and stone." She is more than intrigued by his claim to an understanding of mountains and "all that scale of time." How can he possibly know what she knows? How can he know "what's it all for?" A touch of pathos accompanies her request to hear his poem, for she does not seem to appreciate, at this stage, that the two of them are, after all, together in this venture. It seems a lesson that she too must learn endlessly, even as she teaches the same lesson to others. Without the poem, without the tree, without the rock, there would be no evidence of the spirit. Without the phenomenal world there is no trace of the noumenon. *Shūnyatā* and *tathata* are intertwined; form is emptiness and emptiness is form; "the entire phenomenal universe and the empty sky are nothing but a painting."

The trace of the Mountain Spirit's "time" vanishes among the far reaches of the million-yeared layers of geomorphology that humans continually attempt to measure. Formless herself, her presence may only be glimpsed in the forms she has vivified with her dance. Indeed, as Snyder's poem testifies, she continually inspires new forms, for her "spirit" is the shaping force, as readers may see and hear, of a triple poem: *Mountains and Rivers Without End,* the section-poem "The Mountain Spirit," and the poem-within-a-poem, "The Mountain Spirit." These artistic spiralings, fractal reflections of one another, are mirrored in her own eternally coiling motion. Given that both the narrator-poet of this section and the "real" Gary Snyder have written poems inspired by her, at some level they do indeed know her story well. The narrator's poem begins: "*Walking on walking / under foot earth turns // Streams and mountains never stay the same*" (MRWE 143). Among the patterned turnings of matter over time, he detects her wrinkled being everywhere. The ongoing dynamics of Planet Earth's movements—the rock-diving subduction of continents, the lift of mountains turning the earth inside out, the comings and goings of seas, ooze, and dust—all "display" the "play" of her eternal wandering; one does not always know which way she will turn, but one knows she will always return. Her face may be seen "looming" in the lines of "fractured" cliffs. Observable "flakes" of igneous rock tell the story of her primeval flow, a current of magma consolidating deep within the earth's core long before human existence. Her twisted movements can be detected in the squiggles of fossilized Paleozoic trilobites, in the calcified spiral forms of shells that hearken back to a time before land plants, a time when the Great Basin was covered by a "lime-rich wave-wash" of tidal flats and lagoons. What was once "an old seabed" has been hoisted to heights as "high as alps." From rock to rock, entire ridges composed of waves of sand now arrested in stone testify to millions of years of a constantly shifting drift of wind and water over the grains of eroded rock. One can still see the Mountain Spirit's writing on the wall: "Sandstone layers script of winding tracks / and limestone shines like snow / where ancient beings grow."

Now two-thirds of the way through his performance for the Mountain Spirit, in lines that are reminiscent of Snyder's earlier directive to the reader—"Listen close, the sound gets better"—Snyder's alter ego invites his audience to pause and pay even closer attention to enlightening sound. Quoting Tu Fu's poem—"*When the axe strokes stop / the silence grows deeper*"—readers may find themselves listening, as Su Tung-p'o did, to the "stream with its sounds," in order to hear, as Dōgen heard in his time, the "long wide tongue of the Buddha." Immediately following this significant moment, readers are reminded of the basic dyadic dance that recurs throughout *Mountains and Rivers:* "Peaks [are] like Buddhas" and "waters" are "streaming down" their sides. Then, refracting images once more, the Mountain Spirit hears herself—an "old woman mountain"—spoken of in Snyder's poem. As her never-ending movements teach the lesson of endless interpenetration—that is, emptiness—to the narrator-poet Snyder who has written this poem in her honor, so the Mountain Spirit is told, as Yamamba also learned from Hyakuma, that "nothingness is shapeliness." Snyder further distances the source of this short sermon by putting the phrase in the mouth of the "shifting sand" that "tell[s] the wind." These words, the heart of the *Heart Sūtra,* are the answer to the Spirit's question—"What's it all for?"—and the answer to Snyder's question—"Ah, what am I carrying? What's this load?"—asked long ago in "The Hump-backed Flute Player." Both Snyder and the Spirit recognize their partnership; in their common anguish they search for an answer to the simplest of questions: What's it all for? Why write poems? Where is the end to this ceaselessly turning "wheel of lives"? An answer to these questions would bring an end, yet there can be no end; there is only the dance. In their shared song and dance they become, ultimately, not two. To dance with the Mountain Spirit is to awaken to her agonized knowledge that there is no escape from the endlessly cycling interpenetrating worlds within worlds. Yet, in this grand "emptiness" there is at least a possibility for transformation. Recognizing—in the midst of the ecstatic dance—that we are forever going nowhere even as we go somewhere in time is to discover the basis, the heart, of true compassion. All beings are linked in this spiraling endeavor; there is, ultimately, no hierarchy, no good and evil, nothing to be gained by considering ourselves as separate or better than another being.

This moment of profound recognition in silence is followed by the reassuring lines: "*Mountains will be Buddhas then.*" Before we can ask, perhaps skeptically, "when?" the poet supplies the answer: "when—bristlecone needles are green! / Scarlet penstemon / flowers are red!" Simply put, the moment is now; bristlecone needles *are* green and scarlet penstemon flowers *are* red, right now. They always have been. The mountains are Buddhas *now.* What does this mean? As readers might expect to hear from a poet who has had some fame "for poems of mountains," we are told that "mountains feed the people too." Strictly speaking, within the framework of this poem-within-a-poem the poet is lecturing the "Mountain Spirit," telling her not to agonize over her endless wandering, consoling her that she is a provider for all beings. Similarly, Snyder implies that gratitude and respect for the gifts granted by this turning world would be more appropriate than anguish over a distant future that will play itself out in a time frame beyond human capacity to grasp. The round of seasons eternally cycling about the earth, the planet ball rolling through the vast universe, sustains us. Mountains are the source not only of edible food, but of models for communal living, including storytelling itself as a source of nourishment. As we learned in "The Hump-backed Flute Player," these old landscapes, apparently empty, are actually full. In "Wovoka's empty hat" and "Baby Krishna's mouth," one will find a universe to be recovered. Just below the ridge on which Snyder's poet performs for the Mountain Spirit are the valleys presently named "Salt" and "Death." The entire poem takes place, on the edge, as it were, of the Great Basin, a locale where the flowing ends. By definition it is called a "basin" because rivers that empty into it never leave it; there is no outlet to the sea in these valleys. Yet a body of water, Lake Lahontan, was once alive in this very place; as we have seen, its traces may be found in the wavelike sandstone formations or in the sea shells found on its peaks. As the Mountain Spirit makes her rounds, it is only a matter of time before the waters of Lake Lahontan, teeming with "goose flocks" and "crane flocks," will "come again."

As the poem-within-a-poem concludes, "[t]he Mountain Spirit whispers back" to the poet: "All art and song / is sacred to the real. / As such." As his poem has brought a measure of satisfaction and relief to her, so, in learning about herself from him, she consoles him in words that echo Dōgen's "Unsurpassed enlightenment is a painting." Simply put, art—poetry, or song, in this case—is worth it. It is as if she were answering a poet's question about the value of poetry: "What's it all for?" No mere rhetoric, a poem may be sacred. If distinctions between "good and evil" are "another stupid dream," so antagonism between the "real" and the "artistic" is not only pointless, it is contrary to nature. The poem we have just read has more than adequately demonstrated the intertwining of scientific and poetic "truth"; it should be clear that the "real" and the "artistic" must dance with each other.

And so they do. In *kyū* mode, the Nō play *Yamamba* concludes with a short and vigorous *tachimawari* dance just before Yamamba stamps her foot signaling the end of the play and her exit from the stage. In like manner, Snyder dances with the Mountain Spirit in the last lines of the section. She is once more figured forth as a bristlecone pine: "spiraled standing coiling / dead wood with the living, / four thousand years of mineral glimmer / spaced out growing in the icy airy sky / white bones under summer stars." Together, even as the Lady of Wild Things might have danced with the antlered shaman, the Sorcerer, of Troís Frères, they spiral in the night air, their energetic movements rippling like ancient seas, their entangled arms and limbs "twisting, twining" until finally she "stamp[s] the root-foot DOWN," marking the end of their dance, her visionary appearance before the poet, and the poem itself. Significantly, Snyder speaks of her "root-foot," emphasizing her treelike connection with the ground as well as her disappearance into thin air: "and then she's gone."

It is over. In what we might imagine as the Mountain Spirit's fading voice, picked up and whispered to us now by Gary Snyder, we hear the opening refrain once more—"Ceaseless wheel of lives / red sandstone and white dolomite." It is a phrase that we shall hear again, if not in *Mountains and Rivers Without End* then surely in our heads, in our own visions, reminding us of our encounter in this poem on a high mountain ridge with "a view to the Last Chance range."

For the present, all activity comes to a brisk conclusion: a "few more shooting stars" and then "back to the bedroll, sleep till dawn."

EARTH VERSE

Rapidly approaching the conclusion of part IV, readers have no trouble detecting Snyder's transition into the *kyū* mode. Just as "The Mountain Spirit" ends briskly with a dance and a disappearance, so the short poem "Earth Verse" sets the tone for the swift conclusion of *Mountains and Rivers Without End.*

The poet encountered the landscape that inspired this short section when he traveled to Australia with his friend and fellow poet Nanao Sakaki in 1981. In notes accompanying recent readings of *Mountains and Rivers,* Snyder reveals that the section "was written in the incredibly lonely Musgrave mountains of the central Australian desert" (Snyder, *Gary Snyder Reading*). The Musgrave Ranges, "a series of granite hills, in northwestern South Australia, about 130 miles long" lie "within the arid Central Australian Aboriginal Reserve" ("Musgrave Ranges" *Encyclopaedia Britannica*). The Australian desert-mountain setting has a certain similarity with the landscape of the Great Basin, but it is the contact with aboriginal experience and the all-abiding vision-producing loneliness of the setting that resonates with most significance. *Mountains and Rivers* is alive with visions. We have just experienced one as we danced with a gnarled old tree-woman on a ridge in the White Mountains.

Snyder has kept various journals since he was seventeen. Several years ago, accompanied by a reprinting of "Uluru Wild Fig Song," he published some "notes . . . from [his 1981] ramble in the central Australian desert." As he tells us, his journals often serve as "the source of the first drafts of many poems," for "anything can go in, no special literary pretension, and no obligation to 'make use' of any of it. . . . [T]here is much rich-looking stuff that I have not re-read, let alone copied or edited, lurking back in there" ("Writer's Notebook" 123). Although longer than "Earth Verse," "Uluru Wild Fig Song" obviously draws its inspiration from the same central Australian desert landscape:

> we push through grasses, vines, bushes
> along the damp earth wash-off watershed margin
>   where vertical rock dives
>   into level sand
> . . . . .

stickers & prickles in the sand—

clacking the boomerang beat,
a long walk
singing the land.

.....

Sit down in the sand
skin to the ground
a thousand miles of open gritty land
(*Axe Handles* 95, 96, 97)

With "grasses, vines, and bushes" fed by the "damp earth wash-off watershed margin," the central Australian landscape is "[g]reen enough to go on living"; its "stickers & prickles" are "[p]rickly enough to make you tough" and the sandy, "gritty" ground is "[d]ry enough to make you honest." Both the aboriginal "long walk / singing the land" and the vista of a "thousand miles of open gritty land" indicate that one's perspective on these spaces will be "[w]ide / enough" and "[o]pen enough" to keep on looking and moving.

"Uluru Wild Fig Song" is dated and placed as "*Fall of 40081* [1981], *Uluru, Amata, Fregon, Papunya, Ilpili,* Austral" (*Axe Handles* 98). Several of these names point to small outstations or waterholes difficult to find in an ordinary atlas, but "Uluru" ("Ayers Rock"), "Papunya," and "Amata" may be readily located. Significantly, "Amata" is a small town located within the Musgrave Range, which, of course, connects the 1981 "Uluru Wild Fig" poem to "Musgrave Mountains Gatha," now known as "Earth Verse." The published pages of Snyder's journal do not include references to the time he spent at Amata, but it is likely that his working notes for the poem will be found among unseen journal entries for that visit.

Snyder's essay "Good, Wild, Sacred" provides another avenue for understanding the inner regions of "Earth Verse." In the "Waterholes" section of that essay, Snyder refers again to his Australian experience (*Practice* 81–86). Patrick Murphy points out that Snyder "focuses on the ways in which their [the aboriginal people of Australia] stories about themselves as people are intimately tied to the land in which they live. In that land exist certain sacred places" (*Understanding Gary Snyder* 159). Intimacy with the living land and all its beings becomes the hallmark of "sacredness" for the Australian aborigines, and certainly it is just such a blend of reverence and familiarity for the land that informs Snyder's "Earth Verse." When the poet says the earth is "[o]ld enough to give you dreams," he most certainly has the sacredness of aboriginal dreamtime in mind. As we discovered when we discussed "With This Flesh," dreamtime is "a time of fluidity" and "shapeshifting" that is sometimes viewed as a "mythical past," yet "is not really in *any* time" (*Practice* 84). For the Australian aborigine, dreamtime is the time when ancestral beings inhabited this shapeless planet. In their own time they created

> the natural world, the people and their laws, and provided an understanding of the land. After this period of creation, the ancestral beings returned to become a part of the landscape. It is said that the power of the ancestral beings still exists in the land and the people. ("The Dreamtime")

From ghost marmots and eerie goddesses with their earrings dangling to an apparition of Lake Lahontan's future renewal, readers merely need to recount the abundant "ghosts" that inhabit Snyder's *Mountains and Rivers* to confirm that the poet also believes in "the power of the ancestral beings" still inhabiting the land. Indeed, the land itself is an actor on its own stage. Across the unwinding scroll of Snyder's imagination a veritable flood of ghosts issues forth from Maya's womb. Perceiving one's place in that flow is part of a radically creative moment, an instant of shape-shifting fluidity, that connects the eternal with the now in visionary dreamtime. *Mountains and Rivers Without End* itself is a song of dreamtime, literally filled with actual reveries. Together with the tangible landscape, it provides readers with hints and guesses, tiny illuminations. The long poem is certainly "wide enough and open enough" to keep us looking and moving among its words and visions for years to come.

As D. T. Suzuki explained long ago: "*Gāthā* is a Sanskrit term meaning 'verse' or 'hymn.' In Buddhist literature it is used to designate the versified portion of the sūtras" (*Manual* 13). The *Shambhala Dictionary of Buddhism and Zen* equates the word *gāthā* with "songs." Thus "Earth Verse," formerly "Musgrave Mountains Gatha," is both a poetic song and an intoned prayer. Its repetitive grammatical structure—wide enough to . . . , open enough to . . . , dry enough to . . . —indicates that it could indeed be chanted, yet its final title and deliberate lack of specificity reveal that it is not finally a song of reverence for a specific landscape. For Gary Snyder the realm that we inhabit is a vast interconnecting space that extends from our own local watershed, wherever that might be, to our common planet floating in its universe:

> The earth . . . is fifty-seven million square miles, 3.7 billion human beings, evolved over the last four million years; plus two million species of insects, one million species of plants, twenty thousand species of fish, and 8,700 species of birds; constructed out of ninety-seven naturally occurring surface elements with the power of the annual solar income of the sun. That is a lot of diversity. (*Place* 126)

All of this "diversity" is our "sacred place"; one hears the poet telling us that we should sing this "Earth Verse" on a daily basis as a measure of our gratitude and awe for what we have been given. In *Mountains and Rivers* this small section serves as a quiet and graceful bridge between the climactic section, "The Mountain Spirit," and the final resolution of the entire poem in "Finding the Space in the Heart."

FINDING THE SPACE IN THE HEART

Just as surely as the last unrolling of the Cleveland landscape scroll *Ch'i-shan wu-chin* reveals a relatively level horizontal space after multiple peaks and valleys, so readers, having journeyed through *Mountains and Rivers Without End* to the last section, "Finding the Space in the Heart," find themselves standing on an immensely flat, horizontal space in the Great Basin. Here, amid the "far reaches" of Nevada's Black Rock Desert, Snyder quietly restates his themes one last time before his "wet black brush / tip drawn to a point, / lifts away" (*MRWE* 152). Known to geologists as a *playa,* the Black Rock Desert is "big, flat, and salt-encrusted"; its geological characteristics result from having been the floor of a lake long ago. The Alvord Desert mentioned in the opening lines of the section is another example. The Black Rock Desert was, in fact, once the floor of the "Pleistocene Lake Lahontan" (Grayson 77), the same lake that was conjured up in the closing lines of "The Mountain Spirit." Evidence of the ancient lake may still be seen on the cliffs that surround the Black Rock Desert: "Faint shorelines seen high on these slopes, / long gone Lake Lahontan." On the stone walls one can read the calligraphy of the "wave-etched / beach ledge."

Snyder's verbal route to the playa is not accidental. He retraces his journey there in space and over time. With a touch of wildness equivalent to the freedom of the space he is about to enter, he reminds us of the sexual license of the "sixties"—the "hippie" generation—by mentioning his first trip to the Black Rock Desert with "a fierce gay poet," probably Allen Ginsberg, and a "dangerous girl with a husky voice." Her perilous nature reminds us that mythical female figures in Snyder's world may appear as Kali and Kurukullā just as surely as the benevolent figure of Tārā. In actuality, this '60s' trip "down from Canada" probably took place in the aftermath of Snyder's trip to Glacier Peak with Ginsberg and "Justine" in September of 1965 (*EHH* 94ff). His description of the time they spent together in the Glacier Wilderness contains several topics that are consonant with themes found in *Mountains and Rivers,* not the least of which is the mention of "*Yamauba*" (*Yamamba*) (94).

The choice of the "east side of the ranges" allows Snyder to focus on the geological dynamics of the landscape. The mention of Grand Coulee speaks to the diversion of the Columbia River by the advance of the glacial ice sheet. In between times of great flood and blockage by the ice, drainage from the Columbia Plateau became limited to the Grand Coulee:

> a great canyon, 500 to 1000 feet deep and 1 to 15 miles wide, cut in the basalt flows of the Columbia Plateau. Midway was a gigantic waterfall 400 feet high and nearly 3 miles wide, which, during the Pleistocene, must have thundered with the roar of a thousand Niagaras. Today, no water tumbles over Dry Falls. (Gilluly, Waters, and Woodford 277–78)

The Blue Mountains referred to may contain echoes of Native American "ghost tribes," such as the Nez Percé, who lived among these mountains as well as those of the neighboring Wallowa Range, but it is more likely that Snyder has Dōgen's *Mountains and Waters Sūtra* in mind, since Snyder entitled his essay on Dōgen as "Blue Mountains Constantly Walking" (*Practice* 97). The landscape he chooses to describe is both dynamic and magical. In both the "lava flow caves" and the "track" that is "obsidian-paved," he reminds us of the once turbulent flow of molten rock that took place here. Moreover, travel along these "seldom-seen" roads creates a sheen of enchantment with shining images of "glittering" or "thick frost." In this manner, he prepares us for the startling vision we are about to have: the horizon opens and the "silvery flats" of the Black Rock Desert appear in the distance. Just as the narrator in "Endless Streams and Mountains" finds himself uttering a mantric "ah!" as he steps back to gaze at the awesome rising and subsiding of the land, so here at the end of *Mountains and Rivers* readers hear, once again, that wondrous and mysterious "voice" that speaks "with a sureness and melody of its own, singing out the inner song of the self, and of the planet" (*EHH* 123). "O, ah!" The gleaming landscape brings forth an instant "awareness of emptiness," flooding the onlooker with "a heart of compassion," a sense of "trembling awe, leaving one grateful and humble" (*EHH* 123). Passing on through the town of Gerlach, the town at the edge of the playa "where the roads end," they follow "the tipi path" of "wizards," those who have experienced sacred hallucinogenic visions. These are the lands of the Northern Paiute—Smoke Creek, Pyramid Lake—lands once walked by Wovoka, the visionary prophet of the Ghost Dance, the dance that was to bring about a new world. Indeed, the '60s were full of people who felt "the world might head a new way." Snyder was one of those people, and his statement at the end of the stanza is simultaneously optimistic and wistful.

The '70s pass by in a few lines, primarily to conjure up the dark side once more. There is, as always, a literal truth to Snyder's lines; when only slightly wet, the playa is a dangerous place to be. Still, one cannot help but read more into factual descriptions when correspondences seem so apparent. Wildness may lead to reckless behavior and emptiness has a frightening side; in foolishness one may easily become "stuck," and it is only with help that one is able to be "sucked free" before moving on.

The experiences of the '80s contain the climax of the section. With hindsight the lines lead to the impression that all that has come before them was by way of introducing us, in the *jo* mode, to the fullness of the Black Rock Desert. Now, with "[f]ifteen years passed," we enter the rising developmental mode of the *ha* and return with Snyder and his "lover" to the playa—this enchanted place "where it all drops away." Here we may discover the "path." At first the lines continue prosaically. With the discovery of the "carved stone inscriptions" placed carefully among Artemis's "sagebrush," they become aphoristic: "Stomp out greed" / "The best things in life are not things." The wisdom in these simple yet profound precepts belongs to a sage, one who has clearly felt "at home" in this austere landscape.[25] After a short pause, the poetic lines surge forward again, like the ancient wave action that they image. To this day Pyramid Lake will yield cutthroat trout to anglers, yet ancient fossils of these fish are also uncovered in the silt of the Black Rock Desert. The bones of the "Columbian Mammoth" tell tales of a gregarious animal that grazed the shores of Lake Lahontan in the Pleistocene (Grayson 67–68). In more recent times, the outlines of "desert sheep" have been "pecked into the rock" by Native Americans, much as they had on the walls of Canyon de Chelly in "The Hump-backed Flute Player."

As Snyder turns "the truck onto the playa," suddenly the lines grow intensely poetic. Short lines show an increasing proportion of monosyllables, alliteration, parallel phrasing, and balanced stresses. Much as when we encountered the *kusemai* in "The Mountain Spirit," we know we have come to an essential part—the heart—of the section. Set off from the rest of the section by indention, the lines provide a rhapsodic description of the playa, emptiness itself.

As Snyder and his lover head "for know-not" in this "trackless and featureless" place, readers are led through the "bone-gray dust boiling and billowing" until, like "the car," they "coast to a halt / on the crazed cracked / flat hard face" of the planet. Sandwiched between the extremes of Hamlet's agonizing existential question—"to be or not be"—and the biting reality, or "peak," of King Lear's insanity, these desert images of enormous openness radiate Avalokiteshvara's compassionate message of transcendent wisdom:

> Shāriputra, form is no other than emptiness, emptiness is no other than form; form is exactly emptiness, emptiness exactly form; sensation, thought, impulse, consciousness are also like this. Shāriputra, all things are marked by emptiness—not born, not destroyed; not stained, not pure; without gain, without loss. (Snyder, "Heart Sūtra")

Again we find ourselves at the core of the *Heart Sūtra*, the concise expression of the all-important Buddhist philosophy of emptiness. *Mountains and Rivers* begins with Milarepa's enigmatic utterance that "[t]he notion of Emptiness engenders Compassion." Now, in the title of the last section, "Finding the Space in the Heart," we spiral around, one final time, to Milarepa's words; having made the journey through the poem we are far more attentive now to the meaning of his words. In the tangible desert of the Black Rock, a sand land once immersed under lake water, the spiritual and the physical mirror one another, art and reality intermingle, a "painted rice-cake" and the "entire phenomenal universe" are no longer two. Sounds on the air, images for the eye, words on a page—whether those of an anonymous Chinese landscape artist or Milarepa or Snyder or ourselves—form concepts for the mind, yet remain, after all, impressions sent forth from and engraved on an endlessly changing set of mental mirrors. One cannot eat such emptiness, yet it provides manna for wanderings in the desert and may well serve as a source of vitality:

> To be empty means to be alive, to breathe in and to breathe out. We cannot be alive if we are not empty. Emptiness is impermanence, it is change. . . . [W]ithout impermanence nothing is possible. (Hanh 17)

Out of these spaces we construct, again and again, our vision of fixity and flow; it is the same vision incarnated in the agony of Yamamba's endless rounds. Beginning and ending in emptiness, it is, nevertheless, all that all of us have. In grasping this profound wisdom our compassion for all beings begins. Finding the space in the heart! Ah. Here indeed is an emptiness, a physical space, in which one may find the heart of compassion.

Inspired by the immediately observable flatness, a vision arises. In the "far reaches" of time and space, all is "equal"; there are "no bounds." In the recognition that process is the only fixity, all oppositions are absorbed into the ongoing dance. Where there had once been the sound of activity on and around the lake, the sound is now "swallowed away" and only emptiness can be heard. Where there had once been water, and mountains, and bush, and grass, and shade, there is only the dust and the appearance of flatness, only one's own shadow in the dusty mirror of illusion. Because there are no boundaries, no limits, all is possible; in the fullness of time there can be no loss and no gain. With heads presently bathed by the air, we stand where once we should have been under the waters of Lake Lahontan. Standing here, firm on this ground, we are, nevertheless, "no place between" but always "just."

At home in this amazing locale, their tent mouth arranged properly in the flow of the wind, the "time being here," Snyder and his lover-goddess sit "cross-legg'd" once more, as so many beings have done and will do among the far reaches of both past and future time. Their selfless togetherness once again transforms them. In their nondual, heart-to-heart, leg-to-leg entwining, they both celebrate and create a "space of the heart" where all compassion begins. Their kiss goes deeply "to the bone" even as the Mountain-Spirit-Bristlecone "root-foot" stamped deeply into the soil. It is well to remember that the nonduality associated with emptiness does not fix itself on the void, but includes its very opposite. An understanding of emptiness encompasses the recognition that one is *connected* to all things, all possibilities; it is an awareness of total liveliness. As the dawn sun rises auspiciously over King Lear Peak, one wonders just whose "eye," "tooth," leg," and "mouth" Snyder is speaking of; the imagery of the lines intermingles all things until it is obvious that "[t]he best things in life are not things."

With the '90s, the section moves toward a "fast close" as the *kyū* mode takes over. It is time for the final resolution. Relative to the previous lines describing the experience of emptiness on the Black Rock Desert, the poetic intensity of these lines subsides. However, as if we were witnessing yet another final dance, perhaps a Nō-like *tachimawari,* the communal activities bodied forth in the words are clearly energetic. Circles under the light of the "crescent" moon predominate. Venus, like Tārā a loving goddess, looks down from her abode in the sky. True to the lesson just learned, there seems little hierarchy; "old friends" and "old trucks" are mentioned in the same breath, and both are "drawn around" in a communal circle on the hard-packed sands of the desert. Snyder's lover has also come "around" to a new role as his "wife." Adults and children intermingle. In the darkness of their own futures, the kids cycle in "arcs" on their bikes. As if he were providing a specific instance for his statement that "the boldness of my young people, who ate unlikely manna in the wilderness," finally showed him how to end his poem (*MRWE* 158), Snyder provides unusual food—"grasshoppers roasted in a pan"—for his desert dwellers. Using the word "somehow," he lends a veneer of mystery to their appearance in swarms. Given the desert setting, readers in the Judeo-Christian world will surely remember the strange food eaten by the Israelites as they wandered in search of a new world (Exodus 16:35). Perhaps, the '60's hope that "the world might head a new way" is not dead after all. Yet, syntactically, Snyder deliberately confuses the "they" who "somehow swarm down here" with the "sons and daughters in the circle," leaving readers to wonder whether it is the grasshoppers or the children who have appeared magically, like the manna, as sustenance in the desert. Because readers know Snyder's concept of a *puja* from "An Offering for Tārā" (i.e., that we all bring something to the banquet to be eaten, including ourselves), the notion that the children also provide communal food is not, finally, frightful, even if it were to be taken literally. As he says in *The Practice of the Wild,* "Eating is a sacrament. . . . We too will be offerings—we are all edible" (184). On the one hand it is clear that the children are eating the grasshoppers, "grimacing" at the strange taste of the food they chew. Yet even as the unlikely grasshoppers feed the children, so these children nourish the community; their importance to it—especially in their traditional roles as "sons and daughters"—is underlined by the attention Snyder gives them in the last lines of the section. *Mountains and Rivers Without End,* we remember, is dedicated to his own children: "This book is for Gen, Kai, Mika, Kyung-jin." There is no denying the pedagogical aspect of Snyder's long poem; in the final analysis it is "for the children" of the planet whoever we may be.

Just who is "singing sūtras for the insects in the wilderness"? And who is doing the singing? The Doer, the *shité,* of this action is curiously unspecified. In "The Hump-backed Flute Player" the sound of Kokop'ele, a grasshopper-like petroglyph complete with antennae, was the sound of emptiness: "The ringing in your ears // is the cricket in the stars." The whirr of grasshoppers, a singing of its own kind, is surely implied; insects sing their own songs in praise for all beings. Nor is it possible to avoid the suggestion that in the "far reaches" of time and space all human beings are as "children" and may be seen as tiny "insects." Since we are all together in this forever, surely sūtras must be sung for all beings by all beings. Nothing exists separately. All life exists only in cooperation with and mutual dependence on other beings. An understanding of one's place among the "foolish loving spaces" of the universe engenders compassion and gratitude for all beings, all of whom have been allowed to be part of the process. As Snyder told Ekbert Faas in 1974 when they discussed Snyder's affirmative phrasing of lines from the *Bhagavad Gita,* "the final step, yes, the final step beyond the complete comprehension of the 'emptiness' of the universe" is "the living, simple awareness of the absolute beauty and preciousness of mice and weeds" (Faas 111). Add to those two these tiny splendid insects in "Finding the Space in the Heart" in whose honor sūtras are sung.

Reminding us of the Nō dancer's final foot stamp, the poem concludes, as it began, with its song of a never-ending journey taken upon and by the turning earth:

Walking on walking,
under foot earth turns

Streams and mountains never stay the same.

As fixed as it may seem on its printed paper, *Mountains and Rivers Without End*—like the grains of a Tibetan sand painting scattered by the monks after completion, or Milarepa's houses of stone built and rebuilt again and yet again—is itself impermanent. The scroll takes its final turn. The Chorus sings; the Dancer fades from the stage. The "wet black brush / tip drawn to a point" finally lifts away from the paper in a last flourish of artistic composition. Earnestly encompassed by its current imaginers and fully concluded in the present moment, the scroll nevertheless awaits future unrollings, its spaces ready to leap once more into life as they are reconstituted and re-visioned in the mind . . . again . . . and again . . . and yet again. Even now, the performance goes on.

4

Traveling On . . .

FAAS: But didn't you plan *Mountains and Rivers Without End*
as an open ended endless poem?
SNYDER: Endless? No, not really. . . . [O]bviously, what you do with
"without End" is that you feed it back into itself and make a circle of it . . .

SNYDER: . . . I would like to have the poem close in on itself
but on some other level keep going.
FAAS: What would be the other level? In the reader's mind?
SNYDER: Yes.

(*Faas* 134)

Circumambulations inevitably spiral around to their starting points; a journey through the identifiable landscapes of *Mountains and Rivers* is no exception. Traversing the poem, readers make a virtual journey around the globe, ending where they began. Starting with "Night Highway 99," "Three Worlds, Three Realms, Six Roads," "The Elwha River," and "Bubbs Creek Haircut," the early poems of part I visit locations—urban and wild—parallel to the coastal and inland mountains—the Cascades, the Olympics, the Sierra Nevada—that form the western edge of Turtle Island. "Three Worlds, Three Realms, Six Roads" sketches "things to do" around Kyoto and fills in details of a floating world, life aboard a ship that roams the Mediterranean and the Pacific. With "Boat of a Million Years" we find ourselves on the ancient waterways of the Middle East. Mythically oriented, "The Blue Sky" focuses our attention on the turning globe itself, the interpenetration of its "east" and "west." In general, the poems of part II reconnect these geographical points, while adding to them the westerly push of European civilization into the "new" world. Marketplaces mentioned in "The Market" trace a line from Seattle and San Francisco to the Asian cities of Saigon, Kathmandu, and Benares. With "Night Song of the Los Angeles Basin" and "Covers the Ground" we return to specific California sites. The Kamo, Columbia, and Yosemite Rivers run their courses on East Asian and western American landscapes. "The Hump-backed Flute Player" makes similar geographical connections while extending the ground covered into China and India on the one hand, and into Beringia, the ice-free corridors of Canada, Canyon de Chelly, and the White Mountains on the other. In "With This Flesh" Snyder implies the journey taken across the Atlantic by the Spanish conquistadors who sailed westward to claim Baja California. In part III, he reverses the direction by "Walking the New York Bedrock" and, moving still further "east," pointing us toward an ancient location in the hills of the Czech Republic. We come back to the Alaskan wilderness in "Arctic Midnight Twilight" and visit the mythical lands of the Haida in the Queen Charlotte Islands off the coast of British Columbia. The central landscape of this group of poems is the small town of Leh in northern India where Snyder pays his respect to Tārā and the Tibetan people. "Macaques in the Sky" returns us to a jungle canopy in East Asia. The major poems of part IV—"Old Woodrat's Stinky House," "Earrings Dangling and Miles of Desert," "The Mountain Spirit," and "Finding the Space in the Heart"—emanate from western American landscapes, primarily those of the Great Basin. In addition there are two watery trips to the Pacific Northwest—a raft trip on the Tatshenshini (Raven's Beak) River and a kayak excursion into Glacier Bay—and a side trip into the mythical Japanese landscape of "The Dance."

The trail described by a linear reading of *Mountains and Rivers* ends just east of the Sierra Nevada in the vast open spaces of the Black Rock Desert of Nevada. It is half a day's drive from San Francisco, even closer to Snyder's home in Kitkitdizze, not far from where we began. In this immense landscape of Snyder's imagining there are multiple mythical, cultural, and anthropological tracks to be followed, but in terms of physical geography, connecting the dots reveals a trace that circles the planet. Moving "to the left" much as a landscape scroll unrolls, we travel from western America to East Asia, the Middle East, and into the Mediterranean; then, with the story of Europa and the mythical bull, from Libya to Crete to Spain ("the Thyssen Collection in Madrid"); and, finally, with the Spanish and "Mother *Bos*," across the Atlantic to Baja, once more returning to the landscape of western America.

An exquisite march around the globe, the journey nevertheless ends; the reading is finished. Much as Ginsberg, Whalen, and Snyder concluded their *pradakshina* of Mount Tamalpais in a very mundane "parking lot," so readers who have made their individual imaginative journeys across the landscapes of *Mountains and Rivers Without End* must finally return to whatever "down to earth" worlds they inhabit, however inadequately. The poem itself comes to rest in lines that echo the culminating words of its first section. In "Endless Streams and Mountains" readers were invited to trace the emerging "moist black line" on the broad, unrolling white space. It was there that the consummate chant that comes to exemplify the entire poem was first heard:

> *Walking on walking,*
> *under foot   earth turns.*
>
> *Streams and mountains never stay the same.*
>
> (*MRWE* 9)

Thirty-eight poems later, in the final lines of "Finding the Space in the Heart," the relentless rhythms of the unending song of the Mountain Spirit are heard yet again, even as the tip of the "wet black brush" is lifted away and "the space goes on." Having traversed the magical landscape of Gary Snyder's *Mountains and Rivers Without End* with dedication and attentiveness, at times even outright playfulness and exuberance, readers now finger the final pages in a physical act of closure only to find themselves gazing, once again, at the book's cover: the immense rock of Half Dome, the flow of Yosemite Falls, a lone pine tree. Rock and water, tree and sky; the Nō stage is set once more: "stamp the foot, walk with it, clap! turn, / the creeks come in, ah!" (*MRWE* 8).

Caught by the eye of an ancient spirit, one is compelled to begin again even as lingering images, resonant connections, and new ways of seeing remind readers that nothing can ever be quite the same again. We will be unable to "cease from exploration," as T. S. Eliot said in *Four Quartets,* because each journey's end will find us arriving "where we started," only to "know the place for the first time" ("Little Gidding"). Majestic in both its flow and its fixity, echoing Dōgen's view of mountains and rivers, Snyder's long poem continually awaits new encounters and new readers, including those who have previously taken the journey and find themselves compelled to begin again. In the multiple minds of its community of readers *Mountains and Rivers Without End* will "never stay the same"; complete comprehension of the poem—the fullness of its painted reality—remains beyond any single critical reading of it. Like the seductive form of a goddess seen behind a veil, the allure of the poem's constantly shifting web of associations remains an invitation to transformation for those who attend to its interweavings. Its content espouses tangible metaphors for the metaphysics of emptiness, the doctrine of *vijñaptimātra,* the "philosophy of transcendent wisdom"; we contemplate these images in the pack of the Buddhist scholar-pilgrim Hsüan-tsang, in Milarepa's continual rebuildings, in Wovoka's hat, in Krishna's mouth, in Kokop'ele's hump, in Gary Snyder's backpack, in the all-encompassing, spiraling verbal constructs and "painted" landscapes of *Mountains and Rivers Without End.* In the world of words, the affective and associational techniques of poetry are best suited for transmitting the profound insights associated with emptiness. If we are to believe Dōgen, and then Milarepa, a reading of *Mountains and Rivers,* a veritable vehicle of impermanence itself, will engender compassion.

Compassion is, after all, the primary focus of *Mountains and Rivers.* In Buddhist terminology, the definitive moment of *prajñā* ("wisdom" or "consciousness") occurs when one intuitively experiences the true nature, the emptiness, of reality. This wisdom "cannot be conveyed by concepts or in intellectual terms" ("Prajñā" *Shambhala Dictionary*). Once—and once is never enough—having attained an enlightened view of the interconnectedness of life—at the very least that all beings are equal partners in a global food chain—one is led immediately toward *karunā,* or "compassion, active sympathy, gentle affection," a virtue that "must be accompanied by wisdom (*prajñā*) in order to have the right effect" ("Karunā" *Shambhala Dictionary*). Wisdom and compassion, like mountains and rivers, are an interpenetrating dyad. The English word *understanding* conveys both meanings: to know something completely; to have empathy for another. Avalokiteshvara is the primary Buddhist bodhisattva of compassion; Tārā, his female consort, is equally compassionate; she "ar[o]se from his tears in order to help him in his work" ("Tārā" *Shambhala Dictionary*). Compassionate wisdom, at its simplest, should at least prompt a deep appreciation for the community of Others—other humans, the trees, the plants, the animals—even down to the tiniest of them, even down to the "preciousness of mice and weeds." An enormous range of beings joins us at the ongoing banquet of life. Even ghostly beings come to the table. Their past actions have given shape to our present condition; their presence in our imaginings literally informs our awareness.

On a larger scale, as *Mountains and Rivers Without End* makes clear, we owe a profound sense of gratitude to this whirling blue globe, endlessly pulsing with life: breathing in and breathing out; ebbing and flowing; erupting and eroding; giving and taking. With probing roots and extended leaves, gnarled trees transform the soil's chemicals, extracting energy from the stars. Desert sands trickle through fingers, allowing contact with the ancient age of the globe. Innumerable animals sacrifice and share with us. Somewhere in the encompassing blue sky that bathes the planet lies the unknown play of the future.

In adapting *Yamamba* to "The Mountain Spirit," Snyder has found the perfect symbol to increase the reader's compassion for the planet. As D. T. Suzuki explains, Yamamba is "the principle of love secretly moving in every one of us." Because we notice only the superficial results of love's labors, we easily personify love as "something beautiful to look at, young, delicate, and charming." The reality, according to Suzuki, is far different:

> [L]ove herself, like a hard working peasant woman, looks rather worn out; from worrying about others her face is full of wrinkles, her hair is white. She has so many knotty problems presented for her solution. Her life is a series of pains, which, however, she gladly suffers. She travels from one end of the world to another, knowing no rest, no respite, no interruption. Love in this phase, that is, from the point of view of her untiring labor, is fitly represented as Yama-uba [Yamamba], the old lady of the mountains. (*Zen and Japanese Culture* 419–20)

Using Snyder's chosen token, it is possible to see a certain kind of natural beauty in the twisted shape of a bristlecone pine, but it isn't the beauty of youth. It is easier to see the beauty of natural landscapes—fantastic peaks, sinuous rivers, vast open spaces—but the point Snyder wishes to make has more to do with dynamics: a never-ending, geomorphological tectonic story. Simply put, if the planet has been unendingly kind to us, working tirelessly to provide us with the materials and energy out of which we create our lives, we might at least acknowledge that behavior with respectful actions of our own. A clarion call for literal global compassion, *Mountains and Rivers Without End* is a fundamental wisdom text for the modern ecological movement. Seamlessly woven into this virtual tapestry of words, images, and ideas are significant issues of political and spiritual consequence. Interviewed by Catherine Ingram, who characterizes Snyder as a "spiritual activist," he pointed out that "most of our problems are caused by the human reluctance to accept death, impermanence, ephemerality, and by efforts that people make to build an illusion of permanence . . . which also becomes an illusion of separateness" (Snyder, "Legacy of the Wild" 9). These same themes, of course, fill the pages of *Mountains and Rivers.* Recognizing the illusory nature of permanence and separateness would be a great leap forward for humankind, but it will take place only with a shift to a more compassionate attitude:

> If people can acknowledge their membership in the fabric of the whole, acknowledge that they are part of the habitat, part of the network, part of the web, and feel that the welfare of the web is their welfare, and their welfare is the welfare of the web—in other words, to be mindfully one with the whole—that is an extraordinary spiritual and political step right there, and it dumps the cartridges out of the weapons. It makes people approach things in a different way. ("Legacy of the Wild" 9)

Not that the planet itself is fragile; it is "green enough to go on living," and it will survive the machinations of humans. Yet while we are "here" and "now," we should learn to manage our common house well, to be "at home" with it.

Mountains and Rivers is not a political or religious diatribe. It is a work of art, a long poem conceived in a tradition of modern American long poems that starts with Walt Whitman's flowing line, optimism, and all-encompassing nature. It is certainly not difficult to see the influence of Pound and Eliot. The *Cantos* abound in a similar use of imagistic association, fragmentation, and quotation, not to mention the inclusion of Asian poetic techniques and allusions. In religious terms, Snyder's abiding Buddhism seems an equivalent to Eliot's profound devotion to Christian sensibility in his *Four Quartets.* Formally, the stanzaic rhythms of *Mountains and Rivers Without End* appear to exist somewhere between the tightly structured, measured lines found in Eliot and the idiosyncratic phrasing of Pound. Snyder also shares William Carlos Williams's attention to spoken rhythms, his insistence on the poetry of the common life, and Williams's awareness, however sketchy, of Native American culture. Yet Snyder has a greater familiarity with the extended oral narratives and performances of Native American peoples in addition to those of East Asia. Nor should one forget the influence of his lifelong friend, Allen Ginsberg, whose "Howl" became the hallmark of poetic revolution in the mid-'50s. Like all long poems, Snyder's *Mountains and Rivers Without End* demonstrates an epic intent: a desire to encompass the culture of the times, even perhaps to "make it new" by getting the words to fall on the ears and eyes and mind just so. For all of its apparent mystery at first sight, Snyder's long poem is a metaphor of clarity, an unashamed work of love for the planet and all its beings, perhaps an inkling of a myth for times yet to come.

Adopting the perspective of astronauts on the moon's surface, Lewis Thomas has described the animate Earth in breathtaking terminology:

> Aloft, floating free beneath the moist, gleaming membrane of bright blue sky, is the rising earth, the only exuberant thing in this part of the cosmos. If you could look long enough, you would see the swirling of the great drifts of white cloud, covering and uncovering the half-hidden masses of land. If you had been looking for a very long, geologic time, you could have seen the continents themselves in motion, drifting apart on their crustal plates, held afloat by the fire beneath. It has the organized self-contained look of a live creature, full of information, marvelously skilled in handling the sun. (Thomas 170)

Thomas's vision was intuited by Gary Snyder long before the lunar rockets landed. Similarly, Joseph Campbell also speaks of what has come to be known as the Gaia principle: "the image of the whole planet as an organism"; that "we are the consciousness of the earth . . . the eyes of the earth . . . the voice of the earth." He tells Bill Moyers that "the only myth that is going to be worth thinking about in the immediate future is one that is talking about the planet" (*Power of Myth* 32). Snyder's imagery may be driven by the Paleolithic, but his understanding of the auspiciousness of the present moment for our planet is equally passionate:

> Why this going back into the roots and the past, instead of leaping off into the future, I'm sometimes asked. But it's not *in time* at all that we study our world and ourselves. There's no close or far. We have, simply, the chance to fill out the whole picture now, for the first time in human experience. It is beginning to be possible to look in one wide gaze at all that human beings have been and done on the whole planet, as one small part of the web of Gaia the earth-life-Goddess. . . . GS 13.X.40077 (*Myths & Texts* viii)

A storyteller and singer at heart, Snyder's "gesture," as he says in the preface to *No Nature*, "has been with language" (v), and it is evident that *Mountains and Rivers Without End* is the composed truth of his "one wide gaze," an extraordinary contribution to the mythological edifice of the future.

"Texts," as Snyder tells us, can be read in "the stratigraphy of rocks, layers of pollen in a swamp, the outward expanding circles in the trunk of a tree" (*Practice* 66). In time, rivers and mountains—indeed, entire continents—draw the path of their progress across landscapes. Glaciers advance and retreat, scoring the granite beneath, leaving a string of lakes behind. The bear, the deer, the sheep, the rabbits all leave trails. Year in and year out birds follow unseen routes, the manner of their traveling yet another pattern to observe, their song an audible track in the air. For diverse reasons humans migrate from location to location, their movements to be deciphered in forgotten artifacts or tales of the tribe. All of these traces, and more, enmeshed by Snyder's verbal spirals, wind their diverse ways through *Mountains and Rivers Without End.* The fascinating landscape of his long poem mirrors a world of constant renewal in the process of continual reinhabitation by all of its beings, some of whom are more attentive than others.

Some paths lead off into the wild; others are best followed by staying on the trail. Both directions are necessary; each provides vital knowledge, and each informs the other, as well as those readers who would actively experience this long poem, this vast world. An edifying landscape, it is diverse and yet one space.

> —Coyote says "You people should stay put here,
> learn your place,
> do good things . . . ."
>
> (*MRWE* 121)

Of course, Coyote's long gone, endlessly traveling on . . .

Afterword: An Acknowledgment

Acknowledgment, cloaked in formal statements or an occasion for pleasant intimacies, may run the gamut from reluctant disclosures about one's words to a joyous recognition of the assistance or authority of The Other, whoever or whatever that might be. In the interpenetrating cause-effect time-space framework passed on to me by years of living with Gary Snyder's *Mountains and Rivers Without End,* my debt of acknowledgment appears so vast, so diverse, that only the narrative mode seems appropriate. Before I sum up the story of my indebtedness, I would like to give voice to a simple yet powerful grace, conveyed to me first by Gary Snyder, for those who go unnamed: I give thanks to all my teachers, friends, and especially the "wild" for giving and sharing with me in my own twenty-five-year-long venture, one that I hardly knew I was undertaking.

Behind the making of this book about the imagining and fashioning of a poem is a story of altered personal perspectives mixed in with generational shifts in consciousness that now seem like tiny blips in history, dimly understood, if at all, only in hindsight. As a teacher with over thirty-five years of experience, I can attest that a good proportion of today's high school and university students confuse World War I with World War II, have completely forgotten about the Korean conflict, and know little about Vietnam except what they have gathered from the movies. Somewhere between the '50s and '70s, an optimistic, if anarchistic, revolt against the man in the grey flannel suit and his houses made of ticky-tacky somehow became confused with drugs and dropping out. Beatniks became hippies, and both groups disappeared down some ancient highway with one hand waving free. Somewhere between the '80s and the turn of the century, ideas of community and sharing became lost in a welter of egotism and greed. The stock market ballooned and burst; the Iron Curtain was torn away. Leaders came and went; civil rights come and go. Nothing lasts; all things change. Indeed, *"streams and mountains never stay the same."* Amid the flow of events, the thoughtful eloquence of Gary Snyder's words remains a constant, a steadying place, an intellectual and artistic locus where one may meditate on the dynamics of change. A teacher by nature, Snyder has gone beyond to be a "Master" for successive generations of apprentices, myself included. His *Mountains and Rivers Without End* has enriched my personal and professional life beyond any telling of it. My profoundest acknowledgment is to Gary Snyder for giving me a fuller life, one I could never have imagined or encountered without his presence.

In the spring of 1956, as I completed my high school studies, Snyder had the first inklings of a poem to be called *Mountains and Rivers Without End.* By the end of May, however, he was in Kyoto beginning his formal study of Zen at Daitoku-ji. Hardly a beatnik and with no specific plans in my head, I briefly took to "the road" that summer. It began with a Greyhound bus ride from Philadelphia to San Diego by way of Texas and New Mexico and ended with a month-long return journey in my cousin's 1951 chartreuse convertible. At seventeen, with an untested driver's license, I piloted that Ford from San Francisco across the Sierra Nevada, the mountains and deserts of the Great Basin, the Bonneville Salt Flats, the smoking pools and geysers of Yellowstone, north to Mount Rushmore and the Black Hills, across the plains states, through Chicago and Detroit, until, after a diversion into Canada via the Great Lakes, I landed once more in Philadelphia, Pennsylvania, the fair city and state of my youth. By the end of the journey I knew that I had become hooked on space.

The next four years found me walking a four-block line between my home, the restaurant where I worked on weekends, and the college, St. Joseph's University, I attended. I remember my freshman English instructor, Bill Lynch, patiently teaching me the finer art of explication using Brooks and Warren's *Understanding Poetry* (1950). Thank you William Lynch, wherever you are. As the '60s dawned, I chose the University of Hawaii for graduate school in English. In 1963, tired of my routines and only dimly aware of a "conflict" beginning in Southeast Asia, I filled out an application for the U.S. Peace Corps and wound up in a teacher-training college in the village of Akai-Eket, Nigeria. Within a year I found myself married to a fellow Peace Corps volunteer, Susan Conway, my partner, lover, and friend of over thirty-eight years. She has helped me with untold practical matters involving this book—repetitive and seemingly trivial tasks that she undertook willingly—and with critical feedback to keep me on the path even in times of despair. Yet these matters are not, finally, the debts I wish to acknowledge. There is simply no way to measure the profundity of sensibility and thought ensuing from our years together. In all humility, I bow to her for the luxuriant life she has given me.

Our tour with the Peace Corps came to an end in 1965 just as the first *Six Sections from "Mountains and Rivers Without End"* was published; I had no familiarity whatever with the name "Gary Snyder." Wanting new, and distinctly different, spaces, Susan and I journeyed from tropical West Africa to the mountains, deserts, and red-rimmed mesas of the Southwest where we began graduate studies at the University of New Mexico. For some reason I have long since forgotten, I took Gene Frumkin's course "Literary Movements since 1940" with vague expectations of poems from Dylan Thomas, William Carlos Williams, and James Dickey. Instead, a primary text used for the course was Donald M. Allen's *The New American Poetry* (Grove Press, 1960), and I found myself reading, among others, poets like Charles Olson, Robert Creeley, Denise Levertov, Allen Ginsberg, Lawrence Ferlinghetti, and

Gary Snyder. I thank you Gene Frumkin, wherever you are, and Donald Allen too. And thank you, New Mexico, for truly being a land of enchantment.

New Mexico not only had its bewitching landscapes, imbued with the spirit of Native American culture, it also had a constant stream of poets and writers who spoke to relatively large crowds in the Kiva on weekends. Thus it was that a gathering of meditative listeners at a poetry reading was interrupted one Friday evening by a strange man dressed in an ornate *chaleco* who stood up in the back of the auditorium. It was pretty obvious that he had imbibed an elegant sufficiency of something or other. Rudely, it seemed to me, he implied that the poet then reading before us was mediocre by telling us that a "real" poet would speak to us in the coming weeks. Thank you Robert Bly, for an unforgettable introduction to Gary Snyder. Who could resist? I attended Snyder's reading two weeks later, and from that moment on have never stopped listening. Even now I do not know exactly why I continue in my eagerness to hear his voice, but the word *enchanting*, with its connotations of magic and song, again comes to my mind. At UNM I was to devote hours to studying the "poetry" of Harold Pinter's plays and had little actual time for Gary Snyder, yet one of my graduate school buddies, Bert Almon, was writing his dissertation on Snyder's *Myths & Texts*. Perhaps researching a fact or two for Bert began my affair with Snyder's long poem. Thank you Bert Almon.

My first "real" job as an English professor was at Colby College in Maine. Among other duties, I was given a thoroughly enjoyable assignment to teach a course on modern and contemporary poetry. Additionally, with Gary Lawless, a Colby student whose life would soon be transformed by a hardworking summer spent at Snyder's Kitkitdizze Zen community, I was an organizer of a three-day visit to our campus by Gary Snyder. I remember the poet's kindly advice when I asked him to look at some of my own poems: "give up the left margin," he said; "use the space on the page like music." During his visit to a classroom I remember his chanting, in English, sections from a Japanese Nō play entitled *Yamamba*. How little I knew of that play's importance for my own future. Shortly afterward, while trying to explain Snyder's "After Work" to a class, I discovered its underlying "Asian" motif; I wrote it up, and it became my first real publication. Thank you Colby College, for the opportunities given to a young professor and for colleagues, some now gone, who were invariably as stimulating as they were amiable.

During those Colby years, my wife and I had two children, Julianne and Christopher; both of them grew up to assist me in what I still call "The Search for Kokop'ele," a euphemism for research into the intellectual thought and physical spaces of Snyder's *Mountains and Rivers Without End*. As our nuclear family later camped and hiked throughout the forests of the western United States, it became apparent that Snyder had altered their lives as well. Thank you Julianne and Christopher for thinking I was up to something special. Thank you for all the times you found facts I needed in the libraries you later had access to. Thank you for putting up with my obsession as I dragged you toward unusual, and sometimes uncomfortable, places. We all remember those cold April afternoons and freezing nights on the rim by Canyon de Chelly. Thank you for being my now wonderfully grown-up children.

In the '70s Snyder and his family settled into Kitkitdizze. At the outset of the decade, his long poem resurfaced once more, now called *Mountains and Rivers Without End Plus One* (1970). As for my family, we moved from the cold northlands of Maine to reestablish ourselves in the tropics as I took a job in the English Department at the Mayagüez campus of the University of Puerto Rico. In addition to courses in American literature, I began to teach modern poetry and modern drama on a regular basis. In 1978 I was granted a Summer Seminar award by the National Endowment for the Humanities to study "The Long Poem in American Literature" with Roy Harvey Pearce at the University of California at San Diego. Other seminarians focused on the epiclike poems of Whitman and Williams, Eliot and Pound. Perhaps because little was known or written about it, I selected Snyder's *Mountains and Rivers Without End.* Launched into the world of Zen by D. T. Suzuki, I was soon reading (not necessarily understanding) sūtras. The University of Puerto Rico granted me, now tenured, a yearlong sabbatical in San Diego to follow up on my NEH work. (Thank you UPR–Mayagüez.) It soon became clear that my offhand summer choice of Snyder's long poem was headed in the direction of the book you hold in your hands. (Federal money spent in the service of the humanities does effect change, although sometimes fruition takes more than twenty years! Thank you NEH for the opportunity.) Augmenting the guidance of Roy Harvey Pearce (thank you Dr. Pearce) was excellent advice about little-known litmags by Michael Davidson, then in charge of UCSD's developing Archive for New Poetry, and direct assistance from Dan McLeod, a professor at San Diego State, who shared his audiotapes of Snyder readings. Wherever you are, thank you Michael, thank you Dan. Ensuing years of summer research helped me to discover emerging sections of Snyder's poem. I envisioned their meanings and, at times, some interconnections. Within a few years I knew enough to begin speaking professionally about my "journey" through Gary Snyder's *Mountains and Rivers Without End.* Subsequently I gave presentations in Puerto Rico, across the United States, and even, when in 1986–87 I was granted a Fulbright lectureship in the country then known as Yugoslavia, to an unexpectedly large crowd in Belgrade (Serbia). Obviously by the mid-'80s the work of Gary Snyder had become known around the globe.

Strangely enough, I never connected the word *scholar* with my own activities until I walked through the doors of the Special Collections room in the Shields Library at the University of California at Davis toward the end of the 1980s. There, first with the help of Donald Kunitz who actually called me a "scholar," and then over subsequent years with the monumental assistance and gracious friendship of John Skarstad that continues to the present moment, I grew into the mindful and patient habits of scholarship. Later visits took me to the Cleveland Museum of Art to collect information about *Ch'i-shan wu-chin* (*Streams and Mountains Without End*) and to the Freer Gallery in Washington, DC, to see Hsü Pen's landscape scroll (thanks to the aptly named Tara Coram at the Freer). More library work took me to Reed College in Portland, Oregon, where I examined the Philip Whalen Collection in the Special Collections Library of the Eric V. Hauser Memorial Library, and to San Diego, where I spent time with the Donald Allen Collection housed in the Mandeville Special Collections room at the Geisel Library of the University of California, San Diego. "Facts" are perceived to change over time: the earth, once thought flat, is now round; with new anthropological discoveries near Lake Chad hominid genealogy is surely more diverse and extends further back in time than previously imagined; the origins of human art evidenced by 40,000-year-old cave paintings may be supplanted by 77,000-year-old rock art found in a cave in South Africa; and although Robert Graves and Eric Neumann never had to worry about such things, the existence of "The Goddess" has been called into question by those who are politically correct. No matter . . . to Donald Kunitz, John Skarstad, and to all the research librarians and archivists who have so willingly established the bedrock, such as it is, that this book sits upon, I proffer my deepest thanks. We all live and work in a dynamic world.

To the scholars. In this same time frame I became familiar with the names of individual scholars associated with Snyder's poetry. Patrick Murphy's practical advice and enthusiastic support were, and continue to be, of the highest caliber. Thank you Patrick. I am indebted as well to numbers of other Snyder scholars over the years, some of whom I have met and others for whom correspondence, or just an intellectual appreciation of their scholarship, was the contact. To Tom Lyon, Sherman Paul, David Robertson, Len Scigaj, Katsunori Yamazato, Mark Gonnerman, John Whalen-Bridge, Lin Yao-fu, John Burns, John Suiter, and so many others that go unnamed here, a community of scholars, thank you all. To the editors of the *Journal of Modern Literature*, ISLE, *Western American Literature*, and *Atenea*, thanks for your positive judgments and your meticulous editorial labors. To Ron Latimer, former director of the University of Nevada Press, thanks for your faith in my manuscript and your calm voice. To John Mulvihill, copy editor supreme, so much more than mere thanks for your herculean labors in the fields of precision.

I owe a special debt to several of my colleagues in science at the University of Puerto Rico at Mayagüez who instructed me in the subject matter of their own expertise. Hans Schellekens in geology, and Duane Kolterman, Allen Lewis, and Gary Breckon in biology, all taught me things I needed to know. Both support and insight were furnished by my good friends Jill Barnum of the University of Minnesota and Jeff Holmquist of the University of California at Santa Barbara. There are others, of course, friends and family whose patient anticipatory waiting has kept me going in difficult times.

Finally my sincere gratitude to Jack Shoemaker for taking the time to have coffee with me one fine afternoon in Berkeley; to David Korfhage for being the first to read the entire manuscript with intelligence; and to an unknown park ranger at Canyon de Chelly National Monument, a member of the Navajo Nation, for reverently showing me a way to practice in the wild.

Notes

1. FINDING THE PATHS

1. Katsunori Yamazato also mentions this moment of *satori* in "Seeking a Fulcrum: Gary Snyder and Japan (1956–1975)," 9.

2. "The Circumambulation of Mt. Tamalpais" also appears in *Agenda* 4.3–4 (Summer 1966): 32–35, where it is designated as "from 'Mountains & Rivers'" but does not carry the note about *pradakshina.* Snyder also speaks of a *pradakshina* undertaken in mid-January 1962 in his long letter "To Thea" that first appeared in *Caterpillar* and subsequently was published in book form as *Passage Through India.* See page 26 of that book for the comment on *pradakshina.*

2. COMPOSING THE SPACE

1. Snyder's statement is a version of a text he composed earlier for a poetry reading given at San Francisco State in 1958. From Japan he wrote to Kyger (in San Francisco) asking her to send a copy of that statement to Allen for the anthology. See Snyder's August 17, 1959 letter to Kyger. GSP B104:F11.

2. *Heart Sūtra:* "shortest of the forty sūtras that constitute the *Prajñāpāramitā-sūtra.* It is one of the most important sūtras of Mahāyāna Buddhism and, particularly in China and Japan, it is recited by monks and nuns of almost all schools. The sūtra is especially emphasized in Zen, since it formulates in a particularly clear and concise way the teaching of *shūnyatā,* emptiness, the immediate experience of which is sought by Zen practitioners. The pith sentence of the *Heart Sūtra* is, 'Form is no other than emptiness; emptiness is no other than form,' an affirmation that is frequently referred to in Zen." ("Heart Sūtra" *Shambhala Dictionary*).

3. See the "Statements on Poetics" in Donald Allen's *The New American Poetry* or the essays on poetics gathered in his subsequent book *The Poetics of the New American Poetry.*

4. The India trip is described in great detail by both Joanne Kyger and Gary Snyder, she in her *Japan and India Journals, 1960–1964,* and he first as a letter to his sister Thea in "Now India" and later as a book, *Passage Through India.*

5. Steuding, presumably with Snyder's approval, lists thirteen sections: "Bubbs Creek," "Elwha River," "Night Highway Ninety-Nine," "Hymn to the Goddess San Francisco," "The Market," "Journeys," "Three Worlds / Three Realms / Six Roads," "The Rabbit," "The Blue Sky," "The Hump-Backed Flute Player," "Ma," "Down," and "The

California Water Plan." Steuding's chapter on *Mountains and Rivers Without End* in his book *Gary Snyder* is the earliest critical treatment of Snyder's long poem as a self-referencing sequence. While the poet obviously changed his mind about several things he said at that time, Steuding's book remains a good starting place for anyone interested in tracing the poem's development.

6. Snyder made this comment to me in person. Our conversation took place on the afternoon of November 24, 1996, when our paths crossed quite serendipitously at the Freer Gallery. I had arranged for an appointment to view the scroll. Snyder was in Washington, DC, to read from his newly published poem at the Library of Congress that evening. We viewed the scroll together.

7. This point about the city poems is made by John Whalen-Bridge in "Spirit of Place and Wild Politics in Two Recent Snyder Poems."

8. Snyder speaks of his dislike for the anti-intellectualism of the Beat generation, yet he carefully sets aside Whalen, Robert Duncan, and Kenneth Rexroth as poets who are true intellectuals. (Letter to Joanne Kyger, 14 Sept. 1959. GSP B104:F11.)

9. As Eric Todd Smith relates, Snyder spoke of the *jo-ha-ha-kyu* rhythm of the four parts of his poem to his graduate seminar class at the University of California at Davis in May of 1996. I was also present at that meeting. See Smith 30.

10. Boxes 106 and 107 among the Gary Snyder Papers at the University of California at Davis contain material related to Robin Collins. A classmate of Snyder's at Reed, her presence is strongly felt in many entries of the poet's early journals, and her name surfaces several times in his correspondence with Whalen. The contents of these boxes were unavailable for use before September 21, 2003.

3. INHABITING THE LANDSCAPE

1. Several small line changes and a major rearrangement of the section were made between the time of its journal publication in *Orion* and its appearance in the book. In the Counterpoint version, the section begins by describing the painting. In the *Orion* version, Snyder begins by quoting the colophons, and the description of the painting itself is left to the latter part of the section.

2. These specific tree types are not mentioned in the *Orion* publication. Both species are found in North America and in East Asia.

3. Snyder quotes four of the twenty lines of colophon I as printed in Lee and Fong (51). The lines he selects are not contiguous: "The creator has no original intention; / Mountains and streams are but crystallized pure air, / [two lines skipped] / Who has picked these tasteful forests and springs, / And laid them on this white piece of silk with light ink."

4. Lee and Fong (52) translate these lines from colophon II as: "Other people living with the noise of chickens and dogs / Are happily at peace under a good government. / Why then is my love so foolish / that I crave the company of rocks and streams?" There are twenty-four lines in the complete Lee and Fong translation.

5. The line referred to is a single line of the sixteen-line colophon III in Lee and Fong:

"While the water joins the mountains, the mountains are actually planted in the water" (53).

6. The lines are taken from the four-line colophon VI in Lee and Fong: "It is truly a painting worth / careful keeping. . . . / Its survival from the danger of war and fire is a rarity" (56).

7. Snyder translates the first two and a half sentences exactly as they are found in the seven-sentence prose translation of colophon IX in Lee and Fong (57).

8. The exchange between the old man and Sokei-an is also written out in Snyder's journal entry for June 7, 1959 (Journal—"4.1.1959." GSP B30:F12). Sokei-an is the husband of Ruth Fuller Sasaki, Snyder's original sponsor for Zen study.

9. The mark here, which I've represented as a double quotation mark, may or may not be an ending quotation mark (there is no opening quotation mark). It may be a sign for a musical pause or space break.

10. Donald Allen was the editor of the Four Seasons Foundation, which published the first edition: *Six Sections from "Mountains and Rivers Without End."* He was a major force in the development of American poetry and the editor of the influential 1960 Grove Press anthology *The New American Poetry.* In addition to publishing Snyder, Allen was also instrumental in bringing the work of Charles Olson, Michael McClure, Philip Whalen, Lew Welch, and many others, to the attention of audiences beginning to sense new vibrations in American poetry.

11. "Walking," "Wandering," and "Walking in Place" are major terms used by Eric Todd Smith in his *Reading Gary Snyder's "Mountains and Rivers Without End."*

12. Another poem, entitled "The Sappa Creek," was published in *Earth House Hold* and again in *No Nature.* The "Tanker Blues" poem Snyder later refers to is probably "T–2 Tanker Blues" published in *Riprap, & Cold Mountain Poems.* Many other poems allude to or reflect on Snyder's experience on board the boat.

13. The original reads: "Le reve dont se nourrit obscurement la Recherche humaine, c'est, au fond, de parvenir à maitriser . . . l'Energie de fond dont toutes les autres energies ne sont que les servantes: *saisir,* reunis tous ensemble, *la barre du monde,* en mettant la main sur le Ressort meme de l'Evolution" (Teilhard de Chardin, *Le Phenomene Humain* 278, my emphasis). The English translation is "The dream upon which human research obscurely feeds is fundamentally that of mastering . . . the ultimate energy of which all other energies are merely servants; and thus, by grasping the very mainspring of evolution, *seizing the tiller of the planet*" (Teilhard de Chardin, *The Phenomenon of Man* 250, my emphasis). I am indebted both to Mark Gonnerman of the Department of Religion at Stanford University and, through him, to Father Jacques Séverin Abbatucci for finding the source of this quotation.

14. Snyder spells them as "abt fish" and "yut fish." The former is clearly derived from Budge's "abtu fish"; the latter is problematic. When I asked the poet (in October 1996) about the name "yut," he acknowledged that he may have misspelled it in the notes he took before he wrote the poem.

15. "*Flying Dutchman,* spectre ship of popular legend; it is believed to haunt the waters around the Cape of Good Hope, and its appearance is a sign of imminent disaster. In the most common version of the legend, which forms the basis of the opera *Die fliegende*

Holländer (1843) by the German composer Richard Wagner, Captain Vanderdecken gambles his salvation on a rash pledge to round the cape during a storm and so is condemned to round the cape forever. In another legend the captain, Falkenberg, must sail forever through the North Sea, playing at dice for his soul with the devil. The dice-game motif recurs in *The Rime of the Ancient Mariner* (1798) by the English poet Samuel Taylor Coleridge; the mariner sights a phantom ship on which Death and Life-in-Death play dice to win him" ("Flying Dutchman" *Encyclopaedia Britannica*).

16. Snyder's entry in *Passage Through India* seems to record only a twenty-four-hour period. Joanne Kyger's report of the trip allots December 20–22 to the Saigon stop. See Kyger, *Japan and India Journals, 1960–1964.*

17. See John Whalen-Bridge's article, "Gary Snyder, Dōgen, and 'The Canyon Wren,'" and Leonard Scigaj's chapter on Snyder in his *Sustainable Poetry* for additional commentary on Dōgen's importance to this section.

18. The relevant lines from the original Ladakhi poem read:

> In the lofty sky,
> Is the nest of a vulture,
> There rests a bird, colour of gold,
> May you, the bird, remain unchanged.
> The unchanged bird, may you remain unchanged.
> On the lofty mountain,
> Is the nest of a hawk.
> On the lofty rock,
> The nest of a white hawk,
> Here circles a bird of silver white.
> May you the bird remain unchanged,
> The unchanged bird, may you remain unchanged. (Shakspo 16)

19. The word *arktos* is Greek for "bear." Rhea, child of Ouranos and Gaia, cohabits with her brother Kronos to give birth to the Olympian gods. Kronos sets about to devour the children because he believes one of them will destroy him. Rhea's story is complex (with parallels to the Isis-Osiris-Set-Horos myth), but it reflects her role as conservatrix of her children. She assists her son Zeus when he emasculates his father (her brother-husband), Kronos.

20. The original reads: "A Ernest Delahaye, Parmerde, Juinphe 72 . . . Il y a bien ici un lieu de boisson que je préfère. Vive l'académie d'Absomphe, malgré la mauvaise volonté des garçons! C'est le plus délicat et le plus tremblant des habits, que l'ivresse par la vertu de cette sauge de glaciers, l'absomphe! Mais pour, après, se coucher dans la merde!" (Rimbaud 315). I am indebted to Mark Gonnerman of the Department of Religion at Stanford University for tracking down the original source of this quotation.

21. Cf.: "and through shady mountains and windy peaks / she delights in the chase" (Athanassakis 65). Also: "In mountains of shadow / and peaks of wind / she delights in the chase" (Baring and Cashford 320).

22. I am thankful to Dr. Duane Kolterman, of the Department of Biology at the Univer-

sity of Puerto Rico, Mayagüez, for a concise lesson in Greek etymology and on the botanical species mentioned in this section.

23. In his essay "The Meditation Hall," D. T. Suzuki describes the rituals of meal taking in the Zen monastery. At the end of the meal, "the leader claps the wooden blocks and the serving monks bring hot water. Each diner fills the largest bowl with it, and in it all the smaller dishes are neatly washed, and wiped with a piece of cloth which each monk carries. Now a wooden pail goes around to receive the slops" (*Essays in Zen Buddhism* 325). In a footnote to the word "slops," Suzuki adds: "When the slop-basin goes around, spiritual beings are again remembered: 'This water in which my bowls were washed tastes like nectar from heaven. I now offer this to the numerous spirits of the world; may they all be filled and satisfied! *Om ma-ku-ra-sai . . . svāhā*!'" (325).

24. David Jinsoo Lee's "American Nō: Gary Snyder's *Mountains and Rivers Without End*" is an eighty-five-page honors thesis written under the direction of Professors Steven Goldsmith and Robert Haas while Lee was a student in English H195 at the University of California at Berkeley in the spring of 1997. Mr. Lee's unpublished paper is a detailed investigation into aspects of the Nō theater, with special attention paid to *Yamamba* and its application to Snyder's "The Mountain Spirit." In my own brief comparison of the structure of the two works, I have utilized the same schematic headings set forth by Mr. Lee in his work and, in several places, have compressed his extensive findings into a few lines. I want to express my deep gratitude to Mr. Lee for his careful analysis of "The Mountain Spirit" and for his gracious permission to adapt and summarize from his work.

25. Snyder has chosen these aphorisms from among hundreds of possibilities that, to this day, may be found painted and/or etched on stones lining Dooby Lane, a road at the edge of the Black Rock Desert near Gerlach. As a series of rock displays and memorials, these whimsical yet profound monuments elaborated by the common man began as the work of DeWayne Williams. Additions to his road art have multiplied extraordinarily over the years; everyone who passes by feels compelled to leave behind a new arrangement of stones, or a new saying or drawing on a rock, modern-day pictographs and petroglyphs for future archaeologists to ponder (see DeWayne Williams).

Appendix

MOUNTAINS AND RIVERS WITHOUT END:
THE BOOKS, IN ORDER OF PUBLICATION

Six Sections from "Mountains and Rivers Without End." San Francisco: Four Seasons Foundation, 1965. The book contains "Bubbs Creek Haircut," "The Elwha River," "Night Highway Ninety-Nine," "Hymn to the Goddess San Francisco in Paradise," "The Market," and "Journeys." Referred to as the "first edition."

Six Sections from "Mountains and Rivers Without End" Plus One. San Francisco: Four Seasons Foundation, 1970. The book contains "Bubbs Creek Haircut," "The Elwha River," "Night Highway Ninety-Nine," "Hymn to the Goddess San Francisco in Paradise," "The Market," "Journeys," and "The Blue Sky." Referred to as the "second edition."

North Pacific Lands & Waters: A Further "Six Sections." Waldron Island: Brooding Heron Press, 1993. The book contains "Afloat," "Haida Gwai North Coast, Naikoon Beach, / Hiellen River Raven Croaks" "Greasy Boy," "Raven's Beak River / At the End," "Arctic midnight twilight / cool north breeze / green mountain slopes, white mountain sheep / *dibée* // Song," and "The Bear Mother."

Finding the Space. Reno: The Black Rock Press, 1996. The book contains "Earrings Dangling and Miles of Desert," "Cross Legg'd," "Old Woodrat's Stinky House," and "Finding the Space in the Heart."

Mountains and Rivers Without End. Washington, DC: Counterpoint Press, 1996. Cited in the text as "*MRWE*."

MOUNTAINS AND RIVERS WITHOUT END:
ALL KNOWN SECTIONS, IN ORDER OF PUBLICATION

"Bubbs Creek Haircut." *Origin* 2 (July 1961): 6–10.

"Night Highway Ninety-Nine." *Origin* 4 (Jan. 1962): 27–40.

"The Market." *Origin* 12 (Jan. 1964): 38–42.

"Hymn to the Goddess San Francisco in Paradise." *Fuck You/A Magazine of the Arts VII* 5 (Sept. 1964): [49–59]. Also: *City Lights Journal* 2 (1964): 140–44.

"Journeys." *Wild Dog* 17 (June 8, 1965): 1–4.

"The Elwha River." In *Six Sections from "Mountains and Rivers Without End"* (Four Seasons, 1965).

"The Circumambulation of Mt. Tamalpais." *Agenda* 4.3–4 (Summer 1966): 32–35.

Simultaneously in *Coyote's Journal* 5–6 (1966): 1–5, but not identified as a *Mountains and Rivers* section there.

"Three Worlds / Three Realms / Six Roads." *Poetry* (Chicago) 109.3 (Dec. 1966): 147–52. Also *Three Worlds / Three Realms / Six Roads.* Marlboro: Griffin Press, 1966.

"A Lion Dream." *Coyote's Journal* 8 (1967): 36–37. Snyder refers to it as a *Mountains and Rivers* section on taped recordings of readings given during the time of its publication. Tapes may be heard at The Archive for New Poetry, University of California, San Diego.

"The Black-tailed Hare" ["The Rabbit"]. "Eight Songs of Clouds and Water." *Poetry* 111.6 (March 1968): 353–54.

"The Blue Sky." *Caterpillar* 5 (Oct. 1968): 133–38. Also: *The Blue Sky.* New York: Phoenix Book Shop, 1969.

"Kumarajiva's Mother." *Intransit: The Gary Snyder Issue,* 1969: 47–48.

"Down." *Iowa Review* 1.4 (1970): 85–86.

"The Hump-backed Flute Player." *Coyote's Journal* 9 (June 1971): 1–4.

"The California Water Plan." *Clear Creek* 8 (Nov. 1971): 25. On Steuding's list of sections.

"Greasy Boy." *Caterpillar* 20 (June 1973): 71. Appears in *North Pacific Lands & Waters.*

"Ma." *Coyote's Journal* 10 (1974): 29–32. On Steuding's list of sections.

"The Flowing." *Kyoi Kuksu* 3 (Spring 1974): 67–69. Identified as a *Mountains and Rivers* section with its publication in *Conjunctions* 1 (Winter 1981–82): 20–23. See also: "Flowing." *Head/Waters: A Left Bank Book.* Hillsboro: Blue Heron Publishing, 1994. 65–68.

"Earth Verse." *Tree Rings* 9 (Spring 1996). *Tree Rings* is the newsletter of the Yuba City Watershed Council. According to a personal communication with Gary Snyder, this poem was first published (1981?) in a little magazine in Australia (e-mail: "RE: Spring Seminar," 13 Jan. 1996) but I have been unable to identify the magazine. It first appeared as a *Mountains and Rivers* section with the title "Musgrave Mountains Gatha" in an early (March 1995) unpublished draft version of the long poem.

"The Canyon Wren." *American West* Sept.-Oct. 1983: 47. Also: *Axe Handles.* San Francisco: North Point Press, 1983. 110–12.

"Night Song of the Los Angeles Basin." *The Ten Directions* 7.1 (Spring-Summer 1986): 15.

"Daylight all day / Cool north breeze with low clouds / Midnight twilight / Steep rock slope mountain sheep / Green summer slopes Song." *Zyzzyva* 2.4 (Winter 1986–87): 114–17. Later published in *North Pacific Lands & Waters* as "Arctic midnight twilight / cool north breeze with low clouds / green mountain slopes, white mountain sheep / *dibée* / Song."

"Walking the New York Bedrock / Alive in the Sea of Information." *Sulfur* 20 (Fall 1987): 55–59. See also: "Walking the New York Bedrock Alive in the Sea of Information." *Whole Earth Review* 61 (Winter 1988): 24–29.

"The Bear Mother." *Sulfur* 22 (Spring 1988): 115.

"Jackrabbit." *Sulfur* 22 (Spring 1988): 115–16.
"Raven's Beak River at the End." *Sulfur* 22 (Spring 1988): 118–19.
"Falls." *Sierra* 73 (May-June 1988): 46–47. See also: David Robertson. *West of Eden* 161; and David Robertson, *Yosemite As We Saw It* 73–74. The latter publication identifies it as "Yosemite Falls 1981–82."
"Haida Gwai North Coast, Naikoon Beach, / Hiellen River Raven Croaks." *The Green American Tradition: Essays and Poems for Sherman Paul.* Ed. H. Daniel Peck. Baton Rouge: Louisiana UP, 1989. 284–85.
"Macaques in the Sky." *Wild Earth* 1.4 (Winter 1991–92): 41.
"Earrings Dangling and Miles of Desert." *Yale Review* 80.1–2 (April 1992): 49–51.
"Afloat." *Grand Street* 12.1 (Spring 1993): 147–49.
"Under the Hills Near the Morava River." *Sulfur* 13.2 (Fall 1993): 79.
"Covers the Ground." *Place of the Wild: A Wildlands Anthology.* Ed. David Burks. Covelo: Island Press, 1994. 218–20. See also *The Threepenny Review* 58, 15.2 (Summer 1994): 28.
"With This Flesh" ["Reeds"]. *Sulfur* 14.2 (Fall 1994): 9–12. See also *Poetry Ireland Review* 43–44 (1994): 100–102.
"Cross Legg'd." *Poetry Ireland Review* 43–44 (1994): 103–4. See also *Zyzzyva* 12.1 (Spring 1996): 107.
"An Offering for Tārā." *Yale Review* 43.1 (Jan. 1995): 19–25.
"Endless Streams and Mountains." *Orion* Summer 1995: 38–40.
"Instructions." *Sipapu* 50 25.2 (1995): 25.
"The Old Bones." *The Company of Others: Essays in Celebration of Paul Shepard.* Ed. Max Oelschlager. Durango: Kivaki Press, 1995. 7.
"Boat of a Million Years." *Wild Earth* 6.1 (Spring 1996): 60.
"The Mountain Spirit." *Sulfur* 39 (Spring 1996): 7–14.
"Finding the Space in the Heart." *Shambhala Sun* 4.5 (May 1996): 22–23.
"We Wash Our Bowls in This Water." *Yale Review* 84.3 (July 1996): 69–71.
"Old Woodrat's Stinky House." *Yale Review* 84.3 (July 1996): 72–74.
"The Dance." *Mountains and Rivers Without End.* Washington: Counterpoint, 1996.
"New Moon Tongue." *Wild Earth* 6.4 (Winter 1996–97): 52.

Works Cited

ARCHIVES

Donald Allen Collection, Mandeville Special Collections Library, Geisel Library, University of California, San Diego. Accession number MSS 0003. (Citations include references to box and folder numbers, e.g., DAC B F .)

Gary Snyder Papers, Department of Special Collections, Shields Library, University of California, Davis. Accession number D50. Processed by Pamela Pearl Wilson. March 1995. (Citations include references to box and folder numbers, e.g., GSP B F].)

Philip Whalen Collection, Special Collections Library, Eric V. Hauser Memorial Library, Reed College, Portland, Oregon. (Cited as Reed–PWP.)

OTHER SOURCE MATERIAL

Allen, Charlotte. "The Scholars and the Goddess." *Atlantic Monthly* 287.1 (January 2001): 18–22.

Allen, Donald, ed. *The New American Poetry.* New York: Grove Press, 1960.

Allen, Donald, and Warren Tallman, eds. *The Poetics of the New American Poetry.* New York: Grove Press, 1973.

Almon, Bert. "Buddhism and Energy in the Recent Poetry of Gary Snyder." *Mosaic* 11.1 (1977): 117–25.

The American Heritage Dictionary of the English Language. 1969.

"Artemis." *New Encyclopaedia Britannica: Macropaedia.* 15th ed. 1982.

"Artemis, Temple of, at Ephesus." *New Encyclopaedia Britannica: Micropaedia.* 15th ed. 1982.

"Arts of American Indian Peoples." *New Encyclopaedia Britannica: Micropaedia.* 15th ed. 1982.

Athanassakis, Apostolos. "Second Hymn to Artemis." *The Homeric Hymns.* Baltimore: Johns Hopkins Press, 1976.

Bahn, Paul G. "Triple Czech Burial." *Nature* 332 (24 Mar. 1988): 302–3.

Barbeau, Marius. "Bear Mother." *Journal of American Folklore* 59.231 (Jan.-Mar. 1945): 1–12.

Baring, Anne, and Jules Cashford. *The Myth of the Goddess: Evolution of an Image.* London: Viking Arkana, 1991.

Bertholf, Robert, ed. "Letters from Gary Snyder." *Io* 14 (Summer 1972): 76–113.

Bethe, Monica, and Karen Brazell. *Nō as Performance: An Analysis of the Kuse Scene* of *"Yamamba."* Cornell University East Asia Papers 16. Ithaca: China-Japan Program, Cornell University, 1978.

Beyer, Stephan. *The Cult of Tārā: Magic and Ritual in Tibet.* Berkeley: U of California P, 1973.

Birnbaum, Raoul. *The Healing Buddha.* Rev. ed. Boston: Shambhala, 1989.

Boelscher, Marianne. *The Curtain Within: Haida Social and Mythical Discourse.* Vancouver: U of British Columbia P, 1988.

Bolton, Reginald Pelham. *New York City in Indian Possession.* 1920. 2nd ed. New York: Museum of the American Indian, Heye Foundation, 1975.

Bringhurst, Robert. *The Black Canoe: Bill Reid and the Spirit of Haida Gwaii.* Seattle: U of Washington P, 1991.

Brooks, Cleanth, and Robert Penn Warren. *Understanding Poetry.* New York: Holt, 1950.

Brown, Dale. *Wild Alaska. The American Wilderness Series.* New York: Time-Life Books, 1972.

Budge, E. A. Wallis. *The Book of the Dead: The Hieroglyphic Transcript of the Papyrus of Ani, the Translation into English and an Introduction.* New York: Bell, 1960.

———. *Osiris: The Egyptian Religion of Resurrection.* 2 vols. New Hyde Park: University Books, 1961.

Burks, David Clark. *Place of the Wild: A Wildlands Anthology.* Washington: Island Press, 1994.

Bush, Susan. "Yet Again 'Streams and Mountains Without End.'" *Artibus Asiae* 48.3–4 (1987): 197–223.

Campbell, Joseph. *The Masks of God: Oriental Mythology.* New York: Penguin, 1976. Cited as *Oriental.*

———. *The Masks of God: Primitive Mythology.* New York: Penguin, 1976. Cited as *Primitive.*

———. *The Power of Myth, with Bill Moyers.* Ed. Betty Sue Flowers. New York: Doubleday, 1988.

Chase, Don M. *People of the Valley: The Concow Maidu.* Sebastopol: Don M. Chase, 1973.

Cheng, François. *Empty and Full: The Language of Chinese Painting.* Boston: Shambhala, 1994.

Ch'i-shan wu-chin ["Streams and Mountains Without End"]. Cleveland Museum of Art. Accession Number 53.126. (The dimensions of the scroll in feet are 1.15 wide by 6.99 long.)

Conze, Edward. *Buddhism: Its Essence and Development.* New York: Harper & Row, 1975.

Cook, Francis. *How to Raise an Ox: Zen Practice as Taught in Zen Master Dōgen's "Shobogenzo."* Los Angeles: Center Publications, 1982.

———. *Sounds of Valley Streams: Enlightenment in Dōgen's Zen, Translation of Nine Essays from "Shōbōgenzō."* Albany: State University of New York Press, 1989.

Day, A. Grove. *The Sky Clears: Poetry of the American Indians.* Lincoln: U of Nebraska P, 1964.

Dōgen. "Mountains and Waters Sūtra." *Moon in a Dewdrop: Writings of Zen Master Dōgen.* New York: North Point Press, 1985. 97–107.

———. "Painting of a Rice-cake." *Moon in a Dewdrop: Writings of Zen Master Dōgen.* New York: North Point Press, 1985. 134–39.

"The Dreamtime." Cleveland Museum of Natural History. "Australia: xpressions of the Landscape." http://www.cmnh.org/collections/cultural/aboriginal/dreamtime.html. 15 May 2003.

Eliade, Mircea. *A History of Religious Ideas.* Vol. 1. Chicago: U of Chicago P, 1978.

Eliot, T. S. *Four Quartets.* New York: Harcourt, Brace & World, 1943.

———. *The Waste Land and Other Poems.* New York: Harcourt, Brace, & World, 1962.

Encyclopaedia Britannica. See *New Encyclopaedia Britannica.*

The Encyclopedia of Religion. Ed. Mircea Eliade. 16 vols. New York: Macmillan, 1987.

Exodus. *The Bible.* New International Version. *The Bible Gateway.* http://bible.gosplecom.net/cgi-bin/bible, 7 Dec. 1997.

Faas, Ekbert. "Gary Snyder." *Towards a New American Poetics: Essays and Interviews.* Santa Barbara: Black Sparrow Press, 1978. 89–142.

"Flying Dutchman." *New Encyclopaedia Britannica: Micropaedia.* 15th ed. 1982.

Fresh Tracks (Canada) Inc. "The Tatshenshini River." http://www.freshtracks.ca/river__rafting/tatshenshini.shtml. 15 May 2003.

Genesis. *The Bible.* New International Version. *The Bible Gateway.* http://bible.gosplecom.net/cgi-bin/bible, 7 Dec. 1997.

Gilluly, James, Aaron C. Waters, and A. O. Woodford. *Principles of Geology.* 3rd ed. San Francisco: W. H. Freeman, 1968.

Gimbutas, Marija. *The Language of the Goddess.* San Francisco: Harper Collins, 1991.

Ginsberg, Allen. *Allen Verbatim: Lectures on Poetry, Politics, Consciousness.* Ed. Gordon Ball. New York: McGraw-Hill, 1974.

Gleick, James. *Chaos: Making a New Science.* New York: Penguin, 1987.

Goodchild, Peter. *Raven Tales.* Chicago: Chicago Review Press, 1991.

Govinda, Lama Anagarika. *Foundations of Tibetan Mysticism.* New York: Samuel Weiser, 1969.

Grapard, Allan G. "Visions of Excess and Excesses of Vision: Women and Transgression in Japanese Myth." *Japanese Journal of Religious Studies* 18.1 (1991): 3–22.

Graves, Robert. *The White Goddess: A Historical Grammar of Poetic Myth.* 1948. Amended and enlarged. New York: Farrar Straus & Giroux, 1966.

Grayson, Donald K. *The Desert's Past: A Natural Prehistory of the Great Basin.* Washington: Smithsonian Institution Press, 1993.

Hallowell, Irving. "Bear Ceremonialism in the Northern Hemisphere." *American Anthropologist* ns 28 (1926): 1–175.

Halper, Jon, ed. *Gary Snyder: Dimensions of a Life.* San Francisco: Sierra Club Books, 1991.

Hanh, Thich Nhat. *The Heart of Understanding: Commentaries on the Prajñāpāramitā Heart Sūtra.* Ed. Peter Levitt. Berkeley: Parallax Press, 1988.

Herbert, Jean. *Shintō: At the Fountain-Head of Japan.* New York: Stein & Day, 1967.

Hoff, Frank, and Willi Flindt. "The Life Structure of Noh: An English Version of Yokomichi Mario's Analysis of the Structure of Noh." *Concerned Theatre Japan* (Tokyo) 2.3–4 (1973): 210–56.

Howard, Helen Addison. *American Indian Poetry.* Boston: Twayne, 1979.

Humphreys, Christmas. *A Popular Dictionary of Buddhism.* New York: Citadel Press, 1963.

Hunt, Anthony. "'Bubbs Creek Haircut': Gary Snyder's 'Great Departure' in *Mountains and Rivers Without End.*" *Western American Literature* 15.3 (Fall 1980): 163–75.

———. "'The Hump-Backed Flute Player': The Structure of Emptiness in Gary Snyder's *Mountains and Rivers Without End.*" ISLE: Interdisciplinary Studies in Literature and Environment 1.2 (Fall 1993): 1–23.

———. "Sailing the Metaphorical Seas of the Middle East: Gary Snyder's 'Boat of a Million Years.'" *Atenea* (3rd epoch) 20.1 (Jan. 2000): 67–75.

———. "Singing the Dyads: The Chinese Landscape Scroll and Gary Snyder's *Mountains and Rivers Without End.*" *Journal of Modern Literature* 23.1 (Summer 1999): 7–34.

"In Print: *Mountains and Rivers Without End.*" *UC Davis Magazine* 14.2 (Winter 1997): 22.

An Intermediate Greek-English Lexicon: Founded upon the Seventh Edition of Liddell and Scott's Greek-English Lexicon. Oxford: Clarendon Press, 1972.

Ishibashi, Hiro. *Yeats and the Noh: Types of Japanese Beauty and Their Reflection in Yeats's Plays.* Ed. Anthony Kerrigan. Dublin: Dolmen Press, 1966.

Jetté, Julius. "Riddles of the Ten'a Indians." *Anthropos* 8 (1913): 181–201.

Jobes, Gertrude. *Dictionary of Mythology, Folklore, and Symbols.* 3 vols. New York: Scarecrow Press, 1962.

Kakuzo, Okakura. *The Book of Tea.* 1906. 16th ed. New York: Duffield & Green, 1932.

Keene, Donald. *Japanese Literature: An Introduction for Western Readers.* New York: Grove, 1955.

Kern, Robert. "Recipes, Catalogues, Open Form Poetics: Gary Snyder's Archetypal Voice." *Contemporary Literature* 18.2 (Spring 1977): 173–97.

Kerouac, Jack. *The Dharma Bums.* New York: New American Library, 1958.

Kherdian, David. *Gary Snyder: A Biographical Sketch and Descriptive Checklist.* Berkeley: Oyez, 1965.

Knappert, Jan. *Indian Mythology: An Encyclopedia of Myth and Legend.* London: Diamond Books, 1991.

Kramer, Samuel Noah, ed. *Mythologies of the Ancient World.* New York: Doubleday, 1961.

Kyger, Joanne. *The Japan and India Journals, 1960–1964.* Bolinas: Tomboutou Books, 1981.

Landi, Val. *The Bantam Great Outdoors Guide to the United States and Canada.* Toronto: Bantam, 1978.

Leach, Maria, ed. *Standard Dictionary of Folklore, Mythology, and Legend.* New York: Funk & Wagnall, 1972.

Lee, David Jinsoo. "American Nō: Gary Snyder's *Mountains and Rivers Without End.*" Honor's thesis. U of California at Berkeley, Spring 1997.

Lee, Sherman E. *A History of Far Eastern Art.* 4th ed. New York: Harry Abrams, 1982.

Lee, Sherman E., and Wen Fong. *Streams and Mountains Without End: A Northern Sung Handscroll and Its Significance in the History of Early Chinese Painting.* 1954. 2nd ed. rev. Ascona, Switz.: Artibus Asiae, 1967.

Lomax, John A., and Alan Lomax, comps. *American Ballads and Folk Songs.* New York: Macmillan, 1934.

Lopez, Donald S., Jr., ed. *Religions of Tibet in Practice.* Princeton: Princeton UP, 1997.

"Los Angeles." *Encyclopaedia Britannica: Macropaedia.* 15th ed. 1982.

Martínez, Pablo L. *A History of Lower California (The Only Complete and Reliable One).* Trans. Ethel Duffy Turner. 1st English ed. México City D. F.: Editorial Baja California, 1960.

McClellan, Catherine. *The Girl Who Married the Bear: A Masterpiece of Indian Oral Tradition.* Publications on Ethnology 2. Ottawa: National Museums of Canada, 1970.

McLeod, Dan. "Some Images of China in the Works of Gary Snyder." *Tamkang Review* 10.3 (Spring 1980): 369–83.

McNeil, Katherine. *Gary Snyder: A Bibliography.* New York: Phoenix Bookshop, 1983.

Miner, Earl, Hiroko Odagiri, and Robert E. Morrell. *The Princeton Companion to Classical Japanese Literature.* Princeton: Princeton UP, 1985.

Molesworth, Charles. *Gary Snyder's Vision: Poetry and the Real Work.* Columbia: University of Missouri Press, 1983.

Mooney, James. *The Ghost Dance Religion and the Sioux Outbreak of 1890.* Abridged by Anthony Wallace. Chicago: U of Chicago P, 1965.

Moyers, Bill. *The Language of Life: A Festival of Poets.* New York: Doubleday, 1995.

Muir, John. "The Bee Pastures." *The Mountains of California.* 1894. Atlanta: Cherokee Publishing Company, 1990. 338–81.

Murphy, Patrick D. "Mythic and Fantastic: Gary Snyder's *Mountains and Rivers Without End.*" *Extrapolation* 26.4 (1985): 290–99.

———. *A Place for Wayfaring: The Poetry and Prose of Gary Snyder.* Corvallis: Oregon State UP, 2000.

———. *Understanding Gary Snyder.* Columbia: U of South Carolina P, 1992.

"Musgrave Ranges." *Encyclopaedia Britannica: Micropaedia.* 15th ed. 1982.

Neumann, Erich. *The Origins and History of Consciousness.* New York: Pantheon Books, 1954.

The New Encyclopaedia Britannica. 15th ed. 1982. Cited as *Encyclopaedia Britannica.*

NGS (Nippon Gakujutsu Shinkōkai), ed. *The Noh Drama: Ten Plays from the Japanese Selected and Translated by the Special Noh Committee, Japanese Classics Translation Committee.* Rutland: Charles E. Tuttle, 1955.

———. *Yamamba. The Noh Drama: Ten Plays from the Japanese Selected and Translated by the Special Noh Committee, Japanese Classics Translation Committee.* Vol II. Rutland and Tokyo: Charles E. Tuttle, 1959. 159–78.

Obata, Chiura. *Evening Glow at Yosemite Waterfall* (1930). *Obata's Yosemite: The Art *and Letters of Chiura Obata from His Trip to the High Sierra in 1927.* Ed. Janice Driesbach and Susan Landauer. Yosemite National Park: Yosemite Assn., 1993. 127.

Paul, Sherman. "Arbeiten und Lieben: Gary Snyder." *In Search of the Primitive: Rereading David Antin, Jerome Rothenberg, and Gary Snyder.* Baton Rouge: Louisiana State UP, 1986.

Pearlman, Daniel D. *The Barb of Time: On the Unity of Ezra Pound's "Cantos."* New York: Oxford UP, 1969.

Pound, Ezra. *The Cantos of Ezra Pound.* New York: New Directions, 1970.

Petersen, Will. "September Ridge." *Gary Snyder: Dimensions of a Life.* Ed. Jon Halper. San Francisco: Sierra Club Books, 1991.

Radin, Paul. *The Trickster: A Study in American Indian Mythology.* 1956. New York: Schocken, 1976.

Rimbaud, Arthur. *Rimbaud: Complete Works, Selected Letters. Translation.* Intro. and notes by Wallace Fowlie. Chicago: U of Chicago P, 1966.

Robertson, David. "The Circumambulation of Mt. Tamalpais." *Western American Literature* 30.1 (May 1995): 3–28.

———. "Real Matter, Spiritual Mountain: Gary Snyder and Jack Kerouac on Mt. Tamalpais." *Western American Literature* 27.3 (Fall 1992): 209–25.

———. *West of Eden: A History of the Art and Literature of Yosemite.* [Yosemite National Park]: Yosemite Natural History Assn.; [Berkeley]: Wilderness Press, 1984.

———. *Yosemite As We Saw It: A Centennial Collection of Early Writings and Art.* Yosemite National Park: Yosemite Assn., 1990. (The poem "Falls" appears on pp. 73–74.)

Sargent, Helen, and George Lyman Kittredge, eds. *English and Scottish Popular Ballads.* Boston: Houghton Mifflin, 1932.

Schafer, Edward H. *The Golden Peaches of Samarkand: A Study of T'ang Exotics.* Berkeley & Los Angeles: U of California P, 1963.

Scigaj, Leonard M. *Sustainable Poetry: Four American Ecopoets.* Lexington: The University Press of Kentucky, 1999.

Shakspo, Nawang Tsering. *Songs from the Himalaya: Ladakhi Folk Songs.* Leh-Ladakh, India: Ladakh Ecological Development Group, 1985.

The Shambhala Dictionary of Buddhism and Zen. Ed. Ingrid Fischer-Schreiber, Franz-Karl Ehrhard, and Michael S. Diener. Boston: Shambhala, 1991.

Shaw, Miranda. *Passionate Enlightenment: Women in Tantric Buddhism.* Princeton: Princeton UP, 1994.

Shelley, Percy Bysshe. "The Cloud." *Percy Bysshe Shelley: Selected Poetry.* Ed. Neville Rogers. Boston: Houghton Mifflin, 1968. 367–69.

Shepard, Paul. *The Others: How Animals Made Us Human.* Washington: Island Press, 1996.

Shepard, Paul, and Barry Sanders. *The Sacred Paw: The Bear in Nature, Myth, and Literature.* New York: Viking, 1985.

Shipley, William, ed. and trans. *The Maidu Indian Myths and Stories of Hánc'ibyjim.* Berkeley: Heyday Books, 1991.

Simpson, Richard. *Ooti: A Maidu Legacy.* Millbrae: Celestial Arts, 1977

Smith, Eric Todd. *Reading Gary Snyder's "Mountains and Rivers Without End."* Western Writers Series No. 142. Boise: Boise State University, 2000.

Snyder, Gary. *Axe Handles.* San Francisco: North Point Press, 1983.

———. *The Back Country.* London: Fulcrum Press, 1967.

———. *The Back Country.* New York: New Directions, 1968.

———. "Blue Mountains Constantly Walking." *Practice of the Wild* 97–115.

———. "Cold Mountain Poems." *Evergreen Review* 6 (Autumn 1958): 69–80.

———. "A Conversation with Gary Snyder." With James Van Cleve. *Sallyport* [Reed College] 30.1 (Jan. 1971): 6–9. Also at GSP B19:F5.

———. "Coyote-Mind: An Interview with Gary Snyder." With Julia Martin. *Triquarterly* 79 (Fall 1990): 148–72.

———. "Dharma Queries." *Earth House Hold* 131–34.

———. *Earth House Hold: Technical Notes & Queries to Fellow Dharma Revolutionaries.* New York: New Directions, 1969. Cited as *EHH*.

———. "The Etiquette of Freedom." *Practice of the Wild* 3–24.

———. "The Feathered Robe." *Poetry Score* 1 (Fall 1960): 25–26. (GSP B14:F3). Rpt., without headnote, in *Left Out in the Rain* 68–69.

———. Foreword. *The Divine Woman: Dragon Ladies and Rain Maidens in T'ang Literature.* By Edward Schafer. San Francisco: North Point Press, 1980. Also in *A Place in Space.* Washington: Counterpoint, 1995. 85–90.

———. "From Anthropologist to Informant: A Field Record of Gary Snyder" [interview]. With Nathaniel Tarn. *Alcheringa* 4 (Autumn 1972): 112.

———. *The Fudō Trilogy.* Berkeley: Shaman Drum, 1973.

———. "Glacier Peak Wilderness Area." *Earth House Hold* 94–102.

———. "Good, Wild, Sacred." *Practice of the Wild* 78–96. See also "Good Wild Sacred." *The CoEvolution Quarterly* (Autumn 1983); and *Good Wild Sacred.* Madley, Hereford, England: Five Seasons Press, 1984.

———. "Heart Sūtra." *Gary Snyder Reading His New Long Poem "Mountains and Rivers Without End."* Program notes. 9 Oct. 1997. Stanford Humanities Center, Stanford University.

———. *He Who Hunted Birds in His Father's Village: The Dimensions of a Haida Myth.* Bolinas: Grey Fox Press, 1979.

———. "A High Dry Place Behind the Passes." *Upriver Downriver* 16 (1993): 11, 14–15.

———. Interview with Peter Barry Chowka. *East West Journal* (Summer 1977). Rpt. as "The *East West* Interview" in *Real Work* 92–137.

———. Interview with Hank Fincken. *Indiana Writes* 3.2 (Summer 1979): 42. (GSP B26:F9)

———. Interview with Catherine Ingram. *In the Footsteps of Gandhi: Conversations with Spiritual Social Activists.* Berkeley: Parallax Press, 1990. 225–47.

———. Interview. With John Jacoby. *Espejo* 12.2 (Spring 1974): 37–50. Rpt. in *Real Work* 44–51.

———. "An Interview with Gary Snyder." With Doug Flaherty. *Road Apple Review* 1.4–2.1 (Winter 1969-Spring 1970): 59–68. Rpt. in *Real Work* 15–22.

———. "Interview with Gary Snyder." With Gene Fowler. *Literary Times* (Chicago), 4.2 (December 1964): 7. Rpt. in *Real Work* 3–6.

———. "An Interview with Gary Snyder: 'Language Is Wild.'" With Donald Johns. *Writing on the Edge* 2.1 (Fall 1990): 100–112.

———. Introduction. *Beneath a Single Moon: Buddhism in Contemporary American Poetry.* Ed. Kent Johnson and Craig Paulenich. Boston: Shambhala, 1991. 1–9.

———. Introduction. *Myths & Texts.* New York: New Directions, 1978.

———. "Journey to *Mountains and Rivers Without End.*" *Tokaido. On the Road: Pilgrimage, Travel and Culture.* Spencer Museum of Art: U of Kansas, 1982. 37–45. Six-page typescript, GSP B5:F75.

———. *Left Out in the Rain: New Poems 1947–1987.* San Francisco: North Point Press, 1986.

———. "The Legacy of the Wild: An Interview with Gary Snyder." *The Sun: A Magazine of Ideas* [Chapel Hill] 173 (April 1990): 2–13.

———. Letter to Donald R. Carpenter. Donald R. Carpenter Mini-Collection, Department of Special Collections, Shields Library, University of California, Davis. Accession number D7. (Collection includes multiple letters from Gary Snyder to Donald Carpenter.)

———. Letter to Allen Ginsberg. *Origin* 2nd ser. 2 (July 1961): 63.

———. "Letter to Allen Ginsberg." *The Unspeakable Visions of the Individual.* "The Beat Book" Issue 4 (1970): 114.

———. Letter to Dan McLeod. 6 Nov. 1983. Copy enclosed in personal communication from Mr. McLeod to author.

———. Letter to Will Petersen. "September Ridge." *Gary Snyder: Dimensions of a Life.* Ed. Jon Halper. San Francisco: Sierra Club Books, 1991.

———. "The Making of *Mountains and Rivers Without End.*" *Mountains and Rivers Without End.* Washington: Counterpoint, 1996. 153–58.

———. *Manzanita.* Bolinas: Four Seasons Foundations, 1972.

———. *Mountains and Rivers Without End.* Washington: Counterpoint, 1996.

———. *Myths & Texts.* New York: Totem Press/Corinth Books, 1960

———. *No Nature: New and Selected Poems.* New York: Pantheon Books, 1992.

———. *North Pacific Lands & Waters: A Further Six Sections.* Waldron Island: Brooding Heron Press, 1993.

———. *North Sea Road.* Planet Drum, 1974.

———. Notes. *Mountains and Rivers Without End.* Washington: Counterpoint, 1996. 159–63.

———. "Now India." *Caterpillar* 19, 5.3 (Spring 1972). See also *Passage Through India.*

———. *The Old Ways: Six Essays.* San Francisco: City Lights Books, 1977.

———. "On the Path, Off the Trail." *Practice of the Wild* 144–54.

———. "onward." E-mail to participants of graduate seminar, UC Davis, 26 May 1996, with a copy to Anthony Hunt, 27 May 1996.

———. *Passage Through India.* San Francisco: Grey Fox Press, 1983. A revised version of Snyder's letter to his sister, Thea, first published in *Caterpillar* 19 5:3 (Spring 1972) as "Now India."

———. *A Place in Space.* Washington: Counterpoint, 1995.

———. "Poetry and the Primitive: Notes on Poetry as an Ecological Survival Technique." *Earth House Hold* 117–30.

———. "The Politics of Ethnopoetics." *Place in Space* 126–47.

———. *The Practice of the Wild: Essays by Gary Snyder.* San Francisco: North Point Press, 1990.

———. *Gary Snyder Reading His New Long Poem "Mountains and Rivers Without End."* Program notes. 9 Oct. 1997. Stanford Humanities Center, Stanford University.

———. *A Range of Poems.* London: Fulcrum Press, 1966.

———. "RE: Spring Seminar." E-mail to author. 13 Jan. 1996.

———. "A Reading from *Mountains and Rivers Without End.*" Library of Congress, Washington, 23 Oct. 1996.

———. *The Real Work: Interviews & Talks 1964–1979.* Ed. William Scott McLean. New York: New Directions, 1980.

———. *Regarding Wave.* New York: New Directions, 1970.

———. "Re-inhabitation." *The Old Ways* 57–66.

———. *Riprap.* Ashland: Origin Press, 1959.

———. *Riprap, & Cold Mountain Poems.* San Francisco: Four Seasons Foundation, 1969.

———. "Survival and Sacrament." *Practice of the Wild* 175–85.

———. "Tanker Notes." *Earth House Hold* 54–68.

———. "Tawny Grammar." *Practice of the Wild* 48–77.

———. "To Thea." See "Now, India," and *Passage Through India.*

———. *Turtle Island.* New York: New Directions, 1974.

———. "Uluru Wild Fig Song." *Axe Handles* 95–98.

———. "A Village Council of All Beings: Ecology, Spirituality and Place." *Upriver Downriver* 16 (1993): 10, 12–13.

———. "Voice in the Wilderness: An Interview with Gary Snyder." With Peter Carroll. *San Francisco Review of Books.* Summer 1989: 7–10, 53. (Broadcast live on KPFA/FM, 6 Feb. 1989.)

———. "Walking the Great Ridge Omine on the Womb-Diamond Trail." *Kyoto Journal* 25 (1993): 71–77.

———. "Watershed Perspectives." *Tree Rings: The Forum of the Yuba Watershed Institute* 1.1 (Spring 1991): 3.

———. "When Life Starts Getting Interesting: An Interview with Gary Snyder." With Geeta Dardick. *Sierra: The Sierra Club Bulletin* 70.5 (Sept.-Oct. 1985): 68–73.

———. "The Woman Who Married a Bear." *Practice of the Wild* 155–74.

———. "The Writer's Notebook." *Zyzzyva* 9.3 (Fall 1993): 123–43.

Snyder, Gary, and Anthony Hunt. Seminar discussion of *Mountains and Rivers Without End.* U of California at Davis. 1 May 1996.

Sontag, Susan. "Against Interpretation." *Against Interpretation and Other Essays.* New York: Dell, 1966. 3–14.

Steuding, Bob. *Gary Snyder.* Boston: Twayne, 1976.

Stryk, Lucien, ed. *World of the Buddha: A Reader.* New York: Anchor, 1969.

"Su Tung-p'o." *Encyclopaedia Britannica: Macropaedia.* 15th ed. 1982.

Suzuki, Daisetz T. *Essays in Zen Buddhism: First Series.* 1949. New York: Grove Press, 1961.

———. *Manual of Zen Buddhism.* New York: Grove Press, 1960.

———. *Zen and Japanese Culture.* Princeton: Princeton UP, 1959.

Teilhard de Chardin, Pierre. *Le Phenomene Humain.* Paris: Le Seuil Editions, 1955.

———. *The Phenomenon of Man.* 1955. Trans. Bernard Wall. New York: Harper Books, 1975.

Thomas, Lewis. *The Lives of a Cell: Notes of a Biology Watcher.* New York: Bantam, 1973.

Tyler, Royall, ed. and trans. *Granny Mountains. Granny Mountains: A Second Cycle of Nō Plays.* Cornell East Asia Series 18. Ithaca: Cornell East Asia Program, 1978. 155–75.

———. *Yamamba: The Mountain Crone. Japanese Nō Dramas.* London: Penguin Books, 1992. 309–28.

Walker, Benjamin, ed. *The Hindu World: An Encyclopedia of Hinduism.* 2 vols. New York: Frederick Praeger, 1968.

Waters, Frank. *The Book of the Hopi.* New York: Viking, 1963.

Whalen-Bridge, John. "Gary Snyder, Dōgen, and 'The Canyon Wren.'" *Connotations* 8.1 (1998–99): 112–24.

———. "Spirit of Place and Wild Politics in Two Recent Snyder Poems." *Northwest Review* 29.3 (1991): 123–31.

Williams, DeWayne. *Dooby Lane: A Testament Inscribed in Stone Tablets.* Descriptive text by Gary Snyder. Photographs by students and faculty of The University of Nevada, Reno. Reno: Black Rock Press, 1996.

Windham, Steve. "Unity and the Power of Imagination in Gary Snyder's 'The Elwha River.'" *Western American Literature* 14.4 (Winter 1980): 317–19.

"Yab-yum." *New Encyclopaedia Britannica.* 15th ed. 1982.

Yamazato, Katsunori. "Seeking a Fulcrum: Gary Snyder and Japan (1956–1975)." Diss. U of California at Davis, 1987.

Yeats, William Butler. *Selected Poems and Two Plays of William Butler Yeats.* Ed. M. L. Rosenthal. New York: Collier Books, 1962.

Yee, Chiang. *The Chinese Eye: An Interpretation of Chinese Painting.* 1935. Bloomington: Indiana UP, 1964.

Zimmer, Heinrich. *Myths and Symbols in Indian Art and Civilization.* 1946. Ed. Joseph Campbell. Princeton: Princeton UP, 1972.

Zumak. "Tatshenshini River." *Humanature.* Recorded at Crosstown Studio, North Vancouver, March 1992. Words by Gary Snyder.

Credits

Grateful appreciation is extended to the following individuals and agencies/institutions:

Gary Snyder for permission to print excerpts from his correspondence, journals, and other unpublished and published writing.

The administration, archivists, and staff of the following libraries for access to their special collections: The Philip Whalen Collection, Special Collections Library, Eric V. Hauser Memorial Library, Reed College, Portland, Oregon. The Gary Snyder Papers, Department of Special Collections, Shields Library, University of California at Davis. The Donald Allen Collection, Mandeville Special Collections Library, Geisel Library, University of California at San Diego.

Dan Welch for permission to print excerpts from his correspondence with Gary Snyder.

Donald Allen for permission to print excerpts from his own correspondence, and that of Lew Welch, with Gary Snyder.

Cynthia Archer for permission to print excerpts from the correspondence of Will Petersen.

Michael Rothenberg for permission to print excerpts from the correspondence of Philip Whalen.

David Jinsoo Lee for permission to adapt portions of his honors thesis, "American Nō: Gary Snyder's *Mountains and Rivers Without End*."

The editors and publishers of the following journals in which early versions of sections of my book were first published:

"'Bubbs Creek Haircut': Gary Snyder's 'Great Departure' in *Mountains and Rivers Without End*." *Western American Literature* 15.3 (Fall 1980): 163–75.

"'The Hump-Backed Flute Player': The Structure of Emptiness in Gary Snyder's *Mountains and Rivers Without End*." *ISLE: Interdisciplinary Studies in Literature and Environment* 1.2 (Fall 1993): 1–23.

"Sailing the Metaphorical Seas of the Middle East: Gary Snyder's 'Boat of a Million Years.'" *Atenea* (3rd epoch) xx.1 (Jan. 2000): 67–75.

"Singing the Dyads: The Chinese Landscape Scroll and Gary Snyder's *Mountains and Rivers Without End.*" *Journal of Modern Literature* 23.1 (Summer 1999): 7–34.

Counterpoint Press for permission to print excerpts from *Mountains and Rivers Without End.*

Quotations from Anne Baring and Jules Cashford, *The Myth of the Goddess: Evolution of an Image* (London: Viking Arkana, 1991) copyright © Anne Baring and Jules Cashford, 1991, are reproduced by permission of Penguin Books Ltd.

Myths & Texts, copyright © 1978 by Gary Snyder. Used by permission of New Directions Publishing Corp.

The Back Country, copyright © 1968 by Gary Snyder. Used by permission of New Directions Publishing Corp.

Earth House Hold, copyright © 1969 by Gary Snyder. Used by permission of New Directions Publishing Corp.

Turtle Island, copyright © 1974 by Gary Snyder. Used by permission of New Directions Publishing Corp.

The Real Work: Interviews & Talks 1964–1979, copyright © 1980 by Gary Snyder. Used by permission of New Directions Publishing Corp.

Excerpt from "Foreword" from *The White Goddess* by Robert Graves, Copyright © 1948, renewed 1975 by Robert Graves. Reprinted by permission of Farrar, Straus and Giroux, LLC.

Excerpt from "Painting a Rice-Cake (Gabyō)" from *Moon in a Dew Drop: Writings of Zen Master Dogen,* edited by Kazuaki Tanahashi. Copyright © 1985 by the San Francisco Zen Center. Reprinted by permission of North Point Press, a division of Farrar, Straus and Giroux, LLC.

Excerpt from "Axe Handles" from *Axe Handles* by Gary Snyder. Copyright © 1983 by Gary Snyder. Reprinted by permission of North Point Press, a division of Farrar, Straus and Giroux, LLC.

Excerpts from "Blue Mountains Constantly Walking," "The Etiquette of Freedom," "Good, Wild, Sacred," "The Woman Who Married a Bear," "The Place, the Region, and the Commons" from *The Practice of the Wild* by Gary Snyder. Copyright © 1990 by Gary Snyder. Reprinted by permission of North Point Press, a division of Farrar, Straus and Giroux, LLC.

Excerpt from "Hay for the Horses" from *Riprap and Cold Mountain Poems* by Gary Snyder. Copyright © 1990 by Gary Snyder. Reprinted by permission of North Point Press, a division of Farrar, Straus and Giroux, LLC.

Index